Mariner's
RULES OF THE ROAD

Also by William P. Crawford

Mariner's Weather
Mariner's Celestial Navigation
Mariner's Notebook
Sea Marine Atlas: Southern California

Mariner's
RULES
OF THE
ROAD

William P. Crawford

W. W. NORTON & COMPANY New York London

The text of this book is composed in Times Roman, with display type set in Doric
Black.
Composition by ComCom.
Manufacturing by Hadden Craftsmen.
Book design by The Angelica Design Group.

First Edition

Library of Congress Cataloging in Publication Data

Crawford, William P., 1922-
  Mariner's rules of the road.

  1. Rules of the road, both international and inland. I. Title.
VK371.C7   1983   623.88′84   83–3947

ISBN 0-393-03284-1

W. W. Norton & Company, Inc., 500 Fifth Avenue, New York, N.Y. 10110
W. W. Norton & Company Ltd., 37 Great Russell Street, London WC1B 3NU

1 2 3 4 5 6 7 8 9 0

CONTENTS

ACKNOWLEDGMENTS

No book-length treatment of a complex subject is done by a single person. At least that generality is apt here. For many years I, as teacher, have met with students in classes on Rules of the Road. Seafarers all, these students actually use the Rules daily. Their observations on how they work in practice proved invaluable to my present task. I am very grateful.

While this book was in preparation the navigation rules themselves were undergoing change. The result could have been an author's nightmare, but I was spared. And I attribute my ease of mind to the Rules of the Road section of the U.S. Coast Guard. The staff of this Headquarters unit attended to my inquiries on the new and pending with outstanding courtesy and interest.

In a more personal vein, I am proud to acknowledge the competent and patient assistance of my daughters. Patricia, herself a teacher and writer, endured tiresome hours of manuscript-reading to stave off clumsiness of composition and style. And Christine made her debut as an artist successful by rendering the first-class sketches found throughout the book.

PREFACE

THIS BOOK has several purposes. The major one of course is an understanding of the Rules of the Road. Our procedure will be to dismember the Rules and attempt to reassemble them into a coherent form. Less obvious but perhaps even more primary is another target: to stimulate an appetite for what lies ahead. Decades spent guiding students through technical maritime subjects have taught me that comprehension is directly proportional to enthusiasm. Both instructor and pupil fare better when both look to the subject matter with animation. So the first order of business is to generate a bit of zeal. Passionate concern for the mechanical advantage of a Spanish burton requires special dedication. But a study of the Rules need not be lifeless. We all can muster more than a passing interest in human achievement, and the Rules of the Road are certainly such an accomplishment.

On the no man's land of the high seas appears every nationality operating every variety of vessel for every conceivable reason. Diversity is so rampant that by modern norms the result should be chaos. Yet mariners have managed to fashion a code which works. Why does it work? The only reason is that without such a code maritime commerce would be impossible. The Rules direct every vessel, large and small; they apply to all owners, whether public or private, multinational combines or weekend sailors. Special interest has no status when, on a given night, one encounters a gargantuan bulk carrier following in the wake of a yawl overtaking an oyster dredge.

Here then is our starting point. For more than a century this disparate maritime world has demonstrated a remarkable competence for cooperation. The Hammer and Sickle gives way to the Stars and Stripes; the Red Duster stands on in the presence of the Rising Sun. There are of course violations. Court records from Buenos Aires to Boston reflect the outcomes. But that is not the point. More noteworthy is that the code of acceptable conduct is surprisingly uniform, and for the most part respected. Certainly an overwhelming fear of consequences provides powerful motivation for the Rules' success. Still, we are about to undertake a study of a most unusual accomplishment. The details will become burdensome as we encounter the nits of who keeps clear and what lights are shown. Even so, it is not a burden to maintain a sense of pride in all these nuances. We deal here with voluntary restraints on human conduct. That should prove more captivating than the physics involved in any burton, Spanish or otherwise.

If comprehension is accelerated by enthusiasm, we must enter into the spirit of this important seafaring facet. On the other hand the exercise is not bone-dry. Here is a challenge to the mind. Engender a lively interest and you will join me in respect for a little-recognized feat of international concord.

William P. Crawford

San Francisco, Calif.

Mariner's RULES OF THE ROAD

1
AN OVERVIEW

SEAFARING IS not a contact sport, and the Rules of the Road are designed to keep it that way. One phrase defines their purpose: *regulations to prevent collision.* Every part of the plan pursues this aim. The purpose is neither to expedite voyages nor to decorate ships with colorful lights. Whatever requirement doesn't tend toward keeping ship *A* from striking ship *B* is beside the point.

Today's rules are derived from scores of special disciplines imposed by localities, particular trades, and navies on vessels operating within their scopes. But no array of diverse codes could accommodate everyone at sea. About a century ago maritime nations responded to the confusion with a pattern merging the best of many rules into a uniform set. And every twenty years or so the system is tightened up and modernized to cope with new technology.

The latest international update began in 1972. By mid-1977 the effort was accepted worldwide and new International Rules appeared. Their common name reflects the chronology. 72 COLREGS describes the present *col*lision *reg*ulation*s* stemming from international councils convened in London in 1972. Five years might seem a lengthy interval between the beginning and the end of a convention's work, yet in the arena of international discussion it is almost instantaneous. During that period committees were formed, changes were proposed and argued, the finished product was presented to the world, and a sufficient number of individual governments approved it to make July 15, 1977, the date the new rules went into effect. During similar five-year periods international agreement on such issues as the definition of land and sea frontiers barely progressed beyond formulating a statement of purpose.

Our consideration of the Rules will use the framework of the international set as a guide. Not only is this set essential, it presents a logical skeleton on which to fasten variations. In fact so well do all the parts meld that we must expect some repetitive backing and filling.

There are thirty-eight Rules separated into five Parts and supplemented by four Annexes. The structure, though, can be reduced to this: a *code of conduct* and a *code of signals.* Vessels are given a script to follow when they meet; that is the code of conduct. In addition they are provided with a special set of day shapes, light displays, and sound signals to exchange data essential to following that script.

The rules themselves require more explicit divisions. Here is a roster of the key classifications. *Part A—General* sets the tone and defines terms. *Part B— Steering and Sailing Rules* describes what could be called the script for vessels onstage at the same time to follow. The analogy of a script is apt. Performers acting out parts in a theater are guided by the playwright's specifications of who says what and when. Vessels approaching each other so as to involve risk of collision also require direction, and Part B provides a three-section script. Section I defines conduct in any condition of visibility. Section II is the guide when in sight of one another. Section III specifies conduct in restricted visibility.

Just as cue cards prompt stage actors, so vessels need reminders of which role to play. *Part C* deals with lights and shapes. The essential cues given by one vessel to another are *direction* or *aspect* and *condition* or *limitations on maneuverability.* By day, to see another vessel is to know her aspect. However, an onboard condition which impairs her maneuvers might not be so apparent. So day shapes provide the key. At night the burden of communication is far greater. When the hull form is unseen, light patterns must relate a more extensive story. They furnish the means to judge both aspect and condition.

What, though, if visibility is restricted by atmospheric conditions? Neither lights nor day shapes are adequate to bridge the communication gap. So *Part D* gives the details on sound signals, including audio-visual combinations suitable when vessels are maneuvering in sight of one another. *Part E* is a one-rule division presenting the fine points of exemption from exact compliance with light and sound requirements.

The Rules also standardize technical details. In *Annex I* are the niceties of positioning and size of lights and shapes. *Annex II* describes additional light patterns available to vessels fishing in a group. *Annex III* contains detailed technical information regarding sound signal appliances. *Annex IV* establishes worldwide uniformity for signals of distress.

All in all, this neat arrangement fits the welter of particulars into a snug and shipshape package. In the chapters to follow we'll take an unhurried look at each part and section, with a glance at relevant highlights in an annex or two.

Regulations applicable to United States waters cannot be ignored, but their study need not be as demanding as in the past. By adopting COLREGS, our nation agreed that special rules governing operations on internal waterways navigable by seagoing vessels would conform as closely as possible to the international patterns. Since 1897 our waters have been subject to a somewhat formless maze of regulations. No one should regret the end of that era. We still have special rules when necessary, but the framework of our new Inland Navigational Rules of 1980 is similar to COLREGS. There are the same number of rules, but one of them, Rule 28, is vacant and labeled "Reserved." Inland contains one more annex than does COLREGS. The modern Pilot Rules are in its Annex V.

Now we come face to face with a formidable obstacle: terminology. The rulemakers are not educators. They are not to be expected to phrase and rephrase, to illustrate and give "for instances." And we must anticipate that the rulemakers value precision and economy of words. Mariners in turn must read the words with care. If the limited warranty drafted for a can opener is bewildering, the Rules of the Road are much more so. Legislating for the world is a gigantic task, and the expression of requirements in a babel of languages must be reasonably consistent. Add another element and the task is awesome. The Rules of the Road are directed to the maritime world where the word "ceiling" refers to a shoreside floor and where a "floor" stands in the vertical plane.

One question will constantly recur during our study: "What do the words really mean?" Just as recurrent is the ultimate answer: "What the highest admiralty courts say they mean." Disgruntled seamen sometimes complain that admiralty judges second-guess for months what a mariner must decide within minutes, but that objection is not valid. The mariner is not expected to be as well versed as an advocate at the bar. What is expected is that he understand the Rules and comply with them as would any prudent seaman of ordinary skill in the circumstances. We can assume that the Rules mean close to what they seem to mean.

But the seafarer must recognize a basic principle. At the heart of all Rules of the Road is the concept of risk of collision. Unless such risk exists there is no need to follow a particular script. Yet when does risk exist? Our judicial system does not allow any forecast of binding opinions on hypothetical facts. Rather than speculating on moot inquiries, courts render decisions on real problems. A judge hearing an actual collision case will hardly be influenced by the argument that a rule was not followed because there was no risk of collision. At some point risk must have developed, for how else did the parties gain their day in court? The mariner needs more than "fair-weather" knowledge of the Rules for guidance.

And up pops still another hurdle. An authoritative voice must interpret the words. Courts have the final say, but what guidance is available short of the bench? In the United States the Coast Guard is charged with developing *interpretive rulings.* They serve to shade some gray toward black or white, and they become as much Rules of the Road as the rules they interpret. Such edicts appear in the *Federal Register* and in the *Code of Federal Regulations.*

On an international level there is another source for guidance. Seagoing nations work together through a sort of clearinghouse for maritime matters. Until 1982 it endured the cumbersome title of Intergovernmental Maritime Consultative Organization. Member nations gratefully used the abbreviation IMCO, for mouthing the full designation in languages from German to Japanese was painful. In May 1982 relief arrived with a name change to International Maritime Organization. The abbreviation IMO is not a great improvement over IMCO, but shortening the official title more than justified the switch. Although not a rulemaking forum, the IMO (as we'll now start calling it) is a focus for worldwide maritime concerns. And it makes recommendations which sooner or later seem to turn up as international gospel. Incorporated in our study as *faits accomplis* are amendments slated for June 1, 1983. During our passage through the Rules we'll keep a weather eye on some IMO proposals in the pending file.

These last pages might appear to be teasing avoidance of getting underway, but nothing could be further from the truth. The Rules were not written to assist judges or to challenge advocates. They are to guide the mariner. To plunge heedlessly into "green over white" or "one prolonged followed by two shorts" is to reduce the exercise to a redundancy. Understanding requires us to go farther afield. Here we've been charting the course.

QUESTIONS

A little rest and recreation now and then might help to counteract too earnest an attention to our duties. Each chapter will end with a quiz to relieve the monotonous digestion of the printed page. Now is the time to confront the panel of inquisitors. Oscar, Emmy, and Tony have been recruited from the entertainment world to judge the performance. Turn off the Teleprompter and stow your cue cards. The overture is ending and the curtain is about to rise. On stage, everyone!

1. The present International Rules of the Road
   a. are called the 72 COLREGS
   b. became effective in mid-1977
   c. both a and b
   d. neither a nor b

2. Steering and Sailing Rules prescribe the conduct of vessels
   a. when in any condition of visibility
   b. when in sight of one another
   c. when in restricted visibility
   d. all of the above

3. When in the presence of another vessel, it is important to be informed of her direction or aspect and of her condition or limitations on maneuverabil-

ity. Designed to supply *both* segments of such information are
a. day shapes
b. light patterns
c. both of the above
d. none of the above

4. Distress signals used on the high seas
   a. vary with the nationality of the vessel in distress
   b. are specified by the International Rules of the Road
   c. both of the above
   d. none of the above

5. The ultimate determination of what the Rules of the Road mean and require is made by
   a. admiralty courts
   b. Congress
   c. the U.S. Coast Guard
   d. the IMO

6. When a vessel is on the high seas on a voyage from one U.S. port to another
   a. she is bound only by the Inland Rules of the Road
   b. she is not bound by annexes to the International Rules of the Road
   c. she is bound by the International Rules and annexes
   d. none of the above

7. With regard to the Rules of the Road, technical details of lights
   a. will be found in an annex
   b. apply to all vessels, public or private
   c. both a and b
   d. none of the above

8. IMO stands for
   a. *I*nterpreting *M*aritime *O*ffice
   b. *I*ntergovernmental *M*odifying *O*rganization
   c. *I*nternational *M*aritime *O*rganization
   d. *I*ntemperate *M*ariners *O*rder

9. An interpretive ruling made by the Coast Guard
   a. becomes a part of the Rules of the Road
   b. is advisory to mariners but need not be complied with
   c. is not subject to interpretation by a court
   d. all of the above

10. A decision interpreting a rule of the road by the highest admiralty court in the nation
    a. will be given by that court whenever the Coast Guard requests an interpretation
    b. will prevail over a Coast Guard interpretive ruling on the identical question
    c. both of the above
    d. none of the above

AND ANSWERS

The houselights dim and a hush falls over the audience. Emmy nods to Tony who pronounces the fateful words to Oscar: "The envelope, please!" The scoring? Ten points for each correct response, and here is the tally sheet:

90 or 100	best performance in a documentary
80	"ad libbed" once too often
70	science fiction
under 70	special award for fantasy of the year!

1. c   2. d   3. b   4. b   5. a   6. c   7. c   8. c   9. a   10. b

2

Part A—GENERAL

FOR A PLAYGOER to attend a performance of, for instance, *Hamlet* without the guidance of a program is not only gauche, it can be risky. Knowing who's been murdered and who's about to be makes it easier to understand what's happening onstage. To keep afloat in Shakespeare's Denmark one should recognize the actors, know what roles they play, and have at least a glimmer of the plot. Such a program is even more emphatically necessary at sea, where the dramas are real and the consequences potentially staggering. The "playbill" for the nautical Rules of the Road is *Part A—General.*

The purpose of the introductory rules is to set the scene by describing "who, what, when, where, and how." But first, some attention must be paid to "why," that is, to rewards and penalties. To observe the rules is not to earn echoes of "Bravo!" in the foyer. It is reward enough that an encounter between vessels pass without incident. Not so with penalties. A collision afloat is appalling. Thucydides is supposed to have uttered the banality that a collision at sea can spoil one's entire day, but in reality the anguish is much more disquieting. Unbelievable tumult accompanies the contact of two vessels. What is the price for causing a maritime collision? Destruction, injury, and death. Less apocalyptic tolls are liability for damages and perhaps criminal responsibility. In the United States the Coast Guard has jurisdiction to institute proceedings leading to suspension or revocation of licenses and mariners' documentation, and the imposition of pretty hefty fines.

Enforcement of the Rules can be a problem. No seagoing Interpol courses the waves to nab transgressors. In practice, however, no such international police force is required. When a collision does occur a lawsuit is likely to develop. Then admiralty courts will have the chance to determine fault. We've already heard of the seaman's lament that judges take months to examine what mariners must decide in minutes. Such a whine is not justified. That the mariner has little time is no reason to rush the judge. Conduct will be carefully weighed and liability assessed. There is even a protection against "hit and run." Admiralty courts take a dim view of such conduct as fleeing the scene. By U.S. law any vessel, regardless of flag, which does not, without good reason, render aid or at least proffer identification after a collision will be assumed to have been at fault. This might appear to be a mild penalty; yet if an underwriter is left holding the checkbook because his insured sped over the horizon, the eventual forfeit is substantial enough to deter wrongdoing. Our attention should be to avoidance of such dire consequences. The starting point is a clear understanding of generalities.

Our format will be to examine, in sequence, each official statement of a rule and then to poke around for its meaning. There are some differences between the COLREGS formulation and that of Inland. In addition we must be prepared to cope with another factor. The Inland Navigational Rules Act of 1980 intended to align the regulations for U.S. inland waters with the 72 COLREGS. In fact, though, they are sometimes an improvement. Inland benefits by the operating experience of COLREGS and reflects a good bit of tightening up. One result is that the IMO is now getting some ideas for improvement from Inland. The international community has already approved a number of modifications to align 72 COLREGS with the improvements found in the new Inland Rules, and some other changes are being studied. Even so, the body of each set can be considered complete. In a few instances the U.S. pattern varies substantially from COLREGS, and those infrequent differences will probably persist. But absent one view's prevailing over the other, we can look forward to little more than cosmetic adjustment for some years to come. It is time, then, for a beginning to our survey of the regulations, in Part A—General.

RULE 1—Application

COLREGS

(a) These Rules shall apply to all vessels upon the high seas and in all waters connected therewith navigable by seagoing vessels.

(b) Nothing in these Rules shall interfere with the operation of special rules made by an appropriate authority for roadsteads, harbors, rivers, lakes or inland waterways connected with the high seas and navigable by seagoing vessels. Such special rules shall conform as closely as possible to these Rules.

(c) Nothing in these Rules shall interfere with the operation of any special rules made by the Government of any State with respect to additional station or signal lights, shapes or whistle signals for ships of war and vessels proceeding under convoy, or with respect to additional station or signal lights or shapes for fishing vessels engaged in fishing as a fleet. These additional station or signal lights, shapes or whistle signals shall, so far as possible, be such that they cannot be mistaken for any light, shape or signal authorized elsewhere under these Rules.

(d) Traffic separation schemes may be adopted by the Organization for the purpose of these Rules.

(e) Whenever the Government concerned shall have determined that a vessel of special construction or purpose cannot comply fully with the provisions of any of these Rules with respect to the number, position, range or arc of visibility of lights or shapes, as well as to the disposition and characteristics of sound-signalling appliances, without interfering with the special function of the vessel, such vessel shall comply with such other provisions in regard to the number, position, range or arc of visibility of lights or shapes, as well as to the disposition and characteristics of sound-signalling appliances, as her Government shall have determined to be the closest possible compliance with these Rules in respect to that vessel.

INLAND

(a) These Rules apply to all vessels upon the inland waters of the United States, and to vessels of the United States on the Canadian waters of the Great Lakes to the extent that there is no conflict with Canadian law.

(b)(i) These Rules constitute special rules made by an appropriate authority within the meaning of Rule 1(b) of the International Regulations.

(ii) All vessels complying with the construction and equipment requirements of the International Regulations are considered to be in compliance with these Rules.

(c) Nothing in these Rules shall interfere with the operation of any special rules made by the Secretary of the Navy with respect to additional station or signal lights and shapes or whistle signals for ships of war and vessels proceeding under convoy, or by the Secretary with respect to additional station or signal lights and shapes for fishing vessels engaged in fishing as a fleet. These additional station or signal lights and shapes or whistle signals shall, so far as possible, be such that they cannot be mistaken for any light, shape, or signal authorized elsewhere under these Rules. Notice of such special rules shall be published in the Federal Register and, after the effective date specified in such notice, they shall have effect as if they were a part of these Rules.

(d) Vessel traffic service regulations may be in effect in certain areas.

(e) Whenever the Secretary determines that a vessel or class of vessels of special construction or purpose cannot comply fully with the provisions of any of these Rules with respect to the number, position, range, or arc of visibility of lights or shapes, as well as to the disposition and characteristics of sound-signalling appliances, without interfering with the special function of the vessel, the vessel shall comply with such other provisions in regard to the number, position, range, or arc of visibility of lights or shapes, as well as to the disposition and characteristics of sound-signalling appliances, as the Secretary shall have determined to be the closest possible compliance with these Rules. The Secretary may issue a certificate of alternative compliance for a vessel or class of vessels specifying the closest possible compliance with these Rules. The Secretary of the Navy shall make these determinations and issue certificates of alternative compliance for vessels of the Navy.

(f) The Secretary may accept a certificate of alternative compliance issued by a contracting party to the International Regulations if he determines that the alternative compliance standards of the contracting party are substantially the same as those of the United States.

Rule 1 states that *all* vessels are subject to the Rules. This means public and private, military, commercial, and recreational. Sometimes, though, exceptional conditions exempt a vessel from compliance. When a commanding officer of a naval craft believes her mission is best accomplished "blacked out," then no Rules of the Road signals need be shown. This is true in times of peace as well as war, and whether the ship is in a group or operating alone. She is urged to display running lights when another approaches, but she need not do so. The rationale for this exception is that public interest is best served by permitting the ship to discharge her mission without drumrolls and fanfare. Perhaps the military thereby enters the insurance business, for should there be a collision we would expect the government to pick up the tab. The point in any case is that sometimes a naval vessel may operate without any Rules of the Road lights.

International's Rule 1 goes on to say that COLREGS apply on the high seas and in all waters connected therewith navigable by seagoing vessels. This wording seems to extend the International regulations up the Mississippi, into the Great Lakes, and into San Francisco Bay. Such isolated regions as Lake Tahoe in the Sierras would be exempt, but the scope of COLREGS could still be very wide. Now, though, comes Rule 1(b). By it a sovereign is authorized to make special rules for its own backyard. The United States has done so for more than eighty years with Inland and Pilot Rules. To the distress of deck officer license candidates we have too often done it in a florid manner. Congressional acts separated Inland Rules for the Great Lakes from those for the Western Rivers, and both were distinct from those for the rest of our local waterways. This splitting of internal regulations provided a rich source of question material for license examinations. Furthermore, Congress recognized that convening its membership to adapt basic rules to satisfy local conditions would be cumbersome. The Coast Guard was therefore authorized to prepare Pilot Rules for these areas. The result for decades was a slumgullion of congressional acts and agency regulations to direct maritime operations on our waters.

72 COLREGS brought changes. By endorsing Rule 1(b) the United States agreed that its internal rules would conform as closely as possible to international requirements. Since our rules stemmed from the 1890s they differed considerably from COLREGS patterns. A restatement was inevitable, and it came with the Inland Navigational Rules Act of 1980. A Christmas present for mariners, it became effective in all areas but the Great Lakes on December 24, 1981 (there the change was scheduled for March 1983). But more than an updating was involved. By signing the international treaty we agreed that we had no jurisdiction to require compliance with our local rules on the high seas. What next developed was a recasting of the lines of demarcation or boundary lines between inside waters and those offshore.

Our right to environmental control entitles us to oversee maritime operations on the high seas. And to measure larceny in the heart of smugglers we may board shifty-eyed vessels hovering well offshore. But our own rules to prevent collision don't go to sea. The practice of drawing lines of demarcation is not new. For many years the lines have been spelled out in detail. For just as many years mariners were permitted to fashion one when no specific line was described. In pre–72 COLREGS days we could draw our own line following the general trend of the coast through the outermost aid of a system of aids to navigation. But those days are gone.

Here is the gist of the present approach. The Coast Guard is authorized to draw boundary lines, but when a specific line is not detailed the mariner can no longer improvise. The decision of whether International or Inland Rules apply has been rescued from ambiguity. In the absence of a specific line COLREGS flow in with the tide to all waters connected with the high seas and navigable by seagoing vessels. Since there is now less contrast between conduct on one side of the line and the other, problems will diminish. We should, though, expect a spate of boundary line revisions to clarify what rules are to be followed where. Inland's Rule 1(a) and 1(b) establish a pattern. Our national regulations exercise a COLREGS option to make local rules for local waters. They even extend to U.S. vessels operating on Canada's side of the Great Lakes when no conflict with Canadian rules arises. Of course to say that Inland Rules apply on our inland waters begs the issue and remands us to the discussion of boundary lines. A seamanlike practice is to check with the local Coast Guard district office if there is any doubt as to a local line of demarcation. Inland's Rule 1(b)(ii) is startling. Does it really mean that the use of Inland lights, shapes, and sound appliances is optional? No, it does not, but we'll defer our study to Chapter 8.

Rule 1(c), whether COLREGS or Inland, speaks in unequivocal terms. Flotillas of vessels engaged on special missions might have use for "within the group" signal patterns by sound, light, or shape. These additional signals are permissible for ships of war, vessels in convoy, and vessels fishing in a fleet. There is, though, a commonsense proviso: so long as the signals prescribed by the Rules of the Road are not disturbed in the process.

Rule 1(d) is related to a most important area of international concern. During the last half of the twentieth century Mother Nature has been bruised by man's spewing of chemicals on the seven seas and connected waters. Some controls of maritime traffic are in humanity's best interests. But at odds with complete control is the ancient view that the high seas belong to no one. In fact one of the great appeals of seafaring is the absence of uncomfortable surveillance by officialdom. The high seas is a last frontier, free of Big Brother and his cousins and aunts. Yet it is undeniable that in our world of burgeoning numbers with conflicting interests some measure of prudent direction is necessary.

Vessels congregate in busy areas, congregation risks collision, and collision risks oil spills. COLREGS Rule 1(d) recognizes local maritime "freeways" which channel traffic safely through congested areas. But these "traffic separation schemes" cannot be set up at local whim. To receive COLREGS recognition they must be adopted by the IMO. Rule 10 of the International set has much to say about all this, and later on we'll consider it in detail. For now we need only note that a scheme is not a Scheme until the IMO says so. In passing we should observe something else. A British flavor to COLREGS terminology occasionally surfaces. The English-language version of International Rules harbors a "whilst" or two in place of our colonial "while." And the appearance of "scheme" warrants comment. In the United States that word smacks of the tinhorn's scam or sting. Not so in London where COLREGS saw the light of day. A traffic separation scheme is a legitimate arrangement vouchsafed by IMO credentials.

While (or whilst, as you will) we're still sorting things out, we should note another distinction between COLREGS and Inland. Rule 1(d) of the American set makes no mention of traffic separation schemes. Instead it speaks of "vessel traffic service" regulations. There is a significant difference between a scheme and VTS. Shipmasters are still sovereign on the high seas and COLREGS do not trespass. A traffic separation scheme overlaid on the high seas need not be followed. Not to do so might raise judicial eyebrows to the peruke, but explanations will be listened to. What COLREGS fashion is a code for the conduct of those who elect to follow a traffic separation scheme. Although election is still the shipmaster's prerogative, the rule narrows his freedom. Not even the lordly master can ignore the existence of a nearby scheme. Whether he uses it or not might be his privilege but he must observe COLREGS precepts when an official scheme is in the neighborhood.

In local waters, though, the right of a nation to direct and control traffic is clear. All the sundry shipmasters can be told where to go, when, and how. That is vessel traffic service regulation, or VTS. For many decades the concept has been applied to the Panama Canal. A large measure of his autonomy is surrendered by the master who wishes to transit the canal. The same principle is used to control vessel movements in several U.S. areas. Valdez, Alaska, is an example. Tankers laden with crude oil from the North Slope are not free to pass through Prince William Sound as they wish. Congestion, and the accompanying risk, are minimized by Coast Guard reins directing vessel operation. As such limitations develop they will appear in *Coast Pilots* and in Coast Guard addenda to the Inland Navigational Rules. We need not tarry on such localized requirements, yet we must note that Inland Rule 1(d) warns us that such VTS constraints might be in effect.

Rule 1(e), whether COLREGS or Inland, is a recognition that ships come in all sorts of shapes and builds. A small vessel propelled by an outboard motor would have a difficult time placing a light at her stern over the keel. To require that an aircraft carrier fit masthead lights in a fore-and-aft line over her keel would be to make an obstacle course out of her flight deck. And commercial vessels are by no means standardized in rig. Some have oil-drilling derricks rising from the main deck; some are slab-sided sheds garaging hundreds of automobiles enroute to the marketplace. On others the stern might be the watertight gate of a graving dock formed by her sides and used to raise cargo-laden lighters out of the sea. By Rule 1(e) any vessel, whether military, commercial, or otherwise, may petition her government for certification that her special purpose would be thwarted by strict compliance with the technical requirements spelled out in the Rules for lights, shapes, and sound appliances. So the small ship with the outboard could be allowed to offset a light from her outboard motor well. The carrier is allowed to place masthead displays on her "island." And the cargo ship of unique build can rearrange her lights, shapes, or sound appliances to accommodate her nature. Such departures, though, cannot be without sanction. In the United States permission to vary is granted to warships by the secretary of the navy. Private vessels look to the Coast Guard for a Certificate of Alternative Compliance, which is issued after investigation and is valid for a specified period of time. Inland Rule 1(f) steers clear of redundant paperwork by allowing the Coast Guard to accept a certificate issued by a foreign government if the standards used are substantially parallel to ours.

RULE 2—Responsibility

COLREGS

(a) Nothing in these Rules shall exonerate any vessel, or the owner, master or crew thereof, from the consequences of any neglect to comply with these Rules or of the neglect of any precaution which may be required by the ordinary practice of seamen, or by the special circumstances of the case.

(b) In construing and complying with these Rules due regard shall be had to all dangers of navigation and collision and to any special circumstances, including the limitations of the vessels involved, which may make a departure from these Rules necessary to avoid immediate danger.

INLAND

(a) Nothing in these Rules shall exonerate any vessel, or the owner, master, or crew thereof, from the consequences of any neglect to comply with these Rules or of the neglect of any precaution which may be required by the ordinary practice of seamen, or by the special circumstances of the case.

(b) In construing and complying with these Rules due regard shall be had to all dangers of navigation and collision and to any special circumstances, including the limitations of the vessels involved, which may make a departure from these Rules necessary to avoid immediate danger.

There is no alternative to compliance with Rule 2 on any waters. If one were to name the touchstone of collision regulations, this rule would be it. Its two paragraphs appeared in years past as separate rules straggling along near the end of the regulations. Now they are merged into one rule up front where, in spirit, they have always been.

Rule 2(a) is sometimes called the "Rule of Good Seamanship." It is a stern reminder that the regulations do not overlook common sense. The Rules are fashioned to restrain conduct, but they do not beget seafaring humanoids. When an automaton encounters a situation for which it has no program, a murmured "I do not compute" might excuse inaction. Not so with mariners. The Rules are not silicon discs evoking invariable responses. Nothing, says this admonition, shall bring acquittal from the consequences of stupidity. Mariners are to observe the Rules, but in doing so they must follow the dictates of ordinary seamanship in the context of the situation. The plea that the letter of the law was met will not be tolerated. Seamen cannot abdicate seamanship by a blind adherence to words printed on a page.

Rule 2(b) plugs another burrow for those of passive mind. Sometimes called the "General Prudential Rule," it has roots in a basic standard of human conduct. No one should have the right to disregard the last clear chance to avoid disaster. No matter how culpable other participants might be, he with "the right-of-way" must cooperate to prevent casualty. What Rule 2(b) says is that it is a violation of the Rules to cleave to the regulations when a departure might negate the danger.

A glance now at the tenor of the entire pattern is in order. Both COLREGS and Inland present a script to dictate conduct. They also supply a code of signals to exchange basic data. By no means does Rule 2(b) suborn a capricious disregard of those requirements. Instead it says, "If there is no script, or if what script exists won't work, then be ready to 'ad lib.' " There is nothing advisory about Rule 2(b). It *requires* mariners to improvise. But there must be some restraint on this mandate, for otherwise the entire structure of codes for conduct and for signals could be bypassed. And the last sentence serves as our introduction to a good shipmate, *SELMA*.

No acronym can be expected to squeeze shelfloads of court decisions into a capsule. What SELMA can do is spotlight those situations when Rule 2(b) must be followed by departing from the literal rules. Here is what the letters in SELMA represent.

S

"Signals misunderstood." Your intention was to blow one blast, but somehow the whistle stuttered and out came two blasts. You have just signaled an unintended cue card. What to do? The mariner on the other ship is not aware of the miscue; he must assume that you meant what you said. The result is inevitable confusion. Which script should you now follow: the one you intended or the one you signaled? Which should the other follow: the one he heard or the one he might judge more appropriate? A short conversation by radiotelephone could resolve the mixup. Or could it? Not every vessel, even on U.S. waters, need have such a device. And if balky electrons refused to flow the equipment might be inoperative. On the high seas the problem is more pronounced. Who demands every vessel to carry a radiotelephone out there? Who says you must speak English or Russian or Esperanto? The only safe solution to the Case of the Stuttering Sound is Rule 2(b): under the special circumstances, improvise with caution.

E

"In *E*xtremis." This Latin phrase as used at the Inns of Court might have a variety of technical meanings, but for the mariner there is only one. It tells him that unless somebody does something in a hurry his ship and another are going to strike. Here is a scenario. He and his counterpart on an approaching vessel have a script to follow. One might be required to hold course and speed while the other is obliged to keep clear. Perhaps both are enjoined to keep out of the way. Whatever the roles, there has been a miscue. Now they are in an awkward muddle. A collision is imminent. The British phrase for the situation is "the agony of collision." If contact is actually inevitable, the problem is at least simplified. The duty of each is then to minimize the impact and start writing up an accident report. But so long as there is a last clear chance of avoidance, that ultimate act must be performed. If one ship has the role of holding course and speed, she can no longer hold course and/or speed when the other has run out of options for avoidance. The only answer is, again, departure from the rules.

Fig. 1. Special Circumstances. The limited ability of tug and barge to perform normal duties must be recognized by A.

L

"*L*imitations of the vessels involved." It is all very well to say that *B* should keep clear of *A*. But what if *B* is so handicapped by, for example, weather that keeping clear is not possible? *A* is not allowed to be like Cain. He *must* be his brother's keeper and break off from a collision course. Figure 1 is an example. Power-driven *A* observes *B*, a tug and barge, on the port bow and crossing *A*'s course. *B* is bothered by a current flowing with her at 5 knots. The barge

More than two vessels met R.M.S. Queen Mary *when she entered retirement at Long Beach, California. [Courtesy Port of Long Beach]*

is an unwieldy burden subject to the physical laws of inertia as it lumbers along on the end of a towline. We will learn later that there is a signal which such a tug can display to announce she is severely restricted in ability to deviate from course. But let's suppose no such signal is being shown. Good seamanship and common sense indicate the tug's problem. If she should slow down the barge might run over her. If she changes her course to pass under *A*'s stern the barge might well continue on across *A*'s track. Does *A* have the right to disregard *B*'s predicament? Of course not, says logic. And of course not, says Rule 2(b). The script won't work, so improvise.

M

"*M*ore than two vessels involved." The rules are designed to direct the movements of only two actors. The fundamental theme, as we'll see over and over, is that when feasible, one keeps clear while the other stands on. But what if vessels are presented with contradictory roles, as in Fig. 2? Suppose *A,* a power-driven ship, has steamer *B* on her port bow and crossing. At the same time motor vessel *C* is on her starboard bow and also crossing. *A,* we'll learn, must hold course and speed for *B.* We'll also be told she must keep out of the way of *C.* It is impossible to maintain a constant course and speed, and at the same time to change one or the other. The script won't work, but Rule 2(b) will. A departure from the script is necessary.

A

"*A*ny situation not covered by the Rules." The last letter of SELMA might appear somewhat vague. It seems to say that if no rule is written, then don't follow it. Yet this uncertain statement has a point. The Rules do not represent themselves as having anticipated every situation. Made by humans, they admit to human frailties. Besides, SELMA rolls more easily off the tongue than SELM.

Rule 2(b) emerges as a powerful regulation with strict limitations. It does not profess to make all the other rules optional. Rather, it underscores that seafarers are people. Like Rule 2(a) it requires mariners to be thinking seamen and not puppets.

Fig. 2. A Conflict of Duties. Since A *cannot hold course for* B *and at the same time steer clear of* C, *a departure from normal rules is necessary.*

RULE 3—General Definitions

COLREGS

For the purpose of these Rules, except where the context otherwise requires:

(a) The word "vessel" includes every description of water craft, including nondisplacement craft and seaplanes, used or capable of being used as a means of transportation on water.

(b) The term "power-driven vessel" means any vessel propelled by machinery.

(c) The term "sailing vessel" means any vessel under sail provided that propelling machinery, if fitted, is not being used.

(d) The term "vessel engaged in fishing" means any vessel fishing with nets, lines, trawls or other fishing apparatus which restrict maneuverability, but does not include a vessel fishing with trolling lines or other fishing apparatus which do not restrict maneuverability.

(e) The word "seaplane" includes any aircraft designed to maneuver on the water.

(f) The term "vessel not under command" means a vessel which through some exceptional circumstance is unable to maneuver as required by these Rules and is therefore unable to keep out of the way of another vessel.

(g) The term "vessel restricted in her ability to maneuver" means a vessel which from the nature of her work is restricted in her ability to maneuver as required by these Rules and is therefore unable to keep out of the way of another vessel.

The term 'vessels restricted in their ability to maneuver' shall include but not be limited to:

(i) a vessel engaged in laying, servicing or picking up a navigation mark, submarine cable or pipeline;

(ii) a vessel engaged in dredging, surveying or underwater operations;

(iii) a vessel engaged in replenishment or transferring persons, provisions or cargo while underway;

(iv) a vessel engaged in the launching or recovery of aircraft;

(v) a vessel engaged in mineclearance operations;

(vi) a vessel engaged in a towing operation such as severely restricts the towing vessel and her tow in their ability to deviate from their course.

(h) The term "vessel constrained by her draft" means a power-driven vessel which because of her draft in relation to the available depth of water is severely restricted in her ability to deviate from the course she is following.

(i) The word "underway" means that a vessel is not at anchor, or made fast to the shore, or aground.

(j) The words "length" and "breadth" of a vessel means her length overall and greatest breadth.

(k) Vessels shall be deemed to be in sight of one another only when one can be observed visually from the other.

(l) The term "restricted visibility" means any condition in which visibility is restricted by fog, mist, falling snow, heavy rainstorms, sandstorms or any other similar causes.

INLAND

For the purpose of these Rules and this Act, except where the context otherwise requires:

(a) The word "vessel" includes every description of water craft, including nondisplacement craft and seaplanes, used or capable of being used as a means of transportation on water;

(b) The term "power-driven vessel" means any vessel propelled by machinery;

(c) The term "sailing vessel" means any vessel under sail provided that propelling machinery, if fitted, is not being used;

(d) The term "vessel engaged in fishing" means any vessel fishing with nets, lines, trawls, or other fishing apparatus which restricts maneuverability, but does not include a vessel fishing with trolling lines or other fishing apparatus which do not restrict maneuverability;

(e) The word "seaplane" includes any aircraft designed to maneuver on the water;

(f) The term "vessel not under command" means a vessel which through some exceptional circumstance is unable to maneuver as required by these Rules and is therefore unable to keep out of the way of another vessel;

(g) The term "vessel restricted in her ability to maneuver" means a vessel which from the nature of her work is restricted in her ability to maneuver as required by these Rules and is therefore unable to keep out of the way of another vessel; vessels restricted in their ability to maneuver include, but are not limited to:

(i) a vessel engaged in laying, servicing, or picking up a navigation mark, submarine cable, or pipeline;

(ii) a vessel engaged in dredging, surveying, or underwater operations;

(iii) a vessel engaged in replenishment or transferring persons, provisions, or cargo while underway;

(iv) a vessel engaged in the launching or recovery of aircraft;

(v) a vessel engaged in minesweeping operations; and

(vi) a vessel engaged in a towing operation such as severely restricts the towing vessel and her tow in their ability to deviate from their course.

(h) The word "underway" means that a vessel is not at anchor, or made fast to the shore, or aground;

(i) The words "length" and "breadth" of a vessel means her length overall and greatest breadth;

(j) Vessels shall be deemed to be in sight of one another only when one can be observed visually from the other;

(k) The term "restricted visibility" means any condition in which visibility is restricted by fog, mist, falling snow, heavy rainstorms, sandstorms, or any other similar causes;

(l) "Western Rivers" means the Mississippi River, its tributaries, South Pass, and Southwest Pass, to the navigational demarcation lines dividing the high seas from harbors, rivers, and other inland waters of the United States, and the Port Allen-Morgan City Alternate Route, and that part of the Atchafalaya River above its junction with the Port Allen-Morgan City Alternate Route including the Old River and the Red River;

(m) "Great Lakes" means the Great Lakes and their connecting and tributary waters including the Calumet River as far as the Thomas J. O'Brien Lock and Controlling Works (between mile 326 and 327), the Chicago River as far as the east side of the Ashland Avenue Bridge (between mile 321 and 322), and the Saint Lawrence River as far east as the lower exit of Saint Lambert Lock;

(n) "Secretary" means the Secretary of the department in which the Coast Guard is operating;

(o) "Inland Waters" means the navigable waters of the United States shoreward of the navigational demarcation lines dividing the high seas from harbors, rivers, and other inland waters of the United States and the waters of the Great Lakes on the United States side of the International Boundary;

(p) "Inland Rules" or "Rules" mean the Inland Navigational Rules and the annexes thereto, which govern the conduct of vessels and specify the lights, shapes, and sound signals that apply on inland waters; and

(q) "International Regulations" means the International Regulations for Preventing Collisions at Sea, 1972, including annexes currently in force for the United States.

Our survey of Rule 3 should begin with a preface. The general definitions of this rule present the cast of actors. Just as in a program for a play the identification appears but once. More important, the definitions are loaded with meaning. Behind each is a careful deliberation on decades of court decisions qualified by the impact of modern technology. If Rule 2 is a paramount rule, then Rule 3 might well be the most informative. We should analyze each definition closely to squeeze out the shades of meaning. Ahead of us is a pattern which will assign the roles of "keeping clear" and "standing on." A prime rationale for who does what will involve ranking vessels by relative maneuverability. It is only reasonable that the more nimble should be directed to keep out of the way of those less able to maneuver. And the caste system starts in Rule 3.

First defined is *vessel.* The description seems to include almost everything afloat. However, the words "used or capable of being used as a means of transportation on water" are important. A literal interpretation might suggest that a can of beer perched on a bobbing wooden crate is an example of transportation on water. But the facts of seafaring say otherwise. An international convention of sovereign nations was not convened in London to make rules for flotsam and jetsam. Even so, the meaning is very wide. Note the inclusion of nondisplacement craft and seaplanes. With a nod toward the latest fashions, the Rules recognize that vessels can be exotic craft skimming over the surface on cushions of air or on hydrofoils. Craft whose natural habitat is the sky are included if they are built to maneuver on water. A ditching

Ocean patrol hydrofoil combines gas turbines and waterjet pumps to achieve speeds of up to 50 knots when foilborne. [Courtesy Boeing Marine Systems, Seattle, Washington]

jetliner is not intended of course, but aircraft with floats or hull join hovercraft in the category of "vessel." The high-seas rules have for years been applicable to seaplanes afloat. For just as long on inland waters seaplanes have been subject to Civil Air regulations. The new Inland Navigational Rules include them as vessels when actually on inland waterways.

Power-driven means propelled by machinery. The alternatives are wind-driven, towed, rowed, or just drifting. The method of mechanical propulsion is not important. The intention is to single out a vessel whose maneuverability is not constrained by wind, sea, or fickle fate. Nor is there a distinction made if a vessel combines several ways to go. Should she be under oars with sails rigged while a ram-jet engine belches water out a stern tube, she is under power.

The *sailing vessel*, though, does have limitations. Weather places many more curbs on her movements. To be propelled by sail is to be restrained in maneuverability. Whether a ship has machinery available or not is irrelevant so long as she is not using it. Sail is wind-driven. But this means wind-driven only. A vessel under power as well as sail is not considered wind-driven: she is a power-driven vessel.

The next definition introduces the need for careful attention to terms. What is a *vessel engaged in fishing?* She is not every fishing vessel, no matter how seductive her lures. The distinction is spelled out in Rule 3(d). A vessel engaged in fishing is one whose fishing apparatus restricts maneuverability. If the fishing gear does not hamper her movements, then she is not engaged in fishing. The Rules state flatly that a troller with hook-spangled lines following in her wake is not restricted by her gear. Rule 3(d) might appear to be splitting hairs, but it has a point to make. Although a vessel might not be so hampered as to be unable to keep clear of others, her fishing gear could still make following a script difficult.

Seaplane we've already met. It is an aircraft designed to maneuver on the water. A Hawaii-bound jumbo jet forced down is not a seaplane, even for the few minutes before the cabin fills with ocean. The key words are "designed to maneuver on the water." Since seaplanes rarely taxi under sail, their water-borne status is that of a power-driven vessel.

In Rule 3(f) we meet another term demanding close scrutiny. In fact this paragraph should be read together with Rule 3(g). Both refer to vessels which are unable to keep out of the way of others. Rule 3(f) considers one which, by an exceptional circumstance, is unable to maneuver as required: she cannot play her role; she is unable to keep out of the way. Conduct impossible to perform cannot be demanded; why it cannot be done is the burden of this rule. She is *not under command.* By an exceptional circumstance she is rendered *hors de combat.* Perhaps her rudder fell off. Perhaps her master toppled overboard and his grief-striken officers followed suit, leaving only the unschooled messboy to tend the tiller. For whatever exceptional reason she cannot follow the requirements of the Rules of the Road. Since maritime postmortems are probing, however, attempts at sham will surely be sniffed out. Nautical hypochondriasis will not be tolerated. Nonetheless the possibility of accidental disability must be recognized.

Rule 3(g) speaks of another vessel unable to keep out of the way. But this time the cause is different. A *vessel restricted in her ability to maneuver* is one which from the nature of her work has problems which prevent her from keeping clear. She is just as disabled as one not under command. The impossible can no more be required of her than of one disabled by accident. By Rule 3(g) professional cripples are recognized. In fact six specific types are described: cablelayers, buoy tenders; dredges, vessels engaged in underwater operations, and survey vessels; ships transferring people and commodities while underway; aircraft carriers; minesweepers; and tugs with unmanageable

By rearranging ballast, FLIP *transforms herself from a vessel in normal trim to a platform floating vertically for use in underwater surveys. [USCG photo]*

tows. But the list is not all-inclusive. If a craft has a purpose which makes her unable to keep out of the way, then whether her activity is detailed in the rule or not, she joins the group. Notice how COLREGS deals with mine disposal. We'll have more to say about this later on, but here at the outset we can observe that modern rules accommodate up-to-date technology, even that of warfare. Ridding the sea of pesky mines can be done by more sophisticated means than sweeping.

Next comes a marked contrast between high-seas and Inland regulations. COLREGS Rule 3(h) singles out a *vessel constrained by draft* as worthy of special attention. The definition limits application to power-driven vessels whose draft, compared to water depth, would make changing course ticklish. Inland views such a concept as redundant. Ahead of us is Rule 9, which admonishes vessels not to impede the safe passage of those who cannot safely navigate outside a narrow channel or a fairway. Perhaps not the only reason a ship cannot safely navigate outside a particular channel, but certainly the most obvious, would be draft. The vessel constrained by draft, says Inland, is sufficiently accommodated by Rule 9, and further spotlighting of her disability could incline her toward claiming undue advantage. Such might well be true in congested inland waters where navigation of any kind requires more awareness of the plight of others. The COLREGS view on the other hand finds

Tankers lightering to relieve constraint by draft. [Courtesy Exxon Corp.]

support in areas where unbuoyed waterways might not be so obviously constricted into narrow channels and fairways. In such a case the advertisement of a draft constraint could prove valuable. Whichever rationale might be chosen, the fact is that the rules differ. One result is that for the remainder of Rule 3 the lettering of subparagraphs in COLREGS and Inland falls out of synchrony, for Inland makes no mention of a vessel constrained by draft. COLREGS Rule 3(i) is equivalent to Inland Rule 3(h), and the discord extends into the following subparagraphs. Incidentally, here is a nitpicking note: should a sail vessel be inconvenienced by a 17-foot draft when on the high seas in water 3 fathoms deep, she would not be classified as a vessel constrained by draft. But if she were to start an auxiliary engine she would qualify. Another note on technicalities is this: the IMO has recommended the interpretation that channel width be an added factor for consideration in determining constraint by draft. Although a vessel might be "smelling bottom," perhaps she is not yet constrained if there is ample channel width for maneuvers. Proponents of the Yankee view might now be observed smirking offstage at the complications generated by what COLREGS presents as a fairly simple concept. But neither chauvinism nor pursuit of international accord should draw us into the fray as champions of one view or the other. Due regard having been given to the dispute, we apply weather helm and get back on course.

Underway is a key term defined in COLREGS Rule 3(i) and Inland Rule 3(h). The international paragraph designations don't correspond to Inland, but words and meaning are alike. There are two basic relationships between a vessel and the solid parts of our planet. She can be either in physical contact or not. That contact in turn can stem from having made fast to the shore, being at anchor, or being aground. But when she is not in contact she is underway. The term has nothing to do with motion. So long as she is floating free she is underway; whenever there is contact she is not. The last sentence, not always being true, gives absolute witness that absolute statements have a way of not always being absolute. The Underway Story is not simple.

Courts have pondered on the issue of when a vessel changes status from at anchor to underway. They met no problem with the obvious: the change takes place before the anchor emerges from the water. As soon as the anchor is aweigh (that is, as soon as it leaves the bottom) a ship is underway. What, though, if the anchor, while still on the bottom, is not holding? Ships frequently drop an anchor and then drag it along as an assist in docking or undocking. Sometimes an anchor will bounce around due to insufficient scope of chain or because of weather. Intentional or not, anchors can drag, and courts have had to decide whether a ship dragging an anchor along the bottom was underway or at anchor. The judicial answer is loud and clear: when an anchor ceases to hold, the ship is no longer at anchor. We must rearrange an earlier definition of underway. A vessel is considered underway from an anchorage when the anchor ceases to hold as well as when it is aweigh.

Rule 3's treatment of underway is somewhat cryptic on another score. When we encounter fog signals we'll meet a sound pattern for a power-driven vessel underway and another for the same ship underway and making way. Light displays for vessels engaged in fishing, for ships not under command, and for those restricted in ability to maneuver by the nature of their work will also differ depending on whether the vessel is underway or underway and making way through the water. The specifics on the signals lie far ahead in our

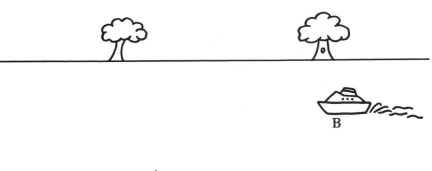

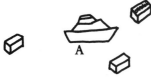

Fig. 3. Making Way. A, *drifting past the trees, is moving with but not through the water. She is underway but stopped.* B *stays abeam of the same tree as she stems the current. She is moving through but not with the water to be underway and making way.*

discussion. But now, when taking a careful look at definitions, we would do well to note the distinction. Underway, we've seen, means floating free. Underway and making way through the water involves the added factor of motion. The rules do not spell out the difference; they only use the terms. Courts, though, have told us the meanings. The extra factor of making way distinguishes a vessel moving from one dead in the water.

Do shades of meaning ever end? Apparently not. But since we've delved this far we might as well wrestle with one more nuance. Accepting the risk of being mired by minutiae, let's hazard a glance at *making way.* What does it really mean? Does it describe making way through the water or does it refer to motion over the bottom? Vessel *A* in Fig. 3 is motionless with relation to the water, but a current is moving her south at 5 knots. Is she making way? Vessel *B*, in the same current, desires to be propelled northward by her engines at 5 knots. Actually, though, she is stopped as far as motion over the bottom is concerned. Is she making way? More than one court case has hinged on the answer. The general conclusion is that making way means making way *through the water* rather than over the bottom. Vessel *A* is not making way in Fig. 3, but Vessel *B* is. Relative to nearby floating objects, *A*'s drift with the flow of current is not propulsion through the water. She and an orange crate floating alongside would be likely to keep company and relative to each other would not be moving. *B*, though, is actually in motion, at least as far as the orange crate is concerned. She, a moving object relative to *A* and to the orange crate, has a direction to indicate by signal lights and can be called on to play a role dictated by a code of conduct. With that, we should scurry back to our course. The point might decide a lawsuit now and then, yet a mariner need not draw such fine lines in the everyday practice of the art.

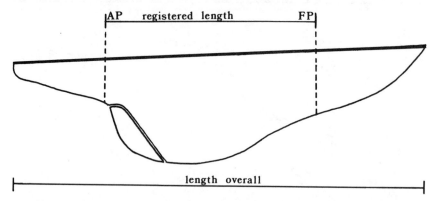

Fig. 4. *Overall Dimensions. The measure of length is overall, not just of water-line or keel.*

Length and *breadth* are next defined. Years ago the determination was by registered dimensions. That measure for length is between perpendiculars. The general idea is indicated by Fig. 4. A vertical line is drawn upward from the forefoot, at the forward end of the keel; that is the forward perpendicular. Another is drawn upward at the other end of the keel; that is the after perpendicular. The distance between them is registered length. To a naval architect the full body of his vessel is between those perpendiculars. He reckons such complexities as buoyancy, freeboard, and loadline regulation on such measures. But all this ignores bow overhang and counter. The Rules of the Road should have concern for more than keel length. More important is the overall geography occupied by the ship, and Rule 3 takes pains to avoid any perpetuation of archaic computations. Length and breadth apply to overall dimensions.

For many decades the phrase *in sight* held no ambiguity. It meant no more than that one could look over intervening water and see another vessel. Binoculars would give greater detail; bifocals might aid those with tired eyes —but in every case "in sight" meant nothing more complicated than observance of the actual object by eye, whether aided by lens or otherwise. Then came radar. A reassessment of meaning was necessary, and Rule 3, whether (k) by COLREGS or (j) by Inland, is the most recent definition of the term. It continues unbroken the older interpretation. "In sight" means in sight *visually.* Lest the modernists object, an explanation is required. Radar is a magical aid to safe navigation, but it is just that—an aid. On many counts it far exceeds the capability of the human eye. On a few crucial counts it falls short. Seas of ink have been spent analyzing its long- and shortcomings. Our purpose is not to support the yeas or nays, but we must place things in perspective. On, then, to a sampling of the pros and cons.

Radar scaled for long range offers poor minimum range. A long pulse of energy required to travel a long distance will mask objects close aboard. On the other hand when short range is important, long range is sacrificed. A short burst of energy necessary to provide nearby delineation will not survive the round trip to and from a distant horizon. Sea clutter, weather interference, and the influences of such things as other radio transmissions add a few more complications. Another factor influencing radar efficiency is beam width. The human eye has no problem on this score. It can distinguish between the turnbuckle on a smokestack stay and the horn-shaped trumpet for the whistle. Radar might show no more than a blob for the entire ship. The electronic beam has a width which can produce misleading images. Still more problems develop. Radar involves reflection of electromagnetic energy. But this requires that the reflecting object be electromagnetically reflective. In general a material which will conduct electric energy will bounce it off. In general a vertical surface will serve as a better backboard than a streamlined curve. Radar detection varies with the electromagnetic detectability of the object to be detected. Radar can overlook small vessels designed to please the eye and built of such nonconductive materials as fiberglass, wood, and canvas.

The eye sometimes needs an occasional drop of boric acid solution on the "morning after," but radar requires much more careful adjustment and maintenance. In addition the radar image is seldom a true photograph. It must be translated to display reality. Careful plotting procedures, whether by man or by machine, are the only means to unravel what radar normally presents. In its simplest form marine radar displays the electromagnetic world around a ship as if the vessel were immobile at the center of the radarscope. If she is in fact at rest, then any motion shown is the true movement of surrounding objects. But if the ship is in motion, then the picture is a relative one. Figure 5 indicates the image which would appear on a vessel traveling due north at 10 knots when its radar picks up a buoy dead ahead. The radar shows that the object detected is moving due south at 10 knots. No telltale winking of a red, green, or a white light appears to identify the buoy. No characteristic skeleton structure indicates its real character. Rather than a buoy it might be a ship dead in the water or an uncharted rock. Visual sighting can be guided by such things as running lights, buoy lights, or breakers. Radar might show only a pip.

On the other hand radar can "see" when the eye is clouded by mist, fog, and a flock of atmospheric disturbances. And radar can indicate with precision the range to another object. Argument and rebuttal have ping-ponged back and forth for years over the pitfalls and strengths of the free electron as a lookout. But none of the discussion lies at the core of Rule 3. A radar so perfect as to satisfy the most skeptical would still fall short of the demands of the Rules of the Road. Later on we'll encounter a script written to guide two vessels when they meet. In order to follow the pattern, each must know that the other is onstage. *B* cannot be expected to follow any pattern to keep out of *A*'s way unless *B* knows where *A* is and what she is doing. Even more important, *B* must rely on a presumption that *A* is also aware of *B*'s presence. Radar, no matter what its limitations, can supply much of the necessary data. But the factor of mutual awareness is missing. We are allowed to assume that the other ship is equipped with human eyes, no matter how bloodshot; we cannot assume that she has radar.

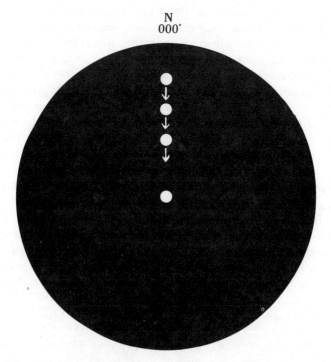

N
000°

Fig. 5. Relative Radar View. Aboard a vessel moving north, radar will show a buoy as if it were moving south.

No law requires that the world's vessels be radar equipped. Without such a requisite, neither *A* nor *B* has assurance that the other is aware of the fog-bound situation. We are not now making a judgment on radar's reliability. The only point is that radar need not be on board. For so long as ships operate without radar there will be no guarantee of mutual radar awareness. To observe another vessel by radar is not to be sure that the other observes you. And until every vessel is required to carry the device, radar cannot replace the human eye in collision avoidance. As already mentioned, we assume that the other has eyes to see us when we see him. Rule 3's definition perpetuates the first and every subsequent reaction of rulemakers to the radar age. "In sight" means "in sight *visually.*" It will probably mean nothing more for years to come.

The next term defined in Rule 3 is *restricted visibility.* To pull a cap over the mariner's eyes is not to plunge him into restricted visibility. The result might be that he is surely blind, but Rule 3 is more concerned with the cause. It lists as grounds for restricted visibility fog, mist, falling snow, heavy rain-storms, and sandstorms. Volcanic ash and a plague of locusts would probably be included as "any other similar causes." But a watchcap over the eyes or deep slumber on a nearby settee would not be in the roster. There must exist some atmospheric impedimenta to screen the mariner's view.

We have finished our survey of Rule 3 of COLREGS, but Inland Naviga-tional Rules present six more subparagraphs, (l) through (q), whose content is neither obscure nor particularly urgent. That the Mississippi is a "Western River" seems a quaint disregard of the population's steady shift toward the setting sun since the days of Davy Crockett. We've already been introduced to the problem of lines of demarcation between the high seas and inland waters. Rules 3(l) and 3(o) speak of such boundary lines as separating International and Inland Rules, but something more is needed to determine how such lines are established.

Rule 3(n), though, warrants some note. It states that the term "secretary" means the head of the department in which the Coast Guard is operating. Since Alexander Hamilton created it the Coast Guard has appeared under the banner of more than one Cabinet secretary. First it belonged to Treasury. In time of strife it becomes part of Defense. At present the standard is that of the Department of Transportation. Congress might not anticipate a transfer to Indian Affairs, yet it protects its options by the noncommittal terminology of Rule 3(n).

Not hazy is where we now find ourselves. Our encounter with Part A—General is at an end and we've earned a catnap on any handy settee. Only one detail remains to be resolved—the chapter quiz.

QUESTIONS

Our judges this time are stern indeed. Moreover, none of them was ever reversed on appeal. By name they are Roy Bean, Cotton Mather, and Caligula. So with gibbett, stake, and hungry lions at the ready, stand by!

1. A naval vessel operating at night in peacetime
   a. may turn off all lights otherwise required by the Rules of the Road
   b. should display sidelights on the approach of or to other vessels
   c. both of the above
   d. none of the above.

2. International COLREGS
   a. apply on the high seas
   b. apply on all United States waters
   c. both of the above
   d. none of the above

3. Failure to maintain a proper lookout is
   a. a violation of the Rules of the Road
   b. a violation of the Rule of Good Seamanship
   c. both of the above
   d. none of the above

4. Considered a violation of Rule 2(b), the General Prudential Rule, would be
   a. not keeping clear when the Rules so provide
   b. not departing from the Rules to avoid immediate danger
   c. both of the above
   d. none of the above

5. A vessel has her anchor down and it ceases to hold. She is
   a. still considered at anchor
   b. considered underway
   c. either of the above
   d. none of the above

6. Not considered a vessel engaged in fishing would be
   a. a vessel engaged in trawling
   b. a vessel engaged in trolling
   c. a vessel fishing with drift nets
   d. a vessel engaged in purse seining

7. A vessel is at anchor in a swift current. The anchor ceases to hold and she begins to drift with the current. She is
   a. underway
   b. underway and making way
   c. both of the above
   d. none of the above

8. A sail vessel is constrained by her draft in relation to the available depth of water. By Inland Rules she is considered
   a. a vessel not under command
   b. a vessel restricted in ability to maneuver
   c. a vessel constrained by draft
   d. none of the above

9. An example of restricted visibility would be
   a. fog
   b. a heavy rainstorm
   c. a sandstorm
   d. all of the above

10. Considered by the rules to be a "vessel restricted in ability to maneuver" would be
    a. a vessel engaged in fishing
    b. a vessel constrained by draft
    c. a vessel surveying
    d. all of the above

AND ANSWERS

Caligula has consulted with a white horse. The result? Bean and Mather agree to follow a Roman standard of measure. Ten points for each correct response, and here is the pattern for scoring:

90–100	a gladiator worthy of the main event
80	suitable for the semifinals
70	saved for another battle
under 70	thumbs down

1. c   2. a   3. c   4. b   5. b   6. b   7. a   8. d   9. d   10. c

3

Part B—CONDUCT IN ANY VISIBILITY

AT LAST, the play begins! Part B presents, in *Steering and Sailing Rules,* the required conduct. Its Section I decrees deportment in any condition of visibility, and Rule 4, whether COLREGS or Inland, merely affirms that.

RULE 4—Application

COLREGS

Rules in this Section apply to any condition of visibility.

INLAND

Rules in this subpart apply in any condition of visibility.

Perhaps repeated comparison of all this to a script might wear thin occasionally, but mariners have been putting up with the tedious since Noah found himself in heavy rain. Besides, the analogy of vessel maneuvers to a stage play is apt. So long as we progress toward a clear understanding of the Rules, any parallel is valuable. Back, then, to greasepaint and curtain calls.

RULE 5—Lookout

COLREGS

Every vessel shall at all times maintain a proper look-out by sight and hearing as well as by all available means appropriate in the prevailing circumstances and conditions so as to make a full appraisal of the situation and of the risk of collision.

INLAND

Every vessel shall at all times maintain a proper look-out by sight and hearing as well as by all available means appropriate in the prevailing circumstances and conditions so as to make a full appraisal of the situation and of the risk of collision.

Rule 5 requires mariners to employ all available means to gain essential data. Judgments are made on facts, and every ship is equipped with factfinders. We must use everything at hand. Of course doing so is an exercise of good seamanship, and Rule 2(a) already dictates that we follow such practices. What Rule 5 adds are some specifics.

The mariner must look and listen at all times, day and night, in fair weather and foul. Moreover, the means he uses to do so must be appropriate to the prevailing conditions. In our modern world these means include such electronic aids as radar. Why must he do so? To gather the data on which to base a full appraisal of the situation and of the risk of collision. The best time to plan avoidance is before avoidance becomes pressing. Rules of conduct are mandatory when risk of collision exists, for then the actors are considered to be on stage together. But no summons will be heard calling them to perform. Each must determine on his own when it is time to start following a script. By judging the situation he must decide when collision risk is upon him.

In rough weather the bow might not be the station for a proper lookout. [USN photo]

Keeping a proper lookout is paramount in such a determination. What this entails might seem obvious, but a few examples are nonetheless valuable. In a thick fog and proceeding bow-first, a lookout should be near the bow and low down. On the other hand when going astern the critical arc of observation is the other end of the ship. To listen for fog signals requires that the ears not be bothered by onboard din. On a small vessel this might require that the engine be stopped occasionally. In heavy weather the safe post for a lookout is in a protected area, but that's not in the galley cradling a cup of coffee. He must bear up under inconvenience, for a protected post does not ensure insulation from the elements.

A lookout cannot be just anyone aboard. He must know what to look and to listen for; he must be instructed in how to observe and how to report. He cannot be an untutored apprentice. When a sail vessel is flying wing-and-wing with everything from BVDs to spinnakers drawing well, yards of sailcloth blocking the view will not excuse failure to look ahead. Someone must be positioned to peer under, over, around, or perhaps through the sails. Should radar be on board and in working condition it must be used. A COLREG isn't necessary to instruct mariners in common sense. The message of Rule 5 is a forceful reminder that certain practices are essential.

RULE 6—Safe Speed

COLREGS

Every vessel shall at all times proceed at a safe speed so that she can take proper and effective action to avoid collision and be stopped within a distance appropriate to the prevailing circumstances and conditions.

In determining a safe speed the following factors shall be among those taken into account:

(a) By all vessels:

(i) the state of visibility;

(ii) the traffic density including concentrations of fishing vessels or any other vessels;

(iii) the maneuverability of the vessel with special reference to stopping distance and turning ability in the prevailing conditions;

(iv) at night the presence of background light such as from shore lights or from back scatter of her own lights;

(v) the state of wind, sea and current, and the proximity of navigational hazards;

(vi) the draft in relation to the available depth of water.

(b) Additionally, by vessels with operational radar:

(i) the characteristics, efficiency and limitations of the radar equipment;

(ii) any constraints imposed by the radar range scale in use;

(iii) the effect on radar detection of the sea state, weather and other sources of interference;

(iv) the possibility that small vessels, ice and other floating objects may not be detected by radar at an adequate range;

(v) the number, location and movement of vessels detected by radar;

(vi) the more exact assessment of the visibility that may be possible when radar is used to determine the range of vessels or other objects in the vicinity.

INLAND

Every vessel shall at all times proceed at a safe speed so that she can take proper and effective action to avoid collision and be stopped within a distance appropriate to the prevailing circumstances and conditions.

In determining a safe speed the following factors shall be among those taken into account:

(a) By all vessels:
   (i) the state of visibility;
   (ii) the traffic density including concentration of fishing vessels or any other vessels;
   (iii) the maneuverability of the vessel with special reference to stopping distance and turning ability in the prevailing conditions;
   (iv) at night the presence of background light such as from shore lights or from back scatter of her own lights;
   (v) the state of wind, sea, and current, and the proximity of navigational hazards;
   (vi) the draft in relation to the available depth of water.
(b) Additionally, by vessels with operational radar:
   (i) the characteristics, efficiency and limitations of the radar equipment;
   (ii) any constraints imposed by the radar range scale in use;
   (iii) the effect on radar detection of the sea state, weather, and other sources of interference;
   (iv) the possibility that small vessels, ice and other floating objects may not be detected by radar at an adequate range;
   (v) the number, location, and movement of vessels detected by radar; and
   (vi) the more exact assessment of the visibility that may be possible when radar is used to determine the range of vessels or other objects in the vicinity.

The concept of safe speed is the same under COLREGS and Inland. It also is dictated by the ordinary practice of good seamanship. Every vessel should be as manageable as possible at all times and under all conditions. Rule 6 lists some guidelines, and by the very act of doing so incorporates them into the roster of seamanlike practices required by Rule 2(a). Were no such guidelines defined, though, they would still come to mind by answering this question: What would a careful mariner consider in selecting a safe speed? He would surely take into account traffic density, weather, and nearness to danger. The prudent mariner would also know something about the capabilities of his ship. How long will it take her to stop and in what distance? How nimble is she in turning and within what radius? Vessels cannot be like strange horses rented in a livery stable for a day's canter in the woods. The shipmaster should be familiar with his mount. Not far ahead of us is a discussion of what he should know about the other master's mount.

The selection of a safe speed involves more factors. The mariner must recognize problems unique to nighttime. Background lights can mask the displays of another vessel. His own illumination, particularly in mist and fog, can envelop him in a blinding glow called "back scatter." The list goes on and on, and so does Rule 6. In the process it might sound a bit pedantic, but its purpose is detail. The Good Seamanship edict of Rule 2 covers much more, but it does so with no specifics. Rule 6 narrows the focus. An example is its consideration of radar as a tool to be used with understanding. In discussing Rule 3 we met some of its shortcomings. Rule 6 requires that we be acquainted not only with its vices, but also with some virtues. To learn electronically that an object is 2 miles off, yet not to see it, is to suspect that visibility is less than 2 miles. When radar beams stab through fog to ricochet electrons off an invisible object, the mariner is told indirectly how far he can see.

The mariner is a sort of "central control" who receives and processes data on which to base crucial decisions affecting, quite literally, life and property. One such judgment is choice of a safe speed. He must take into account every shred of evidence supplied by whatever means. If the theme sounds repetitive, just bear with the annoyance. COLREGS are not the result of committee meetings interrupted by pink gins in London. They arise from centuries of reactions by a score of societies to the vagaries of human conduct afloat. They respond to the threat of the havoc wrought by a rampaging ship. No mariner can be faulted for an occasional sober thought on the seriousness of all this, for each of us perceives how solitary is the responsibility of avoiding collision. Harry Truman could have been a seaman. His philosophy about where the "buck" stops is an onboard way of life.

RULE 7—Risk of Collision

COLREGS

(a) Every vessel shall use all available means appropriate to the prevailing circumstances and conditions to determine if risk of collision exists. If there is any doubt such risk shall be deemed to exist.

(b) Proper use shall be made of radar equipment if fitted and operational, including long-range scanning to obtain early warning of risk of collision and radar plotting or equivalent systematic observation of detected objects.

(c) Assumptions shall not be made on the basis of scanty information, especially scanty radar information.

(d) In determining if risk of collision exists the following considerations shall be among those taken into account:

(i) such risk shall be deemed to exist if the compass bearing of an approaching vessel does not appreciably change;

(ii) such risk may sometimes exist even when an appreciable bearing change is evident, particularly when approaching a very large vessel or a tow or when approaching a vessel at close range.

INLAND

(a) Every vessel shall use all available means appropriate to the prevailing circumstances and conditions to determine if risk of collision exists. If there is any doubt such risk shall be deemed to exist.

(b) Proper use shall be made of radar equipment if fitted and operational, including long-range scanning to obtain early warning of risk of collision and radar plotting or equivalent systematic observation of detected objects.

(c) Assumptions shall not be made on the basis of scanty information, especially scanty radar information.

(d) In determining if risk of collision exists the following considerations shall be among those taken into account:

(i) such risk shall be deemed to exist if the compass bearing of an approaching vessel does not appreciably change; and

(ii) such risk may sometimes exist even when an appreciable bearing change is evident, particularly when approaching a very large vessel or a tow or when approaching a vessel at close range.

Rule 7, the same in both sets, begins to weave subplots into a pattern. Risk of collision is the threshold of collision avoidance. When no risk exists there is little need to follow a script. About now we might bear off from the theater and chance a different kind of analogy. When a person is in a pasture with a raging bull, he is at risk of being gored. Should the bull be a mile away the danger is minimal, particularly if the bull is past his prime. The person might have ample time to vault a fence to safety. Suppose, though, that the bull is young and only 100 yards away. The time frame shrinks frightfully. But in either case that person runs the risk of being gored as soon as he steps into the pasture.

Risk of collision exists as a tug passes a down-bound freighter in the narrow Houston Ship Canal. [USCG photo]

Next comes a fair question: What has this to do with ships? Well, ship *A* is southbound at 15 knots and dead ahead 10 miles away ship *B* is coming north at the same speed. With a closing rate of 30 knots they will see the 10 miles in the middle vanish in 20 minutes. Is there risk of collision? Is the situation akin to the case of the tired old bull furlongs away or does it approach that of the yearling at close quarters? Before fashioning an answer, let's change the facts. The two ships are approaching as before but they are 5 miles apart. It will only be 10 minutes before they are bow-to-bow. What now about risk of collision? What sort of bull is in the pasture now? The answer in either case depends on nimbleness as well as on speed and range.

Ships cannot swerve and stop as readily as either people or bulls. That truism brings us to some generalities on maneuverability. Even though the conversation will be directed toward large vessels, all hands should pay attention. A well-advertised principle of auto operation is defensive driving. We should anticipate the other driver's problems and possible reactions in order not to bend fenders. The same idea applies a thousandfold afloat, where collisions are much more resounding than fender-benders.

A 50-foot cabin cruiser is very handy, indeed. But by sharing the waterways with such lumbering mammoths as supertankers and freighters she has a real concern for their handiness or lack of it. The average merchant vessel is more than large. She is probably single screw, verges on being undermanned and is somewhat underpowered. Were she to have the power/weight ratio of the cabin cruiser her engine would be rated in millions of horsepower. In reality it is less than 5 percent of such a projection. None of us can ignore the facts of modern ship operation. An enormous mass is placed in motion by one propeller churning 90 or so times a minute. Inertia is expected to help keep her in motion once the engine has gotten her up to speed. Here is an eye-popping statistic regarding a 200,000-ton tanker. Suppose she is moving at 16 knots and the engine is abruptly stopped. After 20 minutes she will still be moving forward at 8 knots. She will not come to a standstill in the water for more than an hour (see Fig. 6).

engines stopped	20 mins.	40 mins.	vessel stopped
			60 mins.

Fig. 6. No Sudden Stops. A large vessel will keep moving for a long interval in distance and time after she begins to stop.

No merchant ship is designed for fancy maneuvering. Tugs will usually be in attendance for docking and undocking, even if in a pinch she might be able to do the job on her own. At best, though, she is hard to manage and on occasion is uncontrollable. A smaller vessel might approach the agility of our friend in full flight from a bull; a supertanker, by contrast, can be as unmanageable as a lava flow.

With so many varieties of craft sharing the water, Rule 7 cannot dictate any precise formula to determine when risk of collision exists. Instead it requires each mariner to be aware of what might be involved and then to make his own judgment. We must be prepared for "defensive seafaring." And for us that means attention to some more ins and outs of shiphandling. A few moments ago we considered the prospect of a 200,000-tonner stopping her engine when moving at 16 knots. What if, instead of just ordering "Stop," her master had said "Full astern"? It would take nearly a half hour for her to come dead in the water, and that would take place 6 or so miles beyond the point at which the command was given. But there could be still another frightening consequence. Her machinery might not stand the strain of trying to bring all that weight to a sudden stop. She could end up literally dead in the water, with nuts and bolts bouncing off the engine room bulkheads.

The problem of stopping a heavy ship has caught the attention of professional mariners throughout the world, including the Elder Brethren of Trinity House. And now *we* are inclined to initiate a crash stop. The very mention of such a fellowship demands comment. What we learn might do no more than add an item to a treasure trove of trivia, but we can go no further until the mystery is solved. Such a title could emerge from no place but Britain. Trinity House is a four-century-old organization serving a variety of maritime functions. It was chartered by a British monarch in 1514 and oversees aids to navigation and pilotage within the United Kingdom. Its membership is divided into the Younger Brethren and their gray-thatched seniors, the Elder Brethren. These last include some of the world's foremost mariners and serve as expert advisors to admiralty judges of the House of Lords. The influence of their opinions extends far beyond the shores of England. Now that the Elder Brethern are identified, we can resume our course.

Throughout the world experts are wrestling with the problem of stopping a huge ship. One suggestion to save wear and tear on gears is that a seagoing behemoth reduce its speed in stages as she "fishtails" back and forth across her track. Instead of trying to reverse propulsion, she should offer more resistance to forward motion while ahead-power is diminished. The point for nonbehemoths is that any such huge vessel trying to stop in this manner will require thousands of yards of ocean in which to do so.

What about ability to turn? What if the outsize tanker making 16 knots suddenly goes hard right to change course by 90°? Before she would be heading on the new track she would have advanced more than half a mile in her original direction. And no craft had better be in her side-slipping way! Defining the region of collision risk is getting more elusive as we delve into the problem. And what's been said isn't unique to mammoths. A sleek naval escort with ample reserve power and not 2 percent of the tanker's bulk is no Peter Pan of the sea. It is estimated that her crash stop from 30 knots would take up a quarter of a mile. Her advance while changing course by 90° would be no less. A nuclear-powered carrier with less than half the heft of the supertanker is certainly no better off than her escort.

None of these facts and figures can be ignored by any mariner approaching another vessel. Risk of collision arises long before you can make out the other's name painted on her bow. Large vessels approaching each other might find that risk arises when they are more than 10 miles apart. As size and speed decrease the estimate shortens, but in every case the analogy of the bull applies.

Our friend in the pasture is at no risk if he stays far away from the bull. But he must allow for tripping over bushes and gopher holes as he scrambles to safety. No mariner can define the radius of risk as 1 mile or 10. Everything depends on prevailing circumstances. And if there is any doubt as to whether risk exists, he must assume that it does.

Rule 7 orders the use of radar, including plotting. This can be done manually or by automatic device, but it must be done. Absolute statements have felled

High-speed naval escorts laboring in heavy seas. [USN photo]

us again! To "must be done" we add "nearly always." When a vessel is threading a course along a river, rapt attention to radar plotting might not expand her knowledge of the course of an approaching ship. Perhaps the time would be better spent on a bridge wing. Yet even then periodic consideration of radar data could be helpful. When, though, radar is consulted, no snap judgments based on hurried looks at the scope are tolerated. A study of radar plots is not within our purpose, but "defensive seafaring" requires that some comment be made. A radarscope can present its image in a variety of ways. On smaller vessels not equipped with a gyro compass the view is a *relative* picture. We've already discussed what it shows, but the added emphasis is worthwhile. The observer is at the center of the scope and "pips" move around him as if he were stopped. If in fact he is stopped, then by coincidence he sees a real picture of his surroundings. If he is in motion, though, the actual view is quite different to what his radar offers.

Figure 7 illustrates the following situation. You are proceeding due east at 10 knots. Vessel *A* lies dead in the water and and is directly ahead of you. Radar will show her as moving due west at your speed. Vessel *B* is abeam to starboard and, like you, traveling 090° at 10 knots. Radar shows her as not moving at all. Vessel *C* is abeam to port and heading due west at 10 knots. The scope depicts her as sprinting toward 270° at 20 knots. The scope picture makes your ship a sort of giant pelorus or bearing circle with 000° lined up with your bow and 180° with your stern. And to unravel the relative motion around you is the purpose of radar plotting.

A variation connects the radar presentation to a gyrocompass. Now the scope is "stabilized" by the gyro so that north appears at 000°. Your ship's bow will not be at the top of the scope's circle but will show as a line of light or "heading flasher" somewhere on the rim. Only when you are in fact going north will it coincide with 000°. Now your ship is a king-size compass rose with north at the top of the scope. But even by this "north up" or "stabilized" view the motion of objects is relative to the observer. Your ship still appears as if stopped at the center. Figure 8 recasts the view of vessels *A, B,* and *C.* Change the calibrations on the circle and the picture is the same as in Fig. 7.

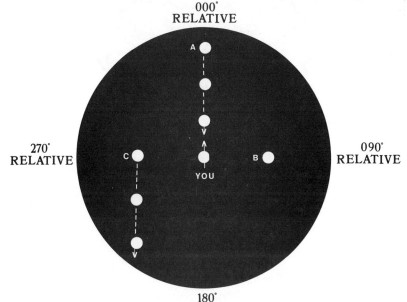

Fig. 7. Interpreting Relative Radar: You are eastbound at 10 knots. Relative radar shows stationary A *moving west at 10 knots, eastbound* B *moving at your speed as stopped, and* C, *westbound at 10 knots, as going west at 20 knots.*

The third radar presentation is more sophisticated. The scope is connected to speed-measuring equipment as well as to a gyrocompass. A special "pip" is created in response to the speed and direction instruments. It represents your ship as it would move across the scope. Your simulated motion will then travel across the radar picture in company with actual "pips" of other vessels. *True motion* approaches a helicopter view of your part of the ocean. Other objects move around as they truly do; you move around as your guidance equipment reports that you do. Figure 9 shows how you and your fellow travelers *A, B,* and *C* would now appear.

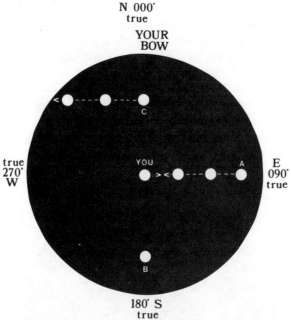

N 000°
true

YOUR
BOW

true
270°
W

YOU

A

E
090°
true

C

B

180° S
true

Fig. 8. A "Stabilized" Radar View. Even when controlled by a gyrocompass, radar depicts relative motion. You, eastbound at 10 knots, see stationary A as moving west. B, moving at your course and speed, seems stopped. C, on an opposite course at your speed, seems to go west at twice her speed.

We need tarry no longer on all this. But we should be aware that most radar observation is founded on relative motion. The scope view can be misleading, with reality not quite the same as it is presented.

Rule 7 is stingy on guidelines to risk of collision, but it is not silent. If the compass bearing of an approaching vessel doesn't appreciably change, then risk exists. That is not to say a bearing change will cancel risk, however. A ship yawing back and forth will appear on different bearings even though she is approaching from a steady direction. A large vessel is more than a shapeless blob, even when far off. Seen broad-on the bow might first be her fo'c'sle head and then her midship house, but the net bearing can remain unchanged. And one of the longest "vessels" is a tug waddling along with a husky barge hundreds of meters astern.

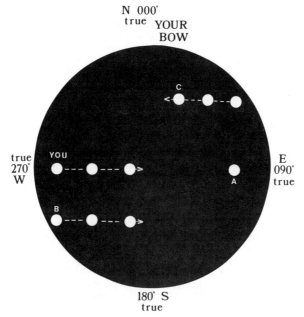

Fig. 9. *True-Motion Radar. Only when the radarscope shows your motion will the view of nearby objects be realistic. Now stationary* A *does not move.* B, *with your course and speed, moves parallel to you.* C, *on an opposite course, moves westward at her true speed.*

What should we conclude from all this? If nothing else, that the approach of any vessel means potential danger. We're back again in the pasture with the bull. Every precaution must be taken to judge when danger might arise. And risk is not measured solely by the capabilities of our own vessel. It takes two to tangle. Defensive seafaring is a must.

RULE 8—Action to Avoid Collision

COLREGS

(a) Any action taken to avoid collision shall, if the circumstances of the case admit, be positive, made in ample time and with due regard to the observance of good seamanship.

(b) Any alteration of course and/or speed to avoid collision shall, if the circumstances of the case admit, be large enough to be readily apparent to another vessel observing visually or by radar; a succession of small alterations of course and/or speed should be avoided.

(c) If there is sufficient sea room, alteration of course alone may be the most effective action to avoid a close-quarters situation provided that it is made in good time, is substantial and does not result in another close-quarters situation.

(d) Action taken to avoid collision with another vessel shall be such as to result in passing at a safe distance. The effectiveness of the action shall be carefully checked until the other vessel is finally past and clear.

(e) If necessary to avoid collision or allow more time to assess the situation, a vessel shall slacken her speed or take all way off by stopping or reversing her means of propulsion.

INLAND

(a) Any action taken to avoid collision shall, if the circumstances of the case admit, be positive, made in ample time and with due regard to the observance of good seamanship.

(b) Any alteration of course or speed to avoid collision shall, if the circumstances of the case admit, be large enough to be readily apparent to another vessel observing visually or by radar; a succession of small alterations of course or speed should be avoided.

(c) If there is sufficient sea room, alteration of course alone may be the most effective action to avoid a close-quarters situation provided that it is made in good time, is substantial and does not result in another close-quarters situation.

(d) Action taken to avoid collision with another vessel shall be such as to result in passing at a safe distance. The effectiveness of the action shall be carefully checked until the other vessel is finally past and clear.

(e) If necessary to avoid collision or allow more time to assess the situation, a vessel shall slacken her speed or take all way off by stopping or reversing her means of propulsion.

Judging risk is but a part of collision avoidance. In any condition of visibility the mariner must have a script to guide his avoiding action. Rule 8 supplies the need. What's in store for us is another dose of common sense. So far nearly every rule we've met has contained a statement or two emphasizing sensible conduct to be expected of any responsible person. The justification for belaboring the obvious? People are not always sensible. Rule 8, though, is more than a litany of reminders. Note the verbs it uses. In four of its five paragraphs we meet the word "shall." Translated into everyday terms that means "You've got to." Only once is conduct suggested by a "may." Rule 8 is not unique in this approach, for throughout all rules the theme is "do" and "don't." In reading any rule of the road we must check each word and look carefully for the "yagottas."

Getting out of the way of another vessel requires forceful action. Sidling unobtrusively left or right will not be appreciated and maybe not even noticed by the other mariner. His decision on collision risk depends on how he judges your action. Avoidance requires seamanlike steps taken early and in ample measure. This "shall" is particularly necessary in the radar age. Such problems as radar beam width might mask from the observer any mincing course changes by another vessel. And radar needs a little time to make any pattern evident.

We've already discussed some details about course and speed alterations by a large vessel. Ships will forge ahead while trying to go astern; they will skid as they change course. But they turn more effectively than they alter speed. When a choice is to be made between a course and a speed change, Rule 8 suggests altering course. There is, though, a predictable proviso: so long as the result doesn't involve you in other dangers.

The next "shall" in Rule 8 requires the mariner to witness the results of any action he takes. A physician-like instruction to take two aspirins and call him in the morning is not acceptable. No shipmaster can order a course change to avoid collision and then go below for schnapps. He must watch the outcome and be ready to invoke other cures.

The final requirement of Rule 8 contains an undiluted capsule of common sense. There is no law against slowing down, stopping, or reversing when necessary. Nor is it illegal to do so when sparring for time. In fact the "shall" in Rule 8(e) makes it illegal not to do so. The rules are designed to prevent collision, and collisions are less likely to happen when vessels are moving slowly or not at all. Now we must take another look ahead. Far along on our course is Rule 17, and it will decree that at times when in sight of an approaching vessel, one must hold course and speed. Yet Rule 8 says that speed shall be reduced to avoid collision or to gain time to sort things out. The two rules must be read together. Rule 17 assigns a specific role and is to be followed first. Rule 8 goes to work when, despite a script, action must be taken or sorting out the unexpected is necessary.

Here is a recap of collision avoidance. Whatever action you take, do it early in the approach so there will be time to undo its effect. Make it a substantial action, and be seamanlike. Consider a course change before a speed alteration. Keep the attempted cure under observation. If you're addled or uncertain, then slow down, stop, or back up.

RULE 9—Narrow Channels

COLREGS

(a) A vessel proceeding along the course of a narrow channel or fairway shall keep as near to the outer limit of the channel or fairway which lies on her starboard side as is safe and practicable.

(b) A vessel of less than 20 meters in length or a sailing vessel shall not impede the passage of a vessel which can safely navigate only within a narrow channel or fairway.

(c) A vessel engaged in fishing shall not impede the passage of any other vessel navigating within a narrow channel or fairway.

(d) A vessel shall not cross a narrow channel or fairway if such crossing impedes the passage of a vessel which can safely navigate only within such channel or fairway. The latter vessel may use the sound signal prescribed in Rule 34(d) if in doubt as to the intention of the crossing vessel.

(e)(i) In a narrow channel or fairway when overtaking can take place only if the vessel to be overtaken has to take action to permit safe passing, the vessel intending to overtake shall indicate her intention by sounding the appropriate signal prescribed in Rule 34(c)(i). The vessel to be overtaken shall, if in agreement, sound the appropriate signal prescribed in Rule 34(c)(ii) and take steps to permit safe passing. If in doubt she may sound the signals prescribed in Rule 34(d).

(ii) This Rule does not relieve the overtaking vessel of her obligation under Rule 13.

(f) A vessel nearing a bend or an area of a narrow channel or fairway where other vessels may be obscured by an intervening obstruction shall navigate with particular alertness and caution and shall sound the appropriate signal prescribed in Rule 34(e).

(g) Any vessel shall, if the circumstances of the case admit, avoid anchoring in a narrow channel.

INLAND

(a)(i) A vessel proceeding along the course of a narrow channel or fairway shall keep as near to the outer limit of the channel or fairway which lies on her starboard side as is safe and practicable.

(ii) Notwithstanding paragraph (a)(i) and Rule 14(a), a power-driven vessel operating in narrow channels or fairways on the Great Lakes, Western Rivers, or waters specified by the Secretary, and proceeding downbound with a following current shall have the right-of-way over an upbound vessel, shall propose the manner and place of passage, and shall initiate the maneuvering signals prescribed by Rule 34(a)(i), as appropriate. The vessel proceeding upbound against the current shall hold as necessary to permit safe passing.

(b) A vessel of less than 20 meters in length or a sailing vessel shall not impede the passage of a vessel that can safely navigate only within a narrow channel or fairway.

(c) A vessel engaged in fishing shall not impede the passage of any other vessel navigating within a narrow channel or fairway.

(d) A vessel shall not cross a narrow channel or fairway if such crossing impedes the passage of a vessel which can safely navigate only within that channel or fairway. The latter vessel shall use the danger signal prescribed in Rule 34(d) if in doubt as to the intention of the crossing vessel.

(e)(i) In a narrow channel or fairway when overtaking, the vessel intending to overtake shall indicate her intention by sounding the appropriate signal prescribed in Rule 34(c) and take steps to permit safe passing. The overtaken vessel, if in agreement, shall sound the same signal. If in doubt she shall sound the danger signal prescribed in Rule 34(d).

(ii) This Rule does not relieve the overtaking vessel of her obligation under Rule 13.

(f) A vessel nearing a bend or an area of a narrow channel or fairway where other vessels may be obscured by an intervening obstruction shall navigate with particular alertness and caution and shall sound the appropriate signal prescribed in Rule 34(e).

(g) Every vessel shall, if the circumstances of the case admit, avoid anchoring in a narrow channel.

It is one thing to speak of maneuvering to avoid collision on the open sea. The scene is much different when the seaway narrows. Rule 9 presents the script for vessels in a narrow channel. And the starting point of our study is this: What is a narrow channel? Certainly it is a bottleneck bordered by shorelines on each side. It would also be a thin strip of deep water between shoals. Courts, though, have not shackled the definition to such obvious situations. They have said that a narrow channel is any area which seamen customarily view as uncomfortably restricted. No riverbanks or chains of buoys are necessary to define a stretch of water as narrow. We should also note that it is within the authority of the Coast Guard, acting on behalf of the secretary

S.S. Maui *threads a narrow channel on her way to sea. [Courtesy Matson Lines]*

of transportation, to designate specific areas as narrow channels. When such might be done, we can expect notice to be given in *Local Notice to Mariners,* on charts, in *Coast Pilots,* and the like. More important, our conclusion should be that Rule 9 then applies.

What Rule 9 attends to is the conduct necessary in any visibility when traversing such a channel. By now we should be anticipating emphasis on plain, ordinary logic shored up with some "shalls" and "musts." Coming up, though, is a new ingredient. In writing the script the rules make frequent use of phrases which sound as if they are merely restatements of each other. Sometimes vessel *B* is told to "avoid impeding the safe passage" of *A.* At other times *B* is ordered to "keep clear" of *A.* Are those instructions synonymous? The technical answer is "no."

Words used in the Rules of the Road are chosen very, very carefully. The purpose is not to shape phrases which roll trippingly off the tongue. Instead the terminology is designed to be as precise and unambiguous as that in an insurance policy. Each word in each sentence will be weighed by judges and assigned a meaning. Considerable time was spent in choosing words so that confusing nuances would be kept at a minimum. When a textwriter varies the introduction of a paragraph from "moreover" to an occasional "in addition," he is trying to avoid a rut. The framers of the Rules of the Road by contrast seek out the ruts of standardized language. If they wanted the phrase "avoid impeding the safe passage" to mean the same as "keep clear," then only one phrase would have been used. Before getting underway in our dissection of Rule 9 we should get used to this important distinction.

Another analogy? We've been on the stage and in a bull-ridden pasture. Now's the time for a glance at Victorian manners. Picture a narrow stairway in a turn-of-the-century house in London. A proper gentleman, arms filled with packages, is maneuvering upward with difficulty. A trim young lady stands on the top landing, ready to descend. She can confidently expect that the proper gentleman struggling up the stairs will follow Victorian rules by trying to keep clear of her path. Yet encumbered as he is, the result could well be parcels, top hat, and masculine pride strewn over the steps. Logic suggests

Blasts of her steam whistle signal a crossing sail vessel as a freighter moves across San Francisco Bay. [Photo by Lawrence Wyatt]

that she not start down the stairs if that would embarrass his safe passage. But prevailing custom grants her the privilege of being deferred to. Common sense says that she should forgo insisting on her rights.

Shift the scene now to a narrow channel edged by buoys with shallow water beyond. A large power-driven vessel is gingerly making her way, unable to stray outside the buoyed limits. A trim shallow-draft sailing vessel is approaching from the opposite direction. The rules of conduct can require the power-driven vessel to keep clear. But should she be forced to attempt clumsy maneuvers when so confined? Wouldn't it be better for the trim sail craft not to insist?

These two scenes indicate the distinction between "avoid impeding the safe passage of" and "keep clear." Once a maneuvering situation arises, then the power-driven vessel, like the Victorian gentleman, keeps clear. But the trim sail vessel, like the young lady, should anticipate what burdens might arise and not impede the safe passage of the burdened oncomer. The terms are not synonymous. The mandate not to impede heads off problems by ordering handy vessels not to place cumbersome ones in difficult situations. The command to keep clear is a straightforward assignment of a duty. When, *however arising*, a situation exists, then the roles of holding course at prevailing speed and that of keeping clear must be acted out. To avoid impeding is to act so that the situation does not arise. Now with another analogy logged and, more important, a significant distinction made, let's return to a consideration of what Rule 9 has to say.

Everyone, dictates its first sentence, will stay to the right. More than that, each will hug the right-hand curb. Rule 9(a) of the International set says no more. Inland echoes COLREGS with its 9(a)(i) and then adds (ii). By it power-driven vessels on certain waters are granted an advantage. When bound down a narrow channel or fairway with a following current, such a vessel has the pattern of currents to contend with and is less maneuverable than one coming against the stream. So in narrow channels and fairways of the Great Lakes, Western Rivers, and wherever else the Coast Guard might specify, the power-driven and downbound vessel calls the tune. She has the right-of-way, proposes how the vessels should pass, and starts the whistle dialogue to clarify procedures. Yet none of this contradicts our Victorian analogy. It just recognizes that when committed to move with the current the downbound vessel has fewer options of avoidance. Like the Victorian lady, such a vessel need not start down the passageway, but once started she is in the toils of gravity.

Next come some encounters with "avoid impeding" phrases. Small vessels of whatever propulsion and sail vessels of whatever size shall not impede the safe passage of those of whatever propulsion which are restricted to the channel. This appears to be reasonable. Trim young ladies should not further burden parcel-laden Victorians struggling on stairways. Just as reasonable are two more "avoid impeding" commands. Long before Saint Peter made a set on the Sea of Galilee, fishing was recognized as a right of man. Neither COLREGS nor Inland challenges the concept. Vessels may fish in narrow channels. But they must recognize that other vessels also have rights. They must avoid impeding the passage of anyone else using the channel, whether the other can safely navigate beyond its limits or not. Such a channel is not primarily a fishing ground; its use as such is subordinate to other traffic. It need hardly be said that a vessel should not cross a channel if that will impede the passage of someone who must remain within the channel limits. The rule mentions a signal to warn the interloper of the problem (more on this when we reach our discussion of signals).

Rule 9(e) previews signals and a script which still lie ahead on our course of study. So in order to grasp what this section is about we must now skip forward a bit. We'll learn shortly that when one vessel is overtaking another she must keep clear and the overtaken one must hold course and speed. That's easy enough when the overtaking vessel has miles of ocean within which to keep clear while moving past. What, though, if they are in a narrow channel? Vessel *B* is moving at 15 knots and coming up astern of *A* which is creeping along at 5 knots. The waterway is so narrow that *B* cannot pass unless *A* changes course or speed or both. The basic script for overtaking requires *A* to hold course and speed. But if she does so, overtaking cannot take place. Must *B* stay behind and travel the next 15 miles in three hours rather than in one? Rule 9(e) gives her a way out. She is still obliged to keep out of *A*'s way, but she can initiate a dialogue to minimize delay. By whistle signals (again, still to come) she can request *A* to move over. It is *A*'s option to agree or not, but the ensuing exchange will clarify the situation. There appear, though, to be significant differences between COLREGS and Inland regarding this paragraph. On international waters the dialogue only develops when it is necessary for the vessel being overtaken to take action. By contrast on inland waters the dialogue ensues whenever *B* desires to overtake *A* in a narrow channel. Each set, by using the word "vessel" without modifying it by "power-driven," has its Rule 9(e) apply to all vessels regardless of propulsion. And Inland's Rule 34(c), although in words seeming to limit overtaking signal exchanges to power-driven vessels, is made applicable in the narrow channel case to everyone. The upshot inside or at sea is a procedure by which *A* and *B,* no matter how propelled, can negotiate an understanding to relieve *B* of delay and consequent nibbled fingernails.

The next paragraph of Rule 9 voices a logical precaution. When any vessel nears an area in a narrow channel where the view of others might be obscured, she is to proceed with particular care. This is another specific expression of a requirement of good seamanship. She must also sound one prolonged blast of her whistle. Note that although the obstruction might often be a channel bend the rule doesn't limit it just to that. Any intervening obstruction will serve. For example, a high seawall or breakwater might fill the bill. And Rule 9 is completed by the prohibition against anchoring unnecessarily in a narrow channel. That should be no surprise. To do so would be like parking a car in the middle of a street.

RULE 10—Traffic Separation Schemes

COLREGS

(a) This Rule applies to traffic separation schemes adopted by the Organization.

(b) A vessel using a traffic separation scheme shall:

(i) proceed in the appropriate traffic lane in the general direction of traffic flow for that lane;

(ii) so far as practicable keep clear of a traffic separation line or separation zone;

(iii) normally join or leave a traffic lane at the termination of the lane, but when joining or leaving from either side shall do so at as small an angle to the general direction of traffic flow as practicable.

(c) A vessel shall so far as practicable avoid crossing traffic lanes, but if obliged to do so shall cross as nearly as practicable at right angles to the general direction of traffic flow.

(d) Inshore traffic zones shall not normally be used by through traffic which can safely use the appropriate traffic lane within the adjacent traffic separation scheme. However, vessels of less than 20 meters in length and sailing vessels may under all circumstances use inshore traffic zones.

(e) A vessel other than a crossing vessel or a vessel joining or leaving a lane shall not normally enter a separation zone or cross a separation line except:

(i) in cases of emergency to avoid immediate danger;

(ii) to engage in fishing within a separation zone.

(f) A vessel navigating in areas near the terminations of traffic separation schemes shall do so with particular caution.

(g) A vessel shall so far as practicable avoid anchoring in a traffic separation scheme or in areas near its terminations.

(h) A vessel not using a traffic separation scheme shall avoid it by as wide a margin as is practicable.

(i) A vessel engaged in fishing shall not impede the passage of any vessel following a traffic lane.

(j) A vessel of less than 20 meters in length or a sailing vessel shall not impede the safe passage of a power-driven vessel following a traffic lane.

(k) A vessel restricted in her ability to maneuver when engaged in an operation for the maintenance of safety of navigation in a traffic separation scheme is exempted from complying with this Rule to the extent necessary to carry out the operation.

(l) A vessel restricted in her ability to maneuver when engaged in an operation for the laying, servicing or picking up of a submarine cable, within a traffic separation scheme, is exempted from complying with this Rule to the extent necessary to carry out the operation.

INLAND

Each vessel required by regulation to participate in a vessel traffic service shall comply with the applicable regulations.

Rule 10 concludes the recital of conduct in any condition of visibility with a COLREGS statement entirely different from that for inland waters. We were warned of this in Chapter 2. *Vessel Traffic Service* regulations (VTS) can subject navigation in certain areas to Coast Guard control. Such specifics are detailed in addenda to the Inland Rules, in *Coast Pilots,* and on charts. Inland Rule 10 says that where VTS exists vessels must meet its demands. Nothing more need be added here, so we can direct our attention to the COLREGS version of Rule 10.

We've already been told what a high-seas traffic scheme amounts to and that the IMO is the agency which reviews proposed schemes and, by adoption, puts them officially to work. What we should particularly note is that although conforming to an Inland VTS pattern can be mandatory, following a COL-REGS Traffic Separation Scheme is not. When a scheme has been adopted mariners are urged to follow it, but they are not ordered to do so. On the other hand even if a shipmaster is not following the scheme he cannot ignore its existence. Some others in the neighborhood will be accepting its direction, so everyone must comply with Rule 10 when navigating in the area.

What the scheme amounts to is a freeway pattern to channel traffic in regions of congestion. As we read the rule we should keep the freeway image in mind. Like a freeway a scheme has one or more lanes for traffic going in one direction and a lane or two nearby for traffic heading the opposite way. Separating the one-way streets is a divider. It can be just that: an invisible line down the middle. It might, though, be a very wide separation zone keeping opposing traffic a mile or more apart. A real freeway manages all this by erecting fences on the sides and by painting lines or planting trees and bushes in the middle. No such obvious barriers are met afloat. Often the pattern is not even marked by buoys, for it might traverse water a half mile deep where no anchored markers can be placed to channel traffic into appropriate lanes. The absence of such guideposts creates the danger of uncertain navigation. On a chart the pattern is clearly evidenced by overprints of purplish ink. Well, the ship's bow might cut through water which appears blue, green, or mud-colored, but only a poet would recognize it as dyed the same purple as appears on a chart. Mariners have a problem of judging when they are actually in a lane or a separation zone.

Prudent seamen recognize that the problem has two sides to it. No matter how certain one navigator is of his position in the scheme he must realize that another, less sure of his position, might be following the wrong script for his actual lane. Operation in or near a traffic separation scheme can bring anxious moments for which there is no absolute cure. Careful plotting is essential in every case. Whether by crossbearings and ranges, whether by eye or electron, the position of the ship must be watched carefully when she is in the vicinity of one of these schemes.

Rule 10 requires vessels to proceed in the general direction of traffic flow, but such an admonition hardly seems necessary. No sensible person would go against the traffic on a freeway. The rule next requires ships to keep clear of the divider, whether it is a line or a zone. It goes on to suggest that they join and leave the patterns at the ends of the lanes. No real freeway has such a problem since a stout fence usually makes it impossible to enter or leave at any place but an on- or off-ramp. The voluntary flavor of seagoing schemes becomes more apparent. It is not expected that a vessel departing from a port midway up the scheme should voyage miles in one direction or another to get on the freeway at the end. She can proceed directly into the flow at any point along the route. If, though, she does not join or leave at an end, she shouldn't jostle in or out at right angles to the traffic. Her course on entering or leaving should make the smallest possible angle with the axis of the lane.

There is another contrast with a shoreside freeway. On land it is usually a bit difficult to cross a freeway without climbing a fence or two. Not so at sea. All it takes afloat is a firm hand on the helm. But vessels should not do so capriciously. On the other hand no one need travel miles out of his way to sail around a scheme from one side to the other. When he does cross, he should do so directly and by the shortest route. His track should be as close as practicable to 90° to the traffic flow. In some areas traffic separation schemes offer multilane patterns in each direction. When that is the format, through traffic should stay offshore and local traffic shouldn't travel in the fast lane.

The middle ground between the traffic lanes is intended as a divider and not a roost for idle vessels. No mariner should cross a separation line or enter a separation zone unless he has a good reason to do so. Actually crossing the entire scheme, avoidance of immediate danger, and a desire to fish in the middle ground are acceptable reasons for such a maneuver. Saint Peter might be purring over this COLREGS deference to his original occupation. Just because officialdom dabs magenta bands of ink on a chart is no reason to infringe on an age-old prerogative.

Obviously careful navigation is required at the ends of freeways. Every motorist knows the hazards to be met when traffic is flowing on or off. The taboo on anchoring in a scheme or in an area near its ends also makes good sense. COLREGS Rule 10 now goes on to suggest that those who are not using a scheme should stay as far away as possible. Don't skirt along the edges of an unmarked highway where neither curbstones nor barriers confine its users to the roadbed. If you are not following the thoroughfare, then keep well clear.

Fishermen receive another concession. They can even fish in a traffic lane. A surprising statement? Not when we consider that a school of skipjack will pay no heed either to Rule 10 or to the IMO. Nets can be cast, trawls can be dragged, and lines can be towed where fishermen fancy the fish might be. That the region also happens to be a marine freeway is no impediment. But now we meet another of those "avoiding impeding" statements. Fishing in any part of a traffic separation scheme is legal *provided* it does not impede the use of the scheme by normal traffic.

As viewed from the bridge of a large ship, the channel she must follow is dotted with traffic. [Photo by Lawrence Wyatt]

Next comes still another "don't impede" instruction. No small vessel and no sailing vessel of any size will impede the safe passage of a power-driven vessel following a lane. We have yet to meet the "in sight" rules which will assign to one vessel a requirement to keep clear of another. Nothing in Rule 10 infringes on that basic script. If by such assignment of roles a power-driven vessel must keep clear of a small vessel or of one under sail, then the power-driven vessel must stand ready to do so even though she is traversing a traffic lane. Just because she is in a scheme is no reason to disregard the fundamental code of conduct. What Rule 10 says is that both the small vessel, regardless of her propulsion, and the vessel under sail, regardless of her size, must anticipate the possibility of embarrassing a power-driven vessel using a traffic pattern. Each must avoid placing the powered ship in an awkward position. We are obviously back to the problem of the proper Victorian gentleman and that sweet young thing on the staircase.

We are also at the end of this chapter. Much has been covered and analogies have been met at every turn. If, though, the dry words of the rules have taken on just a spark of life, then the aim was achieved. One hurdle remains before we can stow Part B, Section I on the shelf. Time for a quiz.

QUESTIONS

Benjamin Disraeli casts a mischievous look at the sheaf of questions he will put and then introduces the judges. Who are they? None other than Queen Victoria, Prince Albert, and the trim young lady of the staircase. Strict compliance with "the code" is the only way to avoid being ostracized. So lean your head against the antimacassar, adjust your pince-nez, and go to work!

1. In determining a safe speed at night the mariner must take into account
    a. the proximity of navigational hazards
    b. the influence of background lights
    c. both of the above
    d. none of the above

2. A lookout
    a. must always be placed forward on the vessel
    b. must never be exposed to the weather
    c. both of the above
    d. none of the above

3. Every vessel should be able to stop her forward motion
    a. in no more than three ship lengths
    b. within three minutes
    c. both of the above
    d. none of the above

4. You are on a vessel going south at 10 knots and equipped with a radarscope presenting a relative picture.
    a. A lighthouse will appear to be going north at 10 knots.
    b. A vessel going south at 10 knots will appear to be stopped.
    c. Both of the above
    d. none of the above

5. Where there is sufficient sea room, the best action to avoid a close-quarters situation would be
    a. to change course
    b. to change speed
    c. either of the above
    d. none of the above

6. Vessels can engage in fishing
    a. in a narrow channel
    b. in a traffic separation zone
    c. in a traffic separation lane
    d. all of the above

7. Sail vessels shall avoid impeding the safe passage of
   a. any vessel which must stay within a narrow channel
   b. any power-driven vessel in a traffic lane of a separation scheme
   c. both of the above
   d. none of the above

8. All vessels shall avoid anchoring
   a. in a narrow channel
   b. in a traffic separation zone
   c. in a traffic lane
   d. all of the above

9. In a narrow channel in international waters
   a. no vessel may overtake another
   b. all vessels shall stay as close as practicable to the right-hand edge of the channel
   c. both of the above
   d. none of the above

10. Vessels engaged in fishing in a narrow channel shall not impede the safe passage of
    a. small vessels under 20 meters using the channel
    b. sail vessels using the channel
    c. large vessels which must remain within the channel
    d. all of the above

AND ANSWERS

Her Majesty the Queen, having consulted with the Prince Consort and the dainty subject of the realm, issues an Honors List. She awards 10 points for each correct answer. Here is the imperial ranking.

90–100	court favorite
80	court friend
70	court visitor
under 70	court jester

1. c   2. d   3. d   4. c   5. a   6. d   7. c   8. d   9. b   10. d

4
Part B—CONDUCT IN SIGHT

THE SCRIPT for conduct of vessels in sight of one another is based on two logical precepts. First off, it is easier to avoid an object of predictable motion than one free to dodge around unexpectedly. Second, the task of avoiding should fall to the more nimble. Section II of Part B adheres to these principles. Whenever possible, one vessel will *stand on* by holding course and speed while the other will take action to *keep clear*. And in the assignment of roles, vessels are ranked by maneuverability. The more agile are required to keep out of the way.

For too many decades a fiction has persisted that one vessel was privileged while the other was burdened. Such terminology, although not in the rules, became gospel. The usage is unfortunate. "Privilege" suggests a freedom of choice granted to the vessel holding course and speed. The word implies that she might hold on or that perhaps she should hold on, but not that she must hold on. There was never a privilege, there is never a privilege, there will never be a privilege. That sentence should be a required exercise in nautical grammar. *Both* vessels are obliged to act out their roles. The stand-on ship must hold course and speed. Her conduct is not optional, for she must be predictable. Here, at the start of our survey, we should expunge the heretical misconception. The rules will not work unless each actor follows a basic script.

In the days of wooden ships and iron men, the British navy might have espoused a different practice. Ships of the line carrying braid-heavy admirals enjoyed the "privilege" of seniority while Sub-Lieutenant Hornblower was burdened to keep out of their way. If that was true, then the faulty concept is several hundred years old. But it is nonetheless faulty. Any admiral worth his epaulets would have the wit to ride a powerful ship and let young Hornblower struggle with a leaky scow overdue for an overhaul. Yet the subaltern was the encumbered one and entitled to consideration of his plight. In a reasonable world, the more fit should watch out for the less fit. Over the side, then, with "privilege" and "burden." Those words have no place in our lexicon. To us, *stand on* means obliged to hold course and speed. *Keep clear* tells us that the role is to stay out of the way.

RULE 11—Application
COLREGS

Rules in this Section apply to vessels in sight of one another.

INLAND

Rules in this subpart apply to vessels in sight of one another.

While tidying up the decks before an assault on Section II, we should pay heed to Rule 11's limitation to "vessels in sight of one another." The concept of *in sight* has already been met. It means that one must be able to see the other visually. Radar surveillance is not enough. The stage on which two vessels perform is no wider than the visible horizon, and it is imperative for each actor to know that the other is present. Such an assurance is only possible when one can see the other by eye.

Before continuing we should note that the chronology of the Rules is about to be disrupted somewhat. After Rule 11 should come Rule 12 and then 13 and so on. But ahead is a bounce or two from 13 to 34 with a visit to 16 and 17 enroute. We'll meet the official text of the Rules in numerical order, but an occasional preview should be anticipated. Eventually, though, all will fit together by a balance of leaps ahead with a touch of repetition. Rule 12 begins the real specifics.

RULE 12—Sailing Vessels

COLREGS

(a) When two sailing vessels are approaching one another, so as to involve risk of collision, one of them shall keep out of the way of the other as follows:

(i) when each has the wind on a different side, the vessel which has the wind on the port side shall keep out of the way of the other;

(ii) when both have the wind on the same side, the vessel which is to windward shall keep out of the way of the vessel which is to leeward;

(iii) if a vessel with the wind on the port side sees a vessel to windward and cannot determine with certainty whether the other vessel has the wind on the port or on the starboard side, she shall keep out of the way of the other.

(b) For the purposes of this Rule the windward side shall be deemed to be the side opposite to that on which the mainsail is carried or, in the case of a square-rigged vessel, the side opposite to that on which the largest fore-and-aft sail is carried.

INLAND

(a) When two sailing vessels are approaching one another, so as to involve risk of collision, one of them shall keep out of the way of the other as follows:

(i) when each has the wind on a different side, the vessel which has the wind on the port side shall keep out of the way of the other;

(ii) when both have the wind on the same side, the vessel which is to windward shall keep out of the way of the vessel which is to leeward; and

(iii) if a vessel with the wind on the port side sees a vessel to windward and cannot determine with certainty whether the other vessel has the wind on the port or on the starboard side, she shall keep out of the way of the other.

(b) For the purpose of this Rule the windward side shall be deemed to be the side opposite to that on which the mainsail is carried or, in the case of a square-rigged vessel, the side opposite to that on which the largest fore-and-aft sail is carried.

This rule considers two sail vessels approaching in sight of each other so as to involve risk of collision. In deference to those who wear belt and suspenders to hedge against misadventure, let's refer back to Rule 3's definition of what the term "sailing vessel" means. Whether or not she has power available is beside the point. When she is under sail and not using propelling machinery she is as much "sailing" as if her auxiliary power were a kedge anchor. Now we can unhook the galluses and get back to Rule 12.

The key phrases are *two vessels, approaching, in sight,* and *risk of collision.* Only three of those keys appear in this rule, but Rule 11 requires us to append "in sight" to each succeeding rule through 18. And those key terms set the tone. Who needs a script unless vessels are getting closer together? When do you know which script applies unless you see the other? Why follow a script if there is no danger? How can you perform one way with one vessel and at the same time another way with another? Roles are played by two vessels approaching, in sight, and at risk. The last sentence serves as the mariner's "Showtime!" summons to perform. Of course, having weathered Chapter 3, we

U.S.C.G. Eagle *under full sail with the wind on her port side. [USCG photo]*

note that the measure for risk of collision is vague. But we do have a starting point. Four factors invoke the script: two vessels approaching in sight with risk of collision.

Rule 12 makes no distinction between an America Cup challenger and a ship's lifeboat. That the sleek 12-meter boat can point close to the wind while the other is lucky to sail at right angles is of no consequence to this rule. Their contrast in nimbleness, though, cannot be ignored. A few leagues back Rule 2 rejected any tolerance for thoughtlessness. Good seamanship would require the racer to recognize the predicament of the clumsy lifeboat. Both must stand ready to improvise if necessary to accommodate limitations, and SELMA is their guide. But subject to common sense, Rule 12 views both vessels as under sail with no allowance for efficiency. Looming ahead, however, is an arbitrary decision.

The vessel with the wind on the port side is told to keep clear of the other with the wind on the starboard. Such a demand has nothing to do with relative agility. Rather, the selection is based solely on our cultural heritage. We live in a right-handed world. We keep to the right on a roadbed. *Right* is synonymous with *correct*. *Left* has links with the Latin word *sinister*, portending vampire fangs threatening the jugular. The balance is somewhat redressed in American baseball with "portsiders" rightfully esteemed. The rulemakers, though, were not influenced by baseball. They had to make a decision and went with the vessel having the wind on the right side. She is to be kept clear of by the sinister one with the wind on the left side.

Anglophiles are entitled to a bit of puzzlement over our custom to keep to the right on roads and highways. Not in Burton-on-Trent, say they! But even the age-old English practice of clinging to the left-hand curb is evidence of Right Supremacy. It is said that such usage stems from the days of bold knights on horseback. Approaching a stranger on a narrow lane, such a warrior wished to be ready for instant combat. To draw one's sword with the correct hand and then have to lean across the saddlehorn for whacking was not efficient. It was much more convenient for right-handed knights to flail away at passersby "starboard to starboard." The modern British custom of driving on the left side of the road is a result. But Sherwood Forest has rarely been the arena for two sail vessels approaching. We had better go back to sea.

What if the two vessels have the wind on the same side? The question of nimbleness is now introduced. The ship upwind is better able to keep clear, and Rule 12(a)(ii) requires the windward vessel to keep out of the way of the vessel to leeward. That seems a trouble-free concept. But here comes another "what if." What if the vessel downwind has the wind on the port side and cannot judge which side the wind is striking a vessel to windward? If the other has the wind on the starboard side, then leeward is sinister and keeps clear since she has the wind on the port side. On the other hand if the windward vessel also has the wind on the port side, then *windward* keeps clear. The Rules decided to be super-cautious. When in doubt as to which side the wind strikes the other, a vessel to leeward with the wind on the port side keeps clear. That way, no matter what the real situation, both will be obliged to exercise care.

The last paragraph of Rule 12 seems a surrender to reality. Not every modern mariner comprehends what "windward side" means. Perhaps the definition is elusive even after a reading of Rule 12(b), but then the rulemakers had no intention to write a primer on sailing. *Windward* is cryptically described as the side opposite to that on which the mainsail is carried. For square-rigged vessels it is opposite that on which the largest fore-and-aft sail is carried. About now we might hear muttered from the shaft alley, "What's that all about?" Propeller proponents could champion a simpler description: *windward* side refers to the gunwale over which the wind blows rather than to the side opposite that over which one or the other sail projects. But devotees of sail have the last word. Rule 12(b) is not so much intended as a definition as to resolve an ambiguity. Consider a sail vessel running "wing-and-wing" before the wind with sails sticking out on *both* sides. Now what would the shaft alley say? Someone on board might be able to judge which rail has the more wind pressure, but not so for a distant observer. This paragraph gives him a handy aid. He is in effect guided by the projection over the side of the largest sail.

Time to skip ahead a few rules. Rule 16 gives further guidance to the *Keep Clear* sailing vessel by reminding her to take early substantial action. This is a restatement of the edicts of Rule 8 and completes the instructions to *Keep Clear*. But the script is one-sided. Not a hint of direction has so far been given to the vessel required to hold course and speed. Finding her role requires us to vault ahead for a quick look at Rule 17. There, in no murky terms, the order is loud and clear: "Where one of two vessels is to keep out of the way, the other shall keep her course and speed." This is a "shall" rule intended to obligate even the most "privileged" luminaries of the Queen's navy.

One option, though, does exist for the *Stand On* vessel playing this role. She has an alternative to inaction. During the progress of approach she is expected to keep a wary eye on the other. And should it become apparent that *Keep Clear* is not taking appropriate action, then *Stand On* has the right to take avoiding action on her own. Although the rules phrase such conduct as optional, some experts predict that by court decision the "may" could well become a "shall." It would not be surprising that the option to take action when another muffs her role could evolve into an exercise of good seamanship. Should that occur, then Rule 2 might transform "may" to a much stronger term. Admiralty courts aside, we should recognize Rule 17 as at least offering a choice. It also contains a further command.

The approach situation might so deteriorate that *Keep Clear* cannot do so on her own. Another mandatory paragraph of Rule 17 dictates what must next follow. *Stand On* shall take whatever action will best aid avoidance. We've just met another injunction to use common sense. When further standing on means collision, then holding course or speed or both can no longer be allowed. Later on we'll spend more time with Rule 17, for it is a keystone to much of the "in sight" script for all vessels.

Chronology is about to be dealt another blow. Part D with its maneuvering signals lies far ahead on our course. But to complete the "sail approaching sail" story we should now sample its content. The sail vessel scenario is normally

Not the billowing spinnaker but the mainsail labels the wind as on the port side.
[Photo courtesy Miller Freeman Publications]

acted out in silence. Neither vessel is given a signal to indicate a course change. But Rule 34(d) provides a very critical alarm and fortifies it with a "shall." Should either vessel, from any cause, be confused or have doubts about the maneuvers being carried out, she shall immediately announce her concern by sounding five or more short and rapid blasts on her whistle. She may also repeat this signal by flashes of a maneuvering light. (More on this when we are formally introduced to Rule 34; for now we should note the *doubt signal* as a part of the script when sail approaches sail.)

We should also recognize that sail vessels in sight of others are allowed to make some other noises. Rule 9(e), we've seen, speaks of the problem of overtaking in a narrow channel or a fairway. The COLREGS version is concerned with the dilemma in which the vessel being overtaken might be placed. She must hold her course and speed; but in a narrow channel the overtaking vessel might not be able to get by unless the overtaken ship changes something. So on international waters a dialogue by sound signals is required of the participants regardless of propulsion. Inland rules go a step further. There Rule 9 specifies that overtaking in a narrow channel requires a dialogue whether the vessel ahead must move or not. The exchanges are detailed in Rule 34 and we can defer discussion until it has approached and is in sight. The point to be noted now is that sail vessels maneuvering in sight of their own kind or even others are not totally mute.

Time for a recap. When a sail vessel approaches another sail, the one with the wind on the port side keeps clear and the other holds course and speed. Should the wind be on the same side, *Windward* keeps clear and *Leeward* holds course and speed. If the vessel downwind with the wind on the port side is not sure on which side the other has the wind, then a conflict in roles might develop. Should *Windward* actually have the wind on the starboard side, then *Leeward* must keep clear. But if *Windward* also has the wind on the port side, then *Leeward* holds course and speed. In case of doubt, *Leeward* with wind on the port side assumes that her role is to keep clear. If the vessel to windward has the wind on the starboard side, then she stands on; if in fact the wind is on the port side, then she keeps clear. Sail vessels do not make signals for course changes but they are obliged to announce doubt.

Veteran sailing mariners might recall that earlier rules distinguished between vessels "close-hauled" on tacks, those "running free," and vessels with "wind aft." Significant differences in maneuverability were attributed to one over the other. By those earlier directions a vessel with the wind aft was required to keep clear of the others. A vessel running free, no matter which side the wind was on, would keep clear of one close-hauled, no matter on which tack. Whether on international waters or inland this is no longer the script. A vessel with the wind on the port side, even if close-hauled, keeps out of the way of one with the wind on the starboard side, even if that vessel is running with sails jutting out on both sides . . . provided her mainsail or largest sail

The two vessels in the foreground have the wind on the starboard side, and the nearest one, being to windward, keeps clear of the other. The two vessels in the background have the wind on the port side, so both keep clear of the others. Between themselves, the nearer one, being to windward, keeps clear of one farthest to leeward. [Photo courtesy Miller Freeman Publications]

extends over the port rail. Of what value is this subtlety to a mariner? Should he be preparing for a license examination it might mean the difference between passing and failure. Should he customarily operate under sail it could explain the outraged glare of a graybeard when maneuvering in sight. Some misunderstanding might be no more than a generation gap.

RULE 13—Overtaking

COLREGS

(a) Notwithstanding anything contained in the Rules of Part B, Sections I and II, any vessel overtaking any other shall keep out of the way of the vessel being overtaken.

(b) A vessel shall be deemed to be overtaking when coming up with another vessel from a direction more than 22.5 degrees abaft her beam, that is, in such a position with reference to the vessel she is overtaking, that at night she would be able to see only the sternlight of that vessel but neither of her sidelights.

(c) When a vessel is in any doubt as to whether she is overtaking another, she shall assume that this is the case and act accordingly.

(d) Any subsequent alteration of the bearing between the two vessels shall not make the overtaking vessel a crossing vessel within the meaning of these Rules or relieve her of the duty of keeping clear of the overtaken vessel until she is finally past and clear.

INLAND

(a) Notwithstanding anything contained in Rules 4 through 18, any vessel overtaking any other shall keep out of the way of the vessel being overtaken.

(c) When a vessel is in any doubt as to whether she is overtaking another, she shall assume that this is the case and act accordingly.

(b) A vessel shall be deemed to be overtaking when coming up with another vessel from a direction more than 22.5 degrees abaft her beam; that is, in such a position with reference to the vessel she is overtaking, that at night she would be able to see only the sternlight of that vessel but neither of her sidelights.

(d) Any subsequent alteration of the bearing between the two vessels shall not make the overtaking vessel a crossing vessel within the meaning of these Rules or relieve her of the duty of keeping clear of the overtaken vessel until she is finally past and clear.

Rule 13 deals with the overtaking situation in no uncertain terms. The vessel astern, no matter what means of propulsion, must keep clear of the vessel she is overtaking. And, it adds, this rule prevails over every other in Sections I and II of Part B's recital of conduct. The Inland version says so, not in terms, but by referring to Rules 4 through 18. They are in fact the rules of the two sections, so both sets amount to the same pattern.

The overtaking situation has a good side and a bad. The good side is that the relative speed of approach can be slow. Suppose vessel B, moving north at 17 knots, is 1 mile astern and closing on northbound A whose speed is 16 knots. One hour will pass before they might collide and the impact would be measured at 1 knot. Should they instead be meeting on opposite courses the 1 mile of separation would vanish in less than two minutes and the impact would be measured as a crushing 33 knots.

On the other hand, a less perceptible approach can be deceptively dangerous. Mariners closing at a slow rate can be lulled into a false judgment of risk. A frequent excuse heard from the fantail of one or the bow of the other is "All of a sudden, there she was!" Actually the situation did not develop "all of a sudden." More likely the slowly decreasing range passed unnoticed until danger was imminent. This might be particularly true on a misty night when the measure of distance would be based on observation of a single white sternlight.

The Rules place the primary burden on the overtaking vessel, and she becomes such when she approaches another in an arc abaft the other's sidelights. Stated another way, this means when she sees only the other's sternlight. Stated a third way, it means when the approach is on a bearing of more than

This deep-draft vessel is cautiously making a turn to port. [USCG photo]

112.5° from the other's bow. Rule 13 is uncompromising. It says that if any doubt exists, the vessel astern must assume that she is overtaking and must keep clear. Moreover once the situation develops she is required to keep clear until she is safely past. No later alteration of bearing will transform her into a crossing vessel. Having assumed the role, she must act it to the end of the scene.

Rule 16 adds the standard instruction on how to keep clear. The overtaking vessel shall take early and substantial action. Idly watching the other's sternlight brighten is not following the Rules of the Road. The vigilance of a proper lookout is demanded to detect the other's presence. Also demanded is that a safe speed be selected to allow opportunity for early and substantial action. The net of requirements tightens. There is no tolerance for the lame lament of ". . . all of a sudden."

Nor is loitering by the sternlight up ahead tolerated. The vessel being overtaken also has responsibilities. She does not have unlimited prior rights to the waterway. She must keep a proper lookout, and that includes looking astern. She must be operated at a safe speed. And, says Rule 17, she must hold her course and speed so that the overtaking vessel can maneuver around her without fear of unexpected changes. Of course Rule 17 does grant her the option to take action on her own when it is apparent the other is not following her script. And a "shall" in Rule 17 requires that the overtaken vessel do something should the overtaker be unable to avoid on her own. We must again recall the narrow channel dealt with in Rule 9. In a narrow channel the overtaken vessel is not bound by Rule 17 to keep course and speed if (an important if) the overtaking vessel will need her cooperation to get by. Rule 9 then goes to work and allows them to negotiate an overtaking arrangement. Unless the narrow channel exception applies, however, the vessel ahead holds course and speed while the faster vessel astern keeps clear on the way by.

The stern light stands out from a background of deck lights on a large tanker. [USCG photo]

RULE 14—Head-on Situation

COLREGS

(a) When two power-driven vessels are meeting on reciprocal or nearly reciprocal courses so as to involve risk of collision each shall alter her course to starboard so that each shall pass on the port side of the other.

(b) Such a situation shall be deemed to exist when a vessel sees the other ahead or nearly ahead and by night she could see the masthead lights of the other in a line or nearly in a line and/or both sidelights and by day she observes the corresponding aspect of the other vessel.

(c) When a vessel is in any doubt as to whether such a situation exists she shall assume that it does exist and act accordingly.

INLAND

(a) When two power-driven vessels are meeting on reciprocal or nearly reciprocal courses so as to involve risk of collision each shall alter her course to starboard so that each shall pass on the port side of the other.

(b) Such a situation shall be deemed to exist when a vessel sees the other ahead or nearly ahead and by night she could see the masthead lights of the other in a line or nearly in a line or both sidelights and by day she observes the corresponding aspect of the other vessel.

(c) When a vessel is in any doubt as to whether such a situation exists she shall assume that it does exist and act accordingly.

This rule writes the script for specific vessels in a specific relationship. When power-driven is meeting power-driven on reciprocal or nearly reciprocal courses, the normal pattern of keeping clear by one and standing on by the other does not apply. Now both vessels must take action to keep clear. And the action required is a course change to the right. They are not knights in armor preparing for the fray. They are ships in a right-handed world and they go right to keep clear.

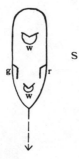

Fig. 10. Meeting Head-on. When power-driven vessels are meeting exactly head-on, each is required to change course to the right to pass port-to-port.

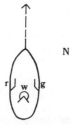

The edict applies to power-driven vessels only. A sailing ship might not be able to go right. This rule speaks only to those having wider options of maneuverability. And to them the order is very clear. But clear statements can sometimes become equivocal. What is meant by the ominous word "nearly" in the statement ". . . reciprocal or nearly reciprocal courses"? Library shelves have bent from Wisby to Washington with court decisions fashioning answers, so we can afford four sketches to pose the question. In Fig. 10 the situation is obvious. Both vessels, *N* and *S*, are on the same track but going in opposite directions. At night each would observe the other's red and green sidelights with a white masthead light or two between. Unless some change is made collision is unavoidable. Rule 14 tells each to go right so the passing will be port-to-port. Rule 8 reinforces the requirement by calling for early and substantial action.

In Fig. 11 they seem lined up to pass clear port-to-port without the need for further adjustments. At night each would see the other's red sidelight. The courses are reciprocal but the parallel tracks should carry them clear of danger. Rule 14 is not needed. Rule 8 might caution them to stand ready for early action to widen the passing distance. But the situation is not what is meant by head-and-head.

In Fig. 12 they appear ready to pass clear starboard-to-starboard. At night the other's green sidelight would be visible to each. Again Rule 14 is not in

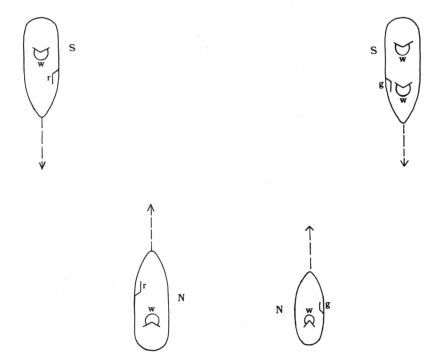

Fig. 11. Meeting Port-to-Port. Since power-driven N *and* S *will pass clear port-to-port, no rudder action is taken.*

Fig. 12. Meeting Starboard-to-Starboard. N *and* S *will pass clear on each other's starboard side, so no maneuver is required.*

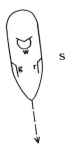

S

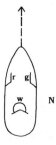

N

Fig. 13. Doubtful Situation. Since wind and weather influence a vessel's track, neither N nor S should assume a safe passage. Rule 14 expects each to change course to the right.

point, for any course change to the right could narrow the passing distance. This relationship is not head-and-head anymore than that shown in Fig. 11.

Figure 13 presents the real problem when power-driven vessels meet. Each would see only the green sidelight of the other and a starboard-to-starboard passing would seem to be the case. That would suggest the same as the situation in Fig. 12, but now the relationship is not so clear-cut. Neither eyesight nor radar might so reliably project the other's course as to resolve any doubt. Should S be yawing as she lurched in a seaway, N might be nagged by doubts when an occasional red sidelight appeared. If the wind were from the east both vessels would make leeway, but perhaps not to the same degree. The result of wind pressure on a vessel's hull can be to make her follow a track downwind from that actually steered. Suppose S were more susceptible to leeway than N. Even though the only sidelight she might show would be green and even though the suggestion might be a starboard-to-starboard passing, her actual track might lead directly down to N's fo'c'slehead.

Collision is a stiff penalty for a mistake in judgment. Let's take a closer look at the approach of N and S. In Fig. 14 N is northbound at 17 knots while S is southbound at 16 knots. The speed of approach would be 33 knots. Each minute the distance between them would decrease by more than half a mile. Were they both large vessels, disaster might be unavoidable when they were

3 miles apart, for within 6 minutes they could collide. In that period any violent maneuvers might be fruitless. Crash stops or "hard over" turns would be out of the question. Now a sobering consideration arises. The minimum range of a large vessel's masthead light is 6 miles and that of her sidelights is 3 miles. *N* might have less than 11 minutes after sighting the white masthead lights of *S* within which to appraise the situation, make a judgment, and act on it. The time limit could be less than 6 minutes after seeing a sidelight.

Nor would smaller vessels be immune to the problem. Consider the situation shown in Fig. 15. Now *N* and *S* are 35-foot power cruisers approaching each other at 10 knots. The closing speed is 20 knots or 1 mile every 3 minutes. As vessels less than 12 meters long they could display sidelights of only 1-mile minimum range. The masthead on each need reach no farther than 2 miles. No sidelight might be visible before they were a mile apart. That would be 3 minutes before collision, the duration of a no-overtime telephone call. The only prior warning of each other's presence could be the sighting of a white mast-

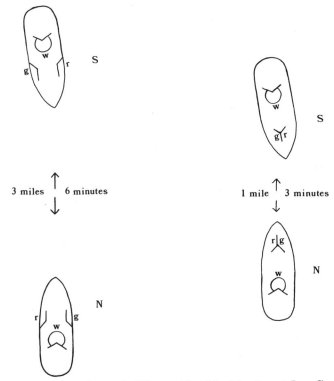

Fig. 14. Meeting at High Speed. When 17-knot N *meets 16-knot* S, *the 3-mile distance will be traveled at 33 knots.*

Fig. 15. Meeting at Low Speed. N *and* S, *each traveling at 10 knots and 1 mile apart, will reach zero range in 3 minutes.*

head light 3 minutes earlier, and that light could be mistaken for anything from a sternlight to Paul Revere's "one if by land" in a church tower. Add yawing, a little spray, or some background glow to mask the green sidelight and the situation could be critical at the outset.

Such grave considerations certainly point up the value of radar. They also emphasize the urgency of keeping a proper lookout and maintaining a safe speed. One other factor also arises. Bare compliance with the minimum ranges for running lights can be risky. Christmas tree bulbs esthetically set in the streamlined curve of a wind screen might earn a fashion award; they might also be dangerously ineffective. The IMO requests maritime nations to discourage the use of strobe lights, but there is plenty of room in the middle between these extremes. COLREGS requirements are not petty annoyances mandated by pompous bureaucrats. More often they are the knowledgeable reaction of professionals to very serious problems.

Glance again at Figs. 13, 14, and 15. In each the approach aspect is unclear and some corrective action is indicated. What, though, should that be? Rule 8 contains a surgeon's answer: amputate the risk of fast approach by slowing down, stopping, or reversing. But if that were done every time two vessels met, the ocean would be a huge parking lot of inactive ships. In an emergency such action must be taken, but it is not required in all cases. There would be a temptation to go left and widen the passing range. That, though, would require both *N* and *S* to yield to temptation together. What if *N* changed course to the left while *S*, judging that they were meeting, turned right? That "what if" could ensure a collision. Rule 14 aims to minimize the risk. It says that if there is any doubt, each shall assume a meeting pattern and each shall go right. It has been said that this instruction is a good antidote to a poorly defined malady. What is head-on is very difficult to describe in practical terms because of the many variables involved. Unless the situation is clear-cut and evident, the only safe procedure is to place on each vessel an unequivocal duty. Rule 14 does so by saying "Alter course to starboard."

In the past some courts have proposed a formula to define what is end-on or "nearly so." It stated that if a vessel observed ahead seems to have a course within one compass point (11.25°) on either side of the opposite to yours, then you are to consider the vessels as meeting end-on or nearly so. Applied to Fig. 16 the formula would have *N* do this arithmetic. Her course is 000° and the opposite is 180°. If she judged the course of *S* as between about 169° and 191° she would consider them as meeting. Some other courts shortened the arc to half a compass point on either side of opposite. *N* would then base a judgment on whether the course of *S* was between about 175° and 185°. By either formula the measure was nebulous. Reaching any conclusion about a yawing vessel miles away and making leeway could hardly be more than a guesstimate. The requirement of Rule 14 is far superior.

We must now recall the Inland Rules exception found in Rule 9(a)(ii). In

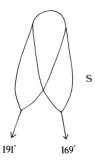

191°   169°

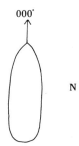

000°

N

Fig. 16. Formula for Meeting. Northbound N, *judging* S *to be on a course within 1 point (11¼°) of opposite, would assume they were meeting.*

a narrow channel or fairway on the Western Rivers, Great Lakes, or other inland waters specified by the Coast Guard, the power-driven vessel bound upstream defers to a power-driven going down with the flow. It is important to recognize that the patterns of river currents, particularly when rounding a bend, might not allow the simple maneuver of going to the right.

Before we leave Rule 14 we should admire how nicely it fits with some of the others we've met. None of the rules is independent of the others. All fit together into a tight pattern. Both *N* and *S* in all the figures are obliged to comply with several related scripts. Rule 2(a) requires each to follow the dictates of good seamanship. Each must be generally prudent and ready to depart from the script when necessary to avoid immediate danger, for that is the edict of Rule 2(b). They must comply with Rule 5's instruction to keep a proper lookout so that a full appraisal of the situation can be made. They must each operate at a safe speed and follow the lead of Rule 6 in selecting that speed. Every means available, says Rule 7, must be used to judge when risk of collision exists. Rule 8 tells them about action to avoid collision. Whatever is done must be early and substantial, and must be watched to observe its effect. The application of these mandates is not restricted to the head-on situation, for they are general commands in any visibility and in any situation. It is well, though, to recognize how they are integrated into this, the potentially most deadly situation of all for power-driven vessels approaching each other.

Meeting a loaded containership on the port bow. [Courtesy Matson Lines]

RULE 15—Crossing Situation

COLREGS

When two power-driven vessels are crossing so as to involve risk of collision, the vessel which has the other on her own starboard side shall keep out of the way and shall, if the circumstances of the case admit, avoid crossing ahead of the other vessel.

INLAND

(a) When two power-driven vessels are crossing so as to involve risk of collision, the vessel which has the other on her starboard side shall keep out of the way and shall, if the circumstances of the case admit, avoid crossing ahead of the other vessel.

(b) Notwithstanding paragraph (a), on the Great Lakes, Western Rivers, or water specified by the Secretary, a vessel crossing a river shall keep out of the way of a power-driven vessel ascending or descending the river.

Now the focus is on two power-driven vessels approaching obliquely. One is not overtaking the other nor are they meeting head-on or nearly so. Instead one is approaching the other in an arc of bearing from fine on a bow to not more than 112.5° on either bow, as shown in Fig. 17. And the speed of approach will be more than in "overtaking" but less than in "meeting." Should the bearing be so close to dead ahead and the courses so nearly opposite that doubt arises, then Rule 14 tells the mariner to assume meeting. At the other end of the pelorus is another doubtful arc. If the bearing is so close to the edge

Fig. 17. *Arcs of Approach. As viewed from your vessel,* meeting *is an approach within about 11° on either bow;* overtaking *is one from more than about 22° abaft your beam on either side;* crossing *is within the remainder of the bearing circle.*

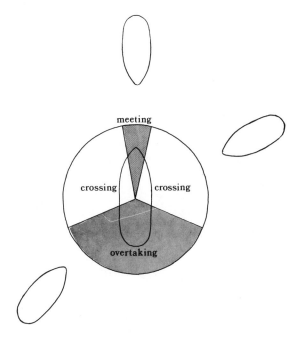

between a sidelight arc and that of a sternlight, and if the courses are similar but the speeds different, then a doubt between crossing and overtaking might arise. In that case Rule 13 commands that overtaking be assumed. But in-between the doubts Rule 15 writes the script.

The basic requirement is simply put: the one with the other on her own starboard bow keeps clear and avoids crossing ahead. Rule 16, speaking as it does to all *Keep Clear* vessels, adds the requirement of taking early and substantial action. However, a wide choice of maneuvers remains. *Keep Clear* can change speed by slowing, stopping, or reversing engines. She can change course to the right or even to the left. She can combine a course and a speed change. The mariner obliged to keep clear finds that his role brings a dividend. During any approach a certain amount of nervous energy is generated. Any requirement to do something eases the pressure of the adrenalin in one's system. When involvement is unavoidable we would all probably rather act than just observe.

A tanker stands on to cross ahead of a freighter keeping clear. [Photo by Lawrence Wyatt]

The Inland version of Rule 15 adds a second paragraph. On any inland river the Coast Guard might specify, a power-driven vessel following the river up or down has the right-of-way over any vessel crossing, and the crossing vessel has the duty to keep clear. No ambiguous "avoid impeding safe passage" statement appears. The crossing vessel, regardless of propulsion, regardless of relative maneuverability, whether the river is a narrow channel or not, shall keep clear. The sweeping words of Inland Rule 15(b) are new to the inland scene. In the past there have been such statements as the one granting preference on Western Rivers to a downbound tug with a tow over a power-driven vessel crossing. Nowadays the instruction is far more positive and is not bound so closely to specific areas. The COLREGS and Inland restraint on crossing ahead are very specific, though, and apply to all areas. In both instances the prohibition is tempered by the phrase "if the circumstances of the case admit," but that should not be read to minimize the basic "ya gotta." You must avoid crossing ahead of another power-driven vessel on your starboard bow unless you have very, very strong justification for acting otherwise. The postcollision lament of the motorist after a try at darting across oncoming highway traffic, "I thought I could make it," is all too common. The nautical code brooks no such delinquency. Nor should the *Keep Clear* vessel feel persecuted by the demand. To have an engine failure a few hundred yards dead ahead of a supertanker's bow wave is not conducive to a healthy old age.

The full crossing script for a *Keep Clear* power-driven vessel on any waters includes Rule 16. We've already met its requirements, for it speaks to all *Keep Clear* ships. Now we'll take a closer look. Beforehand, though, let's tag Rule 15's crossing situation for additional study. The story is only half finished, for we have yet to find what is expected of the *Stand On* vessel. But first, to the further duties of *Keep Clear:*

RULE 16—Action by Give-Way Vessel

COLREGS

Every vessel which is directed to keep out of the way of another vessel shall, so far as possible, take early and substantial action to keep well clear.

INLAND

Every vessel which is directed to keep out of the way of another vessel shall, so far as possible, take early and substantial action to keep well clear.

The words of this rule are simple and apply to everyone in sight of an approaching vessel and required to keep out of the way. Each is told to take early and substantial action. We've heard the lyrics before in Rule 8. That refrain was sung in Section I to any vessel taking action to avoid in any condition of visibility. Rule 16 is not redundant, for it has a narrower aim. But it must be read as if it included the demands of Section I's more general rules. Here is a review, with a few asides to fill out what is expected.

Maintaining a proper lookout and selecting a safe speed are basic. So is taking action to avoid collision. What is done must be done early, in a substantial amount and in the light of good seamanship. Rule 8 says so to everyone; Rule 16 adds "You, too!" for the benefit of vessels required to keep out of the way. The mesh of the pattern is quite fine, with little opportunity for any mariner to plead lack of direction when called to account for his conduct.

Now we must undertake a careful look at Rule 17. It has also already been mentioned when discussing earlier rules. Now is the time to dissect its five short paragraphs which are packed with a cargo of demands.

RULE 17—Action by Stand-On Vessel

COLREGS

(a)(i) Where one of two vessels is to keep out of the way the other shall keep her course and speed.

(ii) The latter vessel may however take action to avoid collision by her maneuver alone, as soon as it becomes apparent to her that the vessel required to keep out of the way is not taking appropriate action in compliance with these Rules.

(b) When, from any cause, the vessel required to keep her course and speed finds herself so close that collision cannot be avoided by the action of the give-way vessel alone, she shall take such action as will best aid to avoid collision.

(c) A power-driven vessel which takes action in a crossing situation in accordance with sub-paragraph (a)(ii) of this Rule to avoid collision with another power-driven vessel shall, if the circumstances of the case admit, not alter course to port for a vessel on her own port side.

(d) This Rule does not relieve the give-way vessel of her obligation to keep out of the way.

INLAND

(a)(i) Where one of two vessels is to keep out of the way, the other shall keep her course and speed.

(ii) The latter vessel may, however, take action to avoid collision by her maneuver alone, as soon as it becomes apparent to her that the vessel required to keep out of the way is not taking appropriate action in compliance with these Rules.

(b) When, from any cause, the vessel required to keep her course and speed finds herself so close that collision cannot be avoided by the action of the give-way vessel alone, she shall take such action as will best aid to avoid collision.

(c) A power-driven vessel which takes action in a crossing situation in accordance with subparagraph (a)(ii) of this Rule to avoid collision with another power-driven vessel shall, if the circumstances of the case admit, not alter course to port for a vessel on her own port side.

(d) This Rule does not relieve the give-way vessel of her obligation to keep out of the way.

The beginning of this rule is explicit. When any vessel, regardless of propulsion, is told to keep clear, the other, regardless of propulsion, is to hold course and speed. That applies to any vessel in sight of another approaching and with risk of collision. So a sail vessel being approached by another sail to windward is not free to do as she wishes. She *must* hold course and speed. The principle is eminently sensible. A more agile vessel should keep clear of a less agile one. The less agile can reasonably be required to continue doing what she has already demonstrated she can do. Whatever course and speed she has achieved she should be able to maintain. That way she'll remain predictable and not startle the other with unexpected twists and turns. The vessel being overtaken cannot sashay back and forth in front of the oncoming overtaker. The mariner to be kept clear of is required to be stable and constant.

A missile-armed warship preparing to play the role of keeping clear of a crossing sail vessel. [Photo by Lawrence Wyatt]

But too much of such passivity might give him ulcers. His *Keep Clear* counterpart can release pent-up emotion by action. Not so for *Stand On*. Adrenalin flow is dammed and blood pressure mounts as the anxious observer performs his role. The rules recognize such cardiovascular punishment and offer some relief. Rule 17(a)(ii) to the rescue! Whenever it is apparent that *Keep Clear* is not taking appropriate action, *Stand On* has an option to take action on her own.

Rule 17(b) now enters with a "shall." When *Keep Clear* has run out of means of keeping clear by her action alone, *Stand On* must turn to and help. This is an application of the "last clear chance" doctrine. No vessel instructed to hold course and speed can follow that script to disaster. She must, when the other no longer is able to avoid on her own, take whatever action might help avoid collision.

Some pages back we fretted over how Rule 8(e) and Rule 17 could coexist. The earlier demand is that when necessary action is taken to avoid collision or to allow more time to assess the situation, a vessel shall slow, stop, or reverse. Rule 17(a)(i), though, demands that the vessel being kept clear of shall hold speed. To slow down when assessing a situation while at the same time standing on would be an incredible feat. Those who go down to the sea are indeed uncommon persons, but they are not magicians. And these two rules do not require hocus-pocus. Rule 17(a)(i) requires standing on until the call comes for action. If, pursuant to Rule 17(a)(ii), *Stand On* wants more time to figure out why *Keep Clear* is not playing her role, then *Stand On* shall slow down, stop, or reverse. And when, in carrying out Rule 17(b), *Stand On* judges that *Keep Clear* cannot fulfill her duty alone, then any action taken must include slowing down, stopping, or reversing. Working together these rules parry the image of vessels swerving away from danger at full speed.

The result of all of this could be viewed as sort of four acts in the play as depicted in Fig. 18. In Act I the vessels are approaching each other but are not yet close enough to be in danger. Perhaps they are in sight of each other, perhaps they are not. In any case each is required to follow the dictates of Part B's Section I. They keep a proper lookout, operate at a safe speed, use all available means to assess risk of collision, and when taking avoiding action, do so by early, substantial, and seamanlike steps.

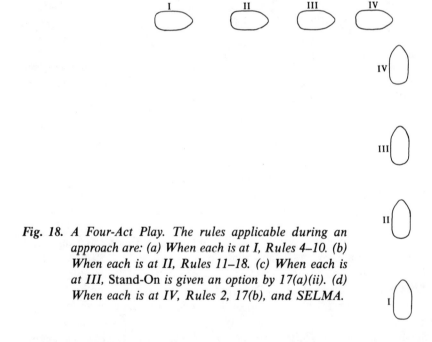

Fig. 18. *A Four-Act Play. The rules applicable during an approach are: (a) When each is at I, Rules 4–10. (b) When each is at II, Rules 11–18. (c) When each is at III,* Stand-On *is given an option by 17(a)(ii). (d) When each is at IV, Rules 2, 17(b), and SELMA.*

Act II begins when, approaching each other, they are in sight and risk of collision exists. The summons to follow a definite script is now heard. Should one be assigned the role to keep clear, the other must stand on. It is basic to the rules that at this stage each must assume that the other will follow the rules. *Keep Clear* is entitled to assume that *Stand On* will do so. On the other hand, *Stand On* must assume that *Keep Clear* will do so by appropriate action. Wariness is not discouraged; in fact it is required by good seamanship. But suspicion and distrust will spoil the performance.

Act III recognizes some facts of maritime life. By now the anxieties of the stand-on mariner might appear well founded. *Keep Clear* is not acting as he should, so *Stand On* has an option to take action on his own. But this third

A large ship stands ready to depart from the Rules when a power-driven vessel on her port bow begins to cross ahead. [Photo by Lawrence Wyatt]

act cannot bypass Act II. Vessels must first be given an opportunity to follow the rules before there is any justification to change the script. And Rule 17(c) adds a prudent caution. If the stand-on vessel is power-driven and is crossing another power-driven vessel on her port bow and elects to exercise her option in Act III, she should not turn left. Just about the time she would do so, *Keep Clear* might awaken to her duties and turn right . . . into a collision.

Act IV brings Rule 2's SELMA onstage. No matter how the regulations have been followed, things have gone awry. Improvisation is all that remains. Conduct in extremis is the common example of what might now transpire. *Keep Clear,* her options exhausted, cannot stay out of the way on her own. So by Rule 17(b) *Stand On* is now obliged to stop standing on. She must take whatever action seems best suited to avoid impact. And if she continues to hold course and speed she violates the Rules of the Road. This, though, might seem unfair. It was not *Stand On*'s fault that the two are ready to tangle. Since *Keep Clear* caused the mess, why shouldn't *Keep Clear* clean it up? The difficulty is that both hero and villain are liable to be badly damaged by collision, no matter who might be at fault. *Stand On* must accept the last clear chance to help prevent disaster. Rule 17(d) offers a reassurance. *Keep Clear* is still obliged to carry out the role of trying to keep clear. *Stand On* does not assume the total responsibility. Moreover, whatever action *Stand On* does take, her performance need not meet the standards of the unruffled. No more is expected of her than that of any seaman suddenly confronted with the spectre of imminent danger.

In retrospect the keep-clear vessel is less pressured during this drama, for she has freedom to act. When the misleading words "privileged" and "burdened" were in style it was no wonder that experienced mariners found little honor in being privileged. The modern rules, while not lessening the burdens of either, at least peel off the subterfuge. Rules 16 and 17 apply whenever *A* is told to keep clear and *B* must stand on. The situation can involve power-driven crossing power-driven, sail approaching sail, any vessel overtaking any other. Whenever the two roles are assigned, the two rules apply.

And that brings us to the subject of casting. What actors play what parts? By what measure is one vessel selected to hold course and speed while another is required to keep clear? The list of dramatis personnae is in Rule 18.

RULE 18—Responsibilities Between Vessels

COLREGS

Except where Rules 9, 10 and 13 otherwise require:

(a) A power-driven vessel underway shall keep out of the way of:
   (i) a vessel not under command;
   (ii) a vessel restricted in her ability to maneuver;
   (iii) a vessel engaged in fishing;
   (iv) a sailing vessel.

(b) A sailing vessel underway shall keep out of the way of:
   (i) a vessel not under command;
   (ii) a vessel restricted in her ability to maneuver;
   (iii) a vessel engaged in fishing.

(c) A vessel engaged in fishing when underway shall, so far as possible, keep out of the way of:
   (i) a vessel not under command;
   (ii) a vessel restricted in her ability to maneuver.

(d)(i) Any vessel other than a vessel not under command or a vessel restricted in her ability to maneuver shall, if the circumstances of the case admit, avoid impeding the safe passage of a vessel constrained by her draft, exhibiting the signals in Rule 28.

(ii) A vessel constrained by her draft shall navigate with particular caution having full regard to her special condition.

(e) A seaplane on the water shall, in general, keep well clear of all vessels and avoid impeding their navigation. In circumstances, however, where risk of collision exists, she shall comply with the Rules of this Part.

INLAND

Except where Rules 9, 10, and 13 otherwise require:

(a) A power-driven vessel underway shall keep out of the way of:
　(i) a vessel not under command;
　(ii) a vessel restricted in her ability to maneuver;
　(iii) a vessel engaged in fishing; and
　(iv) a sailing vessel.

(b) A sailing vessel underway shall keep out of the way of:
　(i) a vessel not under command;
　(ii) a vessel restricted in her ability to maneuver; and
　(iii) a vessel engaged in fishing.

(c) A vessel engaged in fishing when underway shall, so far as possible, keep out of the way of:
　(i) a vessel not under command; and
　(ii) a vessel restricted in her ability to maneuver.

(d) A seaplane on the water shall, in general, keep well clear of all vessels and avoid impeding their navigation. In circumstances, however, where risk of collision exists, she shall comply with the Rules of this Part.

Several pages ago we encountered the Victorian contrast between "keep clear" and "avoid impeding safe passage." We should keep the distinction in mind as we dismember this rule. And note how the list of assignments is introduced: "except where Rules 9, 10, and 13 otherwise require." Rule 9 contains some significant "avoid impeding" cautions in narrow channels with Inland adding a "keep clear" command to a vessel bound upstream. In the COLREGS version of Rule 10 there appear more cautions of the "avoid impeding" type. And the sweeping language of Rule 13 orders all overtakers to keep clear of whomever they overtake, with the overtaken required to stand on. The demand of Rule 13 is supreme over all but the exercise of good seamanship and general prudence. In reading Rule 18, then, we must keep in mind whatever admonitions to avoid impeding or to keep clear are found in Rules 9, 10, and 13. What Rule 18 does is to assign responsibility to keep clear by weighing the relative maneuverability of the participants, subject to the overriding constraints spelled out in the other three rules.

Viewed as a hierarchy with the lower echelons keeping clear of those higher up, the listings in Rule 18(a), (b), and (c) can be rearranged this way:

Vessels not under command and vessels restricted in ability to maneuver
Vessels engaged in fishing
Sailing vessels

Power-driven vessels
Seaplanes on the water

However, recognizing the supremacy of Rule 13 we must advance the overtaken vessel to the top of the pile and place the overtaking vessel on the bottom. Here is the priority list, with annotations:

1. An overtaken vessel stands on while all listed below her keep clear.

2. Both a vessel not under command and a vessel restricted in ability to maneuver stand on while all listed below them keep clear.

3. A vessel engaged in fishing stands on while all listed below her keep clear. She is, though, subject to some "avoid impeding" admonitions. She shall not impede the passage of any vessel in a narrow channel or in a traffic separation lane.

4. A sailing vessel stands on while all listed below her keep clear. But she receives her share of "avoid impeding" cautions. She shall not impede the safe passage of any vessel restricted to a narrow channel or of any power-driven vessel using a traffic lane.

5. A power-driven vessel keeps clear of all those listed above her unless she is being overtaken. If she is under 20 meters long she shall not impede the safe passage of any vessel restricted to a narrow channel or of another power-driven vessel using a traffic separation lane.

6. A seaplane on the water shall try to keep clear of everyone else. But if risk of collision exists she'll follow the normal requirements of conduct. Rule 3 defines her as a vessel, and she is propelled by machinery; so unless she chooses to taxi under sail, the conclusion must be that when risk of collision exists she acts out the role of a power-driven vessel as best she can.

7. Any vessel overtaking any other shall keep clear of the vessel being overtaken. This is the imperious command of Rule 13 for all waters. A sail vessel overtaking a nuclear-powered missile cruiser keeps clear of the cruiser. A sail vessel engaged in fishing on the starboard tack and overtaking the handiest powerboat ever built keeps out of the way.

Let's now sort carefully through the words of Rule 18. First to be noted is the contrast between the "keep clear" command given a vessel engaged in fishing and that given power-driven and sail. Rule 18(a) and (b) leave no uncertainty about the orders given power-driven and sail vessels: they "shall keep out of the way of. . . ." But Rule 18(c) seems more considerate of vessels engaged in fishing. There the command is ". . . shall, so far as possible, keep out of the way of. . . ." Is it possible that St. Peter did some lobbying at the London convention? There's no need for heavenly speculation, for we can find a more ready explanation. Rule 3(d) defines a vessel engaged in fishing as one restricted in maneuverability by the fishing gear in use. She is not considered so hobbled that she cannot keep clear, but she might have difficulty doing so.

So when her turn comes to play the "keep clear" role she is not expected to give an outstanding performance. Rule 18(c) tells her to try her best.

The rationale in our next consideration is not so evident. In fact, should the words be read literally we might well echo the exasperation of the King of Siam: "All is a puzzlement!" According to Rule 3(f) and (g) a vessel not under command and one restricted in ability to maneuver by the nature of her work is each unable to keep out of the way of another vessel. If either should be so nimble as to be able to dodge or, like the fisherman, have even a bare chance of doing so, then she doesn't fit the definition. But when a ship has in fact no ability to keep out of the way then it is idle to command her to do so. What, though, when either of them should be overtaking another vessel? Rule 13 sounds unyielding when it states that notwithstanding what a covey of other rules from 4 through 18 might say, the overtaking vessel keeps clear. Yet the problem will not go away. How can a vessel unable to keep clear be required to keep clear? And the problem is not so academic. Picture an aircraft carrier steaming into the wind at 30 knots and ready to land a wing of expensive planes crewed by even more expensive pilots. She is overtaking a lumbering vessel dead ahead. If the carrier changes course she exposes the aircraft to danger. If she does not, Rule 13 might hold her in violation. At this stage of the game all hands should sing praises to SELMA. The situation is rife with special circumstances and with the limitations of the vessels involved. All hands also know what would happen. The ship being overtaken would sheer off smartly

No course changes are expected when a carrier steaming through sea smoke is about to land a returning plane. [USN photo]

and the carrier would forge on about her business of nesting her eagles. Even so, we can't ignore the point that a script has been written. Rule 13 overrides 18 and commands the overtaker to keep clear. Is this really of any moment to anyone except a judge, a lawyer, and perhaps the pilot of an airplane? Not really. But we can at least enjoy the symmetry of the rules. We should reason that although Rule 13 overrides Rule 18, Rule 2's fiat that common sense, good seamanship, and the occasional need of an ad lib will ultimately prevail.

The aircraft have been recovered, so we can gratefully return to our task. Seven degrees of responsibility are offered and the ranking seems fairly evident. But the emphasis has been on the duty to keep clear. What about the other vessels? During any approach those obliged to hold course and speed will do more than perform the simple role of standing on.

We've heard mention of Act I. Its setting is any condition of visibility and before all the factors of being in sight, approaching, and with risk of collision coincide. Both actors will, pursuant to Rules 2 and 4 through 10, keep a sharp lookout, operate at a safe speed, assess risk of collision by whatever means available, and when action is required, take it early, in substantial amount, and in the light of good seamanship. But neither has yet donned her costume as *Stand On* or *Keep Clear*. The uniform of the day is *Be Wary*.

Then the scene changes. Now they each see the other approaching and each has judged that risk of collision exists. The curtain rises on Act II with the players distinctly robed as *Keep Clear* and *Stand On* in all cases other than when power-driven vessels are meeting. The script for *Keep Clear* is amply detailed throughout the rules of the section we are now studying. Back, though, to reaffirm that *Stand On* must do more than just stand on by holding course and speed. Her actions continue to include compliance with the needs for a lookout, safe speed, and assessment of the unfolding risk of collision. In addition she will keep a keen eye on the other's performance. Should it become apparent that *Keep Clear* is not taking appropriate action, she may ignore the restriction of standing on and take action on her own in Act III. But if the situation so deteriorates that *Keep Clear* cannot solve the problem alone, then Acts II and III are at an end.

Act IV is what SELMA is all about. Either the script won't work or none has been written for the predicament or someone has flubbed her lines or, from whatever cause, the playwright's guidance is ineffectual. There is no rehearsal for this play, and during a live performance there is no curtain to ring down. During Act IV both actors must improvise. *Keep Clear* continues her attempts to do so, but *Stand On* must also participate. In fact she changes her costume to that of *Help Out*.

There are two more acts in the play, and in the next chapter Act V is performed. But now is as good a time as any to discuss the last act. When a happy ending is in store, the performance is cheerfully abbreviated without the staging of this last act. Performers depart from the stage and move on to other theaters. But should the theme be tragedy, Act VI is played out. It deals with inevitable collision. Despite the script, despite all efforts of the actors, the two vessels cannot avoid contact. Understandably the Rules of the Road make no provision for what next should be done. When a collision is unavoidable,

No handy maneuvers can be expected of the Nippon Maru *as she stands down a crowded channel under full sail. [Photo by Harry Merrick]*

regulations to prevent collision are hardly relevant. There is no need for either to play any role other than one designed to lessen the results of the contact. As we saw very early in our study there are separate laws to penalize those who hit and run. And good seamanship makes its own demands. The mariner's first duty is to his own, and if he concludes that the blow is less dangerous when taken by his bow rather than a flank, he will not be summarily condemned for turning toward the other. Of course we presume here that collision is inevitable. While the danger increases, during an approach but before conditions become hopeless, he is expected to follow the Rules. And this would include heeding the caution that he not turn toward others and the requirement that he stand ready to slow down. But when the jig is up he safeguards his people and his ship.

On the other hand he cannot in good conscience remain aloof from the peril of the other vessel. Sea stories galore recount the advantage of trying to keep one's bow in the hole it might have punctured in another. There are many procedures by which one can minimize another's plight. Here, though, is not the place to wander through the subject of seamanlike conduct in a crisis. In fact we should dwell no longer on unwelcome Act VI. Excessive morbidity is unhealthy and, anyway, when the Rules are followed carefully such calamities are not so likely to occur. Let's bury our attention to the dire at this midpoint of our study and return to more genial concerns.

What remains in considering Rule 18 is a glance at a significant difference between the COLREGS version and that applicable on inland waters. COL-REGS Rule 18(d) is not found in the Inland set. Very early in our discussion we learned that the United States finds scant reason to single out a vessel constrained by draft for special deference. But COLREGS give her accommodation. Before we find out what that is, we should review a definition. COL-REGS Rule 3(h) states that a vessel constrained by draft must be power-driven in order to qualify for recognition. And subject to that limitation, here is the tolerance she receives. By Rule 18(d), on the high seas all but vessels not under command and those restricted in ability to maneuver shall, if possible, avoid impeding the safe passage of a power-driven vessel identifying herself as constrained by draft. Further, the constrained ship must bear her condition in mind while she navigates with particular caution. Where, though, does she fit in our hierarchy of responsibilities and duties? Rule 13 maintains that the overtaken vessel is supreme. Those constrained by draft must keep out of her way. Rule 18(d) demotes the constrained vessel below those not under command and those restricted in ability to maneuver by the nature of their work. That follows, for she is not considered unable to keep out of the way. There

S.S. Lurline gracefully turns left after passing under the San Francisco Bay Bridge. [Matson Lines]

is no question that she is below level 2 in our priority list. But does she come next? Does she fit between those unable to keep out of the way and those engaged in fishing who might have a fretful but not impossible time keeping clear? Does she fit between level 2 and level 3? The logic of our Victorian analysis would suggest that this is not the case, and such influential observers as the IMO and the Coast Guard seem to agree.

If the framers of COLREGS meant that a vessel constrained by draft should be kept clear of by vessels engaged in fishing, by sail vessels, and by the power-driven, they should have said so. And they could have done so by listing her in Rule 18(a), (b), and (c) as a type to be kept clear of. Instead, the less peremptory direction is that power-driven, sail, and those engaged in fishing must avoid impeding her safe passage. Our study of the 1890 staircase tells us that such is not a command to keep clear. What it means is that both the constrained vessel and her fellow actor on stage must take into account the constraint and plan ahead to avoid inconvenience.

The silence of Inland's Rule 18 now seems reasonable. Deep-draft ships are already accommodated by the array of "avoid impeding" directions found in Rule 9. A likely restriction in a narrow channel develops from having one's keel perilously close to the bottom. A vessel so constrained is to be granted deference. On analysis the Inland view is even more considerate than that of COLREGS. Regardless of her means of propulsion, a vessel which must remain in the narrow channel is not to be impeded by small vessels, by sail and by crossing vessels, and by vessels engaged in fishing. Again it should not be forgotten that hovering over all the rules, including those directing conduct when vessels are in sight of each other, is Rule 2. Good seamanship must be exercised and everyone must be prepared to depart from the script in order to avoid immediate danger. SELMA can require the actors to extemporize in order to meet special circumstances. The Inland Rules find no cause for more discussion.

Notice that even in COLREGS the deep-draft ship gains no right-of-way. Instead the requirement is that her plight must be taken into consideration. The U.S. view is that since she has no special right-of-way there is no more reason to defer to her than to any other clumsy vessel. Clumsiness is not limited to comparisons of draft to available depth of water. A barge liable to skid because she has little draft and no keel might be worse off. Being under-manned or underpowered or both would certainly forge constraints. How then do we answer the question of the niche for the vessel constrained by draft? She nests in level 5 of our list, along with all other power-driven vessels. By the strict letter of the rules, only seaplanes afloat and vessels overtaking others are strictly obliged to keep out of her way. Sur-rebuttal time, now, for COLREGS. Tucked into Rule 18(d)(i) is the phrase ". . . exhibiting the signals in Rule 28." How does an onlooker know that another's keel is ready to scrape bottom? Must he read the other's draftmarks through a long glass and compare the observation with charted depth after having made appropriate allowance for the state of the tide? Need he carry on board an American Bureau of Shipping list of vessel dimensions or perhaps a Lloyd's Register of Shipping for reference so he can determine the molded depth of a vessel in sight? "No," say the champions of the COLREGS view. Three red lights in a vertical line by night and a black cylinder by day communicate that the vessel displaying the signal is laboring under a constraint. So advised, the onlooker can play the role on the staircase with certainty. What's wrong with a harmless advertisement of a specific constraint? The U.S. reply might be that such an advertisement encourages abuse of status and grants a license for might to snatch first right on the waterways. The points of view have been noted and we should, in good seamanship, react this way. Every time we see a large ship inside the 10-fathom curve we should consider that her keel might be smelling bottom. A comfortable gap of 3 or so fathoms might exist. On the other hand it might only be 3 or so feet. Allow for high-speed squat plus a dab of sag and problems arise. It is probably far better to associate large size with constraints on maneuverability. Then, like the Victorian maiden, we should discreetly not cause a scene.

Our survey of in-sight conduct is complete, and in the exercise of good seamanship we would like to keep out of the way by enjoying a watch below. But a pesky special circumstance disrupts the script. We must now stand by for a chapter quiz.

QUESTIONS

The logbook requires us to make ten entries, some of which will require extra thought. Good seamanship, a flexible term, dictates that we work carefully and cleave to the Rules of the Road. Our position report depends on the outcome.

1. Sail vessels *A* and *B* in the adjoining sketch are in sight of one another and approaching so as to involve risk of collision.

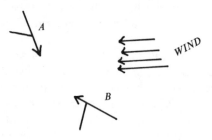

   a. *A* holds course and speed.
   b. *B* keeps clear of *A*.
   c. both of the above
   d. none of the above

2. In the adjoining sketch, *B* is a power-driven vessel and can safely navigate only within a narrow channel. She is overtaking *A*, a sail vessel.

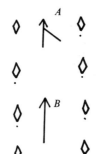

   a. *B* is required to keep out of *A*'s way.
   b. *A* shall avoid impeding *B*'s safe passage.
   c. both of the above
   d. none of the above

3. A naval aircraft carrier is launching aircraft while approaching in sight of a vessel engaged in fishing.
   a. The vessel engaged in fishing shall keep clear if possible.
   b. Since special circumstances exist, both vessels are free to depart from the Rules in order to avoid immediate danger.
   c. The aircraft carrier shall keep clear of the vessel engaged in fishing.
   d. none of the above.

4. A dredge is approaching in sight of a vessel engaged in hydrographic survey.
   a. The dredge keeps clear.
   b. SELMA applies.
   c. The dredge holds course and speed.
   d. none of the above

5. In the adjoining sketch, both *A* and *B* are power-driven vessels and approaching each other in sight.

   a. *A* keeps clear.
   b. *A* avoids crossing ahead of *B.*
   c. both of the above
   d. none of the above

6. A sail vessel in sight of the other keeps out of the way of
   a. a tug and tow severely restricted in ability to deviate from course
   b. a vessel engaged in fishing
   c. both of the above
   d. none of the above

7. In the adjoining sketch, *B* is power-driven. *A*, a sail vessel, is overtaking *B*. *C*, a power-driven dredge, is crossing *B*'s course. All are in sight.

   a. *B* holds course and speed.
   b. *C* holds course and speed.
   c. *A* holds course and speed.
   d. SELMA applies.

8. In the adjoining sketch, *A* is traveling at 6 knots and *B* is traveling at 10 knots. During the approach they were, relative to each other, in positions 1, 2, and 3. Now they are in relative position 4, with *B* on *A*'s starboard bow.

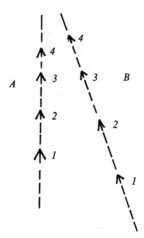

   a. *B* holds course and speed.
   b. *A* keeps clear.
   c. The situation is one of crossing.
   d. none of the above

9. When power-driven *A* observes power-driven *B* approaching on the port bow on a crossing track so as to involve risk of collision,
   a. *A* holds course and speed
   b. *A* may take avoiding action if *B* does not act appropriately
   c. *A* must take avoiding action if *B* alone cannot prevent collision
   d. all of the above

10. Sail vessel *A* on a due-south course observes power-driven *B* dead ahead and on a due-north course.
   a. *A* must change course to the right.
   b. *B* must change course to the right.
   c. both of the above
   d. none of the above

AND ANSWERS

All you now need do is to check your answers and the watch on deck is done. Allow the usual 10 points for each correct response. But since the last session has been trying, SELMA grants a departure from the rules of scoring in order to avoid immediate depression.

80–100	full powered and maneuverable
60–70	navigation restricted to the channel
40–50	engaged in fishing
under 40	not under command

1. d   2. c   3. a   4. b   5. c   6. c   7. d   8. d   9. d   10. d

5

Part B—CONDUCT IN RESTRICTED VISIBILITY

WE ARE ONE section away from completing a survey of the rules of conduct. What remains is the script to follow when in or near an area of restricted visibility. Part B, Section III presents the details in one rule, so our discussion will be short. By no means, though, does that imply that the rule is relatively unimportant. No circumstances can be more demanding of either the mariner or his rules of conduct than those involved when vessels are shrouded in fog. Very careful attention to this chapter is an obvious must.

Devotees of the theater might consider this to be Act V in our drama. Should a power failure suddenly plunge the entire playhouse into darkness, the actors are at risk of bumping into couches and canvas backdrops as well as into each other if they try to carry on. No script applies and it isn't customary that dramatists provide for such an interruption. Not so at sea! Our playwrights, the rulemakers, have indeed provided. In restricted visibility the performers are guided by Rule 19.

RULE 19—Conduct of Vessels in Restricted Visibility

COLREGS

(a) This Rule applies to vessels not in sight of one another when navigating in or near an area of restricted visibility.

(b) Every vessel shall proceed at a safe speed adapted to the prevailing circumstances and conditions of restricted visibilty. A power-driven vessel shall have her engines ready for immediate maneuver.

(c) Every vessel shall have due regard to the prevailing circumstances and conditions of restricted visibility when complying with the Rules of Section I of this Part.

(d) A vessel which detects by radar alone the presence of another vessel shall determine if a close-quarters situation is developing and/or risk of collision exists. If so, she shall take avoiding action in ample time, provided that when such action consists of an alteration of course, so far as possible the following shall be avoided:

(i) an alteration of course to port for a vessel forward of the beam, other than for a vessel being overtaken;

(ii) an alteration of course towards a vessel abeam or abaft the beam.

(e) Except where it has been determined that a risk of collision does not exist, every vessel which hears apparently forward of her beam the fog signal of another vessel, or which cannot avoid a close-quarters situation with another vessel forward of her beam, shall reduce her speed to the minimum at which she can be kept on her course. She shall if necessary take all her way off and in any event navigate with extreme caution until danger of collision is over.

INLAND

(a) This Rule applies to vessels not in sight of one another when navigating in or near an area of restricted visibility.

(b) Every vessel shall proceed at a safe speed adapted to the prevailing circumstances and conditions of restricted visibilty. A power-driven vessel shall have her engines ready for immediate maneuver.

(c) Every vessel shall have due regard to the prevailing circumstances and conditions of restricted visibility when complying with Rules 4 through 10.

(d) A vessel which detects by radar alone the presence of another vessel shall determine if a close-quarters situation is developing or risk of collision exists. If so, she shall take avoiding action in ample time, provided that when such action consists of an alteration of course, so far as possible the following shall be avoided:

(i) an alteration of course to port for a vessel forward of the beam, other than for a vessel being overtaken; and

(ii) an alteration of course toward a vessel abeam or abaft the beam.

(e) Except where it has been determined that a risk of collision does not exist, every vessel which hears apparently forward of her beam the fog signal of another vessel, or which cannot avoid a close-quarters situation with another vessel forward of her beam, shall reduce her speed to the minimum at which she can be kept on course. She shall if necessary take all her way off and, in any event, navigate with extreme caution until danger of collision is over.

First, as usual we should review a definition. Rule 3 describes restricted visibility as the result of fog, mist, falling snow, heavy rainstorms, sandstorms, or other similar causes. We've already been told that a so'wester over the eyes is not a "similar cause." But our interest is in more than why the condition exists. We need to know at what range visibility is considered restricted. That inquiry will lead us somewhat off course. In the next chapter we'll meet a list of minimum visibility ranges for lights. The scope is from at least 1 mile to at least 6. When the atmosphere prevents a light from being seen at its minimum range, surely visibility is restricted. But where does that leave us? Do we have a sliding measure from less than 1 mile to less than 6, depending on the light and the ship size?

It is self-evident that restricted visibility exists when the *weakest* running light cannot be seen. A more prudent measure is that when one cannot see the *strongest* running light, vision is clouded. The Rules formerly required large power-driven vessels to carry masthead lights of at least 5 miles range. By a view of those times restricted visibility was said to prevail when such a light could not be seen. Also attributed to that era is a lighthouse station practice which bore out that measure. At a manned lighthouse the keeper would start the foghorn when visibility fell below 5 miles. Although nowadays the minimum range of a large ship's masthead light is 6 miles, that old yardstick is still worth remembering. But our search for the threshold of restricted visibility is not so easily concluded.

Table 1. Meteorological Optical Range*

CODE NO.	WEATHER	YARDS
0	Dense fog	Less than 50
1	Thick fog	50–200
2	Moderate fog	200–500
3	Light fog	500–1000
		NAUTICAL MILES
4	Thin fog	$\frac{1}{2}$–1
5	Haze	1–2
6	Light haze	2–5$\frac{1}{2}$
7	Clear	5$\frac{1}{2}$–11
8	Very clear	11.0–27.0
9	Exceptionally clear	Over 27.0

*From the International Visibility Code.

Older rules also mentioned that light visibility was keyed to a dark night with a clear atmosphere. Was the adjective "clear" just a capricious choice from among its synonyms or was it selected as a technical term? Probably official precision was not intended; nonetheless the word "clear" leads us to the *International Visibility Code.* This gauge is not usually associated with the Rules of the Road but it is so relevant that we must make its acquaintance. A *meteorological optical range* is the daytime distance that an object can be seen when illuminated by the natural light of sun and sky under a specific atmospheric condition. Such factors as the strength of a light, its height, or the height of the observer are not involved in computing it. The only concern is how atmospheric impedimenta might affect the daytime range of detection. Table 1 reprints from *American Practical Navigator,* Volume 2 (Defense Mapping Agency, 1981) the code's listing of conditions by range and label. Its ten categories describe daytime ranges as from less than 50 yards in a dense fog to over 27 miles when the atmosphere is exceptionally clear. Note that "clear" is the word to describe a meteorological optical range of 5½ to 11 miles. Is this what the makers of the older rules had in mind when they specified minimum ranges "on a dark night in a clear atmosphere"? We can presume that they knew of the International Visibility Code and even that their choice of adjective could have been influenced by it. It is less likely, though, that they intended to be so technical. If that were the purpose they would not have been so coy. The statement would probably have read "on a dark night in a clear (International Visibility Code 7) atmosphere." We must look for a more subjective measure, but in the search the International Visibility Code can be helpful. The fog, mist, and other conditions mentioned in Rule 19 could, under the code, begin at light haze, when the daytime range would be up to 5.5 miles. That seems to harmonize with the 6-mile minimum range of the strongest running light.

Spray sweeps over the flight deck of a nuclear-powered carrier while she is near an area of restricted visibility. [USN photo]

But now the difficulties are compounded. Such a range is daytime and varies with the atmosphere while disregarding such important factors as the height of the object and of the observer. Because of the curve of the earth high objects can be seen (all other factors equal) at greater distances by high observers than can low objects be seen by low observers. Figure 19 presents this fairly obvious concept. And a range at night must consider the strength of the light source as well. The U.S. Coast Guard *Light List* provides a means to adjust nighttime range of a lighthouse to allow for prevailing atmospheric conditions. In effect it brings together the factors of light strength and atmosphere. Figure 20 presents the Luminous Range Diagram used for that purpose. At the top or the bottom margin an entry is made for *nominal range*. This is the distance a particular light should be seen in a "clear" or "Code 7" atmosphere. Then by moving along the vertical line for that nominal range, the corresponding *luminous range* for each coded atmospheric condition can be determined. But all this seems only in point when dealing with lighthouses. What has it to do with the Rules of the Road? Here might be one relationship. Let's consider the minimum visibility of the strongest running light (6 miles) as a nominal range in a clear atmosphere. Now by entering the Luminous Range Diagram in Fig. 20 with that value we can find its corresponding visibility when the meteorological range is less than a "Code 7 clear." The result is a span from slightly less than 5 miles in a "light haze" to under a mile in a "moderate fog." The old rule of thumb used at lighthouse stations seems borne out. The evidence so far presented indicates that restricted visibility sets in when the range drops below 5 miles. But we had better not make a hasty judgment.

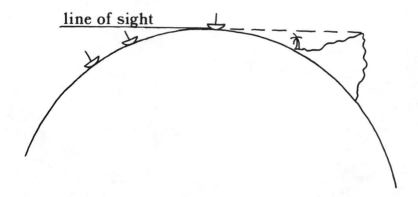

Fig. 19. *Visibility and the Earth's Curve. The range of visibility is subject to the height of both the object and the observer.*

All this is a game with numbers. The International Visibility Code was not prepared for the use of the IMO or any other agency concerned with collision avoidance. As the "only game in town" it can assist, but it doesn't provide the mariner with what he needs. The distance to the horizon where sea and sky meet depends on height of eye as well as atmospheric conditions. From a 10-foot height of eye on a clear day the horizon is 3.7 miles off. From a 100-foot elevation its distance is 11.7 miles. From a 10-foot observer to a 100-foot mast just breaking clear of the horizon would be 15.4 miles. Should "hazel" interpose with her Code 5 atmosphere, the daytime range shrinks to a maximum of 2 miles. If shining from that 100-foot mast were a light of 6-mile strength, "hazel" would translate the range to not much over 2½ miles, regardless of

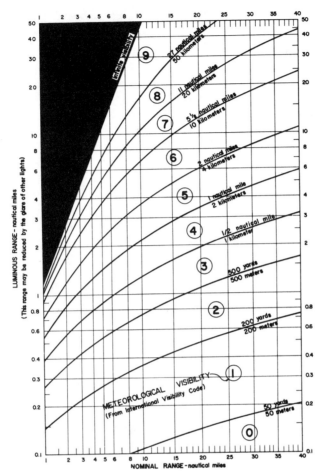

Fig. 20. Luminous Range Diagram. Enter with nominal range at top or bottom and coded number for meteorological optical range to find luminous range at left or right.

the height of the observer's eye. Incidentally, an observer's eye might now be caught by another translation. The simple addition of "l" to "haze" seems to personify an indifferent term. Alas, though, "hazel" has been neutered by the current statement of the International Visibility Code as shown in Table 1. Enough of such dehumanization! We'll speak of her henceforth as "hazel."

There are those, of course, who would urge us to speak no more of this, no matter what the name and gender. We are probably entitled to be impatient, even frankly exasperated. Few will have the onboard facilities, not to mention the inclination, to distinguish "hazel" from "light haze" on one side of her in Table 1 and "thin fog" on the other. The mariner obliged to make the crucial decision of whether or not Rule 19 applies should have less complicated guidance than this sort of luminous range lottery. Our discussion has not ended the search for the meaning of "restricted visibility." At best it has brought to mind some factors which might be involved. The mariner should expect to find no mathematical formula to assist him. Instead he should probably conclude that visibility becomes restricted by atmospheric impediments when his seamanlike common sense says so. He should also recall that Rule 6, in speaking of safe speed, mentioned radar as a guide. Suppose at night the radarscope shows a ship at short range but no light is visible on its bearing. The observer should assume that unless the pip is not from a ship at all, or if so that her lights are out, visibility is restricted. Our final conclusion? The boundary of restricted visibility cannot be determined by formula or fixed by any law. Good seamen on different vessels will make different judgments. One might consider that no significant restriction exists while another, nearby, is operating under Rule 19 and blowing fog signals. Each, though, can only make his own decision based on his own observations. When an atmospheric veil drops between his ship and her normal sea horizon, he should begin to consider that restricted visibility exists.

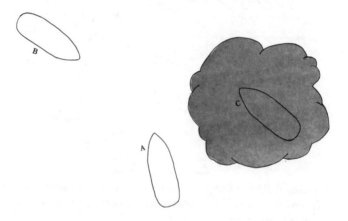

Fig. 21. In or Near a Fogbank. Rule 19 applies to A *as well as* C, *since both have visibility restricted by the fogbank.*

Rule 19(a) contains the phrase "in or near an area of restricted visibility." A vessel need not be totally surrounded by the atmospheric veil. The principle is that poor visibility within any significant arc of the horizon is sufficient to trigger a restriction. Here is an example. Vessel *A* is traveling north and enjoys an uncluttered panorama of moonlit sea on her port side. To starboard, though, lies a fogbank about a half mile off. She is near an area of restricted visibility and must follow Rule 19. By no measure would she be able to see as far as the range of even the weakest sidelight glimmering in the fogbank to the eastward. By anyone's version of good seamanship she should consider her outlook clouded. That same common sense is at work in Fig. 21. There, *A* is skirting a fogbank with *B* in sight on her port bow while *C* lurks in the fog to starboard. Rule 19 only applies to vessels *not* in sight of one another. *A* and *B*, in their dealings, follow the in-sight script of Chapter 4. Toward *C*, though, the conduct is governed by Rule 19.

We have had enough of preambles and it is high time to start sorting out the directions given by Rule 19 to every vessel, to power-driven vessels, and to radar-equipped vessels. The script changes somewhat depending on how well equipped the mariner is. Taking each type in turn, we find the requirements stringent but almost unequivocal. Here are the details.

Every vessel, whether powered or not, whether radar-equipped or not, shall proceed at a safe speed and shall take into account restrictions on visibility when complying with Section I's rules for conduct. All must keep a proper lookout as required by Rule 5. But what is proper must be determined in the light of restricted visibility. Probably the vantage point should be low in the ship and removed from engine noise, for the lookout will be more of a "listen out."

The choice of a safe speed requires allowance not only for limited visibility but also for such factors as sound distortion. Taking avoiding action early and in substantial amounts must also accommodate the restraints on sound and sight. All in all, the demands made of every vessel are quite reasonable. Since she cannot see well, she cannot expect to move quickly and with assurance. And as soon as she hears a fog signal from apparently forward of her beam she is charged with a serious burden. That other vessel might be on an opposite course, might be crossing, might be moving more slowly in the same direction. All data must be used, every shred of information must be considered to judge the situation. If the decision is that no risk exists, then the mariner may proceed at what has been, in his judgment, a safe speed. Unless, though, he makes that bold decision he must immediately reduce speed to bare steerageway. In fact he must, if necessary, stop all motion. In any case he now navigates gingerly.

So far we have outlined the injunctions given to every vessel, small or large, sail or powered. That she is engaged in fishing, dragging a balky tow, or even launching aircraft will do no more than add urgency. There is no privilege to hold course and speed. What exists is a command that everyone put up with the elements and feel his way along.

A *power-driven vessel* is saddled with all those demands, plus one more. As soon as she is in or near an area of restricted visibility she must have her engines ready for immediate maneuver. To small vessels with engine controls near the helm the burden is hardly noticed. On large vessels, though, engine control might not be directly from the bridge. Not all have automated equipment allowing the watch officer to slow down or to reverse by pressing buttons or pulling handles. An older procedure is still used on many ships. On the bridge is an engine order telegraph or annunciator. It is a signaling device by which commands are transmitted to officers on watch in the engine room. Down below is where handles are pulled and valves are turned to alter engine action. The problem is that engineers need not be manning the handles and valves at all times. There is no fog in the engine room. Hearing a periodic moan of the whistle might suggest that the ship is fogbound, yet the engineer is still free to make his normal rounds checking pressures and pumps and ohms and watts. He might even be sitting at a desk catching up on his reading. But none of that watchstanding activity is readiness for immediate maneuver. So when in or near restricted visibility, the bridge must notify the engine room to stand a "throttle watch" until visibility improves.

Even on an automated ship such a watch can be necessary, for remote-control equipment heeds "Murphy's Law." What can go wrong often does at the worst possible time, and therefore mariners cannot ignore the principle. Bridge control of engine action can be overriden by signaling with an annunciator. But there must be someone at the other end to receive the announcements.

What about the *radar-equipped vessel?* Section I has already laden her with burdens and cautions. When onboard and operable the equipment must be used. Such use includes systematic plotting. Section I also requires that allowance be made for radar's long- and shortcomings. In what appears to be a recurring theme, Rule 19 now adds its concern for electronic fallibility. The possession of operable radar is not a license to streak through an atmosphere which clouds the eye. When in or near an area of restricted visibility, even the radar-equipped vessel must operate at a speed judged safe in relation to atmospheric conditions. Not only that, the power-driven vessel whose radar shows that nothing is present for miles around must still have her engines ready for immediate maneuver. This is a clear recognition of radar's inability to detect all objects.

Rule 19(d) places a special burden on a radar observer. Should he detect another by radar alone, he must ask himself two questions: Is a close-quarters situation developing? Does risk of collision exist? If the answer is "no" to each, then he can continue to do what he's been doing.

If, though, the answer to either question is "yes," then he *must* take early avoiding action. One reason for this is to prevent what has been called radar hypnosis. On some unfortunate occasions mariners have been so mesmerized by the soft glow of the scope as to fancy themselves spectators to collision. Rule 19 reminds us that extraordinary foresight requires extraordinary action. What follows next is some more common sense. If course is altered to avoid a vessel detected forward of the beam, the change should not be to the left. Figure 22 illustrates why. Vessels *A* and *B* are crossing in fog and detect each other forward of the beam. If *A* turns left and *B* turns right, a head-on collision could occur. Were *B* to go left and *A* make no change, danger would be increased as they followed parallel courses at close quarters. Should the two vessels have been meeting, a left turn by one could neutralize a simultaneous right turn by the other. But Rule 19(d)(i) adds a logical exception. If the other is ahead and is being overtaken, a left turn is not necessarily hazardous. Rule 19(d)(ii) deals with a radar pip abaft the beam. One should obviously not turn toward it.

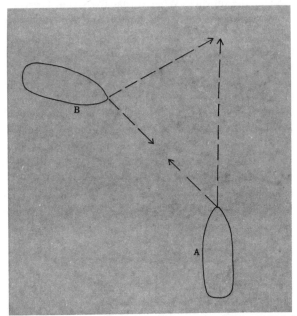

Fig. 22. *Changing Course in Fog.* A *should not turn left since* B *is likely to turn right.*

The last paragraph, Rule 19(e), is a distillation of bitter experience. None but the reckless ignores a fog signal from apparently forward of the beam. Something must be up there somewhere. Unless the mariner is willing to conclude that no risk of collision exists, he must pay heed. Picture this scene. *A*, radar-equipped, has been observing *B*'s pip on the scope. The evidence is clear that *B* is forward of the beam. Then *A* hears a fog signal and it seems to be coming from a point forward of the beam. Perhaps it comes from *B*; perhaps it doesn't. But it comes from someone. *A* must now make a decision. Does risk of collision exist? If *A* decides that there is no risk (and that would be quite cavalier), then she can continue about her business. But should *A* be less optimistic she must reduce speed to bare steerageway. That doesn't mean slow down a little; it means reduction to just enough to stay on course. In numbers the result might be a reduction from 10 knots to no more than 2 or 3. Moreover, *A* must stand ready to stop all motion and in any case must now navigate with extreme caution. Are these unreasonable demands of a vessel whose probing electrons reveal that only *B* is in the neighborhood and whose systematic plotting concludes that *B* is no danger? Not really. From one viewpoint the rule even seems lenient, for it reserves to mariners the option to assume that there is no risk. But don't expect a gray-haired veteran to greet that right with gleeful handsprings. Such a favor cuts the cross and sharpens the nails to crucify the unwary. What if that fog signal heard by *A* had not come from *B* but was sounded by another vessel undetected by *A*'s radar? Even if it had been sounded by *B*, what if radar anomalies merged with plotting blunders to produce a deceptive plot? The oldtimer would consider such "what ifs" as outweighing impetuosity.

Included in Rule 19(e) is another demand. Suppose *A* has not heard any fog signal at all, but is made aware of another's presence forward of the beam by some other means. If her extrasensory perception tells her that a close-quarters situation is unavoidable, she must act just as if a signal had been heard. She must slow to bare steerageway and be ready to stop all motion. The rule is very circumspect in describing the source of such extraordinary knowledge. Since vessels carrying crystal balls are in short supply, there is little doubt that the rulemakers have radar in mind. When in a fog *A* can neither see nor hear *B*, what natural senses for detection are left to use? Collision rules aim to prevent contact, so taste and touch must be excluded. As for smell, well, the aroma of Irish stew bubbling on a nearby galley stove is not recognized as a means of detection. On a modern ship what remains is radar.

Gray-haired veterans would advise that the conclusion should be this. A sound signal from apparently forward of the beam invokes Rule 19(e) unless the mariner is prepared to conclude that there is no risk of collision. Even if no noise is heard, electronics can still put the rule to work. Should radar alone tell that another vessel is forward of the beam and is unavoidably close, Rule 19(e) applies. Either way you must reduce speed to no more than that necessary to stay on course. Either way you must be ready to stop all motion if necessary. And either way you must thereafter navigate with extreme caution until the danger of collision is over. The echoes of some spectacular collisions can be heard in the background. Transatlantic liners *A* and *B*, some years back, detected each other by radar and by sound. They seemed to track each other into a collision. In any event the result was a disastrous detection by touch. Had the modern Rule 19 been in force and followed, the outcome might have been different. Their forward progress would have been so reduced that perhaps only the aroma of Swedish meatballs would have collided with that of Italian pasta. Rule 19 is a closely written restriction on the careless exercise of seagoing power.

We've reached the end of our survey of Part B and its Rules 4 through 19. Our Chapter 3 dealt with required conduct in any condition of visibility and Chapter 4 handled the requirements when in sight. After meeting Chapter 5's treatment of demands when visibility is restricted, we can consider our study of the scripts complete. We've also earned a rest. Unseen but approaching from forward of the beam is the odor of fresh coffee brewed by the watch below. Risk of collision exists and close quarters is unavoidable. In fact it's downright attractive. After a tussle with our customary quiz we should invoke the Rule of Special Circumstance and accept as inevitable a collision with some welcome refreshment.

QUESTIONS

The International Commission on Illumination provides our panel of judges. Amber and Magenta have induced Hazel to join them from her perch in the International Visibility Code. Arrayed in robes of chromaticity trimmed with atmospheric transmissivity, they have prepared the chapter quiz. Amber, by the way, advises that if we have interest in the technical details of their chromatic and transmissive costumes, we may consult Annex I to the Rules.

1. A sail vessel is not equipped with radar and is in an area of restricted visibility
   a. She must proceed at a safe speed.
   b. She must, upon hearing a fog signal from apparently forward of the beam, slow to bare steerageway.
   c. both a and b
   d. neither a nor b

2. A power-driven vessel equipped with radar is in restricted visibility and her radarscope shows no pips within a 20-mile radius.
   a. She must proceed at a safe speed.
   b. She must have her engines ready for immediate maneuver.
   c. both a and b
   d. neither a nor b

3. A power-driven vessel equipped with radar is in restricted visibility. Her radarscope shows no pips within a 20-mile radius, but she hears a fog signal apparently from her port quarter.
   a. She must slow to bare steerageway.
   b. She must have her engines ready for immediate maneuver.
   c. both a and b
   d. neither a nor b

4. A sail vessel equipped with radar is in restricted visibility. Her radarscope shows a pip at a 1-mile range and closing with a steady bearing on the port bow. No fog signal is heard but close quarters is unavoidable.
   a. She must slow to bare steerageway.
   b. She may alter course.
   c. both of the above
   d. none of the above

5. *A,* power-driven, is skirting a fogbank close aboard to port. She hears a fog signal apparently from her port bow and her radar shows a pip bearing to port and apparently crossing. No vessels are in sight.
    a. *A* must slow down to bare steerageway.
    b. Should the vessel on her port bow become visible and be power-driven, *A* would, by Rule 17, be required to hold course and speed.
    c. both of the above
    d. none of the above

6. A power-driven vessel is in restricted visibility. Her radar shows only one pip and that is dead astern with range increasing.
    a. She must slow down to bare steerageway.
    b. She must have engines ready for immediate maneuver.
    c. both of the above
    d. none of the above

7. *A,* a sailing vessel, is overtaking *B,* a power-driven vessel, on *B*'s port side. They are out of sight and in restricted visibility.
    a. *B* should avoid changing course to the left.
    b. *B* should reduce speed to bare steerageway.
    c. *B* should keep clear of *A,* which should hold course and speed.
    d. all of the above

8. Both *A* and *B* are sail vessels in fog and out of sight. *A* is to windward on the port tack. *B* is to leeward on the starboard tack. Each is radar-equipped and by plotting has determined the other's true course and speed.
    a. *A* keeps clear of *B* and *B* stands on.
    b. *B* keeps clear of *A* and *A* stands on.
    c. SELMA and Rule 2 apply.
    d. none of the above

9. The term "restricted visibility" means any condition in which visibility is restricted by, among other causes,
    a. falling snow
    b. heavy rainstorms
    c. sandstorms
    d. all of the above

10. Every vessel in fog and out of sight of other vessels is required to reduce speed to bare steerageway
    a. when she hears the fog signal from any direction
    b. when her radar shows the pip of another vessel on any bearing
    c. both of the above
    d. none of the above

AND ANSWERS

It was proposed by Magenta that the panel of judges derive a pattern of scoring from the following formula in Annex I, Section 8(a) of COLREGS: $I = 3.43 \times 10^6 \times T \times D^2 \times K^{-D}$. But Hazel was as foggy about all that as any mariner. Her view prevailed, and the International Visibility Code is the measure of your progress. Allow 10 points for each correct response, and here is the means to weigh your answers:

90–100	exceptionally clear
80	light haze
70	light fog
under 70	cap over the eyes

1. c   2. c   3. b   4. c   5. c   6. b   7. a   8. d   9. d   10. d

6

Part C—LIGHTS AND SHAPES

PART C OF BOTH COLREGS and the Inland Navigational Rules presents two groups of visual signals to be used in collision avoidance. Neither set of rules actually expresses any such division, but a reading of the official text prompts us to improvise the classifications. So without benefit of either national or international authority, let's indulge ourselves with a simplified approach to this confusing segment of the Rules.

The selection of any avoidance procedure requires that each vessel know something about the other's heading. This exchange of information is fulfilled by the transmission of a signal of *direction* or *aspect*. Just as critical is an awareness of the other's capabilities to avoid collision. And this is handled by a signal of *condition*. The words "direction" and "aspect" are apt to describe how heading is communicated, but the word "condition" might not be completely definitive of what is meant by the second classification. Perhaps *limitation* is better, for often the message signaled is that a vessel has less than normal ability to avoid collision. On the other hand it might be just as crucial for another ship to signal its extraordinary ability. In that case the term *identity* might be appropriate. Whatever the words, we should understand the substance of the thought. Vessels should tell each other of heading and of ability to avoid collision. In our discussion we will use "aspect" to indicate one message and "condition" to indicate the other.

Even though procedures to exchange a variety of messages are spelled out in the International Code of Signals, the collision rules have fashioned their own. The Rules of the Road demand unequivocal signals with no allowance for nuance or overtone. When operating under the Rules a mariner may use some of the forms found in the International Code, so long as they don't interfere with signals specified by the collision rules. But regardless of all else, he *must* display the patterns required by collision regulations. Such an uncompromising attitude has collected its share of catcalls, yet the criticism is largely undeserved. When one considers the scope of signals which might have been specified he marvels at the discretion exercised by the rulemakers. Not much more than the necessary has been demanded.

The code is a visual one. Sound signals are reserved for use when vessels are maneuvering in sight of each other and for identity when they are in restricted visibility. We moderns should expect that communication by radio be recognized, and so it is. But it is not required by COLREGS. On national waters we encounter the Vessel Bridge-to-Bridge Radiotelephone Act, yet it doesn't apply to everyone. The Rules of the Road are willing to presume that even the most ill-equipped mariner has eyes and ears; they do not take for granted that he also owns a radiotelephone. VHF exchanges of maneuvering data are required of some vessels and recommended to all. And when we get to Inland's Rule 34 we'll learn that on U.S. waters when an agreement has been reached by VHF exchanges concerning a maneuvering procedure, no use of Rules of the Road sound signals is required. But a moment's thought shows that VHF cannot be expected to supplant all visual signals. A vessel at anchor continuously declares her condition by display of a day shape and a night light or two. Seafaring would not be advanced were she required to transmit, over and over, "I am at anchor."

By day the signals consist of *day shapes;* at night the patterns involve *lights.* And we should note a basic difference between their tasks. To observe a day shape is also to see the vessel by which it is displayed and to discern, for example, which end is the bow. Day shapes seldom have occasion to signal aspect. But to see a hull form by day is not necessarily to observe a condition or limitation on maneuverability. A day shape can, for example, signal whether a vessel is at anchor or engaged in fishing or is aground. The absence of such a display leaves unclear her ability to maneuver away from danger.

Day shapes are needed to announce that a yacht-like vessel might be engaged in underwater surveying. [USN photo]

Lights, though, carry a far heavier burden. To see them need not mean you've also seen the hull form and are aware of a vessel's heading. In fact the presumption is exactly the opposite. Lights are intended to reveal aspect as well as condition. One result of this dual function is that light patterns are far more numerous than day shapes. Another is that this will be a long chapter. Candidates for deck officer licenses are resigned to such busy detail, for they must become adept at distinguishing one light pattern from another. But most other mariners are annoyed by such nitpicking. They would rather concentrate on no more than the basic signals and sideline the remainder. Yet no seaman should make an arbitrary selection of the subject matter to be discussed. The time for him to choose between the salient and the slight is after he has met a few criteria. And that in turn requires that he allow the collision rules to have their say. By maintaining a receptive frame of mind he might even find the exercise interesting. But whether or not the task is amiable it should be performed, for only by sorting out aspect and condition signals will he acquire workable keys to the patterns.

RULE 20—Application

COLREGS

(a) Rules in this Part shall be complied with in all weathers.

(b) The Rules concerning lights shall be complied with from sunset to sunrise, and during such times no other lights shall be exhibited, except such lights as cannot be mistaken for the lights specified in these Rules or do not impair their visibility or distinctive character, or interfere with the keeping of a proper look-out.

(c) The lights prescribed by these Rules shall, if carried, also be exhibited from sunrise to sunset in restricted visibility and may be exhibited in all other circumstances when it is deemed necessary.

(d) The Rules concerning shapes shall be complied with by day.

(e) The lights and shapes specified in these Rules shall comply with the provisions of Annex I to these Regulations.

INLAND

(a) Rules in this Part shall be complied with in all weathers.

(b) The Rules concerning lights shall be complied with from sunset to sunrise, and during such times no other lights shall be exhibited, except such lights as cannot be mistaken for the lights specified in these Rules or do not impair their visibility or distinctive character, or interfere with the keeping of a proper look-out.

(c) The lights prescribed by these Rules shall, if carried, also be exhibited from sunrise to sunset in restricted visibility and may be exhibited in all other circumstances when it is deemed necessary.

(d) The Rules concerning shapes shall be complied with by day.

(e) The lights and shapes specified in these Rules shall comply with the provisions of Annex I of these Rules.

Neither set of collision rules expresses any exception to these requirements. All vessels are told to show the signals, and to do so in all weathers. A tanker anchored by day in a dense fog shows a day shape. A vessel engaged in fishing by night under a full moon shows lights. In Chapter 2 we learned that military vessels when alone or in a group during times of peace as well as war may operate without lights. That, though, is a necessary concession to an overriding public interest when their mission is best served by invisibility. We also noted in Chapter 2 that any vessel can receive permission for alternative compliance when meeting the letter of the law would interfere with her special build. But absent such extraordinary conditions everyone, says Rule 20, must comply with the demands of Part C.

The need for lights is not limited to nighttime. They must be shown in all weathers from sunset to sunrise but they must also be displayed in restricted visibility from sunrise to sunset. And they may be shown any other time they are considered necessary. Day shapes are of course for daytime use; but they are more than fair-weather signals. They are shown by day in any kind of weather from exceptionally clear to peasoup fog. That tanker we met earlier when she was at anchor by day in fog would certainly be using a variety of ways to communicate her condition. She would have an anchor ball up, she would also be showing light displays, and we'll learn later, she would be making sound signals. One does not have to be carrying low-sulfur crude oil to be required to show both kinds of signals. Shapes, lights, and sounds by day in fog are demanded of all but a few small vessels under specific conditions. The sharp-eyed might have noticed that Rule 20 defines the time for lights by referring to sunrise and sunset while day shapes are ordered by day. One's first reaction to the inconsistency is that the rulemakers just wanted a little variety in their lives so they used alternative wording. Any such reaction, though, is always a bit risky. Rulemakers are supposed to steer clear of variety. And in fact here they exercised no alternative option, for they had a distinction in mind. We've all been on a freeway at twilight and observed that some cars are burning headlights while others are not. One person's nighttime can be another's dusk or dawn. The rules allow no such diversity. Far more definitive is the sun's rising and setting. Nighttime, then, in clear weather starts when the sun goes down and ends when the sun comes up. In restricted visibility the "day" period for lights is from sun-up to sundown.

We've already read that there is no prohibition against showing lights other than those required. But Rule 20(b) adds some qualifications. The additional lights cannot produce confusion or impair the efficiency of specified lights or the keeping of a proper lookout. A flood-lit foredeck while underway, or a strong green light shining through a portside porthole, would be obvious violations. What about strobe lights? They are very effective, but the IMO feels that they should not be used. Too often they overwhelm the aspect and condition lights required by the Rules.

Annex I describes details on positioning and technical matters. The COL-REGS version is reprinted in Appendix A rather than in this chapter for the same reason that COLREGS lists such technicalities in an annex rather than in a numbered rule. Underway, such specifics are rarely needed. Once the lights are rigged there is no need to verify their placement and character every day. We'll consider a few of the more general requirements and then relegate the others to a reference section where they belong. In fact there is no better time than now to sample a bit of Annex I.

Rule 20 introduces day shapes, and other rules in Part C describe their contours, but only in Section 6(a) of Annex I is there mention of their color. We could call this the Henry Ford section since it presents the spectrum he offered buyers of his Model T: "any color you want so long as it's black." The collision rules recognize that a ball viewed from afar is nothing more than a dark blob whether it is red, green, or decorated with orange stripes. Contour is significant but color is not. Section 6(a) of Annex I specifies that all day shapes are black.

By now, though, we should be wary of sweeping generalities, even when they appear in official texts. Before the word "all" we must insert "almost." Far ahead lie Rule 37 and Annex IV, but we must now take a preview. One of the distress signals is a square flag with, above or below it, a ball or anything resembling a ball. Although the elements of the signal are day shapes, they need not be the customary black prescribed by Annex I. We live in a tech-nicolor world, and those arrayed in pastels are not denied use of the flag-and-ball distress signal just because they are colorful. A square shape of any hue above or below a ball shape of any hue means "Help!" Picture the psychedelic seaman dressed in purple shorts and a green T-shirt. He is on a sinking ship and finds nothing left aboard which comes close to blackness. It is hardly proper to deny him the status of distress for the sole reason that he cannot find something black with which to signal. By cutting a purple square from his shorts and a green circle from his shirt he could indicate his misfortune. Any debate on this issue is ended by the answer expected to the following question asked of deck officer license candidates by the U.S. Coast Guard:

By day you observe a black ball below the International Code flag "G." The signal is of a vessel
    a. at anchor requesting a pilot
    b. in distress
    c. aground
    d. none of the above

Answer *a* is tempting but not acceptable, for the required response is *b*. By International Code, "G" is a square flag with vertical stripes of blue and yellow. Its meaning is "I require a pilot." We'll later learn that a black ball indicates a vessel at anchor. The flag would usually be flown above the bridge complex and the anchor ball hung at the bow. But viewed bow-on and from a distance, the combination might appear as if one were directly above the other, uniting to say "I am at anchor and I require a pilot." What the examination question has in mind is clear. The signal of distress does not hinge on the availability of black cloth. Whether the square flag shows vertical bands of blue and yellow or is a remnant of purple "skivvies" is not important when the ship is in need of assistance.

Rule 21 defines required lights. This is a key rule, for hereafter only the name of each light will be used. Later on as we meet the terse outline of each light pattern we must be able to recognize what the brief statement really means. Strict attention now to the exact wording of this rule will pay significant dividends in the future.

RULE 21—Definitions

COLREGS

(a) "Masthead light" means a white light placed over the fore and aft centerline of the vessel showing an unbroken light over an arc of the horizon of 225 degrees and so fixed as to show the light from right ahead to 22.5 degrees abaft the beam on either side of the vessel.

(b) "Sidelights" means a green light on the starboard side and a red light on the port side each showing an unbroken light over an arc of the horizon of 112.5 degrees and so fixed as to show the light from right ahead to 22.5 degrees abaft the beam on its respective side. In a vessel of less than 20 meters in length the sidelights may be combined in one lantern carried on the fore and aft centerline of the vessel.

(c) "Sternlight" means a white light placed as nearly as practicable at the stern showing an unbroken light over an arc of the horizon of 135 degrees and so fixed as to show the light 67.5 degrees from right aft on each side of the vessel.

(d) "Towing light" means a yellow light having the same characteristics as the "sternlight" defined in paragraph (c) of this Rule.

(e) "All-round light" means a light showing an unbroken light over an arc of the horizon of 360 degrees.

(f) "Flashing light" means a light flashing at regular intervals at a frequency of 120 flashes or more per minute.

INLAND

(a) "Masthead light" means a white light placed over the fore and aft centerline of the vessel showing an unbroken light over an arc of the horizon of 225 degrees and so fixed as to show the light from right ahead to 22.5 degrees abaft the beam on either side of the vessel, except that on a vessel of less than 12 meters in length the masthead light shall be placed as nearly as practicable to the fore and aft centerline of the vessel.

(b) "Sidelights" mean a green light on the starboard side and a red light on the port side each showing an unbroken light over an arc of the horizon of 112.5 degrees and so fixed as to show the light from right ahead to 22.5 degrees abaft the beam on its respective side. On a vessel of less than 20 meters in length the sidelights may be combined in one lantern carried on the fore and aft centerline of the vessel, except that on a vessel of less than 12 meters in length the sidelights when combined in one lantern shall be placed as nearly as practicable to the fore and aft centerline of the vessel.

(c) "Sternlight" means a white light placed as nearly as practicable at the stern showing an unbroken light over an arc of the horizon of 135 degrees and so fixed as to show the light 67.5 degrees from right aft on each side of the vessel.

(d) "Towing light" means a yellow light having the same characteristics as the "sternlight" defined in paragraph (c) of this Rule.

(e) "All-round light" means a light showing an unbroken light over an arc of the horizon of 360 degrees.

(f) "Flashing light" means a light flashing at regular intervals at a frequency of 120 flashes or more per minute.

(g) "Special flashing light" means a yellow light flashing at regular intervals at a frequency of 50 to 70 flashes per minute, placed as far forward and as nearly as practicable on the fore and aft centerline of the tow and showing an unbroken light over an arc of the horizon of not less than 180 degrees nor more than 225 degrees and so fixed as to show the light from right ahead to abeam and no more than 22.5 degrees abaft the beam on either side of the vessel.

To begin with, we should note that some romance has disappeared in the newer version of the Rules. Older rules described arcs of visibility in compass points. A hangover from days of "boxing the compass," such a practice was quaint but it was also annoying. No longer need we fret over an arc described as "two points abaft the beam" or "ten points on either bow." Angles are now angles from 0° to 360°.

The Corps of Engineers dredge Biddle *at work clearing a silted channel. [U.S. Army Corps of Engineers photo]*

A *masthead light,* says Rule 21(a), is white, located over the fore-and-aft centerline, and has an arc of 225° from right ahead to 112.5° on either bow. In the past such a light was called a masthead light when it was placed forward and was termed a range light when placed farther aft. Nowadays the term "masthead light" refers to one whether forward or aft so long as it is white, has a 225° arc, and is over the centerline. To the last requirement, though, we must add "on most ships." We've been told that those of special build can be allowed to vary from exact requirements. Such alternative compliance has been granted an aircraft carrier. To place her masthead lights over the centerline would clutter her flight deck. So she may offset those lights. The forward masthead light is placed on a mast located on the starboard side of the flight deck and the after masthead light appears on the "island." Sidelights are placed on the carrier's sides at about half the longitudinal distance between the masthead lights.

Inland Rules are considerate of vessels less than 12 meters long, which on our waters may carry a masthead light "as nearly as practicable" over the centerline. That doesn't mean the same as the unvarnished "over the fore and aft centerline" found in COLREGS. Inland recognizes that a small vessel might not always be able to rig the light directly over the keel, so she need just try her best. But on any waters and no matter where placed, a masthead light is an identity signal. As we'll shortly learn, it is a signal displayed by power-driven vessels, and in nearly every case, only by the power-driven.

The distinctive color of a *sidelight* provides an efficient signal of direction or aspect. Rule 21(b) describes the lights as red on the port side and green on the starboard side, each with an arc of 112.5° measured from right ahead. This last sentence is hardly the bearer of news; even stokers and denizens of the shaft alley know the color of sidelights. Long since pummelled into a cliché is speculation on why green was chosen for the starboard side and red for the port, and for that matter why we use the names port and starboard. That the term "steering board" might have been shortened to "starboard" and that the alternative, "leeboard," somehow became "port" after a sojourn as "larboard" is hardly crucial. No more consequential is the memory aid that port is associated with red wine. And entombed with all late admirals of the ocean seas should be the canard that upon the death of each there was discovered in a desk drawer a small white card bearing the elementary statement "Port is Red and Starboard's Green."

It is common knowledge that sidelights have distinctive colors, but it is less widely known that they need not be isolated from each other on opposite sides of the ship. A vessel under 20 meters long may combine them into one lantern. COLREGS require that such a lantern be over the centerline. Inland is again solicitous of the vessel less than 12 meters long by adding "as nearly as practicable. . . ."

It's time for another visit to Annex I. Its Section 3 requires that when

The Golden Gate gas-turbine ferry Marin *carries her port sidelight within a specially designed slit in her bridge wing. [Courtesy Golden Gate Ferry System]*

separate sidelights are used they must be at or near the ship's sides, and when fitted on a power-driven vessel 20 meters or more long they shall not be forward of the forward masthead light. Section 5 deals with the problem that light sectors cannot be carved out with surgical precision. The wrong color is bound to "bleed" into an adjacent arc. Red will spill over the bow into the province of green. Either sidelight is likely to invade the region of the white sternlight. Section 9 in fact guarantees spill-over by requiring that the practical cutoff for light intensities be a few degrees outside the light's sector. Even so, spill-over should be kept to a minimum, and Section 5 does it by fitting separated sidelights with inboard screens painted flat black.

The *sternlight,* described in Rule 21(c), completes the signals of aspect. The sidelights combine to cover 225° of a circle; the white sternlight appears in the remaining 135°. The result, as shown in Fig. 23, is that centered on each vessel underway is a full circle divided into arcs of green, red, and white to indicate heading or aspect. But before going any further we should note something about the placement of a sternlight. One should hardly question that a stern-light should appear at the opposite end of a ship from the bow. And for decades the collision rules agreed by describing its location as "at or near the stern." But Rule 21(c) is not so restrictive, for it generalizes with the tolerant words ". . . as nearly as practicable at the stern." Such a vagary is due to the peculiarities of modern shipping. In fact one recent type of vessel could per-suade Captain Blood to revert to leeching. She resembles a floating drydock, for at her open stern are either horn-like projections or an elevator to lift 400-ton barges on board or to launch them into a harbor. "Lighter Aboard

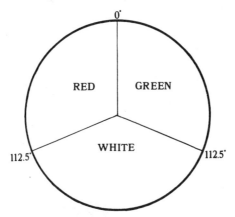

Fig. 23. Light Sectors. Each sidelight shows from dead ahead to 112½° on either bow, and a sternlight completes the circle.

Ship" or LASH is a conformation hardly compatible with a white light placed at the stern. So both COLREGS and Inland allow such a vessel to mount a sternlight forward of any antlered stern. Why should orthodox mariners be concerned with these hermaphroditic rigs? Well, they might not sail on them but they might share the same waters. At night and in fuzzy visibility to see a white sternlight is not necessarily to observe the tail-end of a 1000-foot-long ship. If she is of uncommon build there might be room for the Super Bowl to be played between that white light and her actual bitter end.

To read a few crisp words in a collision rule is not always to appreciate what the few crisp words are all about. An example is Rule 21(d)'s definition of a *towing light*. It seems no more than a yellow sternlight. An important question, though, is "Why?" If a vessel already must display a regular white sternlight, why should she show this extra one? The answer might be found by conjuring up this scene. It is a dark and stormy night and a brisk wind is chasing whitecaps across our course. Dead ahead we pick up a white light. A few degrees on the bow and somewhat closer is another. Radar shows two vessels plodding along in company. We conclude that we are overtaking, but overtaking what? Are the two vessels ahead unassociated fellow travelers or are they connected by a towline? If above the white light dead ahead should be a yellow one, the answer would be clear. A power-driven vessel towing astern displays

The open stern of a 200-foot-long oil industry supply vessel prevents her carriage of a light at her stern. [Courtesy Halter Marine, Inc.]

a yellow towing light. It is a condition signal working with an aspect signal to supply crucial information to an overtaking vessel. Ahead is a brace of vessels yoked into a long, awkward, flexible mass. Incidentally, the yellow also serves as a guiding light on the tug for the tow, if manned, to steer by.

Rule 21(e) describes in straightforward terms what is meant by an *all-round light.* It would seem no more need be said. All-round means visible over an unbroken arc of 360°. In practice, though, compliance with such a requirement might prove impossible. Perhaps the Civil War ironclad *Monitor* could have met the letter of such a law. To mount a 360° light on a stick rising from her solitary turret would have been an easy task. What, though, when scores of cargo containers are piled high on a weather deck? What of the cruise ship whose top hamper shrouds squash courts and swimming pools forward of a simulated smokestack housing kennels for dogs and cats? How feasible is it for a modern vessel to rig a light visible from every degree of the circle? Another visit to Annex I indicates that such problems are recognized and accommodated. In Section 9(b) we find that the superstructure shall not obscure all-round lights within sectors of more than 6°. Translated from technical jargon, this means that all-round lights need not be visible all around. They do the best they can, but they may be obscured in arcs up to 6° wide.

Rule 21(f) describes a *flashing light.* We should note the distinction between a Rules of the Road flasher and one used as an aid to navigation. A flashing light on a buoy goes on and off at the pedestrian rate of no more than 30 times per minute. A quick-flashing buoy light doubles the speed. Neither of them, though, is a match for what collision regulations say is a flashing light. By the Rules of the Road it goes on and off at the attention-getting rate of 120 or more times per minute. Instead of a leisurely flash every other second or a double-time rate of one a second the cadence must be at least two flashes per second.

The COLREGS version of Rule 21(f) completes the international story, but Inland Rules add another paragraph. Rule 21(g) affords a condition or identity signal to vessels being pushed ahead. By supposing another dark and stormy night we might learn why such a warning signal is important. This time let's assume that we observe a red sidelight bearing broad on the starboard bow. Farther to the right appears a vertical string of white lights with another single red light shining below. Something is crossing our track, and that something could be a herd of more than 40 vessels being pushed ahead by a flat-faced, burly tug. The entire string might extend for a quarter of a mile from the single red sidelight on the lead row of barges to the complex display on the tug. That span could make the whole conglomeration larger than the world's largest one-piece ship. The special flashing yellow light on the forward end identifies the procession for what it really is. Required by Inland's Rule 21(g), it affords an essential means to recognize the situation. Without it ambiguity could create a serious problem. Not found as a COLREGS requirement, this identity signal has an arc equal to at least half a circle from the starboard beam through the bow to the port beam. It may be as large as that covered by both sidelights. Its rate of flashing is akin to a quick-flashing buoy light, but far less than the flashing light described by Rule 21(f). Without it our appraisal of the situation on that dark and stormy night could be more guess than judgment. With it the identification is far more positive.

A powerful line boat pushes 45 barges on the Mississippi River. The complex is longer and wider than the largest single ship afloat. [Photo courtesy Joseph Perry]

We are one rule short of being ready to study the actual patterns of lights and day shapes required by the Rules of the Road. What remains is an introduction to intensity and visibility. Section 8 of Annex I sets out how COLREGS expects intensities to be computed. Such remarkable quantities are involved as threshold factors and atmospheric transmissivities seasoned with some candelas thrown in for good measure. The practical mariner is inclined to give such details in an annex as wide a berth as possible. But when a numbered rule such as Rule 22 sets out specifics, he must pay close attention. Here is the text from each set of regulations.

RULE 22—Visibility of Lights

COLREGS

The lights prescribed in these Rules shall have an intensity as specified in Section 8 of Annex I to these Regulations so as to be visible at the following minimum ranges:

(a) In vessels of 50 meters or more in length:

—a masthead light, 6 miles;

—a sidelight, 3 miles;

—a sternlight, 3 miles;

—a towing light, 3 miles;

—a white, red, green or yellow all-round light, 3 miles.

(b) In vessels of 12 meters or more in length but less than 50 meters in length:

—a masthead light, 5 miles; except that where the length of the vessel is less than 20 meters, 3 miles;

—a sidelight, 2 miles;

—a sternlight, 2 miles;

—a towing light, 2 miles;

—a white, red, green or yellow all-round light, 2 miles.

(c) In vessels of less than 12 meters in length:

—a masthead light, 2 miles;

—a sidelight, 1 mile;

—a sternlight, 2 miles;

—a towing light, 2 miles;

—a white, red, green or yellow all-round light, 2 miles.

(d) In inconspicuous, partly submerged vessels or objects being towed:

—a white all-round light, 3 miles.

INLAND

The lights prescribed in these Rules shall have an intensity as specified in Annex I to these Rules, so as to be visible at the following minimum ranges:

(a) In a vessel of 50 meters or more in length:

—a masthead light, 6 miles;

—a sidelight, 3 miles;

—a sternlight, 3 miles;

—a towing light, 3 miles;

—a white, red, green or yellow all-round light, 3 miles; and a special flashing light, 2 miles.

(b) In a vessel of 12 meters or more in length but less than 50 meters in length:

—a masthead light, 5 miles; except that where the length of the vessel is less than 20 meters, 3 miles;

—a sidelight, 2 miles;

—a sternlight, 2 miles;

—a towing light, 2 miles;

—a white, red, green or yellow all-round light, 2 miles; and a special flashing light, 2 miles.

(c) In a vessel of less than 12 meters in length:

—a masthead light, 2 miles;

—a sidelight, 1 mile;

—a sternlight, 2 miles;

—a towing light, 2 miles;

—a white, red, green or yellow all-round light, 2 miles; and a special flashing light, 2 miles.

(d) In an inconspicuous, partly submerged vessel or object being towed:

—a white all-round light, 3 miles.

Table 2. Required Visibility of Lights

LIGHT	50 METERS OR MORE LONG	20 METERS BUT UNDER 50 METERS	12 METERS BUT UNDER 20 METERS	UNDER 12 METERS
Masthead light, 225° & white —on fore-and-aft centerline	6 miles	5 miles	3 miles	2 miles *(Inland:* near as practicable on fore-and-aft line)
Sidelights, separate (112.5° each) —fitted with flat black screens —lower than and not forward of forward masthead light —at or near sides	3 miles	2 miles	not required	not required
Sidelights in combined lantern —on fore-and-aft-centerline	not allowed	not allowed	2 miles	1 mile *(Inland,* near as practicable on fore-and-aft line)
Sternlight, 135° & white —near as practicable at the stern	3 miles *(Inland,* see Rule 23(d) for Great Lakes option)	2 miles	2 miles *(Inland,* see exemption in Rule 38(d)(vi) for "existing vessels")	2 miles
Towing light, 135° & yellow —near as practicable at the stern	3 miles	2 miles	2 miles	2 miles
All-round light —white, red, green, or yellow	3 miles	2 miles	2 miles	2 miles
—white, on inconspicuous, partly submerged tow	3miles	3miles	3 miles	3miles
Special flashing light *(Inland only)* —180° to 225° & yellow —on lead vessel being pushed ahead —as far forward & as near centerline as practicable	2 miles	2 miles	2 miles	2 miles

To some the itemization of light visibilities in Rule 22 is inconsistent with the announced purpose of annexes to the Rules. What is not relevant to actual operation should not, by their view, clutter up the numbered rules. The range of a light, they conclude, might be properly discussed in an annex, but it has little to do with watchstanding. But any such attitude is dangerous. Rule 22's listing of minimum ranges provides valuable operational data. Let's imagine another dark and stormy night to see why. Suppose a mariner observes a single white light dead ahead and getting brighter. High on his list of possible meanings would be a sternlight. In fact his first surmise might be that he was overtaking another vessel. But knowledge of Rule 22 prompts second thoughts. That other vessel could be a small power-driven vessel approaching bow-on with sidelights not yet visible. Unawareness of their minimum ranges could mean selection of the wrong maneuver to avoid collision.

Rule 22 arranges ships by length and then draws around each a series of arcs. The radius of each arc is a minimum light range and the vessel is required to project its aspect and condition signals at least that far. The statement of the rule seems to be a simple pattern of three classes, but in fact there are four. Table 2 recasts the specifics of Rule 22 in company with key requirements selected from Rule 21 and Annex I.

The remaining rules in Part C arrange the lights described by Rules 21 and 22 into patterns for a host of aspects and conditions. Rule 23 starts the process by attending to power-driven vessels. And we must stand ready to tiptoe through subtleties and contrasts. Beforehand, though, we should hark back to Rule 3's definition of "power-driven." The term refers to a vessel propelled by machinery, but not necessarily by machinery *only*. Picture a vessel so eager to reach her destination that she combines an engine-driven propeller with a dozen sails supplemented by a score of hearties toiling at oars. No matter how the engine might be assisted, the ship would be considered power-driven. Rule 23 fashions identification for such a vessel which, regardless of appearance, is actually under power. More obvious than her propeller churning below the surface would be yards of white cloth filling the breeze, accompanied or not by drumbeats giving a cadence to oarsmen. Yet the collision rules are not concerned with appearances. They judge such a vessel capable of power-driven maneuverability, and so she is required to advertise her extraordinary condition.

RULE 23—Power-Driven Vessels Underway

COLREGS

(a) A power-driven vessel underway shall exhibit:

(i) a masthead light forward;

(ii) a second masthead light abaft of and higher than the forward one; except that a vessel of less than 50 meters in length shall not be obliged to exhibit such light but may do so;

   (iii) sidelights;

   (iv) a sternlight.

   (b) An air-cushion vessel when operating in the non-displacement mode shall, in addition to the lights prescribed in paragraph (a) of this Rule, exhibit an all-round flashing yellow light.

   (c)(i) A power-driven vessel of less than 12 meters in length may in lieu of the lights prescribed in paragraph (a) of this Rule exhibit an all-round white light and sidelights;

   (ii) a power-driven vessel of less than 7 meters in length whose maximum speed does not exceed 7 knots may in lieu of the lights prescribed in paragraph (a) of this Rule exhibit an all-round white light and shall, if practicable, also exhibit sidelights;

   (iii) the masthead light or all-round white light on a power-driven vessel of less than 12 meters in length may be displaced from the fore and aft centerline of the vessel if centerline fitting is not practicable, provided that the sidelights are combined in one lantern which shall be carried on the fore and aft centerline of the vessel or located as nearly as practicable in the same fore and aft line as the masthead light or the all-round white light.

INLAND

   (a) A power-driven vessel underway shall exhibit:

   (i) a masthead light forward; except that a vessel of less than 20 meters in length need not exhibit this light forward of amidships but shall exhibit it as far forward as is practicable;

   (ii) a second masthead light abaft of and higher than the forward one; except that a vessel of less than 50 meters in length shall not be obliged to exhibit such light but may do so;

   (iii) sidelights; and

   (iv) a sternlight.

   (b) An air-cushion vessel when operating in the nondisplacement mode shall, in addition to the lights prescribed in paragraph (a) of this Rule, exhibit an all-round flashing yellow light where it can best be seen.

   (c) A power-driven vessel of less than 12 meters in length may, in lieu of the lights prescribed in paragraph (a) of this Rule, exhibit an all-round white light and sidelights.

   (d) A power-driven vessel when operating on the Great Lakes may carry an all-round white light in lieu of the second masthead light and sternlight prescribed in paragraph (a) of this Rule. The light shall be carried in the position of the second masthead light and be visible at the same minimum range.

In essence Rule 23 says that sidelights and a sternlight tell of aspect while condition or identity is shown by a masthead light. The six panels in Fig. 24 demonstrate what the rule intends for a power-driven vessel, and we must look to Rule 21 to be reminded of the color and arc of these lights. The masthead light is white and covers 225°. The sternlight is also white, but covers only 135°. The arc of each sidelight is 112.5°, with green on the starboard side and red on the port. Rule 22 lists minimum ranges from 1 mile up to 6 miles. Rule 21(b) allows a vessel less than 20 meters long to combine its sidelights into one lantern. When a vessel is less than 12 meters long that lantern need not be directly over the keel. But this is all subordinate to the basic theme. Sidelights and a sternlight plus a masthead light or two spell power-driven underway . . . most of the time. Should a vessel be less than 7 meters long and have a top speed of not over 7 knots, COLREGS would like her to show sidelights if that can be done, but allow operation with only an all-round white light.

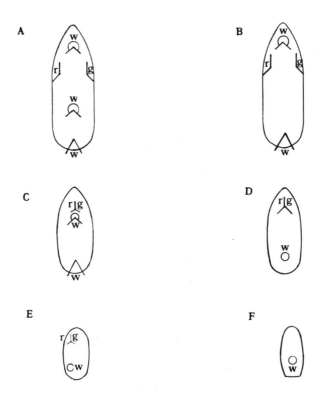

Fig. 24. COLREGS Lights for Power-Driven Vessels. Vessels (A) 50 meters or more long; (B) between 20 and 50 meters long; (C) between 12 and 20 meters long; (D) under 12 meters; (E) under 12 meters; (F) under 7 meters long and speed under 7 knots.

The Inland version of Rule 23(c) is deceptively simple, for it creates some distinct variations from COLREGS patterns. It restates the COLREGS Rule 23(c)(i) deference to small power-driven vessels less than 12 meters long. They have the option to combine masthead and sternlight into one all-round white light to be displayed with a sidelight pattern. But sublety develops when Inland

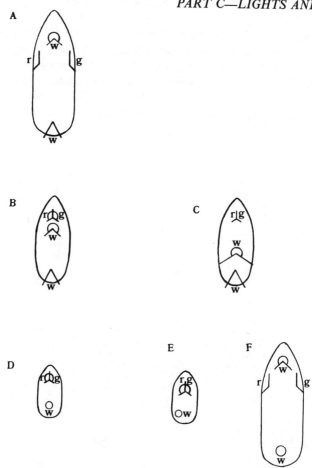

Fig. 25. *Inland Lights for Power-Driven Vessels. Vessels (A) between 20 and 50 meters long; (B) between 12 and 20 meters long; (C) under 20 meters long with masthead light abaft midlength; (D) under 12 meters long; (E) under 12 meters long with all-round white light offset from centerline; (F) on Great Lakes with all-round white light aft in lieu of after masthead light and sternlight.*

Rule 23(c) says no more. Small vessels using our inland waterways are considered usually capable of speeds in excess of 7 knots and probably will not be inconvenienced by a demand to show sidelights, therefore no dispensation from sidelights is mentioned for inland vessels under 7 meters long and not capable of over 7 knots. So no counterpart to COLREGS Rule 23(c)(ii) appears.

Nor did COLREGS Rule 23(c)(iii) seem any more appropriate on inland waters. In fact it was viewed as unduly restricting. Both on the high seas and inside, vessels under 12 meters long are not required to place a masthead light, all-round white, or a combined red-and-green sidelight lantern directly over the centerline. They are told to rig them as nearly as practicable there; however, if necessary they can be off-center. But if either of the white lights is offset, what about the red-and-green lantern? The COLREGS requirement is that no matter how they are placed athwartships, the result must be they are in the same fore-and-aft line as the white light. When an offset is made of either a white light or of the combined sidelight lantern, then the other must conform. Not so on inland waters, and the difference is not the result of a semantic accident. The drafting committee for the Inland Rules intended the difference. When presenting an analysis for congressional guidance during consideration of the new Rules, it drew attention to its proposal that an allowance to offset the masthead light or its all-round white counterpart should be independent of the location of the sidelights. No official words of the final text say so, but Rule 23(c) of Inland accepts that proposal by saying nothing. Echoes of the old Motorboat Act are heard, for it allowed the required all-round white on the stern of motorboats less than 26 feet long to be placed outboard from the centerline so that room would be left for securing an outboard motor.

What then does Rule 23(c) of Inland require? All it states is that the small vessel may combine masthead and sternlight into one all-round white light and show it together with sidelights. It leaves to Rule 21(a) and (b) the specification of the manner of rigging sidelights and the topic of offsets. The resulting light patterns can be any of those shown in Fig. 25. An understandable question is "Why need any but the most dedicated mariner be concerned with these options?" Well, owners of power-driven vessels less than 12 meters long should be interested. And of course license examination candidates must care. And the rest of us might find here an explanation for an otherwise puzzling night-

The S.S. Hawaiian Enterprise *(renamed the* Manukai*) indicates her great length by placing a forward masthead light on the mast above her bridge and an after masthead light on another mast just forward of her smokestack. [Courtesy Matson Lines]*

time encounter. In any case we should remember that no such casual mixture of masthead light and sidelights is tolerated on the high seas.

It's time now to shake off the torpor induced by the last few paragraphs and consider a section far more complicated than any discussion of offsets. Rule 23(a)(ii) introduces the subject of a second masthead light. Required of power-driven vessels 50 meters or more long and optional for those of less length, it is carried abaft of and higher than the forward masthead light. Much more detail is found in Annex I, but we need not go exploring in that direction. It is sufficient now to mention that its Sections 2 and 3 give the particulars on technical details and the positioning of these lights.

This second masthead light is not a new requirement. Power-driven ships have displayed it for many years. What is new is its name. Until 72 COLREGS appeared it was called a range light; but now, by both high-seas and Inland rules it is an *after masthead light.* Its companion, the other white light forward and lower, was earlier called the masthead light. Now by both sets of rules it is the *forward masthead light.* Whatever their labels, these two work together and supply more than identification as a power-driven vessel probably 50 meters or more long. In fact the older name of range light for the after one

Fig. 26. A Range of Masthead Lights. The angle between masthead lights on an eastbound vessel closes as she turns right and then begins to open as she completes her reversal of course.

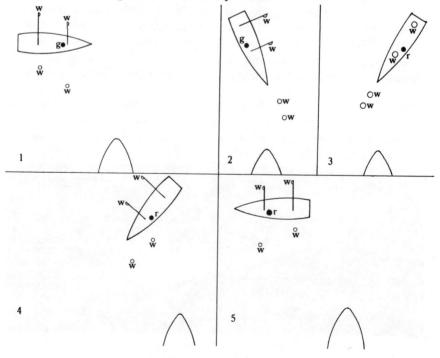

was quite apt to suggest another purpose. Where the after one appears in relation to the forward masthead light depicts aspect. Masthead lights are usually more powerful than sidelights, so there can be a gap between detection of a white light and sighting a red or a green. Measured in distance, the span can be as much as 3 miles. Measured in time, the interval depends on the speed of the vessels involved. An important task of the after masthead light is to supply an indication of direction or aspect before a sidelight or two should heave into view.

Figure 26 illustrates the function of the two masthead lights. We are presumed to be northbound with a large ship about 4 miles off bearing broad on our port bow. She crosses our track and then reverses course to head back westward. In the first of the five panels she is heading due east. We know that our view is of her starboard side, for the forward masthead light is to the right of the higher one farther aft. In the second panel she is turning toward us to begin her reversal of course. Now the angle between the two masthead lights has decreased. We know she is turning toward us, for if she were turning away both masthead lights would disappear and a lone sternlight would be pointing our way. In the third panel she has just passed through being bow-on. The fourth view shows the forward masthead to the left of the after one with the angle between them increasing. And in the last panel, with the turn complete, she is heading due west. A range of about 4 miles would place us beyond the reach of her sidelights and sternlight. Only the two masthead lights working together would then indicate to us what is taking place.

Of course for those two lights to act effectively they must be sufficiently far apart, and not every vessel can meet this requirement. One masthead light just a few feet abaft the other might never open up enough to indicate any significant change in bearing and aspect. So Rule 23(a) does not expect that all vessels will be long enough to make the pattern work. As we've seen, the dividing line between those vessels which may carry the second light and those which must is a length of 50 meters. It is worth pondering for a moment how smaller vessels should react to this part of Rule 23. There is no question that they must understand the display and be ready to recognize it when worn by others. Need they, though, consider mounting the two lights on their own short platforms? One conclusion would be that since both are not required they should not be shown. According to fo'c'sle cynics, in order to retire as an admiral one should never volunteer. That is poor counsel in naval circles and no better here. Any display, required or not, which might afford others a better understanding of what you are doing is to be considered. If in fact your ship is not long enough to make an extra masthead light useful, then don't mount it. But how short is too short? An inquiry to learn if such an extra light might be helpful could be very worthwhile.

Inland adds a paragraph to its version of this rule. In it are found echoes of older regulations for domestic waters. By Rule 23(d) a power-driven vessel on the Great Lakes is given the option to combine the after masthead light with the sternlight by carrying an all-round white light in the position of the after masthead light. The reason for consolidating the two is better detectability in a low-lying fog when the observer is within the arc of a sternlight. Those of us who have lived with the older rules might find nothing new in this requirement. For decades an all-round white light was shown by inland power-driven vessels abaft of and higher than the "masthead" light. In those less permissive days not only was that light imperative but the mandate was extended to all power-driven vessels whether on the Great Lakes or not. We ancient mariners, though, should not presume too much on scanty data. A new twist has been given to the old command.

Under the new Inland Rules, all power-driven vessels except those operating on the Great Lakes are subject to Rule 23(a), (b), and (c). This means that when they are 12 meters or more long they must display one or two white lights of 225° arc; that is, they must show one or two *masthead* lights. There is no authority for them *ever* to display an all-round white light in lieu of an after masthead light. The age-old 32-point range light has disappeared into history. The basic modern requirement is one masthead light when the length is less than 50 meters and two when that length or greater. There are only two exceptions to this decree. One is the option offered power-driven vessels less than 12 meters long. They may combine their one and only masthead light with a sternlight into an all-round white light. The other exception is that found in Rule 23(d) and presented, as we've just seen, to vessels on the Great Lakes. How important is all this? Not critical when an observer is afloat. Whether a light is all-round or only partly so can hardly be detected when one's vantage point is on the surface. A seagull wheeling high above the ship might be able to tell, but not the likes of the waterborne.

Both COLREGS and Inland devote Rule 23(b) to requirements for an air-cushion vessel when in the nondisplacement mode. The mention of this water creature entitles us to ask three questions: What is an air-cushion vessel? What is meant by nondisplacement mode? Why should conventional mariners bother to inquire? Steering clear of scientific fine points, we might be content with the following answers.

Air-cushion refers to a hovercraft, a vessel in the category of surface effect. She skims over the surface rather than pushing an immersed part of her hull through the sea. When a ship has a submerged form she displaces water. When she skims over the surface without an immersed shape she is in the nondisplacement mode. But not all skimmers skim the same way. The hydrofoil rises up on nautical skis. The hovercraft, however, directs a fan downward from her underside to create a cushion of air on which she rides. The technology for such radical shipping is constantly evolving and has generated considerable controversy. But the rulemakers proffer neither opinions nor advice. They merely establish signals for maverick vessels whose peculiarities merit identification. By Rule 23(b) an air-cushion vessel need only be identified as such when she is in the nondisplacement mode. Without her pillow of air she sinks into the water and is propelled through it the same as nearly everyone else. And in that mode her immersed part resists sideways skimming. No matter how tub-like her bottom contours she will tend to follow the track toward which she is steered. But when her fan is operating she mounts her cushion of air to dance across the surface almost free of contact. And that creates a problem. She might not follow her nose. A hydrofoil is not so beset, for she

In the nondisplacement mode this military hovercraft can transport a fully laden company and its vehicles at speeds up to 60 knots. [Photo courtesy Vosper Thornycroft (UK) Ltd.]

is less likely to ski sideways. But the hovercraft's skittishness must be signaled.

Rule 3 defines her as power-driven, and she remains so whether she rides her air cushion or not. Rule 23(a) requires that since she is power-driven, she must display a masthead light or two (depending on length), plus sidelights and a sternlight. As we've learned, the task of sidelights and a sternlight is to indicate direction or aspect. Now, though, comes the problem. When an air-cushion vessel hovers over the sea, free to drift from her track, neither sidelights nor sternlight might be valid indicators of direction. Her leeway could equal the downwind drift of an aircraft. In Fig. 27 we are northbound with the wind from the northwest. We observe a masthead light and a red sidelight on the port bow. The direction and aspect story is that the other is power-driven, is presenting her port side, and is probably not dangerous. She should pass clear to the westward of our track. But that need not follow if she is a hovercraft in the nondisplacement mode. With neither hull nor keel to keep her constant she might drift with the wind to the left of her course. She might in fact skim directly toward our bow. We should be forewarned that the directional lights of this exotic craft can be misleading, and Rule 23(b) provides the alarm. Such a vessel in the nondisplacement mode must supplement her normal power-driven display with an all-round flashing yellow light.

This is a commendable provision, for it establishes a simple signal to adver-

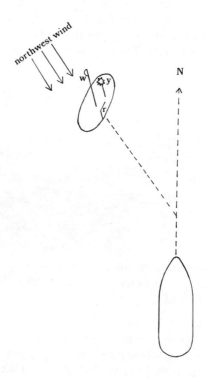

Fig. 27. *Hovercraft and Leeway. Because of wind drift, a hovercraft apparently passing clear on the port side might be on a collision course.*

tise a danger. But when COLREGS first appeared this simple signal ran afoul of another one intended to advertise another danger. At night a submarine on the surface can appear to be a small vessel. Instead it is a large, clumsy, deep-draft ship. So naval regulations require United States submarines to display a special identification signal both on international and inland waters. Until the advent of 72 COLREGS this special signal was a rotating yellow light flashing 90 times per minute. Then came Rule 23(b) with its demand that an air-cushion vessel flash an all-round yellow light at the rate of 120 times or more per minute. The resemblance was too close and one of the displays would have to be changed. By an unsung act of deference, U.S. naval authorities condoned the COLREGS intrusion on their signal and fashioned a substitute.

The submarine identification signal is now an intermittent flashing yellow beacon emitting one flash per second for three seconds followed by a three-second off period. And it is shown in addition to normal navigation lights, with placement either above or below the masthead lights. The importance of this display is clear when we consider a sobering reality of submarine operation. Fully submerged the submarine enjoys the fruits of careful design. She can speed and swerve like her living prototypes. Fully surfaced, though, she deserves the epithet "pigboat." Those in command often achieve a more comfortable in-between ride by speeding along neither surfaced nor submerged but at a level combining a little of each. The part of the hull visible might be smaller than a fishing boat and any running or identity lights might be veiled by the spume of whitecaps. Perhaps nary a soul is on an open deck, for the periscope might well be the only lookout other than electronic and acoustical gear. And all this is moving faster than the top speed of a World War II destroyer! We should harbor no illusions: a semisurfaced submarine is a dangerous vessel. Charts define her coastal operating lanes in many areas. Whenever such a zone is traversed we should be ready for the prospect of a nuclear-powered complex moving at 30-plus knots and showing no more effective light pattern through her halo of spray than that of a vessel under oars. Submarine operating areas are not safe places to dally. When crossing one, do so quickly. While in one, overcome any urge toward wanting to see the Silent Service at work. And don't be surprised if a submarine, displaced from its submerged habitat, doesn't conform to all the signal tenets of the Rules. Her flashing yellow beacon should be enough warning to keep well clear.

Veteran observers of collision rule mutation might detect a subtle change

The nuclear-powered U.S.S. Ohio requires more than masthead light, sidelights, and a sternlight to give adequate warning of her surface operation at night. [USN photo]

in the description of a color. Older rules spoke of an amber light while current ones refer to it as yellow. According to scuttlebutt, which is never to be trusted, the reason for the change is this. A mariner accused of not recognizing a light the color of which bore the same name as the hue of low-calorie beer silenced his critics with a resourceful defense. Amber might be fossilized tree sap, he argued, but it is not a color. So, says this story, it was decreed that the misnomer be expunged. If this recounting is factual, civilization's concern with trivia might have reached new heights. But there is still reason for optimism. That we can indulge ourselves in such a fribbling issue is a tribute to our advanced state. In any event a transition from amber to yellow will not occur all at once. The offending term for tree sap will probably masquerade as a primary color for some time to come.

Inland's Annex V presents Pilot Rules and another flirtation with colors other than plain red and green. Section 88.11 of that annex offers a special identity signal to law enforcement agencies. High-speed chases of miscreants while under sail are hardly likely, so we can fit this unique signal in with power-driven displays. Here is what Section 88.11 has to say:

ANNEX V, PILOT RULES, SECTION 88.11—LAW ENFORCEMENT VESSELS

§ 88.11 Law enforcement vessels.

(a) Law enforcement vessels may display a flashing blue light when engaged in direct law enforcement activities. This light shall be located so that it does not interfere with the visibility of the vessel's navigation lights.

(b) The blue light described in this section may be displayed by law enforcement vessels of the United States and the States and their political subdivisions.

A primary mission of the medium-endurance cutter U.S.C.G.C. Dependable *is law enforcement. [USCG photo]*

We should have no problem this time with tints and shades. Blue is blue and not azure, indigo, or even lapis lazuli. The signal is a sort of visual siren. When racing in hot pursuit a police vessel may clear the way with a flashing blue light so long as it doesn't interfere with her normal navigation lights. And the law enforcement can be by federal, state, or local officialdom. Note, though, the "may" in the regulation. If stealth is the better way to stalk villains, then no such identity light need be shown.

Whether a power-driven vessel is conventional, air-cushioned, or more at home beneath the sea, she is at least free of hangers-on. That is not true, though, when she is towing. Both she and whatever depends on her for propulsion are awkward enough to warrant special identification, and Rule 24 recites the requirements. But before looking at the specifics we should note to whom the rule applies. It speaks only to the power-driven. A sail vessel towing is not included.

RULE 24—Towing and Pushing

COLREGS

(a) A power-driven vessel when towing shall exhibit:

(i) instead of the light prescribed in Rule 23(a)(i) or (a)(ii), two masthead lights in a vertical line. When the length of the tow, measuring from the stern of the towing vessel to the after end of the tow exceeds 200 meters, three such lights in a vertical line;

(ii) sidelights;

(iii) a sternlight;

(iv) a towing light in a vertical line above the sternlight;

(v) when the length of the tow exceeds 200 meters, a diamond shape where it can best be seen.

(b) When a pushing vessel and a vessel being pushed ahead are rigidly connected in a composite unit they shall be regarded as a power-driven vessel and exhibit the lights prescribed in Rule 23.

(c) A power-driven vessel when pushing ahead or towing alongside, except in the case of a composite unit, shall exhibit:

(i) instead of the light prescribed in Rule 23(a)(i) or (a)(ii), two masthead lights in a vertical line;

(ii) sidelights;

(iii) a sternlight.

(d) A power-driven vessel to which paragraph (a) or (c) of this Rule apply shall also comply with Rule 23(a)(ii).

(e) A vessel or object being towed, other than those mentioned in paragraph (g) of this Rule, shall exhibit:

(i) sidelights;

(ii) a sternlight;

(iii) when the length of the tow exceeds 200 meters, a diamond shape where it can best be seen.

(f) Provided that any number of vessels being towed alongside or pushed in a group shall be lighted as one vessel,

(i) a vessel being pushed ahead, not being part of a composite unit, shall exhibit at the forward end, sidelights;

(ii) a vessel being towed alongside shall exhibit a sternlight and at the forward end, sidelights.

(g) An inconspicuous, partly submerged vessel or object, or combination of such vessels or objects being towed, shall exhibit:

(i) if it is less than 25 meters in breadth, one all-round white light at or near the forward end and one at or near the after end except that dracones need not exhibit a light at or near the forward end;

(ii) if it is 25 meters or more in breadth, two additional all-round white lights at or near the extremities of its breadth;

(iii) if it exceeds 100 meters in length, additional all-round white lights between the lights prescribed in subparagraphs (i) and (ii) so that the distance between the lights shall not exceed 100 meters;

(iv) a diamond shape at or near the aftermost extremity of the last vessel or object being towed and if the length of the tow exceeds 200 meters an additional diamond shape where it can best be seen and located as far forward as is practicable.

(h) Where from any sufficient cause it is impracticable for a vessel or object being towed to exhibit the lights or shapes prescribed in paragraph (e) or (g) of this Rule, all possible measures shall be taken to light the vessel or object towed or at least to indicate the presence of such vessel or object.

(i) Where from any sufficient cause it is impracticable for a vessel not normally engaged in towing operations to display the lights prescribed in paragraph (a) or (c) of this Rule, such vessel shall not be required to exhibit those lights when engaged in towing another vessel in distress or otherwise in need of assistance. All possible measures shall be taken to indicate the nature of the relationship between the towing vessel and the vessel being towed as authorized by Rule 36, in particular by illuminating the towline.

INLAND

(a) A power-driven vessel when towing astern shall exhibit:

(i) instead of the light prescribed either in Rule 23(a)(i) or 23(a)(ii), two masthead lights in a vertical line. When the length of the tow, measuring from the stern of the towing vessel to the after end of the tow exceeds 200 meters, three such lights in a vertical line;

(ii) sidelights;

(iii) a sternlight;

(iv) a towing light in a vertical line above the sternlight; and

(v) when the length of the tow exceeds 200 meters, a diamond shape where it can best be seen.

(b) When a pushing vessel and a vessel being pushed ahead are rigidly connected in a composite unit they shall be regarded as a power-driven vessel and exhibit the lights prescribed in Rule 23.

(c) A power-driven vessel when pushing ahead or towing alongside, except as required by paragraphs (b) and (i) of this Rule, shall exhibit:

(i) instead of the light prescribed either in Rule 23(a)(i) or 23(a)(ii), two masthead lights in a vertical line;

(ii) sidelights; and

(iii) two towing lights in a vertical line.

(d) A power-driven vessel to which paragraphs (a) or (c) of this Rule apply shall also comply with Rule 23(a)(i) and 23(a)(ii).

(e) A vessel or object other than those referred to in paragraph (g) of this Rule being towed shall exhibit:

(i) sidelights;

(ii) a sternlight; and

(iii) when the length of the tow exceeds 200 meters, a diamond shape where it can best be seen.

(f) Provided that any number of vessels being towed alongside or pushed in a group shall be lighted as one vessel:

(i) a vessel being pushed ahead, not being part of a composite unit, shall exhibit at the forward end sidelights, and a special flashing light; and

(ii) a vessel being towed alongside shall exhibit a sternlight and at the forward end sidelights.

(g) An inconspicuous, partly submerged vessel or object being towed shall exhibit:

(i) if it is less than 25 meters in breadth, one all-round white light at or near each end;

(ii) if it is 25 meters or more in breadth, four all-round white lights to mark its length and breadth;

(iii) if it exceeds 100 meters in length, additional all-round white lights between the lights prescribed in subparagraphs (i) and (ii) so that the distance between the lights shall not exceed 100 meters: *Provided,* That any vessels or objects being towed alongside each other shall be lighted as one vessel or object;

(iv) a diamond shape at or near the aftermost extremity of the last vessel or object being towed; and

(v) the towing vessel may direct a searchlight in the direction of the tow to indicate its presence to an approaching vessel.

(h) Where from any sufficient cause it is impracticable for a vessel or object being towed to exhibit the lights prescribed in paragraph (e) or (g) of this Rule, all possible measures shall be taken to light the vessel or object towed or at least to indicate the presence of the unlighted vessel or object.

(i) Notwithstanding paragraph (c), on the Western Rivers and on waters specified by the Secretary, a power-driven vessel when pushing ahead or towing alongside, except as paragraph (b) applies, shall exhibit:

(i) sidelights; and

(ii) two towing lights in a vertical line.

(j) Where from any sufficient cause it is impracticable for a vessel not normally engaged in towing operations to display the lights prescribed by paragraph (a), (c) or (i) of this Rule, such vessel shall not be required to exhibit those lights when engaged in towing another vessel in distress or otherwise in need of assistance. All possible measures shall be taken to indicate the nature of the relationship between the towing vessel and the vessel being assisted. The searchlight authorized by Rule 36 may be used to illuminate the tow.

A study of this complex rule will not be easy. In fact the anguished howl of a nontowing mariner already echoes from the vault of the heavens. "Why," he complains, "need I be vexed by all this chapter and verse? A few white lights in a vertical line and a sidelight or two are enough to tell me a towboat is nearby. Then, being a prudent seaman, I'll give the whole works a wide berth without prying into whether the tug is big or small or where her tow might be." To this a chorus of pragmatic seafarers appends, "Hear! Hear!" No such grumbles should be dismissed out of hand, for they might contain grains of truth. There is much detail to be found in this rule and undue attention to such particularities might create confusion. The art, though, is to know when to stop, for not enough attention can be as bad as too much.

A deep-sea rescue tug taking a disabled liner in tow with heavy chain hawser. [USCG photo]

That howling mariner who expresses such a lean interest in lights and shapes is really not a prudent seaman. Tows are not all alike, and perceiving their differences is essential. For example, keeping clear of a long tandem tow is not the same as maneuvering around a tug pushing ahead. Recognition of the difference in their identity signals is a part of good seamanship. A study of Rule 24 and its complications might not be pleasant, yet it is necessary. We should quell mutinous thoughts and prepare for a tedious watch.

This rule states four ways that a power-driven vessel can propel another craft. The vessel or object being moved can be towed astern, towed alongside, or pushed ahead. The fourth mode reflects modern technology by speaking of a rigid composite unit. We can dispose of that towing method in short order. A towboat designed for pushing ahead can be fashioned in such a way that its flattened bow nests snugly into a cleft in the stern of its barge. Then both are rigidly bound together into a composite unit. Rule 24(b) views the issue of such a marriage as a single power-driven vessel subject to Rule 23. She carries one or two masthead lights, depending on her length; she displays one set of sidelights; she mounts a stern light as near as practicable to her stern. In other words she wears the raiment of a powered vessel. However, the Coast Guard has forged a safeguard against indifferent nuptials. Exercising its authority to make an interpretive rule, it has, in Title 33 of the *Code of Federal Regulations,* proclaimed this definition for "composite unit":

88.3 PUSHING VESSEL AND VESSEL BEING PUSHED: COMPOSITE UNIT.

Rule 24(b) of the 72 COLREGS states that when a pushing vessel and a vessel being pushed ahead are rigidly connected in a composite unit, they are regarded as a power-driven vessel and must exhibit the lights under Rule 23. A "composite unit" is interpreted to be a pushing vessel that is rigidly connected by mechanical means to a vessel being pushed so they react to sea and swell as one vessel. "Mechanical means" does not include the following: (a) lines; (b) hawsers; (c) wires; (d) chains.

When clear of channel buoys the diesel tug Winquatt *will pay out her towline to take the* Islander *to sea. [Courtesy Matson Lines]*

That wasn't so bad! One towing pattern is already abaft our beam. We move on with confidence, if not enthusiasm, to the remaining three. Since meeting Rule 1 the need to weigh each word carefully has been evident, and here again we must do so. In COLREGS Rule 24(a) we read about a power-driven vessel towing; the same paragraph of Inland Rules speaks of towing astern. The meaning, though, is the same. The rulemakers in London seemed overly chary with words, for when referring to power-driven vessels dragging something behind, they used the imprecise word "towing" instead of the more descriptive words "towing astern." We must keep this COLREGS shorthand in mind, for the confusion is liable to recur in later paragraphs of the International Rules. At least, though, such obscurity is limited to the mode of towing astern. Rule 24(c) in both sets of rules uses no ambiguous description when referring to towing alongside and pushing ahead.

First up in our study of the remaining three relationships between tug and tow is the display on a power-driven vessel *towing* on the high seas and *towing astern* on inland waters. The customary signals of direction or aspect must appear. Required on the tug are sidelights and a sternlight. The real meat of Rule 24 is found in the patterns to signal identity or condition. The tug is known as such by showing two masthead lights in a vertical line when the length of the tow is not over 200 meters and three of them when it exceeds that measure. "Length of the tow" in turn is defined as a measurement from the stern of the towing vessel to the after end of the tow. That means to the end of the last vessel or object astern. Figure 28 illustrates the idea.

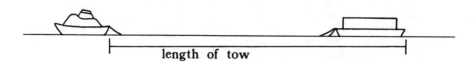

length of tow

Fig. 28. Measuring a Tow. When a tug and her tow are in tandem the rules measure length of tow from the stern of the tug to the end of the last in line behind her.

We should pay particular heed to Rule 24(a)(i), for it incorporates a change. The original COLREGS statement specified that the cluster of masthead lights, whether two or three, was required to be forward. That placement created, among other problems, the potential for bothersome glare on the bridge. Now by both sets of rules the identity or condition pattern of 225° white lights can appear either forward or aft.

In order to grasp the consequence of this we must skip ahead to Rule 24(d). By Inland a tug must also comply with Rule 23(a)(i) and (ii) by carrying a forward masthead light and, if long enough, an after one. COLREGS mentions only the after masthead. By the time a large tug with a long tow astern could meet all these demands she might be enveloped in a blizzard of white lights. So common sense prevailed. By Section 2(e) of Annex I, if the tug's identity cluster of tow or three white lights in a vertical line is located forward,

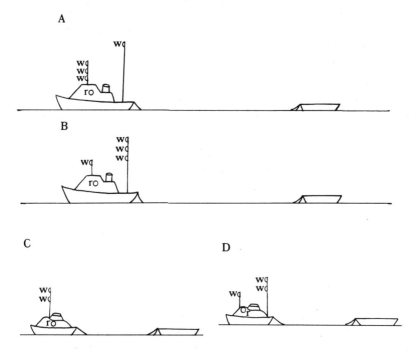

Fig. 29. Towing Astern. Panels A and B show a tug 50 meters or more long with a tow astern more than 200 meters. Panels C and D depict a tug less than 50 meters long with a short tow astern. (B and D: Inland only.)

then one of them does double duty by fulfilling the requirement for a forward masthead light. If, though, the identity cluster is placed aft, one of them serves as the after masthead light. The sketches in Fig. 29 illustrate some possible displays. In Fig. 29A we see a power-driven tug 50 meters or more in length with a tow more than 200 meters astern. She is carrying her three towing identity lights forward, so one of them serves as the forward masthead light. But since she is 50 meters or more in length she must also carry the after masthead light. Figure 29B illustrates her sister ship under the same conditions of towing. This time, though, the identity cluster is aft, so one of them is accepted as the after masthead light required of a long power-driven vessel. She must, however, as a powered vessel, carry a forward masthead light. The next panel, Fig. 29C, has a small tug with a short tow astern. She has elected to show her identity cluster of two white towing lights in the forward position.

One of them also serves as the forward masthead light required of a power-driven vessel. Since she is less than 50 meters long, she need not carry the after masthead light and does not do so. In Fig. 29D we see the same short tug with the short tow astern. This time she is carrying the identity lights aft. Neither of them can serve as the forward masthead light because they are not forward, so she must still display a masthead light in the forward position.

The murmur of the malcontents is getting louder! In fairness we should admit that this discussion seems bound to incite mutiny. A latter-day Mr. Christian can be seen readying a longboat to cast Captain Bligh and his loyal students of the literal word adrift with a dictionary and a seabag full of lights and shapes. Should he delay that mutiny a while he'll have more cause to rebel, for there are still more irritants to consider. A power-driven vessel towing astern must show a distinctive signal to those behind her: Rule 24(a)(iii) requires a normal white sternlight and Rule 24(a)(iv) adds a towing light in a vertical line above it. By darting back to Rule 21(d) we can recall that a towing light has the same 135° arc as a sternlight, but is yellow. Figure 30 presents the stern view of a power-driven vessel towing astern. Regardless of the tug's length and no matter how long the tow, "yellow-over-white" is shown from the stern of the tug. It is worth noting that nothing else would be seen by someone astern, for the white identity lights and any accompanying masthead light are only 225° in arc.

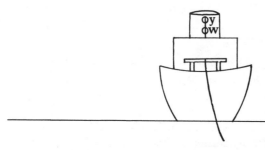

Fig. 30. Stern View of Tug Towing Astern. A power-driven tug of any length with a tow astern of any length shows this stern view.

In the daytime we should have little difficulty recognizing a tug at work. If her unique build doesn't set her apart we can look to her telltale companion bobbing astern, alongside, or ahead. Sometimes, though, the separation between the tug and a tow astern is so great that they seem disconnected. Such deception is hazardous, for a towline lies between them. Rule 24(a)(iv) and Section 6(a) of Annex I combine to provide a warning. When her tow astern is more than 200 meters, a power-driven tug must display by day a black diamond shape.

Powerful diesel engines occupy much of the Olmstead's *hull as this pusher tug is seen on the Mississippi River at St. Louis, Missouri. [Courtesy St. Louis Ship]*

When power-driven vessels are towing alongside or pushing ahead they look to Rule 24(c) for their signals. The night display is two vertical white masthead lights for identity. And like those towing astern, they may locate the pattern either forward or aft. Again like the tug towing astern, they must show the after masthead light if the identity cluster is forward and the tug is 50 meters or more long, and (Inland) show the forward masthead light if the identity cluster is aft, regardless of tug length. What about directional signals? Well, perhaps Mr. Christian should belay that mutiny, for Bligh might have a point after all. There is a curious and even alarming contrast between COLREGS and Inland. Rules 24(c) of each requires that sidelights be mounted, but the stern display justifies Bligh's rigorous attention to detail.

The International rule calls for no more than a sternlight to be exhibited by the power-driven tug when her tow is either alongside or stretching far out ahead. In neither case is she allowed to show the yellow towing light. It seems inadequate that we might see only a white light when overtaking a snub-nosed tug pushing a file of long barges ahead. Of course we shouldn't expect to overtake such a parade in mid-Atlantic, but COLREGS also govern many national waters. In any case the United States can tolerate no such miscue. Inland Rule 24(c)(iii) demands that a positive signal be shown. Two towing lights in a vertical line and no white sternlight marks the powered tug pushing ahead or towing alongside. And Fig. 31 illustrates a variety of possible displays.

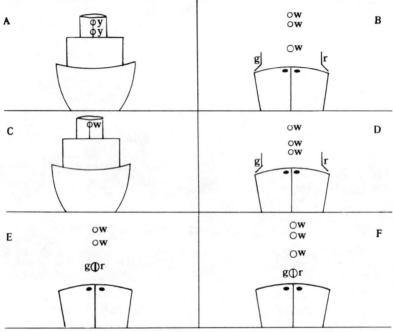

Fig. 31. *Bow and Stern View of Tugs. (A) Stern view of any-length tug with any-length tow ahead or alongside, tow not visible* (Inland only); *(B) bow view of any-length tug with tow alongside, ahead, or not over 200 meters astern, tug carrying two upper white lights aft* (specified by Inland); *(C) stern view of any-length tug with any-length tow ahead or alongside, tow not visible* (COLREGS only); *(D) bow view of tug 50 meters or more long with tow alongside, ahead, or not over 200 meters astern, tug carrying two lower white lights forward* (COLREGS and Inland); *(E) bow view of tug under 20 meters long with tow alongside, ahead, or not over 200 meters astern, tug carrying two lights forward* (COLREGS and Inland); *(F) bow view of tug under 20 meters long with tow alongside, ahead, or not over 200 meters astern, tug carrying two upper white lights aft* (specified by Inland).

Our friend the malcontent Mr. Christian is quick to disapprove. He observes that we have only attended to lights on the tug. What about the tow? His "bare bones" approach to learning finds no utility in fussing with the lights on the tug and disregarding those on the barge. He even goes further and intones that *any* lights moving along with a tug will obviously tell the story of whether they are keeping company astern, alongside, or by being pushed ahead. If the study could be that simple we surely have been gulled into wasting time. Yet his argument seems plausible. It also offers the lure of less work. Seamen since Ulysses have been easy marks for seductive wiles of all sorts, and high on anyone's list of flimflam is the promise of saving work.

But the case for a thorough study of towboat lights is easy to state. The most incompetent of mariners will conclude that the appearance of two green side-lights plus a swarm of other lights suggests the starboard view of vessels traveling in company, with one of them being carried along by the other. What, though, if the lights on the tow are weak or burned out? If the separation of tow from tug can be confusing by day, it can be far more so at night. The fair-weather sailor who hawks shortcuts to competence is only rationalizing ignorance. The Rules of the Road tell the mariner to make a full appraisal of each situation by using all knowledge and data at hand. He is cautioned to resolve doubts in favor of possible danger. He is advised not to make snap judgments on scanty information. During the short moments while risk of collision escalates toward disaster, more is expected of the seaman than that he only recognize a towboat because it is accompanied by something being towed. Whenever during this study we are disposed to question the worth of our dedication to detail we should recall this paragraph. If we can tolerate a study of towing lights and shapes we should have no difficulty pondering over any of the signal patterns.

Inland's Rule 24(i) describes a special pattern designed to accommodate the problems of towboats on certain domestic waters. A Western Rivers night display is specified for power-driven vessels pushing ahead or towing alongside, and general authority is given the Coast Guard to extend the requirements to other areas. Nothing extra is required. Instead the display is pared down, as shown in Fig. 32. In addition to the aspect signals of sidelights and a sternlight, towboats need only show two towing lights in a vertical line. They do not display either the forward or the after masthead light, for Rule 24(i) says " . . . notwithstanding paragraph (c)." And that section speaks of the white masthead lights. Here is the Coast Guard explanation for the change. Tow-boats on the Western Rivers place the pilothouse as high above the water as possible so the pilot will have better visibility. But the higher he goes the closer he gets to any masthead lights. Were such white lights to be shown together with identity signals, the back scatter could dangerously reduce the night vision of the tug operator. So a trade-off was made. The need for masthead lights to warn oncomers is overridden by the need for better vision while maneuvering a clumsy tow.

Lurking in this discussion has been a question now voiced by a Hawaiian mariner on behalf of western Americans from Prudhoe Bay to Point Loma.

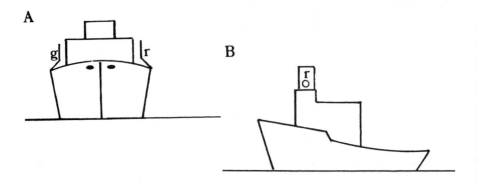

*Fig. 32. Western Rivers Tugs. (A) Bow view of tug towing alongside or pushing
        ahead* (Inland only); *(B) port profile of tug towing alongside or pushing
        ahead* (Inland only).

"Where," he asks, "are the Western Rivers?" We've already met the answer
in Rule 3(l) of the Inland Rules. *Western Rivers* means the Mississippi and its
tributaries as well as the Port Allen–Morgan City Alternate Route and that
part of the Atchafalaya River above its junction with the Port Allen–Morgan
City Alternate Route including the Old River and the Red River. Such a
description might be understandable to those conversant with the waterways
of middle America and the Gulf States but not to our lei-laden seaman. Even
so he is enlightened, for this special rule does not apply on whatever might
qualify as a river in Hawaii. And his fellow westerners conclude that it has no
application on the Yukon, the Columbia, or even the dusty Los Angeles.
Western Rivers are west of Westchester County but east of the Continental
Divide.

While we are on the subject of parochial terms, we might as well dispose
of another pearl. Students of older rules might experience accelerated eye blink
when they read mention of the Red River. Where is it? For nearly a century
it seems to have been a part of Inland Rules. Well, just as the Wizard of Oz
had to distinguish between witches east and west we must separate Red Rivers
north and south. The Red River of the north, featured in older rules, flows
from the United States into Canada's Lake Winnipeg. It garnered its share of
attention when it was of navigational significance. Traffic, though, seems to
have decreased to the point that further mention is not necessary. Inland Rule
3(l) speaks of a different Red River. The one now referred to is in Louisiana.
With rivers, whether Red or Western, set aright, let's drift back to midstream.

Must every power-driven vessel engaged in towing abide by Rule 24? The
zeal of a Good Samaritan would be dampened if towing a disabled vessel

involved hoisting strings of lights fore and aft. Both COLREGS and Inland recognize that except for professional tugs, vessels seldom tow unless in emergency circumstances. Moreover, the amateur towboat usually finds it impracticable to rig Rule 24 lights. So, say the Rules, she need not. What she must do, though, is advise the nautical world of her connection with her tow. And the use of a searchlight is specifically authorized.

This Bureau of Indian Affairs supply ship in Alaskan waters with one barge alongside and another astern is not the usual towboat. [Photo by Lawrence Wyatt]

The scrupulous student of the Rules might churn over an uncertainty which now is detectable. COLREGS Rule 24(i) and Inland Rule 24(j) release amateurs from the burden of showing lights but make no mention of a day shape. What if the length of the disabled tow is more than 200 meters? Is it then required that a day shape be shown when sunlit even though a special light display would not be required from sunset to sunrise? Advocates of a close study of the Rules are grieved by this obvious imperfection. In public they might excuse the oversight as evidence that, after all, the Rules were made by men and not received from the Almighty on a Near Eastern mountain. Privately, though, they lament the absence of the words "or shapes" from the offending paragraphs. Those of less literal persuasion have no difficulty making a free translation. Surely, if no volunteer towboatman is expected to rummage around for spare lights, he need not sculpt a black diamond day shape from his onboard stock of miscellany.

The same spirit of free translation provides clues to an answer to another problem. Rule 24 assumes that all modern professional tugs are power-driven and able to carry standardized lights and shapes. Not even the most diehard defender of sail can object. No one could ward off bankruptcy were he to operate a topsail towboat for hire. But that doesn't mean sailing vessels are not allowed to tow. So a good question: What should be the signal displayed by a sailing vessel engaged in towing? The white and yellow lights of a power-driven tug are barred, yet she must show something to alert approaching vessels of her condition. Even occasional tugs propelled by wind are not exempt from the obligation to practice good seamanship. Some effective notice must be given to indicate that a dangerous and encumbering operation is underway. The means used will of course depend on what equipment is available. A searchlight by night would serve, but not all vessels carry a searchlight. The Rules do not require that one plan ahead for such an eventuality, but they will hardly tolerate inactivity. The mariner aware of the danger must make it known to oncomers by whatever means available, whether that be some efficient modern device or something as basic as gestures and shouts. We should read these permissive paragraphs as applicable to any irregular tug, regardless of her means of propulsion.

So far the concentration has been on lights and shapes shown by the shepherd. But what about the sheep? Rule 24(e) requires that on both the high seas and on inland waters a vessel or object being towed astern must show the aspect signals of sidelights and a sternlight. We should not be surprised by that command, for when there is a direction or aspect to indicate, then such should be done. But veteran students of the Rules might lift an eyebrow over the reference to whatever is astern as being a "vessel or object." Prior to the advent of COLREGS only "vessels" were mentioned. The result, though, was a pall of doubt among a corps of earnest mariners. What if whatever might be in tow was not so patently a vessel? The present Rule 3(a), a model of universality, would seem to settle the problem by defining a vessel as ". . . every description of watercraft . . . used or capable of being used as a means of transportation on water." Yet the conscientious might still be concerned. What, for example, is the status of a buoy being towed to its station? Is it really a Rule 3(a) vessel? It was solemnly suggested prior to COLREGS that a case of beer be lashed to its bell tower; then it would surely be used as a means of transportation on water. Rule 24(e) renders the discussion academic. Its "vessel or object" covers everything from a warship to a wine cask. And when bobbing astern, whether vessel or object, each such entity must show sidelights and a sternlight when able to do so.

By day a special hazard can require advertisement. We've read that a long tow astern is one measuring more than 200 meters from the stern of the tug to the after end of the last unit in line. Rule 24 already demands that the tug identify its nib of the procession by showing a black diamond day shape. Rule 24(e)(iii) orders that the other end be marked with a similar shape, as illustrated in Fig. 33.

Rule 24(g), both COLREGS and Inland, makes special allowance for a tow which is probably more object than vessel. A wide variety of floating craft is being towed nowadays, and some types have so little freeboard that they are hard to see. Whether awash by design or by adversity, they are not suitable platforms on which to mount sidelights and sternlights. On the other hand they are capable of displaying some kind of signal. Were that not the case, Rule 24(h) would go to work. By it, when a tow is unlightable the tug must do whatever is feasible to indicate its presence. But our present concern is with an "in-between" fellow traveler who is capable of displaying some lights but not the customary ones expected of an object under tow.

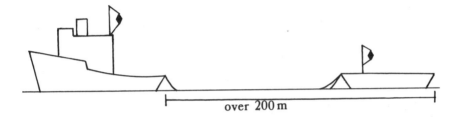

over 200 m

Fig. 33. Day Shapes When Towing. Black diamonds mark a tug of any length and a long tow astern.

Rule 24(g) requires that an all-round white light be placed at each end of the object. And if that craft is 25 meters or more wide, similar lights will be mounted at each corner. Make it more than 100 meters long and additional white lights will mark the length. The daytime identification is a black diamond near the after end of the last "thing" wallowing astern. Figure 34 illustrates what we might expect from such a bizarre craft. What is not indicated, though, is how often such a combination might be encountered. Things awash and in tow don't regularly ply the northeastern Pacific bound for Honolulu. Even so, there are areas on both high seas and inland waters where logs are rafted together for transit to sawmills. Securing sidelights and a sternlight to the bark of floating tree trunks would be at the very least

Fig. 34. Lights on Tows Awash. A wide inconspicuous object or group in tow is marked with white lights on each corner.

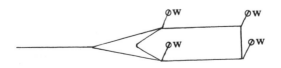

challenging, but hanging a fore-and-aft string of white lights on pikestaffs might be feasible. Most of us will have little need to rig the day and night signals displayed by an unstable log raft. In fact it won't be long before only the geriatric mariner will recall that older rules spoke of rafts as being cribs, bags, and booms. But there are nonetheless valid reasons for us to bother with Rule 24(g).

First of all we should sample that paragraph just because it was written. Our present task is to look at every word contained in the Rules before we decide what is and what is not worthwhile. A second reason holds more interest. Even the most discriminating of us harbor a secret hoard of little-known facts hardly worth knowing. COLREGS Rule 24(g) can add to such a fund of dross. In some parts of the world a synthetic rubber sausage called a *dracone* is used to deliver petroleum by water. When filled it bulges into a cylinder riding partly submerged. Empty, it might not shrivel enough to stow under the mate's bunk, but it is sufficiently dwarfed to assure easy delivery back to the starting point. Like the log raft, an undulating dracone is not the proper scaffold on which to hang regulation running lights. And Rule 24(g) serves as a neat accommodation to its shortcomings. Note that COLREGS Rule 24(g)(i) exempts a dracone from displaying an all-round white light at its forward end. A logical reason might be that the weight of the hawser dips the front end of the sausage beneath the waves. And while we are studying COLREGS 24(g) we might as well glance at its subparagraph (iv). A complex of inconspicuous, partly submerged "things" will always have a black diamond at the after extremity, but it is also required, when the tow is more than 200 meters long, to have another as far forward on the tow as possible. The market for black diamonds seems expanding. Power-driven tugs with long tows need them; long tows behind power-driven tugs need them. Inconspicuous objects when com-

Fig. 35. Groups Towed Alongside. A cluster in tow on the port side is lighted separately from the group on the starboard side.

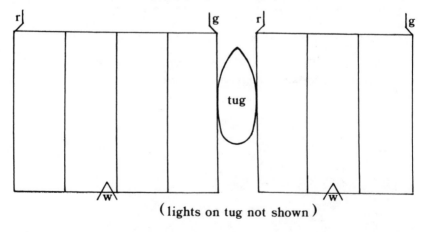

(lights on tug not shown)

prising a long tow need two. And our new friend, the dracone, will sport one on its after end. Of course, dracones are rarely met so we need hardly emphasize having made their acquaintance. But in today's surprising world we might one day be asked to rig a dracone with lights and a day shape. At least we should be prepared to recognize its raiment. And if such is not our fate, we've at least augmented our arsenal of words for use in crossword puzzles, Scrabble bouts, and awkward lulls in cocktail conversation.

Whether on the high seas or inland waters, a vessel towed alongside shows sidelights and a sternlight. Moreover, Rule 24(f) lights a group as one. But common sense demands that the term "group" apply to vessels on the same side of the tug. Three barges on one side and four on the other constitute two groups and not a single assembly of seven. Each cluster would show sidelights and a sternlight, as depicted in Fig. 35.

What of the vessel being pushed ahead? Unless she and her propellant are a rigid composite unit, she must display sidelights. But a sternlight would do more harm than good by dazzling the helmsman on the tug a few meters back.

Clearing an Antarctic channel, icebreakers do an unusual job of pushing ahead.
  [USCG photo]

But Inland Rule 24(f)(i) adds an identity signal. The lead unit being pushed ahead displays the special flashing light described in Rule 21(g). With an arc from dead ahead to at least abeam on each side, this yellow light flashes about once a second. The only complaint about this signal is that it is not also required by COLREGS. Anyone meeting a caravan of a pusher and one or more pushees stretching a quarter of a mile ahead is grateful for advance warning. Figure 36 contrasts the signals to be expected under COLREGS with those required on inland waters.

A seaman's lot is happier than it once was. Taking the place of the "Cat-o-Nine-Tails" and holystone on Sundays are videocassettes and microwave ovens. But this Draconian chapter we've just survived threatens a reversion to more melancholy days. Page after page has addled us with lights and day shapes for vessels moving through the water and over the water as well as pulling and shoving others along the way. Such cruelty would have brought Billy Budd to the noose long before his time. We deserve a more clement fate. The Sailing Board has been posted and we've been granted a sufficient lull from duty to collect our scattered wits. "But there must be a catch," says the Old Salt. "No Bully Mate worth loathing would ever be so considerate." And of course he's correct. Before going off watch we must dispense with the the matter of a chapter quiz.

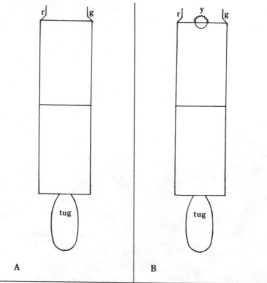

Fig. 36. Vessels Pushed Ahead. Although both sets of rules allow a group to carry only one set of sidelights, the Inland Rules add a flashing yellow identity light forward (lights on tugs are not shown). (A) COLREGS only; (B) Inland only.

QUESTIONS

It is alleged that this chapter includes cruel and inhuman drills on lights and shapes, so a Board of Inquiry will deal with the issue. Members are Capts. Frank Queeg, Edward Teach, and Wolf Larsen. All are noteworthy for their familiarity with crew complaints as well as their views on the efficacy of harsh discipline. A taste of the cat or a keelhaul, to them, is not at all outrageous.

To these masters of taut ships, any taint of kindliness is more than felonious. If we pass this quiz they have concocted they will laud the chapter for its savagery. But should we blunder, the penalty is that future studies be much more severe. To avoid a scholastic reign of terror we must prove the allegations of inhumanity by passing this test!

1. A power-driven vessel 25 meters long and underway
   a. shall display separate sidelights at night
   b. shall display a sternlight at noon in a thick fog
   c. both of the above
   d. none of the above

2. At night you observe a flashing yellow light and, lower down, a fixed white light. This would indicate
   a. an air-cushion vessel in the nondisplacement mode
   b. a stern view of a vessel towing astern
   c. both of the above
   d. none of the above

3. The minimum range for sidelights is
   a. 3 miles on vessels 50 meters or more long
   b. 2 miles on vessels 12 meters but less than 50 meters long
   c. 1 mile on vessels less than 12 meters long
   d. all of the above

4. A power-driven vessel less than 12 meters long may carry an all-round white light in lieu of a masthead light and a sternlight
   a. on the high seas
   b. on inland waters
   c. both of the above
   d. none of the above

5. A single vessel is being pushed ahead in inland waters.
   a. She would display a black diamond shape by day.
   b. She would display sidelights and a special flashing light at night.
   c. both of the above
   d. none of the above

6. A black diamond day shape would be displayed by
   a. a power-driven tug with a tow astern more than 200 meters long
   b. a vessel in tow astern when the length of the tow exceeds 200 meters
   c. an inconspicuous, partly submerged vessel or object in tow astern
   d. any of the above

7. At night you observe three white lights uniformly spaced in a vertical line.
   a. This would indicate a power-driven vessel towing astern.
   b. The stern view of that vessel would be a single white light.
   c. both of the above
   d. none of the above

8. A 15-meter-long power-driven vessel has lost her propeller and is taken in tow astern of a 25-meter sail vessel.
   a. The power-driven vessel could show a forward masthead light, a stern-light, and a combined red-and-green lantern for sidelights.
   b. The sail vessel would, in addition to her normal running lights, show three white lights in a vertical line.
   c. both of the above
   d. none of the above

9. On a power-driven vessel 10 meters long operating on inland waters, a combined red-and-green sidelight lantern
   a. may be offset from the fore-and-aft centerline
   b. must be in a vertical line with a masthead light or all-round white light shown in lieu of a masthead light and a sternlight
   c. both of the above
   d. none of the above

10. A 15-meter-long power-driven vessel is being towed astern of a power-driven commercial tug. She may carry
   a. a combined red-and-green lantern for sidelights
   b. an all-round white light in lieu of her masthead and sternlight
   c. both of the above
   d. none of the above

AND ANSWERS

As our ghastly tribunal deliberates we hear the click of ball bearings in Queeg's clenched fist. Wolf Larsen idly scars the bench of justice with his wicked-looking knife while he watches Teach plait the strands of a coal-black beard. What quarter can we expect from a paranoid, a bully, and a bloodthirsty fiend? Each correct response means 10 points toward appeasement of their wrath. Use the following table to learn whether more cruelty lies ahead.

90–100	rogues of distinction salute you!
80	a promising blackguard
70	soft on benevolence but still corruptible
under 70	incorrigibly humane

1. c   2. a   3. d   4. c   5. b   6. d   7. a   8. d   9. a   10. a

7

Part C—MORE ON LIGHTS AND SHAPES

THIS CHAPTER will complete our survey of lights and shapes. Measured by our experience in Chapter 6, what looms ahead might seem overly ambitious. Behind us are dozens of pages spent on only five rules from Part C and dead ahead are seven more. In fact, though, the tedium is past. We've invested time to establish "whys" and "wherefores" of signal patterns. Now we can savor the dividends by a faster passage through what remains of Part C.

The lights and shapes already met have been associated with power-driven vessels and those dependent on them for propulsion. But there remain two other means of moving over the waves. One is literally to be self-propelled by oars; the other relies on sails to commandeer movement from the wind. Rule 25 lists aspect and identity signals for these vessels.

RULE 25—Sailing Vessels Underway and Vessels Under Oars

COLREGS

(a) A sailing vessel underway shall exhibit:

  (i) sidelights;

  (ii) a sternlight.

(b) In a sailing vessel of less than 20 meters in length the lights prescribed in paragraph (a) of this Rule may be combined in one lantern carried at or near the top of the mast where it can best be seen.

(c) A sailing vessel underway may, in addition to the lights prescribed in paragraph (a) of this Rule, exhibit at or near the top of the mast, where they can best be seen, two all-round lights in a vertical line, the upper being red and the lower green, but these lights shall not be exhibited in conjunction with the combined lantern permitted by paragraph (b) of this Rule.

(d)(i) A sailing vessel of less than 7 meters in length shall, if practicable, exhibit the lights prescribed in paragraph (a) or (b) of this Rule, but if she does not, she shall have ready at hand an electric torch or lighted lantern showing a white light which shall be exhibited in sufficient time to prevent collision.

  (ii) A vessel under oars may exhibit the lights prescribed in this Rule for sailing vessels, but if she does not, she shall have ready at hand an electric torch or lighted lantern showing a white light which shall be exhibited in sufficient time to prevent collision.

(e) A vessel proceeding under sail when also being propelled by

155

machinery shall exhibit forward where it can best be seen a
conical shape, apex downwards.

INLAND

(a) A sailing vessel underway shall exhibit:
   (i) sidelights; and
   (ii) a sternlight.

(b) In a sailing vessel of less than 20 meters in length the lights
prescribed in paragraph (a) of this Rule may be combined in one
lantern carried at or near the top of the mast where it can best be
seen.

(c) A sailing vessel underway may, in addition to the lights
prescribed in paragraph (a) of this Rule, exhibit at or near the top
of the mast, where they can best be seen, two all-round lights in a
vertical line, the upper being red and the lower green, but these
lights shall not be exhibited in conjunction with the combined
lantern permitted by paragraph (b) of this Rule.

(d)(i) A sailing vessel of less than 7 meters in length shall, if
practicable, exhibit the lights prescribed in paragraph (a) or (b) of
this Rule, but if she does not, she shall have ready at hand an
electric torch or lighted lantern showing a white light which shall
be exhibited in sufficient time to prevent collision.

(ii) A vessel under oars may exhibit the lights prescribed in
this Rule for sailing vessels, but if she does not, she shall have
ready at hand an electric torch or lighted lantern showing a white
light which shall be exhibited in sufficient time to prevent
collision.

(e) A vessel proceeding under sail when also being propelled by
machinery shall exhibit forward where it can best be seen a
conical shape, apex downward. A vessel of less than 12 meters in
length is not required to exhibit this shape, but may do so.

Being eager to absorb the content of this rule we might be tempted to dash
pell-mell into the middle of it. On the other hand, being prudent seamen we
should first review some definitions of sailing vessels and of what is meant by
"under oars." Rule 3(c) circumspectly tells us that a sailing vessel is under sail.
She may have an engine, says that rule, but it cannot be in operation. Should
it be running, then Rule 3(b) would catalog the vessel as power-driven. In
separating sail from power the measure is not which mode is primary. Rather
it is whether, to any degree, sail is aided by an engine. If a vessel moving at
7 knots derives 6 of them from sail and only 1 of them from an engine, she
is just as much power-driven as would be a nuclear-powered submarine. A
pinch of power added to a pound of sail means exclusion from the perquisites
and duties of "ragmen."

Not nearly so definite is the line between sail and under oars. Nowhere do
the rules set out exactly what is meant by "a vessel under oars." At one extreme
is Hiawatha paddling a birchbark canoe upstream. At the other are banks of
galley slaves rowing their lives away in heavy triremes. Apparently, though,
oars are more compatible with sail than are clanking valves and gears. No
matter that leather-wrapped sweeps should toil between thole pins while sails

billow aloft. So long as no engine is working the vessel would probably be classed as sailing. Perhaps the most logical distinctions are these: oars alone mean *under oars;* oars and sail or sail alone mean *under sail;* oars, sail, and power, or sail and power, or power alone mean *under power.* Our earlier study of roles and scripts assigned by comparative maneuverability is now in point. The use of an engine adds the extra dimension of extraordinary maneuverability freed from the elements and from the constraints of human endurance. And now, having demonstrated a laudable degree of seamanlike prudence, we can start to work on the requirements of Rule 25.

A vessel under oars in the Central Pacific. [Courtesy NOAA]

All but small sailing vessels less than 7 meters long must carry sidelights and a sternlight, as specified in Rule 21, to show aspect. For vessels 20 meters and more in length the sidelights must be separate and the sternlight must be all by itself facing astern. But when the length drops below 20 meters, then all three aspect signals may be combined in one lantern placed at or near the top of the mast. The result is that sailing vessels underway at night have quite a variety of aspect displays available to them. Figure 37 shows a series of down-views of what might be encountered, and here is a discussion of each panel. Figure 37A depicts what sail vessels 20 meters or more long must show on both the high seas and inland waters. Separate sidelights must be placed outboard and a regulation sternlight must be placed as nearly as practicable at the stern.

Figures 37B and 37C present options offered smaller vessels. By both sets of rules a vessel less than 20 meters long may combine the separate sidelights into a single two-colored lantern, an option granted by Rule 21 to all ships that small. And as we've seen, that two-colored lantern may be offset from the centerline when the vessel is less than 12 meters long. But when a red-green lantern is used, a separate sidelight must be fitted. Small ships, though, are granted another accommodation. As shown in Figure 37D, those sailing and

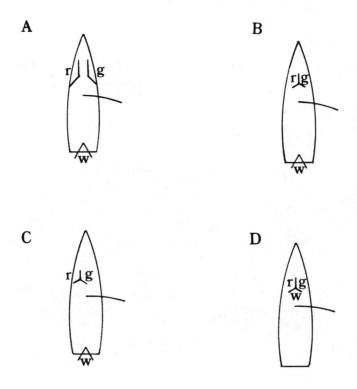

Fig. 37. Sailing Vessels. (A) 20 meters or more long (COLREGS and Inland); *(B) between 12 and 20 meters long* (COLREGS and Inland); *(C) under 12 meters long with sidelight lantern offset* (Inland only); *(D) under 20 meters long with tricolored lantern at or near the top of the mast* (COLREGS and Inland).

less than 20 meters long may use a tricolored red-green-white lantern to combine the entire circle of aspect signals. And that "one for all" display is to be placed at or near the top of the mast.

At night the billowing sail would mask a sidelight and prove the value of an identity pattern at the masthead. [Photo courtesy Miller Freeman Publications]

Rule 25(c), both COLREGS and Inland, creates an identity signal for those under sail. All-round red over all-round green placed at or near the top of the mast tells the nighttime world that a sailing vessel is in sight. The signal is optional, but there is a time when it cannot be shown. Placement, says the rule, is at or near the top of the mast. But that is where the rule specified that the tricolored lantern combining sidelights and sternlight be carried. Were a ship allowed to combine both of these patterns she could well be top-heavy with a cluster of reds, greens, and white at or near the top of the mast. So Rule 25(c) voices a logical prohibition. When a smaller vessel elects to combine all the aspect signals into one lantern of red-green-white, she cannot at the same time identify herself as under sail with red-over-green. Figure 38 shows, in several panels, the combinations of aspect and identity signals for sailing vessels.

Rule 25(d)(i) recognizes the practical problems of very small vessels under sail. Rigging a number of different colored lights on a vessel not much longer than a station wagon might be difficult. And when she heels in the wind the light patterns would range from confusing to meaningless. The Rules order her to try her best to show aspect lights, but if the task is impracticable she may limit her array to a bare minimum. All she need display is a white light in time to prevent collision. And whether an electric torch or a lighted lantern, it need not be fixed in position. Rather, it can be something like a battery-powered lantern flashed toward an approaching vessel.

The next paragraph, Rule 25(d)(ii), extends consideration to a vessel under oars. Regardless of length, she is allowed to show no more than a white light

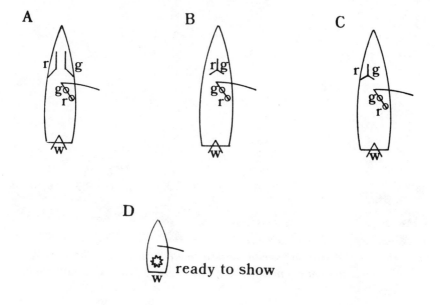

Fig. 38. Sailing Vessel Options. (A) 20 meters or more long showing identity lights (COLREGS and Inland); (B) between 12 and 20 meters long showing identity lights (COLREGS and Inland); (C) under 12 meters long with sidelight lantern offset and showing identity lights (Inland only); (D) under 7 meters long (COLREGS and Inland).

in time to prevent collision. Cleopatra's navigators would have recognized that signal. As they guided the famous femme fatale over the Ionian Sea to witness Marc Antony's defeat at the Battle of Actium they may have used such a basic

display on her Egyptian galley, the *Antonia.* Modern COLREGS and Inland
go a step further and allow a vessel under oars to show, if she desires, the lights
of a sailing vessel. History offers no hint of what might have passed for
COLREGS in 31 B.C., but colorful Cleopatra would hardly have been satisfied
with a simple white light. To decorate her multibanked warship with sidelights
would have been more her style. And if she had thought of it, a red-over-green
display at the masthead would have been irresistible. The drab facts, though,
are probably that a night view of Cleopatra's barge was in black-and-white
rather than technicolor. What is left to the reader is the judgment as to whether
or not this next statement adds to his knowledge of the Rules. Having in mind
the modern concepts of roll-on/roll-off container ships and the LASH type
we've already met, a student mused whether the *Antonia* was the first "Ro-Ro"
or perhaps nothing more than an early LASH. It is a sufficient point for us
that by modern rules Cleopatra would have had an option.

No option is given by Rule 25(e). This unequivocal command requires a
vessel under both sail and power to advertise her true condition. She is power-
driven and by night she must show the lights of the power-driven rather than
those for sail. Sidelights and a sternlight must be topped with at least one
masthead light to identify her means of propulsion. In the daytime, though,
the presence of her sails could be misleading. Others might view her as under
sail rather than under power and entitled to the deference reserved for the
purely wind-driven. On the high seas such subterfuge is forbidden all vessels
of dual propulsion. By day they must hang a black cone forward, point down,
as shown in Fig. 39. Inland rules are a bit more realistic, for although black
cones have been required on the high seas for generations, the demand has
usually been ignored. Inland recognizes such mutinous conduct and copes with
it by lessening the number of potential miscreants. On our waters vessels under

Fig. 39. *Under Power and Sail. A sailing vessel with her auxiliary engine in
operation by day must identify herself as power-driven.*

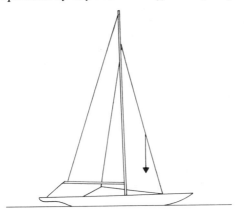

12 meters long are protected from guilt feelings by being exempt from showing the day shape. Even so, the widespread violation of Rule 25(e) is not prudent. There are two general categories of civil penalties for not heeding the commands of the Rules of the Road. One, hardly attractive to underwriters, is being held liable for damages in a collision. The other is a monetary fine, and the value Inland places on each violation is up to $5000. So far, enforcement does not seem to be energetic; but with such a high price tag this part of the rules can catch the eye of the enforcers as well as enforcees. Rule 25(e) uses the word "shall," and t'at means "ya gotta." Occasionally one reads of the unfortunate merchant who finds himself overstocked on spats, buttonhooks, or some other item in little demand. Perhaps he might be someone who has cornered the market on black cones to sell to vessels under power and sail. Should officialdom decide that this rule must be obeyed, the merchant whose warehouse bulges with black cones worth up to $5000 apiece might yet be hailed as very shrewd.

Time now for another appearance of vessels engaged in fishing. Rule 26 will require close study, but first we should meet its exact terms which, incidentally, are the same in Inland as in COLREGS.

RULE 26—Fishing Vessels

COLREGS

(a) A vessel engaged in fishing, whether underway or at anchor, shall exhibit only the lights and shapes prescribed in this Rule.

(b) A vessel when engaged in trawling, by which is meant the dragging through the water of a dredge net or other apparatus used as a fishing appliance, shall exhibit:

(i) two all-round lights in a vertical line, the upper being green and the lower white, or a shape consisting of two cones with their apexes together in a vertical line one above the other; a vessel of less than 20 meters in length may instead of this shape exhibit a basket;

(ii) a masthead light abaft of and higher than the all-round green light; a vessel of less than 50 meters in length shall not be obliged to exhibit such a light but may do so;

(iii) when making way through the water, in addition to the lights prescribed in this paragraph, sidelights and a sternlight.

(c) A vessel engaged in fishing, other than trawling, shall exhibit:

(i) two all-round lights in a vertical line, the upper being red and the lower white, or a shape consisting of two cones with apexes together in a vertical line one above the other; a vessel of less than 20 meters in length may instead of this shape exhibit a basket;

(ii) when there is outlying gear extending more than 150 meters horizontally from the vessel, an all-round white light or a cone apex upwards in the direction of the gear;

(iii) when making way through the water, in addition to the lights prescribed in this paragraph, sidelights and a sternlight.

(d) A vessel engaged in fishing in close proximity to other vessels engaged in fishing may exhibit the additional signals described in Annex II to these Regulations.

(e) A vessel when not engaged in fishing shall not exhibit the lights or shapes prescribed in this Rule, but only those prescribed for a vessel of her length.

INLAND

(a) A vessel engaged in fishing, whether underway or at anchor, shall exhibit only the lights and shapes prescribed in this Rule.

(b) A vessel when engaged in trawling, by which is meant the dragging through the water of a dredge net or other apparatus used as a fishing appliance, shall exhibit:

(i) two all-round lights in a vertical line, the upper being green and the lower white, or a shape consisting of two cones with their apexes together in a vertical line one above the other; a vessel of less than 20 meters in length may instead of this shape exhibit a basket;

(ii) a masthead light abaft of and higher than the all-round green light; a vessel of less than 50 meters in length shall not be obliged to exhibit such a light but may do so; and

(iii) when making way through the water, in addition to the lights prescribed in this paragraph, sidelights and a sternlight.

(c) A vessel engaged in fishing, other than trawling, shall exhibit:

(i) two all-round lights in a vertical line, the upper being red and the lower white, or a shape consisting of two cones with apexes together in a vertical line one above the other; a vessel of less than 20 meters in length may instead of this shape exhibit a basket;

(ii) when there is outlying gear extending more than 150 meters horizontally from the vessel, an all-round white light or a cone apex upward in the direction of the gear; and

(iii) when making way through the water, in addition to the lights prescribed in this paragraph, sidelights and a sternlight.

(d) A vessel engaged in fishing in close proximity to other vessels engaged in fishing may exhibit the additional signals described in Annex II to these Rules.

(e) A vessel when not engaged in fishing shall not exhibit the lights or shapes prescribed in this Rule, but only those prescribed for a vessel of her length.

First of all we must recognize that although the title of this rule says "Fishing Vessels," its first paragraph correctly identifies the application as only to "vessels engaged in fishing." Long ago we learned that Rule 3(d) made an important distinction: not every fishing vessel is to be considered "engaged in fishing." Even though we've been through this before, a repetition is valuable. A waterborne Izaak Walton must only advertise his activity when the fishing gear employed restricts his maneuverability. No matter how successful his catching of fish, his operation constitutes no maritime danger worth noting until his appliances interfere with his vessel's ability to play its role in the codes of conduct. So a troller is expressly considered unaffected by the hooks and lines streaming astern. But when fishing apparatus make inroads on normal agility, the plight must be signaled. Rule 26 states how that is done by day and by night, and its introductory paragraph sets the tone. Vessels engaged in fishing at anchor as well as underway make no other signals than those prescribed here. So off go all lights and down come all shapes. We start with neither aspect nor condition signals and will hang up only what this rule specifies.

A trawler at work with her day shape hanging from the yardarm. [USCG photo]

In setting out its requirements Rule 26 first divides fishing impedimenta into two groups: that used by a trawler and that used by a nontrawler. Those of us not involved in fishing had better make sure we know what all this means. A trawler bags its quarry by dragging some sort of apparatus astern to scoop up fish. The gear used by a nontrawler, whether astern, ahead, or spread out on either side, is more like a trap into which the fish swim on their own. An example is a purse seine. It is a large bag with purse strings to seal it tight around the catch.

Annex II, with which we'll soon have a fleeting affair, speaks further about trawlers and intrigues us by mentioning the terms "demersal" and "pelagic," ominous words which sound like dreadful diseases. In its *Glossary of Oceanographic Terms* (Special Publication 35, 1966), the Naval Oceanographic Office labels *demersal* as referring to "fishes which live on or near the bottom." This seems to square with a trawl skimming over the seabed in search of a catch. But *pelagic* is more resistant to easy definition. In general it refers to a division of the sea beyond the region of tidal action. The malady worsens with such complications as *neritic* and, most vile of all, *epipelagic*. The first term deals with the block of water above a continental shelf; the other is said to refer to the upper portion of an ocean, extending from the surface to a depth of about 100 fathoms. Happily, since neither term seems hazardous to health, we can stow away the medicine chest. And for our less-than-expert needs we can view a demersal trawl as one designed to take deep-living fish and pelagic gear as that designed to collar those swimming closer to the surface, whether in a neritic or epipelagic province of an ocean.

Regardless of the depth of the gear, the nighttime trawler must show an identity signal of an all-round green light over an all-round white light. From any aspect, green-over-white means trawling at night. Since the trawl will nearly always be astern of the ship, provision is made for indicating its direction. When the trawler is 50 meters or more in length she must show a masthead light abaft of and higher than the green-over-white array. Smaller vessels may display this added light if they wish, but they need not. The required day shape for trawlers 20 meters and more long consists of two black cones point to point. Smaller ships are given the alternative of a basket.

What, though, about aspect or directional signals? Rule 26 decrees that no such are shown until the vessel has a direction to indicate. By Rule 26(b)(iii) a trawler actually moving through the water adds sidelights and a sternlight. The panels of Fig. 40 depict the day and night signals for trawlers underway, underway and making way, and at anchor. We less-than-expert fishermen need raise no eyebrows at the prospect of a vessel trawling at anchor. Not hampered by technical knowledge, we can blithely assume that trawling at anchor is a common occurrence. In any case the point is that a trawler at work never shows an anchor signal by day or night. Nor would she, when power-driven, show a forward masthead light. The white light in her green-over-white combination is all-round, and is not a masthead light. And the after masthead light required of larger trawlers is not the mark of a power-driven vessel. Since its purpose is to point out the general direction of the trawl, it is required of large sailing trawlers as well as those propelled by machinery.

Rule 26(c) speaks to nontrawlers underway or at anchor. They identify themselves by day with the same signal as do trawlers: two black cones point-to-point, or if under 20 meters long, a basket. But the night identity requirement is different. Nontrawlers mark themselves by an all-round red light over an all-round white light. So red over white is nontrawling at night. At anchor, neither anchor lights nor day shape are shown; when underway and moving they add sidelights and a sternlight. These vessels have no occasion to exhibit an after masthead light, for the nontrawling gear might not be stretched out astern. It could be on the beam or it might be streamed out ahead.

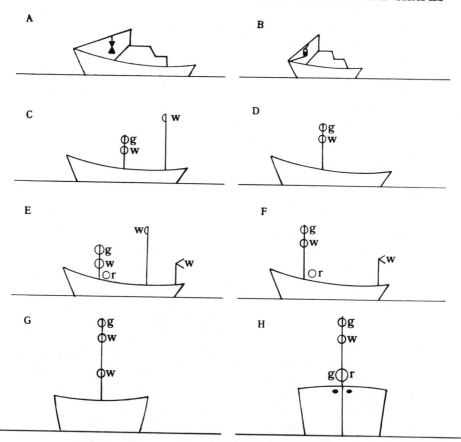

Fig. 40. *Trawler Lights and Shapes. (A) Port profile of vessel 20 meters or more long trawling by day while underway or at anchor (COLREGS and Inland); (B) port profile of vessel under 20 meters long trawling by day while underway or at anchor (COLREGS and Inland); (C) port profile of vessel of any propulsion 50 meters or more long, trawling while underway but stopped or at anchor (COLREGS and Inland); (D) any aspect of vessel of any propulsion under 50 meters long, trawling underway but stopped or at anchor (COLREGS and Inland); (E) port profile of vessel of any propulsion 50 meters or more long, trawling while underway and making way (COLREGS and Inland); (F) port profile of vessel of any propulsion under 50 meters long, trawling while underway and making way (COLREGS and Inland); (G) stern view of vessel of any propulsion and any length, trawling while underway and making way (COLREGS and Inland); (H) bow view of vessel of any propulsion under 20 meters long, trawling while underway and making way (COLREGS and Inland).*

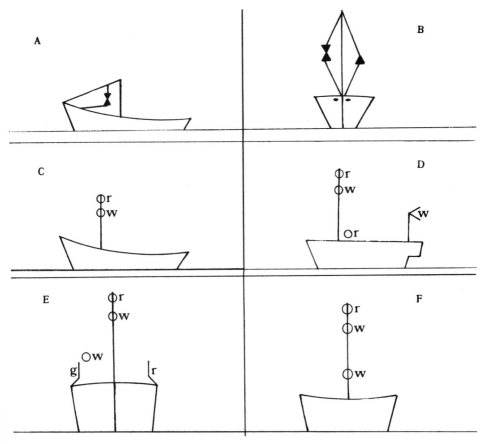

Fig. 41. *Fishing Vessels (Other Than Trawlers) Lights and Shapes. (A) Port profile of vessel 20 meters or more long engaged in fishing by day with gear not over 150 meters outboard while underway or at anchor (same as trawler)* (COLREGS and Inland); *(B) bow view of vessel 20 meters or more long engaged in fishing (except trawling) by day with gear extending more than 150 meters while underway or at anchor* (COL-REGS and Inland); *(C) any view of vessel of any length or propulsion engaged in fishing (except trawling) while underway but stopped or at anchor* (COLREGS and Inland); *(D) port view of vessel of any length or propulsion engaged in fishing (except trawling) while making way* (COLREGS and Inland); *(E) bow view of vessel 20 meters or more long of any propulsion engaged in fishing (except trawling) with gear extending over 150 meters while making way; (F) stern view of vessel of any length and propulsion engaged in fishing (except trawling) while making way,* or *any view if at anchor or not making way with gear out more than 150 meters* (COLREGS and Inland).

But Rule 26(c)(ii) provides a warning when the gear, no matter where it lies, extends a good distance out from the fishing vessel. If the gear reaches more than 150 meters out, then the ship must tell the world of its presence by displaying an all-round white light in the direction of the equipment. By day she displays a black cone point up in place of the white light. We must emphasize that Rule 26 has no concern for the means of propulsion in use. No power-driven vessel engaged in fishing by any means will ever identify herself as power-driven by displaying a masthead light; no sail vessel so engaged will tell the world she is under sail by the display of red-over-green at the top of the mast. It is more important, says this rule, to declare that the appliances she employs interfere with her ability to live up to the code of conduct normally required. Figure 41 depicts views of nontrawling vessels engaged in fishing. Rule 26(e) restores her to the company of Rules of the Road regulars when she is not engaged in fishing. She is then considered freed from her restrictions and thus capable of performing the demands customarily made of one of her propulsion and length. So off go the Rule 26 displays and on go those specified by other rules for normal power-driven, sail, or "under oars."

Saved for last in our study of signals by vessels engaged in fishing is Rule 26(d). There we are formally introduced to Annex II and its recognition of problems unique to such vessels. The upshot is a pattern of lights, so we should take a closer look. Here is the text of the annex, with the same details in Inland as those in COLREGS.

ANNEX II—ADDITIONAL SIGNALS FOR FISHING VESSELS FISHING IN CLOSE PROXIMITY

COLREGS

1. General

The lights mentioned herein shall, if exhibited in pursuance of Rule 26(d), be placed where they can best be seen. They shall be at least 0.9 meter apart but at a lower level than lights prescribed in Rule 26(b)(i) and (c)(i). The lights shall be visible all around the horizon at a distance of at least 1 mile but at a lesser distance from the lights prescribed by these Rules for fishing vessels.

2. Signals for trawlers

(a) Vessels when engaged in trawling, whether using demersal or pelagic gear, may exhibit:

(i) when shooting their nets: two white lights in a vertical line;

(ii) when hauling their nets: one white light over one red light in a vertical line;

(iii) when the net has come fast upon an obstruction: two red lights in a vertical line.

(b) Each vessel engaged in pair trawling may exhibit:

(i) by night, a searchlight directed forward and in the direction of the other vessel of the pair;

(ii) when shooting or hauling their nets or when their nets have come fast upon an obstruction, the lights prescribed in 2(a) above.

3. Signals for purse seiners

Vessels engaged in fishing with purse seine gear may exhibit two yellow lights in a vertical line. These lights shall flash alternately every second and with equal light and occultation duration. These lights may be exhibited only when the vessel is hampered by its fishing gear.

INLAND

§ 85.1. General

The lights mentioned herein shall, if exhibited in pursuance of Rule 26(d), be placed where they can best be seen. They shall be at least 0.9 meter apart but at a lower level than lights prescribed in Rule 26(b)(i) and (c)(i) contained in the Inland Navigational Rules Act of 1980. The lights shall be visible all around the horizon at a distance of at least 1 mile but at a lesser distance from the lights prescribed by these Rules for fishing vessels.

§ 85.3 Signals for trawlers

(a) Vessels when engaged in trawling, whether using demersal or pelagic gear, may exhibit:

(1) When shooting their nets: two white lights in a vertical line;

(2) When hauling their nets: one white light over one red light in a vertical line;

(3) When the net has come fast upon an obstruction: two red lights in a vertical line.

(b) Each vessel engaged in pair trawling may exhibit:

(1) By night, a searchlight directed forward and in the direction of the other vessel of the pair;

(2) When shooting or hauling their nets or when their nets have come fast upon an obstruction, the lights prescribed in paragraph (a) above.

§ 85.5 Signals for purse seiners

Vessels engaged in fishing with purse seine gear may exhibit two yellow lights in a vertical line. These lights shall flash alternately every second and with equal light and occultation duration. These lights may be exhibited only when the vessel is hampered by its fishing gear.

It is probable that most nonfishing vessels will never observe any of these signals. In fact there is no intention that these lights be displayed for the benefit of anyone except other nearby vessels engaged in fishing. Yet there would be a gap in our survey of the Rules of the Road if we were to sail past these patterns without at least a fleeting look. The background for the inclusion of the annex is this. Some very productive fishing grounds attract fleets of vessels often flying a variety of flags and operated by particular ownership groups. The traffic jams on such banks are sometimes severe and very likely to be aggravated by intense competition for a catch. In an effort to regulate the milling around with resulting tangles of nets and lines, participants have agreed upon signals which would announce what a particular ship might be doing. The concern was sufficiently deep that international treaties were concluded between the governments involved. However, there was no standardization of the

signal patterns, so Rule 26(d) introduces Annex II to do that job. The displays
are optional but presumably the prospect is that their value will encourage
their use. So now to a look at this annex.

*A modern king crab boat near another engaged in fishing. [Courtesy Halter
    Marine, Inc.]*

The statement in Section 1 regarding strength of the lights emphasizes that
the signals are intended for use within the fishing fleets. In every case they must
have less range than the lights prescribed by Rule 26. There are two basic sets.
The first, discussed in Section 2 of the annex, applies to trawlers; the other,
found in Section 3, refers to purse seiners. It is in the trawler section that we
encounter our newfound friends demersal and pelagic.

Whether dragging their gear deep or shallow, trawlers are invited to advertise three conditions which might affect the degree of their limited maneuverability. One is shooting nets. When engaged in that activity, they may add to
their required fishing signals two all-round white lights in a vertical line.
Another is when hauling nets, and then the signal which may be added is
all-round white over all-round red. The third and least desirable predicament
arises when the net has come fast upon an obstruction. The optional signal in
that case is all-round red over all-round red. Section 2(b) provides patterns for
trawlers working together in one sweeping operation. Annex II allows each
member of a *pair trawling team* to display the patterns for any of the three
conditions, as well as shining a searchlight forward and in the direction of the

teammate. Of what interest is any of this to the rest of the maritime world? Well, at least an explanation for some dazzling arrays. But before we veer off from trawlers we should heed the exasperated cry of the nontrawler: "What in the world is meant by shooting nets?" Navigators shoot the sun, daredevils shoot the rapids, and gamblers shoot craps. Is one of these activities akin to shooting nets? The answer is "yes." Crapshooting by aristocrats might be termed "casting the dice." Net shooting by trawlers is no more than casting nets.

Section 3 of Annex II allows a purse seiner to alert nearby vessels engaged in fishing that she is hampered by her gear. The display is only allowed if the fishing apparatus is troublesome, and when shown it must be in addition to the regular fishing signals required by Rule 26. The signal is a vertical line of two all-round yellow lights flashing alternately off and on.

To complete our inspection of the signals of vessels engaged in fishing, we see in Fig. 42 a selection of combinations required by Rule 26 and as they might optionally be enhanced by Annex II.

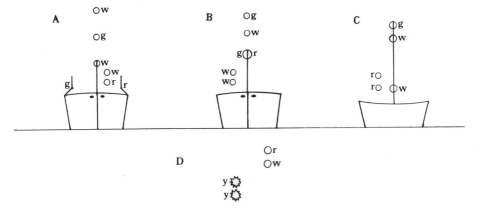

Fig. 42. *Optional Fishing Lights. (A) Bow view of trawler 50 meters or more long of any propulsion while making way and hauling nets with other vessels fishing nearby (COLREGS and Inland); (B) bow view of trawler under 20 meters long of any propulsion while making way and shooting nets with other vessels fishing nearby (COLREGS and Inland); (C) stern view of trawler of any length and propulsion while making way with nets fast to an obstruction and other vessels fishing nearby (COLREGS and Inland); (D) any view of purse seiner of any length and propulsion while underway but stopped or at anchor and hampered by gear with other vessels fishing nearby (COLREGS and Inland).*

Dead ahead on our track lies Rule 27, laden with subtleties and overtones. After glancing over the words we must attend to their shades of meaning.

RULE 27—Vessels Not Under Command or Restricted in Their Ability to Maneuver

COLREGS

(a) A vessel not under command shall exhibit:

(i) two all-round red lights in a vertical line where they can best be seen;

(ii) two balls or similar shapes in a vertical line where they can best be seen;

(iii) when making way through the water, in addition to the lights prescribed in this paragraph, sidelights and a sternlight.

(b) A vessel restricted in her ability to maneuver, except a vessel engaged in mineclearance operations, shall exhibit:

(i) three all-round lights in a vertical line where they can best be seen. The highest and lowest of these lights shall be red and the middle light shall be white;

(ii) three shapes in a vertical line where they can best be seen. The highest and lowest of these shapes shall be balls and the middle one a diamond;

(iii) when making way through the water, a masthead light or lights, sidelights and a sternlight, in addition to the lights prescribed in subparagraph (i);

(iv) when at anchor, in addition to the lights or shapes prescribed in subparagraphs (i) and (ii), the light, lights or shape prescribed in Rule 30.

(c) A power-driven vessel engaged in a towing operation such as severely restricts the towing vessel and her tow in their ability to deviate from their course shall, in addition to the lights or shapes prescribed in Rule 24(a), exhibit the lights or shapes prescribed in subparagraphs (b)(i) and (ii) of this Rule.

(d) A vessel engaged in dredging or underwater operations, when restricted in her ability to maneuver, shall exhibit the lights and shapes prescribed in subparagraphs (b)(i), (ii) and (iii) of this Rule and shall in addition, when an obstruction exists, exhibit:

(i) two all-round red lights or two balls in a vertical line to indicate the side on which the obstruction exists;

(ii) two all-round green lights or two diamonds in a vertical line to indicate the side on which another vessel may pass;

(iii) when at anchor, the lights or shapes prescribed in this paragraph instead of the lights or shape prescribed in Rule 30.

(e) Whenever the size of a vessel engaged in diving operations makes it impracticable to exhibit all lights and shapes prescribed in paragraph (d) of this Rule, the following shall be exhibited:

(i) three all-round lights in a vertical line where they can best be seen. The highest and lowest of these lights shall be red and the middle light shall be white;

(ii) a rigid replica of the International Code flag "A" not less than 1 meter in height. Measures shall be taken to ensure its all-round visibility.

(f) A vessel engaged in mineclearance operations shall in addition to the lights prescribed for a power-driven vessel in Rule 23 or to the lights or shape prescribed for a vessel at anchor in Rule 30 as appropriate, exhibit three all-round green lights or three balls. One of these lights or shapes shall be exhibited near the foremast head and one at each end of the fore yard. These lights or shapes indicate that it is dangerous for another vessel to approach within 1000 meters of the mineclearance vessel.

(g) Vessels of less than 12 meters in length, except those engaged in diving operations, shall not be required to exhibit the lights and shapes prescribed in this Rule.

(h) The signals prescribed in this Rule are not signals of vessels in distress and requiring assistance. Such signals are contained in Annex IV to these Regulations.

INLAND

(a) A vessel not under command shall exhibit:

(i) two all-round red lights in a vertical line where they can best be seen;

(ii) two balls or similar shapes in a vertical line where they can best be seen; and

(iii) when making way through the water, in addition to the lights prescribed in this paragraph, sidelights and a sternlight.

(b) A vessel restricted in her ability to maneuver, except a vessel engaged in minesweeping operations, shall exhibit:

(i) three all-round lights in a vertical line where they can best be seen. The highest and lowest of these lights shall be red and the middle light shall be white;

(ii) three shapes in a vertical line where they can best be seen. The highest and lowest of these shapes shall be balls and the middle one a diamond;

(iii) when making way through the water, masthead lights, sidelights and a sternlight, in addition to the lights prescribed in subparagraph (b)(i); and

(iv) when at anchor, in addition to the lights or shapes prescribed in subparagraphs (b)(i) and (ii), the light, lights or shapes prescribed in Rule 30.

(c) A vessel engaged in a towing operation which severely restricts the towing vessel and her tow in their ability to deviate from their course shall, in addition to the lights or shapes prescribed in subparagraphs (b)(i) and (ii) of this Rule, exhibit the lights or shape prescribed in Rule 24.

(d) A vessel engaged in dredging or underwater operations, when restricted in her ability to maneuver, shall exhibit the lights and shapes prescribed in subparagraphs (b)(i), (ii), and (iii) of this Rule and shall in addition, when an obstruction exists, exhibit:

(i) two all-round red lights or two balls in a vertical line to indicate the side on which the obstruction exists;

(ii) two all-round green lights or two diamonds in a vertical line to indicate the side on which another vessel may pass; and

(iii) when at anchor, the lights or shape prescribed by this paragraph, instead of the lights or shapes prescribed in Rule 30 for anchored vessels.

(e) Whenever the size of a vessel engaged in diving operations makes it impracticable to exhibit all lights and shapes prescribed in paragraph (d) of this Rule, the following shall instead be exhibited:

(i) Three all-round lights in a vertical line where they can best be seen. The highest and lowest of these lights shall be red and the middle light shall be white;

(ii) A rigid replica of the international Code flag "A" not less than 1 meter in height. Measures shall be taken to insure its all-round visibility.

(f) A vessel engaged in minesweeping operations shall, in addition to the lights prescribed for a power-driven vessel in Rule 23, exhibit three all-round green lights or three balls. One of these lights or shapes shall be exhibited near the foremast head and one at each end of the fore yard. These lights or shapes indicate that it is dangerous for another vessel to approach closer than 1,000 meters astern or 500 meters on either side of the minesweeper.

(g) A vessel of less than 12 meters in length, except when engaged in diving operations, is not required to exhibit the lights or shapes prescribed in this Rule.

(h) The signals prescribed in this Rule are not signals of vessels in distress and requiring assistance. Such signals are contained in Annex IV to these Rules.

It is hardly a surprise that definition time is here again. We must look back to Rule 3 for the meanings of the terms "not under command" and "vessel restricted in her ability to maneuver." As we were told in Chapter 2, the reason these vessels must identify themselves with special signals is that they are unable to keep out of the way of other shipping. They cannot follow a script which would ask them to play the role of keeping clear. Since the predicament might not be obvious to others, they must signal it in the manner required by Rule 27. A vessel not under command is one unable to keep clear because of some circumstance which is out of the ordinary. A vessel restricted in her ability to maneuver, on the other hand, is crippled on purpose. She is unable to keep out of the way because of the nature of her work. Perhaps the word "restricted" is not strong enough. The meaning should be taken as requiring more of an inability than a discomfit. Rule 3(g), as we've seen, lists six operations which meet the requirements. Those six are not intended to be the only six. If other "on purpose" causes of inability prevail, then the definition applies. The rule mentions these activities: working with a navigation mark, submarine cable, or pipeline; dredging, surveying, or engaging in underwater operations; replenishment or transfer of persons or cargo underway; launching or recovery of aircraft; minesweeping or clearance; towing astern while severely restricted in ability to change course.

On both the high seas and inland waters, a *vessel not under command* tells the world of her plight by showing two all-round red lights in a vertical line by night and two black balls in a vertical line by day. She is not in distress and she does not need any help. Her message is strictly that those around must not expect her to carry out her normal role and should be ready for some erratic behavior. Her exceptional condition overrides any need to announce whether she is power-driven or under sail, so neither the masthead light of power-driven nor the optional red-over-green for sail will be seen. In fact no other light patterns will appear unless she is actually moving through the water. Then, since she has a direction to indicate, Rule 27(a)(iii) requires that she show the directional signals of sidelights and a sternlight. It should be noted again that she does not turn on her masthead light or lights, or if sailing, her red-over-green lights. And the not-under-command condition is signaled only when a vessel is underway. When she is at anchor there is no need to tell the world about her accident. The Rules presume that since she already cannot keep out of the way by the ordinary circumstance of having an anchor or two down, any announcement of why she is otherwise unable to maneuver is irrelevant. Rule 27, unfortunately, is not explicit on this point; but the inference is clear when its words are set alongside Rule 30. Later on we'll see that the signal for a vessel aground seems to combine the not-under-command display with that for a vessel at anchor.

The following scenes from a maritime drama indicate what all this means. A vessel moving at 10 knots loses her rudder. Obviously she is now unable to keep clear of other ships, so by day she would hoist two black balls. Her nighttime signals would depend on some other circumstances. If she were power-driven and still moving through the water, she would douse her masthead light or lights, put up all-round red over all-round red, and keep on her sidelights and sternlight. If she were sail and still moving she would put out any identity lights, keep burning her sidelights and sternlight, and add the two red lights in a vertical line. In the next scene she has come to a stop in the water and is lying to. Now off would go the sidelights and sternlight, no matter what her propulsion. Only the two red lights would be visible. What next occurs is that she decides to drop the anchor while she awaits a tug. Down goes the anchor and with it down go the two red lights at night and the two black balls by day. Up, instead, would go anchor displays as specified in Rule 30. There is only one exception to this scenario, and we find it mentioned in Rule 27(g). Neither set of rules considers it necessary for vessels under 12 meters long to signal such traumatic occurrences, so they are exempt from the requirements for any not-under-command display. One picture is worth scores of lines of type, so we should now look at Fig. 43. There the not-under-command displays appear for various vessels by day and by night.

Not nearly so succinct is a review of the signals required of *vessels restricted in ability to maneuver* by the nature of their work. We must reduce speed while we take a close look at what COLREGS and Inland require of vessels from buoy tenders to aircraft carriers. The basic signal by night for all but one of the six types is a vertical line of red-white-red lights, and by day a vertical line of black ball–black diamond–black ball. (The one not included is a minesweeper, and we'll meet what is specified for her shortly.) Whatever her specific occupation, each of these ships means to transmit a very important message.

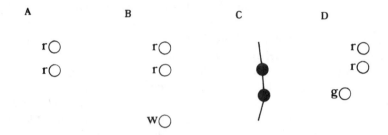

A   B   C   D

Fig. 43. Vessels Not Under Command. (A) Any view of vessel 12 meters or more long of any propulsion while underway but stopped and not under command (COLREGS and Inland); (B) stern view of vessel 12 meters or more long of any propulsion while underway and making way not under command (COLREGS and Inland); (C) day shapes for vessel 12 meters or more long of any propulsion while underway and not under command (COLREGS and Inland); (D) starboard profile of vessel 12 meters or more long of any propulsion while making way and not under command (COLREGS and Inland).

Antenna whiskers, radar domes, and a wedge-shaped structure aft mark the U.S.N.S. Observation Island as a vessel whose special mission can restrain her ability to maneuver. [USN photo]

She cannot keep out of the way by reason of her employment. The reaction of ships receiving that signal should in every case be to keep out of the way. None of these hobbled mariners needs assistance. Rather, each is warning all nearby seafarers that the ongoing operation could be dangerous to safe passage and is none of their business.

As with vessels not under command, those whose disability stems from their profession do not show directional signals until there is a direction to indicate. Then Rule 27(b)(iii) dictates that they add running lights. For power-driven vessels this means more than just sidelights and a sternlight. They must also turn on a masthead light display commensurate with their length. Moreover Rule 27(b)(iv) does not overlook signals for these ships when at anchor. In contrast to vessels not under command, they then combine anchor signals with those specified by Rule 27 for being restricted by the nature of the work.

Research vessel Atlantis II, *operated by Woods Hole Oceanographic Institution. [Courtesy National Geographic Society]*

Here would be the patterns of such a vessel passing through several conditions. A 60-meter power-driven vessel equipped for hydrographic surveying is moving at 15 knots through the water at night. A surveyor is polishing the lens in his theodolite, but has not yet aimed it at any reference mark. The light signals would be masthead lights, separate sidelights, and a sternlight. The surveyor completes his preparations and squints through the instrument. The vessel is now engaged in hydrographic surveying, so the bridge personnel must make a change in signals. The full kit of running lights remains on, but the vertical display of red-white-red would be added. In order to be more certain of his bearings, the surveyor requests that the ship be stopped, and when she lies dead in the water a signal light change must be made. Red-white-red remains on, but all the running lights are extinguished. Next he decides that his observations would best be made at anchor, so the windlass brake is released and out rumbles the port anchor and a good scope of chain. As for signals, now the anchor lights would be turned on as well as the vertical line of red-white-red. The sequence shown in Fig. 44 would also be required for

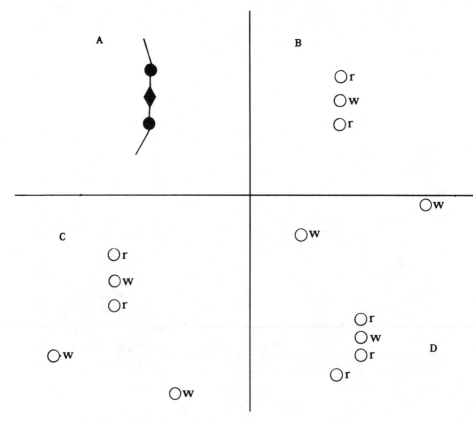

Fig. 44. *Vessels Restricted in Ability to Maneuver. (A) Day shapes of vessel 12 meters or more long while underway and restricted in ability to maneuver* (COLREGS and Inland); *(B) any view of vessel 12 meters or more long while underway but stopped and restricted in ability to maneuver or a small diving tender* (COLREGS and Inland); *(C) port profile of vessel 50 meters or more long while at anchor and restricted in ability to maneuver* (COLREGS and Inland); *(D) port profile of vessel 50 meters or more long while making way and restricted in ability to maneuver* (COLREGS and Inland).

such ships as buoy tenders, cable ships, diving tenders, aircraft carriers, and many dredges.

Now, though, we must touch on some of the complications of this rule. When a tug and barge are so hamstrung by the operation that they cannot readily change course, both sets of collision rules would consider them unable to keep clear by the nature of their work. So they must signal two messages. The displays of Rule 24 will tell the world about the towing operation, and

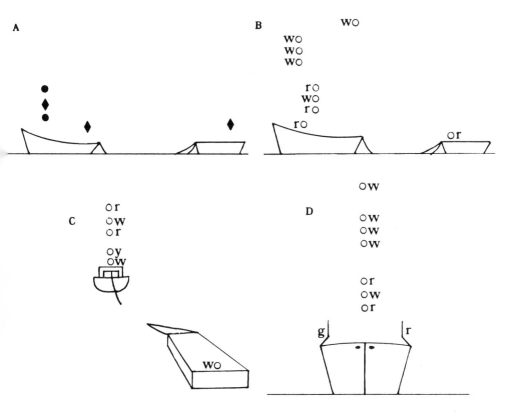

Fig. 45. *Tug and Tow Restricted in Ability to Maneuver. (A) Day shapes of tug with tow over 200 meters astern while severely restricted in ability to change course (COLREGS and Inland); (B) port profile of tug 50 meters or more long with tow over 200 meters astern while severely restricted in ability to change course (COLREGS and Inland); (C) stern view of tug and tow of any length astern while severely restricted in ability to change course (COLREGS and Inland); (D) bow view of tug 50 meters or more long with tow over 200 meters astern while severely restricted in ability to change course (COLREGS and Inland).*

An offshore oil drilling platform at work on the waters of Southern California.
[Courtesy Western Offshore]

the basic signals of Rule 27 must be added to advise that the nature of their
work leaves them with a greatly diminished ability to change course. Figure
45 depicts the resulting patterns for large and small tugs with long and short
tows.

When a vessel is engaged in dredging or in an underwater operation, the
concern of other shipping can be more than that the restricted ship is not able
to keep out of the way. All sorts of gear might stream out from the mother
ship and oncomers should be advised which is the clear side and which side
is cluttered. Rule 27(d) addresses the problem and comes up with this solution.
When such an obstruction exists, the cluttered side is marked by two red lights
in a vertical line at night and by two black balls in a vertical line by day. Nearby
shipping can recognize the clear side as that marked by a vertical line of two
green lights at night and two black diamonds in the daytime. When so obstructed and making way through the water she advertises direction by her
normal full running light display. That means, if she is power-driven, a masthead light or two with sidelights and a sternlight. Should she be in tow or under
sail, though, no masthead light should be expected to appear.

A realist might impatiently object to the nit just picked. As the year 2000 approaches, sailing dredges are if not extinct at least an endangered species. Even the Corps of Engineers of such a backward society as Lower Slobbovia would be unlikely to operate a sailing dredge. No matter where deployed, wouldn't a modern dredge be under power? The answer, surprisingly, is "not necessarily." Barges fitted out for dredging are still in use. In fact a lately demised Pilot Rule applicable through 1981 provided expressly for a non-self-propelled suction dredge being pushed ahead while dredging. It would be presently unwarranted to expect that such a dredge barge would show mast-

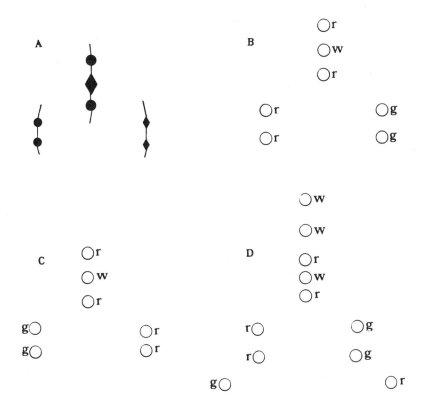

Fig. 46. Underwater Operations. (A) Day shapes of dredge or vessel engaged in an underwater operation while underway or at anchor with an obstruction to the observer's left (COLREGS and Inland); (B) stern view of dredge or vessel engaged in an underwater operation while making way with an obstruction to her starboard (COLREGS and Inland); (C) bow view of dredge or vessel engaged in an underwater operation while underway but stopped or at anchor with an obstruction to the observer's right (COLREGS and Inland); (D) bow view of dredge or vessel 50 meters or more long engaged in an underwater operation while making way with an obstruction to her starboard.

head lights when in motion. Even more noteworthy is another point. Rule 27(d) is not just limited to dredges. It refers to "A vessel engaged in dredging or underwater operations. . . ." That includes a vessel tending a diver; and even in advanced societies divers on occasion descend from auxiliary sail vessels whose engines are not engaged. Granted, we are sorting through technicalities, but at least we should observe that diving mother ships as well as dredges must warn onlookers of their impediments.

No reading between the lines is necessary to learn the display required of an obstructed dredge and a diving platform at anchor. Both COLREGS and Inland specify that they forgo anchor displays. Instead they warn of their problems by the basic day and night signals for vessels restricted in ability to maneuver while they point out the cluttered side by red lights and black balls and the clear side by green lights and black diamonds. The result is that such vessels seen without running lights can be either at anchor or underway but not moving through the water. In either case, though, with no direction to indicate, they have little call to be overprecise. Whether at anchor or dead in the water, their main concern is to warn of dangerous encumbrances. Figure 46 illustrates the signals of Rule 27(d).

Annex V of Inland, which contains the Pilot Rules, provides for more lights to be displayed by a dredging complex. In addition to whatever lights the dredge shows, some marking on her pipelines must be visible. Here is the wording of the requirement.

INLAND ANNEX V

§ 88.15 Lights on dredge pipelines.

Dredge pipelines that are floating or supported on trestles shall display the following lights at night and in periods of restricted visibility.

(a) One row of yellow lights. The lights must be—

(1) Flashing 50 to 70 times per minute,

(2) Visible all around the horizon,

(3) Visible for at least 2 miles on a clear dark night,

(4) Not less than 1 and not more than 3.5 meters above the water,

(5) Approximately equally spaced, and

(6) Not more than 10 meters apart where the pipeline crosses a navigable channel. Where the pipeline does not cross a navigable channel the lights must be sufficient in number to clearly show the pipeline's length and course.

(b) Two red lights at each end of the pipeline, including the ends in a channel where the pipeline is separated to allow vessels to pass (whether open or closed). The lights must be—

(1) Visible all around the horizon, and

(2) Visible for at least 2 miles on a clear dark night, and

(3) One meter apart in a vertical line with the lower light at the same height above the water as the flashing yellow light.

An anchored dredge obstructed by a pipeline leading outward from one side and crossing a navigable channel with safe passage available on her other side can become a very colorful scene, as shown in Fig. 47. Common sense would dictate that passersby keep well clear of the entire complex. But since that might not be so easy to do in confined inland waters, recognizing the light patterns could be of very great assistance.

While we are sorting out items in the Pilot Rules, we might as well dispose

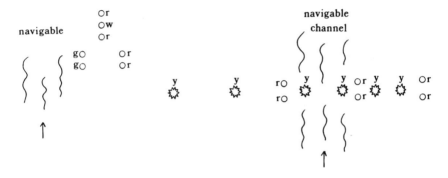

Fig. 47. Dredge and Her Pipeline. The dredge on the left indicates the passage to navigable water. The pipeline extends to the right and marks the opening for the navigable channel (Inland only).

of Section 88.13 of Inland's Annex V. It deals with lights on barges tied to the bank or to a dock on inland waters. Its long-winded recital of requirements includes a careful specification of areas in the Illinois River where barges are exempt from the demands. We should consider ourselves exempt from so much wordage and limit ourselves now to a glance at the basic requirements.

INLAND ANNEX V

§ 88.13 Lights on barges at bank or dock.

(a) The following barges shall display at night and, if practicable, in periods of restricted visibility the lights described in paragraph (b) of this section—

(1) Every barge projecting into a buoyed or restricted channel.

(2) Every barge so moored that it reduces the available navigable width of any channel to less than 80 meters.

(3) Barges moored in groups more than two barges wide or to a maximum width of over 25 meters.

(4) Every barge not moored parallel to the bank or dock.

(b) Barges described in paragraph (a) shall carry two

unobstructed white lights of an intensity to be visible for at least one mile on a clear dark night, and arranged as follows:

(1) On a single moored barge, lights shall be placed on the two corners farthest from the bank or dock.

(2) On barges moored in group formation, a light shall be placed on each of the upstream and downstream ends of the group, on the corners farthest from the bank or dock.

(3) Any barge in a group, projecting from the main body of the group toward the channel, shall be lighted as a single barge.

(c) Barges moored in any slip or slough which is used primarily for mooring purposes are exempt from the lighting requirements of this section.

(d) Barges moored in well-illuminated areas are exempt from the lighting requirements of this section. These areas are as follows:

What follows now in the full annex is a long string of names listing areas of exemption. We can find the whole works set out in Appendix A. For now, though, the gist of things is sufficient. Whenever a single barge projects from its berth into a buoyed or restricted channel or narrows the channel width to less than 80 meters or is not parallel to the bank, it must show two white lights. Each must be visible for at least 1 mile with one on each of the two corners farthest from the bank. If a group more than two barges wide or, regardless of number, more than 25 meters wide is tied up, then the two white lights are placed on the two corners farthest from the bank with one at the upstream end and the other at the downstream end. And if one of the group should project toward the channel, in addition it will be lighted as a single barge. No signals are required of any barges in a slip or slough used primarily for mooring. And well-lighted areas detailed in the regulation are also exempt.

Critics of close study might, as usual, view attention to these details as unnecessary. This time we could well agree. Two points, though, might mollify our irritation. First of all, we can at least conclude that our review is complete. Second, we can be thankful that the barge lights were not encountered until after Fig. 47 was behind us. Picture a flock of barges working with a dredge and tied up to the bank on the clear side of the channel. The prospect would be like entering the port of Metropolis on New Year's Eve. A mariner approaching that cluster might be well advised to make a U-turn and return from whence he came.

Rule 27(e) aims to accommodate the plight of a small vessel involved in a diving operation. The visibility range of a day shape is in direct proportion to size. A black basketball is more detectable at 1000 yards than a licorice jelly-bean. On the other hand were a small ship required to mount a vertical line of basketballs athwart a line of diamonds with a string of ball-diamond-ball in the middle, she might have no deck space left for tending divers within her forest of necessary masts and rigging. So both sets of rules allow her to substitute a rigid replica of the International Code flag "A." Divided vertically with white to the mast and blue to the fly, it has a single-letter meaning of "I have a diver down; keep well clear at slow speed." Even when the minimum 1 meter high it should not interfere with deck activity on anything but a pirogue.

At night the small diving ship need not show red lights on the dangerous side and green lights on the side safe for passing. Instead she displays the same vertical string of red-white-red lights as others restricted in ability to maneuver without pointing out whether the encumbrance is on one side or the other. What is not clear, though, is whether she must add running lights when making way and anchor lights when tending a diver at anchor. We are probably entitled to do some "Good Seamanship" interpolation to fill the gap. Surely when moving she should be expected, as are all vessels restricted in ability to maneuver, to indicate direction by applicable masthead light, sidelights, and a sternlight. By extension there would seem merit in her showing an anchor display when the diving operation finds her in that condition. Figure 48 tells the story of Rule 27(e).

Fig. 48. *Small Diving Operation. (A) Day shape of small vessel (no minimum length) engaged in diving operations* (COLREGS and Inland); *(B) lights of small vessel (no minimum length) engaged in diving operations* (COLREGS and Inland).

One more operation restricts maneuverability. A vessel engaged in mine-sweeping operations should not be expected to keep clear of other vessels. Moreover, if the others have any sense at all they would rather the mine-sweeper keep her mind on her dangerous business. She is working for everyone's good. Requiring her to dodge off course to keep clear might cause her to leave a mine or two undiscovered. Identity signals of the minesweeper engaged in her profession are specified by Rule 27(f). At night when underway she shows normal power-driven running lights and adds a triangle of three all-round green lights near her foremast head with the apex up. Her day display is a similar triangle of black balls. And Fig. 49 depicts the views to be expected.

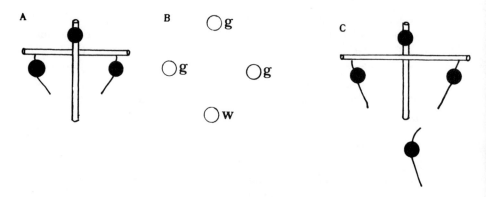

Fig. 49. Mine Clearance Vessels. (A) Day shape of vessel engaged in mine clearance while not at anchor (COLREGS only) *or vessel engaged in minesweeping* (Inland only); *(B) stern view of vessel underway and engaged in mine clearance or minesweeping* (COLREGS and Inland) *or bow or stern view of vessel clearing mines while at anchor* (COLREGS only); *(C) day shape of vessel engaged in mine clearance while at anchor* (COLREGS only).

But before the discussion goes a word further we should put to rest the prospect of encountering a *sailing* minesweeper. No such patently inefficient craft would seem conceivable to the average mariner. Such horrors as the thrashing sounds of propellers while stalking mines with acoustical sensors must worry minesweepers. But relying on wind shifts and tacks to keep the vessel on her course is hardly a remedy. We should safely assume that all minesweepers worthy of their paravanes will be power-driven, so their identity signals will be in addition to power-driven running lights. But there has been speculation on the placement of the top green light of the triangle with reference to the forward masthead light. If it appears above the white masthead light, it could violate paragraph 2(f) of Annex I, which we have yet to study. There a mandate is stated that masthead lights shall, subject to a few exceptions, be above and clear of all other lights and obstructions. Should the minesweeper's top green light appear higher than the forward masthead light, the bow view would show a green triangle with a white light in its middle. Were the forward masthead light higher, as it should be, then the bow view would be a green triangle pointing up toward a white light. Flexibility results when Rule 27(f) says "near the foremast head." Of course the discussion is probably academic since naval vessels can vary specific requirements to allow for special builds and missions. Those of us not expert in the nuances of mine warfare should have no extra concern. A triangle of green lights, no matter how it appears in conjunction with masthead lights, tells us that a minesweeper is at work and that we should keep out of its way.

A few more comments, though, are necessary. The state of the mine-disposal art has progressed far beyond the streaming of paravanes and similar wirecutting paraphernalia. During two World Wars the approach involved not much more than snipping the umbilical cords holding floating mines in position. But it seems that the modern mine is often "smart," with a host of insidious and crafty capabilities. Detection and disposal, though, have kept pace. Today's "minesweeper" makes use of highly sophisticated electronic gear which need not ever come in physical contact with either the mine or its wire tether. COLREGS recognizes this by replacing the word "minesweeping" with "mineclearance." That move brings with it another accommodation of futuristic defense. Minesweeping suggests that the sweeper be in motion so there would be little need for signals when the sweeper would be at anchor. Apparently, though, the mineclearer can do her thing without leaving a mooring or berth. So COLREGS specifies that a mineclearing vessel at anchor combine her triangle of lights or shapes with anchor displays. Our concern, though, is not so much with where or how she is at work, but that by some means or other she is doing the job of searching out mines. When such a vessel identifies herself, the rest of us should stay far, far away. Inland warns us to stand off at least 500 meters on either side and 1000 meters astern. COLREGS demand a more prudent minimum of 1000 meters in any direction.

The requirements of Rule 27 could border on the ludicrous if imposed strictly on all vessels. So in 27(g) a modicum of reason is exercised. There a minimum length limit is specified as the threshold for application of the requirements. By it, lilliputian aircraft carriers need not show Rule 27 signals

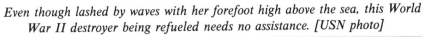

Even though lashed by waves with her forefoot high above the sea, this World War II destroyer being refueled needs no assistance. [USN photo]

when launching or recovering aircraft and dinky derelicts are not expected to signal that they are not under command. We've noticed, though, that with annoying regularity COLREGS and Inland seem capable of snatching complex statements from the jaws of simplicity. How dinky must a vessel's measure be before she is considered as hailing from Lilliput? Rule 27(g) exempts most vessels less than 12 meters long from showing the light displays. This would exempt a 39-foot aircraft carrier, dredge, minesweeper, or the like. But the exemption is only partial, and the nonexempt class embraces many small recreational vessels. An under-12-meter vessel engaged in a diving operation must show day shapes and lights.

It is time now to wrap up this discussion by looking at Rule 27(h). Lest the overzealous misconstrue the portent "not under command" or "restricted in ability to maneuver," it cautions them that these are not signals of distress and need for assistance. Neither mineclearers nor aircraft carriers engaged in their duties are requesting shipping to stand by. In fact every vessel showing a signal pattern dictated by Rule 27, including those not under command, is transmitting a message of exactly the opposite meaning. In each case other shipping is warned to keep clear since the vessel showing the signal is unable to do so herself. Good seamanship considers it irresponsible to approach unnecessarily close to any vessel. Rule 27 merely affords warnings for vessels that are particularly dangerous to approach.

Far back in our discussions we wrestled with the concept of a vessel constrained by her draft and with the contrast between the high-seas viewpoint and that prevailing on our inland waters. Rule 3 of Inland, in presenting general definitions, does not even proffer a mention of the status. Before us now is Rule 28. The COLREGS version offers day and night patterns to identify such a vessel. Since Inland doesn't even recognize that such a vessel exists, its Rule 28 is vacant and reserved for future use. The only reason the vacancy is numbered is to keep Inland in step with the COLREGS numerical progression. Here are how the words of the rule appear.

RULE 28—Vessels Constrained by Their Draft

COLREGS

A vessel constrained by her draft may, in addition to the lights prescribed for power-driven vessels in Rule 23, exhibit where they can best be seen three all-round red lights in a vertical line, or a cylinder.

INLAND
RULE 28
[Reserved]

Our starting point as usual must be with a definition. In COLREGS Rule 3(h) we read that a vessel so constrained must first of all be power-driven. No sailing ship in a shallow basin is deemed constrained. We also learned that in reconsidering the matter COLREGS feel that more than just a draft constraint is required. "Smelling bottom" in a delta several miles wide is not nearly as hampering as waddling through a narrow channel with one's keel perilously near grounding. Such an observation, we've already noted, strengthens the U.S. view that no special rule is required. The narrow channel rules, we say, are adequate to define the predicament. Nonetheless COLREGS disagrees and we must look to the high-seas demands. Three red lights in a vertical line can be added to the running light display. By day the warning can be a black cylinder. We should note, though, that the signal is optional. By its display a vessel warns of a limitation and demands from others an added measure of caution. Its absence then would suggest that oncomers are absolved from presuming that lumbering giants might have difficulties. But we all know what Good Seamanship would say to that! Should you observe the approach of a huge tanker in a narrow channel, you cannot disregard your knowledge of channel depth and of the possibility of her discomfort. By any measure of common sense, whether it be Good Seamanship or its companion, General Prudence, you must stand ready to accommodate her limitations. What COL-REGS Rule 28 amounts to is a means for the oncoming monster to remind you of her plight. Figure 50 demonstrates what could be seen by day and by night.

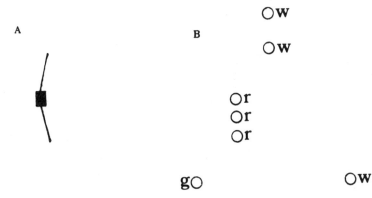

Fig. 50. Vessels Constrained by Draft. (A) Day shape of power-driven vessel while underway and constrained by draft (COLREGS only); (B) bow view of power-driven vessel 50 meters or more long while underway and constrained by draft (COLREGS only).

With a remarkable economy of words Rule 29 describes the identity signal for a pilot vessel. For millennia pilots have extended to wandering seafarers welcome and guidance to unfamiliar ports. One might expect then that they come arrayed in the trappings befitting an official greater. Not so. They are "all business" professional mariners advising strangers on safe approach through local dangers, and their signal pattern is a model of simplicity. Here is the wording for both COLREGS and Inland.

RULE 29—Pilot Vessels

COLREGS

(a) A vessel engaged on pilotage duty shall exhibit:

(i) at or near the masthead, two all-round lights in a vertical line, the upper being white and the lower red;

(ii) when underway, in addition, sidelights and a sternlight;

(iii) when at anchor, in addition to the lights prescribed in subparagraph (i), the light, lights or shape prescribed in Rule 30 for vessels at anchor.

(b) A pilot vessel when not engaged on pilotage duty shall exhibit the lights or shapes prescribed for a similar vessel of her length.

INLAND

(a) A vessel engaged on pilotage duty shall exhibit:

(i) at or near the masthead, two all-round lights in a vertical line, the upper being white and the lower red;

(ii) when underway, in addition, sidelights and a sternlight; and

(iii) when at anchor, in addition to the lights prescribed in subparagraph (i), the anchor light, lights, or shape prescribed in Rule 30 for anchored vessels.

(b) A pilot vessel when not engaged on pilotage duty shall exhibit the lights or shapes prescribed for a vessel of her length.

"White over Red means Pilot Ahead" has been the slogan for many years. Its straightforward message remains basically unchanged. But there are still some new developments worth noting. The function of a pilot vessel on duty is to deliver pilots to incoming vessels and to retrieve them from ships outward bound. Their duty station can be at anchor, underway, or even, infrequently, alongside some sort of dock. Whenever they are so engaged they display, at night, an all-round white light over an all-round red light. If they are also at anchor they add the display required by upcoming Rule 30 for vessels at anchor. If, instead, they are, by disconnection from the planet, considered underway, they add the aspect signals of sidelights and a sternlight appropriate to their size. And here are the few points worth noting. The Rules of the Road specify no day shape to identify a pilot vessel, and in fact none is necessary. Often a nameboard of some kind prominently displayed shows her occupation. By the International Code of Signals the red-and-white "H" flag declares that she has a pilot on board. And such publications as *Coast Pilot* and *Sailing Directions* usually describe her build and where she might be expected to be found. By day, though, she is expected to display an anchor ball when she is working at anchor.

Of particular importance is a difference between the running light requirements for a pilot boat and other "special operation" vessels. A vessel engaged in fishing at night doesn't show sidelights and a sternlight until she is actually moving through the water. "Underway" is not enough; she must be in motion. The same is true of a vessel not under command and one restricted in her ability to maneuver. Both Rules 26 and 27 stipulate that they display directional signals only when they have a direction to indicate. But a pilot vessel turns on her sidelights and sternlight when she is underway, whether she is making way or not. Why the difference? The answer lies in recognition of how a pilot vessel works. Sometimes she goes alongside a large ship to deliver or recover a pilot, but on other occasions she lies immobile while the large ship maneuvers nearby to effect the transfer. The pilot vessel is required to signal her aspect rather than her direction. It can be important for the nearby ship to know whether she is approaching the pilot vessel on the port side, the starboard, ahead, or astern. What is unimportant, though, is how the pilot vessel is propelled. So even though power-driven, she does not add her masthead light display. Figure 51 shows what could be seen by night when in sight of any pilot vessel, power-driven or sail, when underway or at anchor.

The last sentence of Rule 29 returns an off-duty pilot vessel to the ranks of

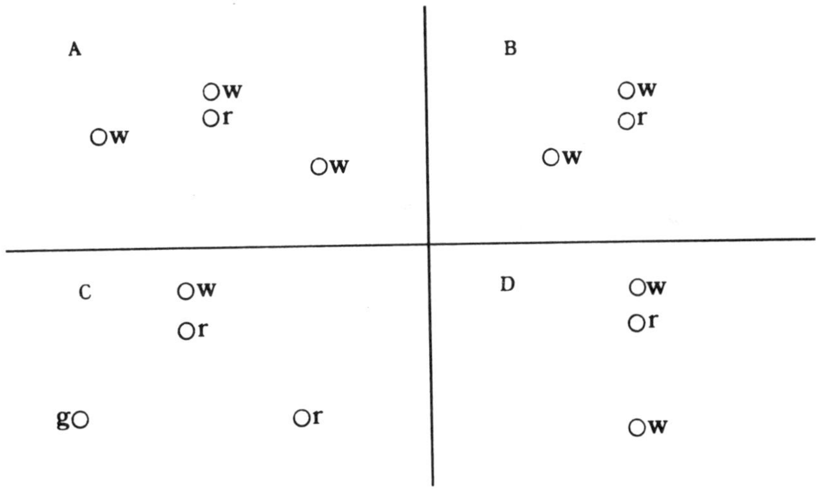

Fig. 51. Pilot Vessel Lights. (A) Port profile of pilot vessel 50 meters or more long while on duty and at anchor (COLREGS and Inland); (B) any view of pilot vessel between 20 and 50 meters long while on duty and at anchor (COLREGS and Inland); (C) bow view of pilot vessel 20 meters or more long of any propulsion while on duty and underway, whether making way or not (COLREGS and Inland); (D) stern view underway or bow or stern view of pilot vessel of any length and propulsion while on duty and at anchor (COLREGS and Inland).

just another ship. She will then douse her identity lights and be governed by Rule 23 if power-driven and by Rule 25 if under sail, or perhaps propelled by oars.

The end of lights and day shapes is in sight! Two more rules remain to complete our survey of these signal patterns. Next up are the requirements for vessels at anchor and aground, as set forth in Rule 30. First off, then, to a statement of the COLREGS version with the words of Inland Rule 30 tagging along in its wake.

RULE 30—Anchored Vessels and Vessels Aground

COLREGS

(a) A vessel at anchor shall exhibit where it can best be seen:

(i) in the fore part, an all-round white light or one ball;

(ii) at or near the stern and at a lower level than the light prescribed in subparagraph (i), an all-round white light.

(b) A vessel of less than 50 meters in length may exhibit an all-round white light where it can best be seen instead of the lights prescribed in paragraph (a) of this Rule.

(c) A vessel at anchor may, and a vessel of 100 meters and more in length shall, also use the available working or equivalent lights to illuminate her decks.

(d) A vessel aground shall exhibit the lights prescribed in paragraph (a) or (b) of this Rule and in addition, where they can best be seen:

(i) two all-round red lights in a vertical line;

(ii) three balls in a vertical line.

(e) A vessel of less than 7 meters in length, when at anchor, not in or near a narrow channel, fairway or anchorage, or where other vessels normally navigate, shall not be required to exhibit the lights or shape prescribed in paragraphs (a) and (b) of this Rule.

(f) A vessel of less than 12 meters in length, when aground, shall not be required to exhibit the lights or shapes prescribed in subparagraphs (d)(i) and (ii) of this Rule.

INLAND

(a) A vessel at anchor shall exhibit where it can best be seen:

(i) in the fore part, an all-round white light or one ball; and

(ii) at or near the stern and at a lower level than the light prescribed in subparagraph (i), an all-round white light.

(b) A vessel of less than 50 meters in length may exhibit an all-round white light where it can best be seen instead of the lights prescribed in paragraph (a) of this Rule.

(c) A vessel at anchor may, and a vessel of 100 meters or more in length shall, also use the available working or equivalent lights to illuminate her decks.

(d) A vessel aground shall exhibit the lights prescribed in paragraph (a) or (b) of this Rule and in addition, if practicable, where they can best be seen:

(i) two all-round red lights in a vertical line; and

(ii) three balls in a vertical line.

(e) A vessel of less than 7 meters in length, when at anchor, not in or near a narrow channel, fairway, anchorage, or where other vessels normally navigate, shall not be required to exhibit the lights or shape prescribed in paragraphs (a) and (b) of this Rule.

(f) A vessel of less than 12 meters in length when aground shall not be required to exhibit the lights or shapes prescribed in subparagraphs (d)(i) and (ii) of this Rule.

(g) A vessel of less than 20 meters in length, when at anchor in a special anchorage area designated by the Secretary, shall not be required to exhibit the anchor lights and shapes required by this Rule.

The first six paragraphs are the same on the high seas as on inland waters. By day, vessels at anchor display a black ball forward. By day when aground they show three black balls in a vertical line where these best can be seen. At night, though, the anchor signal depends on the length of the vessel. Three classes are specified. When the length is under 50 meters, one all-round white anchor light is hung where best seen. When the length is at least 50 meters but less than 100 meters, one such white light is suspended forward and another appears lower and at or near the stern. When the length is 100 meters or more an additional requirement is that the decks between the two anchor lights be illuminated. Should a vessel ground at night she adds to her anchor display the signal of two all-round red lights in a vertical line where they can best be seen. Before delving into the variations which appear in the extra paragraph (g) added to the Inland rule we should carefully examine the basic signals. They represent the meat of the entire rule.

Table 3 lists the day and night patterns for long and short ships at anchor or aground. A single black ball identifies anyone at anchor. Well, we really can't make such a sweeping statement if we remember Rule 27(c). There we learned that vessels restricted in ability to maneuver when at anchor combine the ball-diamond-ball of Rule 27(c) with the anchor ball. And Rule 27(d) told us that an obstructed dredge dispensed with any anchor ball when at anchor it directs traffic with two black balls on the obstructed side and two black diamonds on the passing side. The generalization that "one black ball is a vessel at anchor" is further weakened when we recall the signals given vessels engaged in fishing by Rule 26. In no uncertain terms, whether underway or at anchor, they are told to display only the signals prescribed by Rule 26. It says nothing about anchor balls. But absent those few exceptions most ships at anchor will show only a black ball forward. This sounds reasonable. When the ball is visible so is the hull form. An observer can then tell the long or short of it at a glance without further guidance. All he need know is that the form is at anchor, and the placement of the ball forward even hints which is the likely end for the hawse pipe and around which the ship will swing. The instigator who now speculates on the infrequent case of a ship swinging to a *stern* anchor should be drummed out of the corps. Should she then show the anchor ball from that end? Strip him of his epaulettes and break his sword for he seeds confusion and discontent! The statement of the rule unequivocally

Table 3. Day and Night Signals

VESSEL AT ANCHOR	DAY	NIGHT	RULES
100 m or more long	anchor ball forward	all-round white light forward + all-round white light aft and lower + illuminate decks between	COLREGS and Inland
50 m but under 100 m long	anchor ball forward	all-round white light forward + all-round white light aft and lower	COLREGS and Inland
Under 50 m and in frequented area	anchor ball forward	all-round white light where best seen	COLREGS and Inland
Under 20 m in Special Anchorage Area	—	—	Inland only
Under 7 m and not in frequented area	—	—	COLREGS and Inland
Engaged in fishing	Rule 26 shapes only	Rule 26 lights only	COLREGS and Inland
Not under command	anchor shape only	anchor light(s) only	COLREGS and Inland
Restricted in ability to maneuver and 12 m or more (except dredge with encumbrance, small diving ship, and mine-clear-ance vessel)	anchor shape + Rule 27(b) shapes	anchor light(s) + Rule 27(b) lights	COLREGS and Inland
Dredge with encumb-rance 12 m or more long	Rule 27(d) shapes only	Rule 27(d) lights only	COLREGS and Inland
Small diving ship	anchor shape +rigid replica of "A" flag	anchor light +red-white-red in vertical line	COLREGS and Inland
Mine-clearance vessel 12 m or more long	triangle of 3 black balls + anchor ball	triangle of 3 green lights + anchor light(s)	COLREGS only
Pilot vessel	anchor ball forward	white-over-red + anchor light(s)	COLREGS and Inland

AGROUND	DAY	NIGHT	RULES
12 m or more long	3 black balls in vertical line	2 red lights in vertical line + anchor light(s)	COLREGS and Inland
Under 12 m long	—	—	COLREGS and Inland

Her cargo delivered, a bulbous-bow giant rides easily with her port anchor down. [Photo by Lawrence Wyatt]

places the single black ball in the forepart of the vessel. Not so, though, when a vessel is aground in the daytime. Now the rule requires three black balls in a vertical line, but places them where they can best be seen. That might be on the forestay, but then again it might be on the poop. Even more likely is someplace above the bridge or wheelhouse.

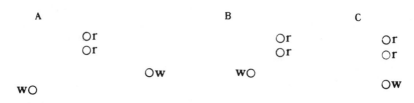

Fig. 52. Lights of Vessels Aground. (A) Starboard profile of vessel 50 meters or more long while aground (COLREGS and Inland); (B) any view of vessel under 50 meters long while aground (COLREGS and Inland); (C) bow or stern view of vessel aground (COLREGS and Inland).

The night signals appear in Fig. 52. Recognizing again that Rule 27 can bring differences for special craft, to begin with we find an artful approach for signaling when a vessel is aground. In that situation she is, as at anchor, connected to the planet but involuntarily so. She is not in command of her ability to disengage. So her signal combines an anchor display with the separate hoist of two red lights associated in Rule 27 with being not under command. In fact the day shapes for aground are similar. There a single anchor ball is suspended in a vertical line with the two not-under-command balls to tell the story. All this, incidentally, explains why a vessel not under command *at anchor* does not show Rule 27 identity signals in addition to her anchor display. That combination, by Rule 30, is given to those aground.

Notice that vessels under 50 meters long need not hang their single anchor light forward. It can be placed where best seen. But length might be important when shaping up to maneuver past something large at anchor, so one light is forward and the other is aft, with the cutoff point at 50 meters. Placing the higher light in the fore part seems intended to indicate, as mentioned before, the probable end from which the anchor chain will range. And that snicker just heard was our incorrigible "cashiered" disturber bringing up the pesky problem of a stern anchor. We'll pay no more attention to him now than we did before.

Rule 30(c) is very valuable, as an example will demonstrate. In San Francisco Bay southward of the Bay Bridge an anchorage has been set aside for large tankers to rest while being lightered prior to moving northward via bays and straits to nearby refineries. Suppose it is the dead of a dark night and a southbound craft, having passed under the bridge, is approaching that anchorage. On the port bow is a white light and on the starboard bow is another. Thinking that there are two vessels at anchor up ahead to left and right, she decides to pass between them. That would be a mistake, for in between stretch 300 meters of hull cradling a million barrels of crude oil. Rule 30(c) combats the problem by requiring that ships 100 meters or more long light up their decks between their anchor lights.

Now for some accommodations granted by Rule 30. Paragraph (e), whether COLREGS or Inland, speaks to those under 7 meters long and grants an exemption when anchored but not in or near a narrow channel, fairway, or anchorage, or where other vessels normally navigate. The realist might tag this as not much of an advantage, for few areas seem left except a backwater and a graving dock. In any case, when not near traffic these small craft need not at times display some of the Rule 30 signals.

Not found in COLREGS, and for obvious reasons, is a counterpart to Inland Rule 30(g). There a long-standing reference to "special anchorage areas" is perpetuated. For many years Congress has given administrative authority for the establishment of special zones within which regulated anchoring is allowed. Early in the game it was the secretary of the army as the superior of the Corps of Engineers who made the assignments. Nowadays it is the secretary of the department in which the Coast Guard is operating. That currently means the secretary of transportation. In any case, when proper authority

The World War II S.S. Joplin Victory *is unquestionably aground at Inchon, Korea. [Photo by Richard Haller]*

establishes such an area and when vessels under 20 meters long are using them at anchor, then Inland's Rule 30(g) exempts them from showing any anchor signals by day or night. Since, though, the long arm of the secretary does not reach far into the high seas and foreign areas, this exemption is not found in COLREGS.

It is always welcome to conclude a difficult task on an easy note. We find such in Rule 31. COLREGS and Inland are identical, and here is the reading.

RULE 31—Seaplanes

COLREGS

Where it is impracticable for a seaplane to exhibit lights and shapes of the characteristics or in the positions prescribed in the Rules of this Part she shall exhibit lights and shapes as closely similar in characteristics and position as is possible.

INLAND

Where it is impracticable for a seaplane to exhibit lights and shapes of the characteristics or in the positions prescribed in the Rules of this Part she shall exhibit lights and shapes as closely similar in characteristics and position as is possible.

The unambiguous words obviously recognize that seaplanes on the water don't suddenly sprout masts and rigging on which to mount arrays of lights and shapes. Should one, for example, be engaged in a diving operation, she would find it frustrating to display from wing and fuselage such things as black balls and diamonds or even a rigid replica of the code flag "A." So Rule 31 says to her, "Do the best you can." We should note, though, what type of creature rulemakers consider a waterborne seaplane to be. The rule refers to her as a "she," and even in today's liberated world of seapersons a "she" is a vessel. That statement just echoes the spirit of Rule 3. There, in paragraph (a), "vessel" is defined to include a seaplane. Rule 3(b) goes further in specifying that a power-driven vessel is any vessel propelled by machinery. Seldom are seaplanes seen sporting spinnakers. We are justified in the generalization that when waterborne as well as when in the air they will be power-driven. The result? In doing the best she can, as Rule 31 invites, a seaplane will aspire to power-driven lights and shapes.

We may now aspire to relief from the clouds of light patterns and shapes met in this chapter. The review is over and class is dismissed. Wait a minute! What did we just hear from Teacher's Pet in the front row? A quiz? Thanks to our earnest pupil for the reminder. As for the rest of you, please leave no marks or bruises when you get him outside.

QUESTIONS

It is only civilized that Teacher's Pet be judged by his peers. Since none of his equals are handy, we've chosen three dock wallopers. Tom Sawyer, Huckleberry Finn, and Peck's Bad Boy have enthusiastically volunteered for the panel. While they are about it, they will also present you with the chapter test. Approach it, though, with suspicion. Seapersons have learned that Bully Mates were once rowdy fo'c'sle hands. These cut-ups have already doubled the normal ration of ten questions!

1. A sailing vessel 10 meters long underway at night
   a. may display a tricolored red-green-white lantern at or near the top of the mast
   b. may also display an all-round red light over an all-round green light
   c. both of the above
   d. none of the above

2. A sailing vessel 10 meters long at night
   a. may carry a red-green lantern for sidelights
   b. may carry separate sidelights
   c. may display all-round red over all-round green at or near the top of the mast
   d. all of the above

3. A vessel 15 meters long propelled by sail and power
   a. shall, by day, show a black cone point down
   b. shall, by night, show a masthead light
   c. both of the above
   d. none of the above

4. A power-driven vessel underway at night and engaged in fishing other than trawling
   a. shall show an after masthead light
   b. shall show all-round red over all-round white
   c. both of the above
   d. none of the above

5. A power-driven troller 20 meters long and trolling at night underway
   a. shows the same lights as any power-driven vessel 20 meters long and underway at night
   b. shows the same lights as a power-driven trawler 20 meters long and underway at night but not trawling
   c. both of the above
   d. none of the above

6. By night a power-driven vessel not under command by reason of having lost her rudder
    a. shows a masthead light or lights, depending on her length
    b. shows an anchor light or lights, depending on her length, when at anchor
    c. shows two red lights in a vertical line when at anchor
    d. none of the above

7. By day you observe the day shape pattern as illustrated. This could be displayed by
    a. a power-driven vessel towing   ●
    b. a vessel engaged in fishing   ◆
    c. both of the above
    d. none of the above   ●

8. By day you observe a vessel engaged in an underwater operation with an obstruction existing on one side. Visible, with other shapes, is the day shape pattern illustrated.   ●
    a. This would indicate the side on which you may pass.   ●
    b. This would be shown whether the vessel was underway or at anchor.
    c. both of the above
    d. none of the above

9. By day three black balls may be shown by
    a. a vessel engaged in minesweeping
    b. a vessel aground
    c. either of the above
    d. none of the above

10. On the high seas at night a power-driven vessel is constrained by her draft in a narrow passage while underway.
    a. She must display a forward masthead light.
    b. She need not display a vertical line of three all-round red lights.
    c. both of the above
    d. none of the above

11. At night, which of the following displays sidelights when underway but not making way?
    a. a vessel engaged in fishing other than trawling
    b. a vessel engaged in an underwater operation
    c. a vessel engaged on pilotage duty
    d. none of the above

12. A pilot vessel engaged on pilotage duty at anchor
    a. shows anchor lights at night
    b. need not show an anchor ball by day

c. both of the above

d. none of the above

13. Three red lights in a vertical line is a signal for a vessel constrained by draft
    a. on the high seas
    b. on inland waters
    c. both of the above
    d. none of the above

14. By day an anchor ball is shown by a 30-meter vessel surveying at anchor
    a. on the high seas
    b. in inland waters
    c. both of the above
    d. none of the above

15. At night you observe a vessel displaying a green light over a white light. Also visible are two red lights in a vertical line. This would indicate
    a. a vessel engaged in trawling and not under command
    b. a vessel engaged in trawling with her net fast upon an obstruction
    c. either of the above
    d. none of the above

16. A sailing vessel 25 meters long underway but stopped at night and not under command would show
    a. all-round red over all-round green
    b. a combined red-green-white lantern at or near the top of the mast
    c. two all-round red lights in a vertical line
    d. any of the above

17. Dead ahead at night you observe a red light over a green light with, lower down, a white light.
    a. You are overtaking a vessel under sail.
    b. You are approaching a vessel engaged in fishing other than trawling and she has fishing gear extending more than 150 meters outboard in your direction.
    c. You are observing the port side of a vessel engaged in trawling.
    d. none of the above

18. A vessel under oars at night and underway
    a. may show only a white light in time to prevent collision
    b. may show sidelights and a sternlight
    c. either of the above
    d. none of the above

19. A sailing vessel engaged in fishing other than trawling and underway at night but not making way
    a. shows sidelights when she is 20 meters or more long
    b. may show all-round red over all-round green at or near the top of the mast
    c. shows a stern light
    d. shows all-round red over all-round white

20. A seaplane on the water
    a. is considered a power-driven vessel
    b. is exempt from showing sidelights
    c. both of the above
    d. none of the above

AND ANSWERS

Seafarers might be easy marks in many ways, but they can sense trouble when it is hull-down on the horizon. Those three truants selected as judges were certainly up to no good! If this is an example of their tyranny, what must they have done to poor Teacher's Pet? Before they drifted off on their raft they instructed us to correct the quiz in this manner. Allow 5 points for each accurate response and then use the following table to learn how you fared. Not having a reputation for literacy, the trio has chosen to use day shapes to indicate the scoring pattern.

90–100   (a clean sweep and homeward bound!)

75–85   (still surveying in unfamiliar waters)

60–70   (not under command)

under 60   (hard aground with a diver down and launching search planes)

1. a   2. d   3. c   4. b   5. c   6. b   7. a   8. b   9. c   10. c   11. c   12. a
13. a   14. c   15. b   16. c   17. a   18. c   19. d   20. a

8

Part D—SOUND/
LIGHT SIGNALS
Part E—EXEMPTIONS

THERE ARE OCCASIONS when a vessel must have a voice to declare her actions or intentions when in sight of another, and to announce her presence when she is not. Part D of both COLREGS and Inland provides the means. More so, it goes further to authorize special signals for vessels in distress. This chapter will examine all this in detail. And then, having arrived within one rule of completing our survey of the body of the Rules, we'll close with a study of Part E. Lest that should sound like too ambitious an undertaking, we can be cheered by the knowledge that Rule 38 is the sole occupant of that part. It is also the last of the numbered rules.

Part D begins with some definition of terms. Here is the text of Rule 32.

RULE 32—Definitions

COLREGS

(a) The word "whistle" means any sound signalling appliance capable of producing the prescribed blasts and which complies with the specifications in Annex III to these Regulations.

(b) The term "short blast" means a blast of about one second's duration.

(c) The term "prolonged blast" means a blast of from four to six seconds' duration.

INLAND

(a) The word "whistle" means any sound signaling appliance capable of producing the prescribed blasts and which complies with specifications in Annex III to these Rules.

(b) The term "short blast" means a blast of about 1 second's duration.

(c) The term "prolonged blast" means a blast of from 4 to 6 seconds' duration.

The definition of "whistle" seems clear enough. It requires an appliance for signaling by sound which can make short and prolonged blasts and satisfies the technical demands of Annex III. A quick glance at those pages, though, can be frightening. Unless the reader is familiar with the likes of a Hertz and a decibel he must prepare for some heavy weather. Inland, profiting by trouble encountered with the COLREGS annex, has made some changes. There is hardly a need for us to sort all this out during our practical study, but there are some details of the annex worthy of note.

A pattern is set up for different sounds to be made by vessels of different size. Deep tones come from vessels 200 meters or more long, middle-range sounds are made by those from 75 to 200 meters long, and higher pitched noise issues from those under 75 meters long. A seagoing chorus of a basso, an alto, and a soprano is specified. Also set out in Annex III is a table of approximate minimal ranges. That, however, is cushioned by the realistic caution that weather and similar factors can greatly reduce the range. Here, in any case, is the list:

vessels 200 meters or more long	2.0 miles
vessels 75 but less than 200 meters	1.5 miles
vessels 20 but less than 72 meters	1.0 mile
vessels less than 20 meters long	0.5 mile

Inland Annex III refers to the last group as "12 but less than 20 meters," and the reason introduces us to some ambiguity. Rule 33 will tell us that on both sides of the line of demarcation vessels under 12 meters long need not carry a device meeting the full definition of "whistle" so long as they are provided with an alternative to emit an efficient sound signal. Since the table of audibility range expressly refers to whistles, what the rule and annex require of smaller vessels is wrapped in fog. What *is* expected of a 39-foot boat? Need she carry a whistle? If not, how far need her alternative noisemaker be heard? We can expect to hear more on this confusion later on, for it involves a great number of mariners. We'll mark this vague area for future study.

There is a temptation to skip over any more attention to Annex III, and we can succumb in great part. Its intricate detailing of the technical requirements for noisemakers is certainly not of daily interest. So it appears in Appendix A, standing ready for such infrequent reference. But imbedded in its minutiae is mention of multiple whistles on one vessel. Not everyone will be shipmates with such a rig, yet we all might hear its din. We had best inquire.

The discussion centers on modern behemoths and on those whose exotic builds offer significant obstruction to a sound field. The speed of sound in air is somewhat more than 1100 feet per second. Blow a ship's whistle and one second later the sound will have traveled about that far. But on some vessels 1100 feet is barely a shiplength. With the sound source on a smokestack near the stern the noise will barely clear the stem in the first second. Furthermore the sound loses pep as it courses over the weather deck, with a resulting reduction in effective range. So provision is made for mounting two sound sources. One horn might be on the stack and a second on the foremast or some other location allowing more effective dispatch of a sound away from the ship.

Annex III, though, makes a logical proviso. When the whistles are more than 100 meters apart they shall not be synchronized and the sounds shall be of different tones. Otherwise they are bound to be heard as closely spaced toots easily mistaken for a different signal.

Maneuvering in a Los Angeles turning basin, the huge S.S. Manulani *may use sound signals from bow or stern to announce her intentions. [Courtesy Matson Lines]*

A similar problem arises when a ship's whistle is buried behind ventilators, high bridge complexes, or cargo containers piled like building blocks on the decks. It is unavoidable that sound will be baffled and blocked in some arcs. Both COLREGS and Inland recommend that a *combined whistle system* be the remedy. The details on such a complex are found in Annex III, with Inland's description in Section 86.13 more positive than that found in COLREG's paragraph 1(g). Each describes a number of sound-emitting sources working together. So one horn might be on the fore part of a smokestack with another one or more artfully placed on nearby perches to aim in other directions clear of obstructions. It is required of such a system that all sources sound off together, emitting tones suitable to the length of the ship. But each source must have a fundamental frequency different from the others. Even so, the entire system is viewed as one whistle under the rules, and that makes the next requirement unavoidable. All the sound sources must be clustered in the same general onboard area; they must be within 100 meters of each other. An exaggerated example might be the way to justify our attention and also to extricate us from this discussion. Should you see a huge tanker underway with a horn on her foremast and 1000 feet away her smokestack studded with more horns, you are looking at a ship with two whistles. The one forward is a single whistle; the brass band aft is a combined whistle system. The soloist forward would not sound off with the others, but the after chorus would all make music together. And the whole works would be emitting different tones. To encounter that orchestra in a thick fog might be to suspect you have stumbled on an armada, but at least you would know "something" was out there. Hearing such cacaphony in sight while maneuvering, though, could be dangerous. Rule 34 provides a protection, but we'll wait until we reach that rule to meet its requirements.

One more item will see us clear of Annex III. Section 86.15 of Inland grants to power-driven tugs a welcome concession. Although they might be short enough to be sopranos, they and their consort towed alongside or being pushed

By Inland Rules the whistle signal from a small tug may be as deep-toned as that from the largest ship. [Photo by Lawrence Wyatt]

ahead might be long enough to qualify as bassos. Must they then use a high pitch when running alone and deepen the sound when moving a tow? Rather than changing pitch with the towline they are allowed at all times, even when running alone, to use a whistle whose characteristics accommodate the longest customary composite length of tug and tow. A 20-meter tug which customarily handles 200-meter tows alongside or ahead can emit a roar like the mating call of a bull moose. When running alone she approaches the effrontery of a compact car sounding the klaxon of a freight train. So far, though, COLREGS Annex III has ignored the problem. The nitpicker would have small tugs chirping on the high seas when running alone and bellowing when hitched to a tow.

More welcome than any concession granted tugs by Inland should be our retreat from Annex III. Let the nitpicker indulge himself with speculation while we return to Rule 32. Two more definitions need our attention. A *short blast* is said to be about 1 second long; a *prolonged blast* is about 4–6 seconds long. And consigned to history at last is the age-old tussle with a now-gone Inland specification of a "long blast." The problem confronting generations of inland mariners was that although Congress prescribed the signal, no definition was given. The courts filled the gap by saying that "long" was longer than "prolonged," and that it should be considered as 8–10 seconds long. The lifetime of that enigma was far too long. It passes from the rules with no laments by mariners.

Next up is Rule 33, which lists the soundmakers required on board. Here is the text.

RULE 33—Equipment for Sound Signals

COLREGS

(a) A vessel of 12 meters or more in length shall be provided with a whistle and a bell and a vessel of 100 meters or more in length shall, in addition, be provided with a gong, the tone and sound of which cannot be confused with that of the bell. The whistle, bell and gong shall comply with the specifications in Annex III to these Regulations. The bell or gong or both may be replaced by other equipment having the same respective sound characteristics, provided that manual sounding of the prescribed signals shall always be possible.

(b) A vessel of less than 12 meters in length shall not be obliged to carry the sound signalling appliances prescribed in paragraph (a) of this Rule but if she does not, she shall be provided with some other means of making an efficient sound signal.

INLAND

(a) A vessel of 12 meters or more in length shall be provided with a whistle and a bell and a vessel of 100 meters or more in length shall, in addition, be provided with a gong, the tone and sound of which cannot be confused with that of the bell. The whistle, bell and gong shall comply with the specifications in

Annex III to these Rules. The bell or gong or both may be replaced by other equipment having the same respective sound characteristics, provided that manual sounding of the prescribed signals shall always be possible.

(b) A vessel of less than 12 meters in length shall not be obliged to carry the sound signaling appliances prescribed in paragraph (a) of this Rule but if she does not, she shall be provided with some other means of making an efficient sound signal.

Three classes of vessels are specified. Those 100 meters or more long must each have a whistle, a bell, and a gong. When the length is at least 12 meters but less than 100 meters, only the whistle and the bell are needed. Note, though, that neither COLREGS nor Inland makes means of propulsion a factor. Whether propelled by sail, power, or extraterrestrial energy, a vessel is bound by the list of soundmakers appropriate to her length. We should also observe that our deferred attention to soundmakers on board vessels less than 12 meters long is due. But first we should dispose of some other items.

The last sentence of Rule 33(a) makes a noteworthy statement. It allows either the bell or the gong or both to be replaced by other equipment making the same sound, but insists that manual sounding must always be possible. The meaning of the sentence is keyed by the provision for manual sounding and, as we might expect, relates to large ships. In Rule 35 we'll encounter requirements for large ships at anchor in a fog to sound at least once each minute a 5-second clanging of a bell forward and a 5-second gonging of a gong aft. Manual sounding would require the seamen stationed fore and aft to have keen hearing, be conversant with the speed of sound in air, and possess a good sense of rhythm. Otherwise they would sooner or later mess up the beat, causing bells to jam gongs and oncoming vessels to be in confusion. So Rule 33 obliquely authorizes the use of automatic devices with provision to be overridden by hand. Annex III goes further by recommending that the striker on a bell should, when practicable, be power-driven. This demonstrates laudable recognition of the seaman's lot. It is not a happy one when he is required to stand a long anchor watch forward in fog on a cold and clammy night. To swing a lanyard for 5 seconds out of every minute of the hour will sooner or later mean giving a ragged performance. It also is to risk overdevelopment of biceps, triceps, and a stray unicep or two. A power-driven clanger would do more than reduce the consumption of analgesic balm. It should better assure that the required cadence is kept and that proper signals go out to those nearby.

Procrastination must come to an end! It is time for our delayed consideration of how vessels less than 12 meters long cope with sound. Since COLREGS and Inland give scant guidance we must not expect precise detail. In fact our discussion will cast two rules we've not yet met against a few no longer in force. And here is the justification for such a curious approach. Rules 34 and 35, just over the horizon, will prescribe particular signals to be sounded when in sight and when in restricted visibility. Rule 32 defines a whistle and describes the blasts which it must be able to produce. The first paragraph of Rule 33 itemizes the various soundmakers which vessels 12 meters or more in length must have on board. Before we become too enmeshed in a study of the signals we must consider a very basic question: Need vessels less than 12 meters long be concerned with any of this?

A partial answer seems unassailable. Whether small vessels need *make* the signals or not, they must surely be prepared to recognize them when sounded by others. So no matter what equipment options exist, the mariner on a small vessel must have an understanding of the patterns. A complete study of Rules

Although not required to do so, a vessel less than 12 meters long might, in good seamanship, sound the signals prescribed in Part D of the Rules. [Courtesy Morgan Yacht Corp.]

34 and 35 lies ahead for all hands. We should then restate the basic question by dividing it into two inquiries. The first is "Need the vessel under 12 meters long sound the maneuvering and warning signals prescribed by Rule 34?" The second is "Need she make the sound signals of Rule 35 when in restricted visibility?"

We'll soon learn that Rule 34 describes patterns of short and prolonged whistle blasts to be given during maneuvers and for warnings. And Rule 35 prescribes the use of whistles, bells, and gongs in restricted visibility. But Rule 33(b) excuses the small vessel from carrying a whistle, bell, or a gong so long as she is provided with "some other means of making an efficient sound signal." One can hardly be expected to sound the short and prolonged whistle blasts demanded by Rule 34 when he need not have a whistle. No more is he to be expected to ring bells or gongs in fog when he need not carry either a bell or a gong. In fact paragraph (h) of Rule 35 would seem to be a model of clarity. There we'll see that a vessel under 12 meters long need not sound the prescribed fog signals so long as she makes "some other efficient sound signal" no less frequently than once every 2 minutes. So although no such express exemption is found in Rule 34, why need we fret further? Since the Rules don't require that small vessels carry the appliances designed to make the prescribed sounds, the question seems moot.

But that viewpoint would leave unresolved at least one other matter. When Rule 33(b) speaks of an alternative means of making an efficient sound signal, what does it have in mind? It need not be Rule 32's whistle, a device capable of measuring its sounds into short blasts of 1 second and of 4–6 seconds when prolonged. It need not be the peal of a bell or the deep tone of a gong. Could that other means be as casual as a soup ladle banged on a galley dishpan or perhaps a large-lunged cat with a sensitive tail? There is no express guidance to be found in the current Rules, so perhaps we should look elsewhere.

The reason for a small-ship exception is not so obscure. Finding a place to secure such devices on board a vessel less than 40 feet long might be awkward. Being required to sound off every time one changed course, and in fog every 60 seconds, would at least be inconvenient. Perhaps COLREGS, sympathetic to the plight of canoes and curraghs, concludes that a rule fated to be honored in the breach is worse than no rule at all. But in a country such as the United States many vessels under 12 meters long would experience no difficulty in fitting the prescribed appliances. A horn sounded by a can of compressed air gives more seamanlike notice than the clatter of kitchen utensils or the anguished yowl of a tomcat. Yet the writers of the Inland Rules elected to be just as noncommittal as those of COLREGS. The Motorboat Act of 1940 specified that an efficient whistle or "other sound-producing mechanical appliance" be carried by motorboats from 16 through 65 feet long and that those from 40 through 65 feet in length add a bell. But those sections were repealed at the advent of the new Inland Rules. Earning the privilege to display the U.S. Coast

Having just crossed the line of demarcation between International and Inland Rules, an inbound freighter readies to change the meaning of her maneuvering signals under the Golden Gate Bridge. [Photo by Lawrence Wyatt]

Guard Auxiliary decal can involve having on board a whistle and bell similar to those prescribed by the Rules. But conforming to any such standards is voluntary. When a vessel's employment subjects her to inspection by the U.S.

Coast Guard the demand that she carry prescribed equipment might be forth-coming. The care and feeding of insurance underwriters might suggest that carrying a whistle and a bell helps cement a relationship. But none of these musings answers our questions.

It is safe to conclude that vessels under 12 meters long are exempt from carrying sound appliances which conform to the technicalities set out in Annex III of the Rules. The sound of a whistle need not be of x decibel intensity and the mouth of a bell need not be of y millimeters diameter. But that is not to say that whistles and bells need never go onboard. Rule 2 must be heeded, and it prohibits neglect of precautions required by seamanlike practices or by prevailing circumstances. Let's not conclude that small vessels can always make do with catcalls and stew pots. It would seem reasonable that a 26-foot tug, required by law to carry a radiotelephone, also have a whistle on board. And it is no more outrageous to suggest that a sleek powerboat laden with electronics from computer games to radar should find the cranny to hang a whistle or a bell. Let's not, though, prolong our speculation any longer. This area of the Rules is uncharted and, all things considered, our guide is reason-ableness. Back we go to the main channel.

Stand ready to receive good news and bad. We are about to pass through the eddies and currents swirling around Rule 34. The good news is that there will be little tolerance for weak attempts at humor. The bad is the reason for such sobriety. This material is so important and so intricate that we can't afford the shadow of a smirk. We must for a while attend strictly to our duties.

Rule 34 of COLREGS differs fundamentally in approach from its Inland counterpart. The decades-old demand that power-driven vessels make certain sound signals to announce the *execution* of a maneuver is maintained on the high seas. Inland, on the other hand, clings to the also-hoary concept that sound signals be made to announce an *intention*. The contrast is that between a monologue and a dialogue. COLREGS has in mind a unilateral statement of fact by one vessel with no expected repartee with another. It signals action being taken. Inland, by contrast, views the matter as a conversation or perhaps even a negotiation, with every anticipation of reply. More on that later. Now we should look at the official statements of the rules. Since the two versions are so different we would do well to study them separately before attempting much comparison. Let's start, then, with the COLREGS requirement.

RULE 34—Maneuvering and Warning Signals

COLREGS

(a) When vessels are in sight of one another, a power-driven vessel underway, when maneuvering as authorized or required by these Rules, shall indicate that maneuver by the following signals on her whistle:

—one short blast to mean "I am altering my course to starboard";

—two short blasts to mean "I am altering my course to port";
—three short blasts to mean "I am operating astern propulsion".

(b) Any vessel may supplement the whistle signals prescribed in paragraph (a) of this Rule by light signals, repeated as appropriate, whilst the maneuver is being carried out:

(i) these light signals shall have the following significance:
—one flash to mean "I am altering my course to starboard";
—two flashes to mean "I am altering my course to port";
—three flashes to mean "I am operating astern propulsion";

(ii) the duration of each flash shall be about one second, the interval between flashes shall be about one second, and the interval between successive signals shall be not less than ten seconds;

(iii) the light used for this signal shall, if fitted, be an all-round white light, visible at a minimum range of 5 miles, and shall comply with the provisions of Annex I to these Regulations.

(c) When in sight of one another in a narrow channel or fairway:

(i) a vessel intending to overtake another shall in compliance with Rule 9(e)(i) indicate her intention by the following signals on her whistle:
—two prolonged blasts followed by one short blast to mean "I intend to overtake you on your starboard side";
—two prolonged blasts followed by two short blasts to mean "I intend to overtake you on your port side".

(ii) the vessel about to be overtaken when acting in accordance with Rule 9(e)(i) shall indicate her agreement by the following signal on her whistle:
—one prolonged, one short, one prolonged and one short blast, in that order.

(d) When vessels in sight of one another are approaching each other and from any cause either vessel fails to understand the intentions or actions of the other, or is in doubt whether sufficient action is being taken by the other to avoid collision, the vessel in doubt shall immediately indicate such doubt by giving at least five short and rapid blasts on the whistle. Such signal may be supplemented by a light signal of at least five short and rapid flashes.

(e) A vessel nearing a bend or an area of a channel or fairway where other vessels may by obscured by an intervening obstruction shall sound one prolonged blast. Such signal shall be answered with a prolonged blast by any approaching vessel that may be within hearing around the bend or behind the intervening obstruction.

(f) If whistles are fitted on a vessel at a distance apart of more than 100 meters, one whistle only shall be used for giving maneuvering and warning signals.

The first paragraph speaks to a power-driven vessel underway and maneuvering and in sight of another craft. She is to announce the execution of her maneuvers by one short blast, two short blasts, or three short blasts. First of all we should observe that COLREGS require that the signals be given to the other vessel whether that other is propelled by power, sail, oars, or whatever. The second consideration is that no minimum length is expressed, and that we have muddled through already. A bit more comment, though, is worthwhile. A literal reading would suggest that a two-meter punt driven by an outboard motor should make the blasts, but that seems niggling. When, though, does niggling become of consequence? Is a length of under 12 meters to be excused and could that be why Rule 33(b) does not insist that such craft carry such soundmakers as whistles and bells? Yet Rule 34 contains no hint of an intention to exempt small vessels. Beset by such vagueness, those under 12 meters long should presume a requirement, and when feasible to do so, be prepared to make the signals.

A third observation is more enlightening. There is a direct correlation between the signals described in Rule 34(a) and both the Morse Code and the International Code of Signals. *One short* means, in Morse Code, the letter "E" (Echo). The International Code of Signals defines that letter as meaning "I am altering my course to starboard." And COLREGS give it the same meaning. *Two shorts,* says the Morse Code, is "I" (India). By both International Code and COLREGS it means "I am altering my course to port." *Three shorts* signal "S" (Sierra). Current International Code says that it means "My engines are going astern." COLREGS vary that slightly to mean "I am operating astern propulsion."

Who gives these signals? A power-driven vessel when underway. When? In sight of another vessel and maneuvering as authorized or required by the rules. How? On a whistle emitting 1-second blasts. To whom does she give it? To that other vessel, whether she be power-driven, sail, seaplane, or under oars. She is not proposing a maneuver nor is she asking permission to make it. She has already decided on a course of action and is now carrying it out.

Courts have wrestled with the problem of the three-short-blasts signal. In the past when it meant "My engines are going full speed astern" they made short work of that requirement. It was judged too limiting and the meaning was enlarged to include engines going astern at any speed. More troublesome was the issue when, although the engines were not backing down, the vessel was actually moving backward. And there exists substantial judicial support to include it in the signal's meaning. What if the engines are actually working ahead but the ship is still moving astern? There is even precedent for the view that in such a case the three-blast signal is appropriate. What if, although the engines are operating astern, the ship is actually moving forward? Again that situation has gained judicial support as justifying the astern signal. We are best served to adopt a liberal interpretation. The three-blast signal covers engines operating astern at any setting regardless of which way the ship is moving and it also covers the case of the ship moving astern regardless of which direction the engines are working. At least then the other vessel will know that motion backward is either in fact happening or will shortly commence, and that would seem to be what the other vessel should be told. How the propeller shaft might turn is not as critical as how the ship might move. Setting that nuance aside, though, we find COLREGS Rule 34(a) quite clear.

Rule 34(b) introduces the *maneuvering light.* Vessels, say COLREGS, may carry an all-round white light visible at least 5 miles and capable of emitting flashes so that the one-, two-, and three-blast sounds may be supplemented by one, two, and three flashes of light. Particularly to be noted is the fact that COLREGS allows the light signals to be repeated during the maneuver, but no such provision is made for repetition of the sound. In turn it follows that the light flashes need not be synchronized with the sound signals. Light flashes are prescribed as about 1 second long with an interval between flashes of the same length. And should a light signal be repeated, at least 10 seconds must elapse between successive signals.

Annex I of COLREGS, in its section 12, sets out a startling provision regarding the placement of this maneuvering light. A general statement in the annex requires that the masthead light or lights shall always be placed above all other lights. But section 12 countermands that provision. It requires that a vessel carrying a forward and an after masthead light should place the maneuvering light above the forward masthead light and either above or below the after one. If only one masthead light is carried, the maneuvering light will be either above it or below it. So the maneuvering light can be the highest light on a power-driven ship. This, though, should cause not even momentary confusion since the maneuvering light will only be visible for a matter of seconds.

Rule 34(c) harks back to our discussion in Chapter 3 of COLREGS Rule 9, the problem of overtaking in a narrow channel. Although normally an overtaking vessel must keep clear while the vessel being overtaken holds course and speed, that script could defeat many attempts to overtake in a narrow channel. What if the vessel astern cannot safely overtake unless the vessel ahead takes some action to move out of the way by altering either course or speed or both? Rule 9 authorizes a dialogue or a negotiation to agree on a change of the script. And Rule 34(c) presents the whistle signals to hammer out the deal.

The result is a departure from the high-seas philosophy that sound signals are part of a monologue but the outcome is a workable exchange. When crowded circumstances justify, the overtaking vessel sounds two prolonged blasts followed by one short to express an inclination to overtake on the other's starboard side and two prolonged followed by two shorts if the desire is to pass on the port side. There is no corollary with either the Morse Code or the International Code of Signals here. "Dah-dah-dit" is the letter "G" (Golf). Its meaning by International Code is either "I require a pilot," or when given by a fishing vessel "I am hauling nets." Neither is relevant to overtaking in a narrow channel. "Dah-dah-dit-dit" is the letter "Z" (Zulu). Its code meanings are either "I require a tug," or when from a fishing vessel "I am shooting nets." And that is hardly appropriate for the impatient vessel anxious to get by. What might serve as a COLREGS rationale is this. Each request starts with two prolonged blasts and then is followed by one short for "starboard side" or two shorts for "port side." Why not consider the introduction of "dah-dah" as an attention-getter? It seems to say to the slower vessel ahead, "Pardon me, but. . . ." From the less gracious it can be taken as "Hey, you!" Then follows the announcement of intention, and it squares with the basic pattern of one short for going right and two shorts for going left. Rule 34(c) assigns specific

A U.S. Coast Guard patrol vessel clears the way for an LNG (liquefied natural gas) carrier. [USCG photo]

meanings to the signals and we should of course have them in mind. Two prolonged followed by one short is to mean "I intend to overtake you on your starboard side"; two prolonged followed by two shorts is "I intend to overtake you on your port side." But those meanings carry a flavor of independence. The overtaker seems not so much making a request as making a flat statement. Clarity might be served by recasting the matter as more of an overture or petition. "Hey, you! What about my going up your starboard side?" is the outburst in one case. "Pardon me, but may I go up your port side?" is the entreaty in the other.

In either situation the vessel to be overtaken now is entitled to reply. Since she has first use of the waterway with the speedster astern required to keep clear, she cannot be coerced into taking action other than holding course and speed. Should she accept the offer and agree to take the necessary action, however, she replies with "prolonged, short, prolonged,-short." By the code this is the letter "C" (Charlie) and does have a relationship to the Rules. The general meaning is "yes" and by Rule 34(c) it is the same. What, though, if she rejects the suggestion? Rule 34(c) is not clear on the point, but Rule 9(e) has an answer. There the overtaken vessel is given the use of the doubt signal (our next subject). It would seem practical that should the vessel ahead have misgivings about the proposed maneuver, she would be in doubt and so would deny the request with five or more short and rapid blasts. In that case the overtaker might sulk in her rejection but would not be entitled to crowd ahead.

Time for a "who, what, when, and where" recap. Who participates in the exchange? Any vessel, regardless of propulsion. An overtaking sail vessel as well as power-driven will make the request. And a vessel being overtaken, whether sail or power-driven, will respond. The "what" of the signals we've already seen. And the sound appliance will be a whistle. We'll shortly learn that the doubt signal may also be given on the maneuvering light, but there is no provision for flashing "G," "Z," or "C." When are they given? When in sight of each other would seem a logical proviso, but that statement seems to clash with something encountered far back in our study. It was in Section I of Part B that we met Rule 9, and that segment of the Rules deals with conduct in *any* condition of visibility. That would seem to countenance the sensitive maneuvers of overtaking in a narrow channel in fog. But Rule 34(c) conditions its signals with the words "when in sight." We had better try to reconcile the conflict.

It has been suggested that Rule 9(e) extends Rule 34(c)'s in sight signals to cover the circumstance of overtaking in a narrow channel when out of sight of the other vessel. The argument is that Rule 9 appears in a section describing conduct in *any* condition of visibility, so 9(e) would literally apply when the overtaking takes place in fog. There are at least two very persuasive retorts. One is that the only use for "G," "Z," and "C" is during a Rule 9(e) maneuver, and that Rule 34(c), in describing those signals, limits their use to vessels in sight of one another. If one insists that Rule 9(e) would allow such tricky overtaking maneuvers in fog, he must concede that Rule 34(c) just as literally denies the actors an exchange of "Gs," "Zs," and "Cs" unless they are in sight.

The prudent seaman offers an equally strong rebuttal. To rely solely on shipboard radar while acting out an overtaking maneuver in a narrow channel would wrack nerves. Playing such roles without radar would be irresponsible. A ship should not grope toward a channel edge in thick fog to make room for someone equally sightless coming up her flank. The procedure might be feasible under the direction of shore-based radar with high definition; at some future time it might even be safe with sophisticated shipborne radar. But at present vessels ahead should not accept invitations to be overtaken in fog-shrouded confined waters and vessels astern should not make such overtures. The paramount demands for Good Seamanship and General Prudence of Rule 2 would require at least some second thoughts.

In any case this exchange is not for every overtaking situation. The occasion is limited to a narrow channel or a fairway *and* when overtaking can take place only if the vessel ahead takes action other than holding course and speed. On open waters no request is made by the vessel astern and no permission is granted by the slower vessel ahead. She just holds her course and speed in silence while the overtaker makes her maneuvers. Even were they in a narrow

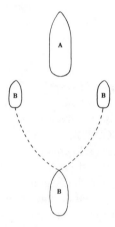

Fig. 53. Sound Signals When Overtaking on Open Water. Vessel A sounds no signals unless in doubt; vessel B, except when in doubt, makes signals only if power-driven and changing course (COLREGS only).

channel there would be no exchange if there is sufficient room for safe passage. Some examples would probably help. Figure 53 depicts an overtaking case on the open sea free of any confinement. Vessel *A*, being overtaken, holds course and speed with no normal need to make any signals regardless of her propulsion. *B*, astern and overtaking, goes by as she desires but with the obligation to keep clear. When *B* is power-driven she follows Rule 34(a)'s dictates by blowing one or two shorts, but only if she should change course while passing by. If *B* is under sail she doesn't signal course changes. If all goes well she will pass in silence. In Fig. 54 we find the vessels hemmed in by a narrow channel or fairway, but there is room for *B* to overtake without *A*'s assistance. The sound requirements would be no different than those applicable in Fig. 53.

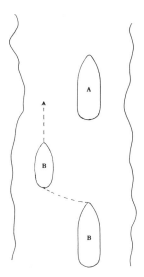

Fig. 54. Sound Signals in a Narrow Channel But with Room to Pass. Vessel A sounds no signals unless in doubt; vessel B, except when in doubt, makes signals only if power-driven and changing course (COLREGS only).

But now comes Fig. 55. Now *A* so blocks the narrow channel that unless she sidles over to the right or left *B* will not be able to go by in safety. So Rule 34(c) becomes applicable when they are in sight of each other. *B*, regardless of her mode of propulsion, makes a request and *A*, also regardless of propulsion, makes a reply. Thereafter, and this is important, sound signals may or may not be heard. If either of them is power-driven then she will add the signals for her course changes as required by Rule 34(a). Should either be under sail, though, she will change course without fanfare. The result when power-driven overtakes power-driven in a narrow channel could be a noisy waterway. *B* requests to overtake on the starboard side of *A* by blowing "dah-dah-dit." *A* agrees with "dah-dit-dah-dit." Now *A* starts edging to port to give *B* some clearance. *A* now sounds "dit-dit" as she executes her left turn. To keep from going ashore on the left bank she straightens up with a right turn and blows "dit." Meanwhile a grateful *B* slants to the right to gain more room and sounds "dit." When she straightens out to keep from grounding on the bank she sounds "dit-dit" for her left turn. Should they, after the maneuver, go back to midstream, more "dits" and "dit-dits" might follow. Would all this hubbub really take place? Probably not in most cases. Having made their deal with "G" or "Z" and "C," they would be inclined to perform it without a lot of clamor. But to gain the spirit of the law we must understand its literal meaning. Our exercise in keeping *A* and *B* apart during the passage might have been ear-splitting but it should be worth the noise.

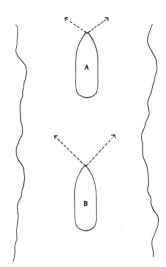

Fig. 55. Sound Signals When Vessel Ahead Must Move. Vessel B, *of any propulsion, requests passage by "dah-dah-dit" or "dah-dah-dit-dit" and vessel* A *complies with "dah-dit-dah-dit." Power-driven vessels then sound signals for course changes* (COLREGS only).

No unnecessary din is involved in Rule 34(d). When what can go wrong does, a panic button is supplied. The *doubt signal* is intended to alert both vessels to a mixup. It consists of at least five short and rapid blasts of the whistle and may be supplemented by the maneuvering light. Back again to the "whos" and "wheres." This signal is to be given by any vessel, whether under power, sail, or otherwise. More than that, it *must* be given when in sight of another and in doubt. No options are granted in confusion. If, states the rule, from any cause either fails to understand intentions or actions, or doubts whether sufficient action is being taken by the other, then the doubting vessel shall signal her concern. Nor should she interpret too literally the prerequisites. Failure to understand another's intentions or actions or doubting the sufficiency of the other's maneuver are specified as reasons to sound this alert. Good seamanship, though, suggests that it be given when any dangerous condition suddenly arises. In the past this sound pattern was called the "danger signal," and the reason is still worth noting. For example, if a vessel suffers a sudden rudder failure while maneuvering in sight of another she would be expected to blow five or more short and rapid blasts. Even though she understands the other's intentions and is satisfied with the sufficiency of the other's actions, she should still alert the other to a dangerous development.

Troublesome Rule 9(e) overtakes us again in our narrow channel. It mentions that the overtaken vessel in a narrow channel and being asked to take action *may* use this signal when in doubt. That seems to be a curious statement in light of Rule 34(d). By it, she and everyone else *shall* use the doubt signal when in sight of another and in doubt. Why does 9(e) run the risk of weakening the "ya gotta" command of 34(d) by use of the watered-down word "may"? One who views Rule 9(e) as countenancing the drama of overtaking in a foggy narrow channel says, "I told you so!" He finds vindication in this analysis. Since Rule 34(d) demands that everyone when in sight and in doubt sound the doubt signal, the mention in 9(e) only has meaning when viewed as allowing the vessel being overtaken in a narrow channel to use the doubt signal in any condition of visibility. Moreover, he argues that his view justifies another paragraph of the narrow channel rule. Rule 9(d) states that a vessel restricted to a narrow channel *may* warn off someone crossing by use of the doubt signal. If, he says triumphantly, the doubt signal is an in-sight "must," it follows that 9(d) and (e) make it a "may" at certain times in any condition of visibility. Probably we should accept this as sound reasoning on a minor point of slight obscurity and move along. In any case it is clear that the doubt signal is a most important tool to be used by everyone when in sight of another and disconcerted.

Mention of obscurity brings us to Rule 34(e) and what is sometimes called its *bend signal.* Every motorist is expected to drive cautiously as he approaches a blind corner. Not only that, he would do well to blow his horn. No less demand is made of the mariner. Visibility can be blocked by a grove of trees, a shed on the end of a dock, a breakwater jutting out from shore. All sorts of obstructions can interfere with a clear view, and no vessel is entitled to proceed blithely past without concern for hidden traffic. Rule 34(e) requires her to signal her approach with one prolonged blast. Going further, it expects a vessel on the far side of the obstruction and within earshot of the blast to reply with her own prolonged blast. But labeling this the bend signal is too restricting. It applies even on a straight channel reach. A container ship with her bow hard aground on a shallow will surely block the channel view. Her piles of vans would be just as obstructing as any cluttered bend. To sound one prolonged blast as you approached would be a proper way to probe for oncoming traffic. And we should observe that the demand for this signal applies to all vessels, no matter what their type of propulsion. It is worth noting that a radiotelephone announcement of approach is no substitute. Were a mariner upbound on a winding river to hear over the airwaves "This is the motor vessel *Stalwart* downbound and a half mile above Horseshoe Bend," he would be thankful for the courtesy; but he should still expect a prolonged blast and be prepared to give one in reply. And perhaps we should consider how this signal might bear on an overtaking situation, particularly in a narrow channel. Vessel *B* is dead astern of very bulky vessel *A* and preparing to overtake. *A,* though, is so gargantuan that vision of the waterway ahead is blocked. Would the Rules require that *B* sound one prolonged blast to probe beyond the obstructing *A?*

Deck license candidates sometimes fancy that what heaven amounts to is the opportunity to test Coast Guard examiners on the Rules of the Road. Should that be true, our present speculation might be a likely test question in Valhalla. We lowly mortals are best served to approach the problem with realistic humanism. *B*'s making of one prolonged blast would at least jar the concentration of bulky *A*. The result could well be total confusion. It would be better for *B* to follow normal overtaking signal procedures. He should certainly be wary of oncoming traffic as he sidles left or right while making his overtaking move, but he should not perplex *A* with any one prolonged blast.

Shortly we'll be discussing the Inland version of Rule 34 and meet a signal to be given by power-driven vessels leaving a dock or berth. They, we'll see, are obliged to sound one prolonged blast. Historically this seemed an extension of the bend signal by considering the end of the dock as an obstructed channel turn. Previous high-seas rules did not follow that reasoning so a signal for leaving a berth was not provided. What should be our interpretation of the present COLREGS statement? If we are not swayed by history we should have no problem. The shed on the end of the dock is an obstruction to visibility and traffic might be "around the bend," so why not use the one-prolonged signal? On the other hand it was not so considered under prior high-seas rules. We've met another misty area. Not to sound such a signal would be no reason for keelhauling. But if it is given, any oncomer would be given worthwhile information. Something, he would be told, lurks on the far side of that shed. One schooled in the ways of diplomacy could avoid reaching a conclusion by the bland view that no provision was spelled out for the situation. He would also neatly dodge another problem. If the vessel leaving the dock should make the signal, would it then be expected that a vessel moving down the channel make a reply? It's time for us to stop speculating and get on with more pressing business.

Rule 34(f) of COLREGS recognizes the predicament of a vessel fitted with more than one whistle. Multiple sources of sound placed more than 100 meters apart blowing together could wreak havoc with the signals of Rule 34. A vessel announcing a course change to the right would blow one short from each whistle, and the listener might receive the signal as two shorts. That the sounds would be of different tone is not sufficient distinction. So Rule 34(f) requires her to use only one whistle for maneuvering and warning signals. What, though, about a combined whistle system with sound outlets not more than 100 meters apart? Might not one short blast issuing at once from each of the sound sources clustered in the same general area be heard as a staccato signal? Paragraph 1(g) of Annex III instructs us to consider a combined whistle system as a single whistle, and no mention is made of any problem caused by multiple blasts whether staccato, allegro, or otherwise. If the possibilities do not disturb the rulemakers, we have no occasion to fuss.

We've finished our survey of COLREGS Rule 34! With some resignation, though, we should expect this to be a long watch on deck. Coming up is a study of Inland's version, and then we move on to the remaining numbered rules. Let's take time out for coffee and a cruller before we forge ahead.

That slavedriving mate is singing out for us to turn to, so with pea jackets buttoned and so'westers strapped we go back out on the bridge wing. Close quarters with Inland's Rule 34 is imminent and unavoidable. Here are the official words.

INLAND

(a) When power-driven vessels are in sight of one another and meeting or crossing at a distance within half a mile of each other, each vessel underway, when maneuvering as authorized or required by these Rules:

(i) shall indicate that maneuver by the following signals on her whistle: one short blast to mean "I intend to leave you on my port side"; two short blasts to mean "I intend to leave you on my starboard side"; and three short blasts to mean "I am operating astern propulsion".

(ii) upon hearing the one or two blast signal of the other shall, if in agreement, sound the same whistle signal and take the steps necessary to effect a safe passing. If, however, from any cause, the vessel doubts the safety of the proposed maneuver, she shall sound the danger signal specified in paragraph (d) of this Rule and each vessel shall take appropriate precautionary action until a safe passing agreement is made.

(b) A vessel may supplement the whistle signals prescribed in paragraph (a) of this Rule by light signals:

(i) These signals shall have the following significance: one flash to mean "I intend to leave you on my port side"; two flashes to mean "I intend to leave you on my starboard side"; three flashes to mean "I am operating astern propulsion";

(ii) The duration of each flash shall be about 1 second; and

(iii) The light used for this signal shall, if fitted, be one all-round white or yellow light, visible at a minimum range of 2 miles, synchronized with the whistle, and shall comply with the provisions of Annex I to these Rules.

(c) When in sight of one another:

(i) a power-driven vessel intending to overtake another power-driven vessel shall indicate her intention by the following signals on her whistle: one short blast to mean "I intend to overtake you on your starboard side"; two short blasts to mean "I intend to overtake you on your port side"; and

(ii) the power-driven vessel about to be overtaken shall, if in agreement, sound a similar sound signal. If in doubt she shall sound the danger signal prescribed in paragraph (d).

(d) When vessels in sight of one another are approaching each other and from any cause either vessel fails to understand the intentions or actions of the other, or is in doubt whether sufficient action is being taken by the other to avoid collision, the vessel in doubt shall immediately indicate such doubt by giving at least five short and rapid blasts on the whistle. This signal may be supplemented by a light signal of at least five short and rapid flashes.

(e) A vessel nearing a bend or an area of a channel or fairway where other vessels may by obscured by an intervening obstruction shall sound one prolonged blast. This signal shall be answered with a prolonged blast by any approaching vessel that may be within hearing around the bend or behind the intervening obstruction.

(f) If whistles are fitted on a vessel at a distance apart of more than 100 meters, one whistle only shall be used for giving maneuvering and warning signals.

(g) When a power-driven vessel is leaving a dock or berth, she shall sound one prolonged blast.

(h) A vessel that reaches agreement with another vessel in a meeting, crossing, or overtaking situation by using the radiotelephone as prescribed by the Bridge-to-Bridge Radiotelephone Act (85 Stat. 165; 33 U.S.C. 1207), is not obliged to sound the whistle signals prescribed by this Rule, but may do so. If agreement is not reached, then whistle signals shall be exchanged in a timely manner and shall prevail.

The design of this Inland rule produces a signal pattern much different from that required by COLREGS, and here is the Inland reasoning. Signals of action or execution of a maneuver while it is being performed might be all very well on the high seas, but on confined waters a greater measure of agreement is safer. So a dialogue is to be initiated by one vessel's signal of intention with a reply expected from the other. The Inland rulemakers also found this practice so much a part of U.S. maritime usage that to deviate was not viewed as

View from the wheelhouse of a large ship overtaking a vessel under sail. [Photo by Lawrence Wyatt]

desirable. Whatever the rationale, the result is a very pronounced contrast to COLREGS.

The first two paragraphs, 34(a) and 34(b), speak only to the power-driven. The instructions are even more exclusive, for they apply only when power-driven vessels are meeting or crossing. They do not apply to sail approaching sail or to power-driven approaching sail. When both vessels are power-driven *and* they are in sight of each other *and* they will meet or cross at a distance within half a mile of each other, then they are subject to these two paragraphs. One short blast will mean "I intend to leave you on my port side"; two short blasts will mean "I intend to leave you on my starboard side"; three short blasts will mean "I am operating astern propulsion."

The nuclear-powered Savannah *meets an outbound tanker while entering Los Angeles Harbor stern first. [Courtesy Los Angeles Harbor Department]*

To begin our analysis of these demands we should recall the discussion about the COLREGS three short blasts and engines going astern. We should assume that the signal covers engines going astern at any speed regardless of the ship's motion and even ship movement astern at any speed regardless of the engines.

Those familiar with Inland and Pilot Rules of yesteryear will note the very neat manner in which the meanings of one and two short blasts have been clarified. In the past, one blast had a choice of meanings, depending on whether a vessel was to stand on or to keep clear. In the one case it indicated intention to hold course and speed; in the other it meant intent to direct course to starboard. Now, with simplicity, it means that the other is to be kept on the port side, without implying how that will be done.

Consider the situation of two power-driven vessels coming together on reciprocal courses in a meeting situation, as shown in Fig. 56. If they are to approach within a half mile of each other, Rule 34(a) considers signals as

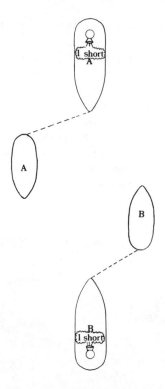

Fig. 56. *Sound Signals for Power-Driven Vessels Meeting on Inland Waters. Whether changing course or not, power-driven vessels A and B ex-change one-blast signals when meeting within a half mile of each other (Inland only).*

necessary whether they take rudder action to change course or not. Each would realize that Rule 14 requires them to pass port to port. Whether that might involve changing course or not is subordinate to agreement that they pass in the required manner. So even if no course change were necessary, they would exchange one-blast signals to confirm "I intend to leave you on my port side."

Figure 57 has them crossing. The script in Rules 15 and 17 requires that *A* hold course and speed while *B* keeps out of the way and avoids crossing ahead. How do they make their arrangements? *A,* even though not changing course, sounds one short blast to say she intends to keep *B* on her port side. And *B,* obliged to keep clear and avoid crossing ahead, will sound one if her intention is to pass under the other's stern either by changing course to the right or by slowing down. On the other hand if *B* considers it preferable to back down while *A* crosses ahead, then *B*'s signal will be three short blasts to

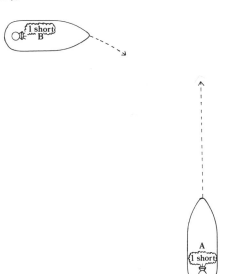

Fig. 57. Sound Signals for Power-Driven Vessels Crossing Inland.

announce operation of engines astern. Normal practice would have *A* cross ahead, which would place *B* on her port side. It would also be normal to have *B* cross *A*'s wake, which places *A* on *B*'s port side. All that would make the exchange of one-blast signals appropriate. And when meeting or crossing, a proposed maneuver is rejected by the use of the danger or doubt signal.

The modern containership S.S. President Tyler *keeping clear with a wide right turn in San Francisco Bay. [Courtesy American President Line]*

Rule 34(b) is the Inland counterpart of the provision for a maneuvering light. Again, though, there are key differences from the COLREGS version. On inland waters the maneuvering light can be white or yellow; COLREGS specifies white only. Inland's light may be of 2-mile range while COLREGS require a minimum of 5 miles. On the high seas the flash signal may be repeated and need not be synchronized with the sound. On inland waters they must be synchronized. At least, though, placement of the light relative to masthead lights is the same by Inland rules as on the high seas. It should, says section 84.23 of Inland's Annex I, be higher than the forward masthead light when two such are carried, and above or below the after masthead light. Should only one masthead light be carried, then the maneuvering light can be above or below it. And the meanings of the flash sequences conform to those assigned the whistle blasts.

Inland's Rule 34(c) attends to the signals exchanged when a power-driven vessel is overtaking another vessel also under power. A request is made by sounding one or two short blasts. One blast means an intention to overtake on the starboard side of the other; two blasts announce an intention to go up the port side. And the vessel being overtaken grants permission by replying with the same signal. The vessel overtaken gives the doubt signal (coming up shortly) to indicate disapproval.

Notice, though, that there is no mention of any special pattern when the situation is overtaking in a narrow channel. And our earlier reading of Inland's Rule 9(e) supplies a clue. There we learned that the overtaking vessel in a narrow channel or fairway indicates intention by Rule 34(c) signals and the overtaken vessel sounds approval or disapproval as Rule 34(c) describes. Until clarified by some authority, consideration of how Rules 9 and 34(c) work together might well drive some nitpickers over the edge. Inland's Rule 9(e) doesn't restrict its application to situations in narrow channels when overtaking can only take place if the vessel ahead takes some action other than holding course and speed. That unique demand is found in COLREGS alone. So even if there is plenty of room in an inland narrow channel for the vessel astern to get by, a dialogue is required. Inland does, however, parallel COLREGS by recognizing that method of propulsion is not important when overtaking in a narrow channel. Rule 9(e) speaks to "the vessel overtaking" and to "the overtaken vessel" with nary a mention of how they might be driven through the water. Does 9(e) intend that sail vessels involved in a narrow channel overtaking situation make 34(c) overtaking signals even though 34(c) speaks only to the power-driven? Saturday matinee serials of long ago urged moviegoers not to miss the next episode. Perhaps we should not miss what courts might have to say about this Rules of the Road puzzle. But the answer seems clear. A "vessel" is not the same as a "power-driven vessel." We should consider that in a narrow channel sail as well as power-driven is expected to participate in the exchange of signals.

So where do we stand? When power-driven overtakes power-driven on inland waters, whether narrow or not, a dialogue ensues. But that pesky problem of the narrow channel just won't go away. What if, on an inland narrow channel, overtaking cannot take place unless the vessel ahead moves over? Rules 13 and 17 require the overtaken vessel to hold course and speed unless inaction or miscues arise. COLREGS grants her an option to move aside after a signal exchange, but who gives her any such license on inland waters? Rule 9 of Inland doesn't raise the issue, but an inference can be made. Although Inland prescribes different signals, the problem met by COLREGS Rule 9(e) was intended to be solved. Yet mariners shouldn't speculate too much on the meaning of the Rules. It would have been better if Inland spelled out whether or not consent to be overtaken in a narrow channel authorized *Overtaken* to alter course or speed. It is likely that Inland wants *any* vessel engaged in narrow channel overtaking to speak out with one or two blasts and then to perform whatever maneuver for safe overtaking might be necessary. Should that mean that the vessel ahead may take action, then the contrast with COLREGS is lessened. The several panels of Fig. 58 depict what Inland seems to require.

A reading of Rule 34(d) raises no suspicions of murkiness. It speaks plainly to say that *any vessel in sight of any other vessel* and concerned about the maneuvers being performed *shall signal her confusion* by at least five short and rapid blasts. We should, though, view it as giving evidence that appearances deceive. The Inland doubt signal lives up to its name by generating more than its share of uncertainty, and has been doing so for decades. Older Inland and Pilot Rules specified it as four or more short and rapid blasts and referred to it as the "danger" or "doubt" signal; new Inland's Rule 34 also tags it as "danger" or "doubt" and raises the minimum blasts to five. But the purpose of this signal would seem to remain unchanged. Those older rules seemed even more unequivocal about when it could be given. Not only did they specify that it be given when in sight, they left no question that in fog, mist, falling snow, and the like, fog signals only were to be given. No question might have been left, but a question certainly arose. It is unavoidable for us to glance at the interpretations given that older danger signal so we can anticipate what might be in store for the new one.

Despite the seemingly positive words used by older rules, respectable authority urged that the danger signal be allowed when out of sight in restricted visibility. A very common question on deck officer license examinations boiled down to "Can you use the danger signal when in fog on inland waters and out of sight of others?" Even though the rules seemed clearly to say "no" the expected answer was "yes." And the argument in favor of such a looking-glass reply was strong. When shrouded by fog, would you be confused to hear a danger signal from "out there"? If so, the confusion would be on the credit side. At least you'd learn that someone is "out there" and is also confused.

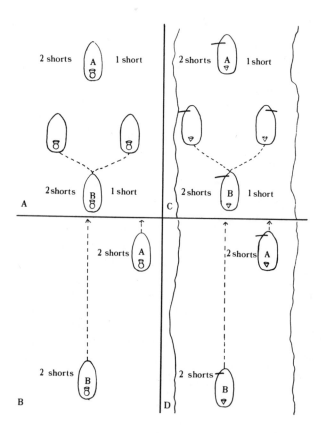

Fig. 58. *Sound Signals While Overtaking on Inland Waters. (A) On open water, only power-driven vessels exchange overtaking signals (Inland only); (B) on open water, power-driven vessel A replies to power-driven vessel B's proposal even though vessel A takes no action (Inland only); (C) on confined waters, even sail vessels exchange one- or two-blast signals when overtaking (Inland only); (D) on confined waters, sail vessel A replies to sail vessel B's proposal even if vessel A takes no action (Inland only).*

That's better than not knowing that he and his doubts are in the vicinity. By semantic contortions the proponents of that view tried to suggest that they were not in conflict with the Rules, but there was ample evidence that at least the letter of the law was being bent. Now we have a new rule. Does that mean we have a new viewpoint, or more contortions, or what? The issue never arose

over International Rules, even prior to COLREGS. Everyone, including license examiners, accepted that the high-seas doubt signal was only to be given
when in sight. Preparation of the present Inland Rules granted legislators the
opportunity to settle the problem if they meant us to use the inland doubt
signal when out of sight. All they had to do was to say so, but they didn't.
Instead they included in Rule 34(d) the words "when in sight" but removed
the older admonition that in fog, mist, and so forth only fog signals would be
given. To an extent then the matter is still indefinite, with the jury still ou..

But we do have a glimmer of interpretation. In anticipation of the advent
of new Inland Rules, an authoritative Coast Guard periodical offered a series
of articles commenting on the upcoming requirements. It contained an opinion
on the use of the doubt signal in restricted visibility, and the comment makes
good sense. Although Inland does not say in words that the doubt signal can
be used in fog and out of sight of others, it doesn't say in words that it cannot
be so used. And for as long as the exercise is not abused, using it under those
conditions can be helpful. The suggestion seems to carry on the earlier approach, and since the opinion stems from Coast Guard personnel, we should
give heed. At least license candidates should consider the Inland doubt signal
usable in restricted visibility and out of sight of others. But no musing of
nonjudicial citizens, official or otherwise, will control COLREGS, whose
words are to be followed literally.

A recap is surely in order, and here it is. By COLREGS the doubt signal
is for in-sight use only, except for two narrow channel situations. Rule 9(d)
allows a vessel being crossed to sound it; Rule 9(e) grants it to a vessel being
overtaken. And we've already been plagued with the pro and con arguments
regarding in sight. As for Inland, Rule 34(d) is clear as a bell. It requires
everyone to use it when doubtful and in sight. Rule 9 also seems specific. Its
paragraphs (d) and (e) go further than COLREGS to say that vessels being
crossed and being overtaken and in doubt *shall* use it. We've been bruised too
much already by the side issue of whether Rule 9 (an any-visibility rule)
extends Rule 34(d) (an in-sight one). Assuming, though, that it does, we are
still left with the problem of the general use of Inland's doubt signal when out
of sight. Until the matter is resolved we should probably recognize the practice
as permissible.

With troublesome Rule 34(d) astern we take care of 34(e) with neatness and
dispatch. The Inland words are the same as the COLREGS running mate, so
we can refer back to our discussion when studying it. And it is our pleasure
to do the same for Rule 34(f). On all waters the vessel equipped with more than
one whistle will use only one during maneuvering. COLREGS now ends its
Rule 34, but Inland continues on for two more paragraphs.

We should recall our speculation over sounds made by a vessel leaving a
dock on international waters. COLREGS seemed to consider the problem
inconsequential. Should structures on the pier create a channel obstruction we

might consider COLREGS to require a prolonged blast, but there is no indication that such signal is always given as a matter of course on departure. Not so by Inland. Its Rule 34(g) commands a power-driven vessel to blow one prolonged blast when leaving a dock or berth, and the manner in which that command appears requires our attention. It is not stated in the same paragraph as the "bend or obscured area" signal so it should not be viewed as one. Certainly it is a warning, but it is *not* only given when traffic in the channel is obscured. Power-driven vessels are expected to give it whenever they depart. Now, though, we have something else to note. Any vessel on the far side of a channel obscurity and hearing a prolonged blast must reply with the same signal. Does that apply to vessels in the channel which hear the one-prolonged from a departing steamer? The answer should be "no" if the departing one is in sight. And sheer fatigue discourages our consideration of what should happen when the vessel leaving a dock is not seen. Oh, well, since we've gone this far we might as well run the risk of going "a bridge too far." Figure 59 shows an example to spotlight the issues. *A*, a power-driven vessel, must always blow one prolonged blast when leaving a dock. If *B*, a vessel traversing the channel, is in sight, she now knows that *A* is underway and requires attention. But *A* needs no special warning from *B* of her presence. She sees

Fig. 59. Sound Signals When Leaving a Dock. Whether in sight of other vessels or not, a power-driven vessel undocking in inland waters sounds one prolonged blast (Inland only).

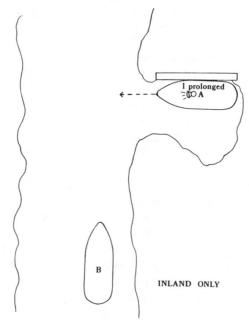

B and is guided by her observations. So no reply from *B* is required. Suppose, though, that *B* is not in sight. *A* has given warning of her approach but has no warning from *B*. Under those circumstances it would seem logical for *B* to sound a reply. In other words, what would be wrong with *B*'s accepting *A*'s signal as having been sounded pursuant to Rule 34(e) and not (g)? That would require an exchange of warnings and be all to the good. A minor point? Perhaps so, but it could reach epic proportions were *B* to make a sudden appearance as *A* was emerging from the slip.

We should be grateful for Rule 34(h). It rescues us from the tedium of the last discussions and it also brings Inland into the age of radio. When agreement is reached by VHF radiotelephone there is no need to blow horns and flash lights to signal Rule 34 maneuvers. And inching its way through international

The passenger liner S.S. Royal Viking Star *dead ahead. [Courtesy Royal Viking Line]*

circles is a proposal to fashion a similar provision on a worldwide basis. However, included in Rule 34(h) is the wise provision that if no such agreement is reached the requirements for whistle signals snap back into force. The advantages of radiocommunication need hardly be mentioned. The range is many times that of sound and the scope for negotiation is almost boundless. But problems are just as obvious. Not every vessel has the equipment, and even if it is aboard it might not be working. Certainly a proper caution would be to use it early so that there will be time left to sound horns if a negotiation falls through. Not to make a radio call early enough and then at the last minute to realize that the other has no ability to converse could be disastrous.

One dangling issue still remains. Agreement by VHF relieves vessels of the obligation to make the signals of Rule 34. However, what about the signal patterns required by troublesome Rule 9(e) when overtaking in a narrow channel? Would agreement by VHF between vessels of any propulsion exempt them from making the sound signals required by 9(e)? Court decisions will eventually resolve the question, but until then mariners must indulge in some imaginative interpretation. The chances are that they will consider VHF accord as sufficient, even though that judgment might widen the scope of exemption as prescribed by the Rules. In any case it is quite clear that proper use of the radiotelephone is far more valuable than the more imprecise blasts of a whistle.

We are finished with a study of Rule 34's words, but now we must glance at what it doesn't say. Required by its paragraph (a) is a three-blast signal from a power-driven vessel when operating astern propulsion. Its paragraph (b) states that the signal may also be given by light flashes. But in no other part of Inland is this signal mentioned, and that creates bewilderment. We should look for any unannounced limitations on its use. COLREGS has no problem, for its Rule 34(a) says that when vessels are in sight of one another a maneuvering power-driven vessel operating astern propulsion sounds three short blasts. The signal is made to any and all vessels regardless of propulsion and whether meeting, crossing, overtaking, or even perhaps immobile. The signaling vessel is warning the visible world of concerned shipping that rudder and screw are now or shortly will be her "head." Older Inland and Pilot Rules avoided any concern by using language similar in principle to present COLREGS, and that makes the current Inland approach even more curious.

Inland's Rule 34(a) addresses power-driven vessels when they are meeting and crossing each other and requires the three-blast signal when one is operating astern propulsion. Rule 34(b) merely authorizes that that signal be supplemented by the maneuvering light. But there are three ways a power-driven vessel can approach another power-driven. Rule 34(a) covers meeting and crossing, but what about overtaking? Rule 34(c) describes the sounds to be exchanged in that situation and defines the meanings of one-short and two-shorts without a whisper about three-shorts. Does this mean there is no authority for a power-driven vessel to blow three short blasts when involved in an overtaking situation? If so, the discovery is startling. Imagine A, under power, being overtaken by power-driven B. Surely A would be expected to signal that she is operating astern propulsion! In exasperation a defender of the "Keep It Simple School of Study" charges that if B needs whistle blasts to tell her which way A is going they are already in serious trouble. He might also add that we have no call to get exercised over this. If A would like to blow three blasts, then what is so heinous if she does so? Advocates of that viewpoint run a grave risk of being tagged as simpletons. Only the knowledgeable should make judgments on what is or is not important. Let's keep digging into this peculiar issue.

The mention of three blasts in Rule 34(a) is even more limiting. Meeting and crossing are the situations, and then only when both actors are power-driven. Does this mean that power-driven *A* does *not* blow three blasts when maneuvering in sight of sailing vessel *B?* The plot is beginning to thicken, for the modern Inland viewpoint seems in stark contrast to COLREGS and to its own past history. Until we are told in no uncertain terms to cease and desist, we should probably elect to blow three blasts to anyone in sight and approaching in any situation when we are operating astern propulsion. It would seem no more than good seamanship to advise an approaching vessel, regardless of how you are getting closer and of how she is propelled, that you now are or shortly will be moving astern.

At last we're clear of Rule 34 and all its snags. Now we can move along to study what signals are required when vessels are out of sight in restricted visibility. The script prescribing their conduct appeared in Rule 19. We learned that since no presumption can be made about who is hidden in the fog, or where, or even if, everyone must move with great caution. In the same spirit, the sound signals required are not bound up with too many sophistications. Rule 35 tells the story, and here are its words.

RULE 35—Sound Signals in Restricted Visibility

COLREGS

In or near an area of restricted visibility, whether by day or night, the signals prescribed in this Rule shall be used as follows:

(a) A power-driven vessel making way through the water shall sound at intervals of not more than 2 minutes one prolonged blast.

(b) A power-driven vessel underway but stopped and making no way through the water shall sound at intervals of not more than 2 minutes two prolonged blasts in succession with an interval of about 2 seconds between them.

(c) A vessel not under command, a vessel restricted in her ability to maneuver, a vessel constrained by her draft, a sailing vessel, a vessel engaged in fishing and a vessel engaged in towing or pushing another vessel shall, instead of the signals prescribed in paragraphs (a) or (b) of this Rule, sound at intervals of not more than 2 minutes three blasts in succession, namely one prolonged followed by two short blasts.

(d) A vessel engaged in fishing, when at anchor, and a vessel restricted in her ability to maneuver when carrying out her work at anchor, shall instead of the signals prescribed in paragraph (g) of this Rule sound the signal prescribed in paragraph (c) of this Rule.

(e)   A vessel towed or if more than one vessel is towed the last vessel of the tow, if manned, shall at intervals of not more than 2 minutes sound four blasts in succession, namely one prolonged followed by three short blasts. When practicable, this signal shall be made immediately after the signal made by the towing vessel.

(f)   When a pushing vessel and a vessel being pushed ahead are rigidly connected in a composite unit they shall be regarded as a power-driven vessel and shall give the signals prescribed in paragraphs (a) or (b) of this Rule.

(g)   A vessel at anchor shall at intervals of not more than one minute ring the bell rapidly for about 5 seconds. In a vessel of 100 meters or more in length the bell shall be sounded in the forepart of the vessel and immediately after the ringing of the bell the gong shall be sounded rapidly for about 5 seconds in the after part of the vessel. A vessel at anchor may in addition sound three blasts in succession, namely one short, one prolonged and one short blast, to give warning of her position and of the possibility of collision to an approaching vessel.

(h)   A vessel aground shall give the bell signal and if required the gong signal prescribed in paragraph (g)   of this Rule and shall, in addition, give three separate and distinct strokes on the bell immediately before and after the rapid ringing of the bell. A vessel aground may in addition sound an appropriate whistle signal.

(i)   A vessel of less than 12 meters in length shall not be obliged to give the above-mentioned signals but, if she does not, shall make some other efficient sound signal at intervals of not more than 2 minutes.

(j)   A pilot vessel when engaged on pilotage duty may in addition to the signals prescribed in paragraphs (a), (b) or (g)   of this Rule sound an identity signal consisting of four short blasts.

INLAND

In or near an area of restricted visibility, whether by day or night, the signals prescribed in this Rule shall be used as follows:

(a) A power-driven vessel making way through the water shall sound at intervals of not more than 2 minutes one prolonged blast.

(b) A power-driven vessel underway but stopped and making no way through the water shall sound at intervals of not more than 2 minutes two prolonged blasts in succession with an interval of about 2 seconds between them.

(c) A vessel not under command; a vessel restricted in her ability to maneuver, whether underway or at anchor; a sailing vessel; a vessel engaged in fishing, whether underway or at anchor; and a vessel engaged in towing or pushing another vessel shall, instead of the signals prescribed in paragraphs (a) or (b) of this Rule, sound at intervals of not more than 2 minutes, three blasts in succession; namely, one prolonged followed by two short blasts.

(d) A vessel towed or if more than one vessel is towed the last vessel of the tow, if manned, shall at intervals of not more than 2 minutes sound four blasts in succession; namely, one prolonged followed by three short blasts. When practicable, this signal shall be made immediately after the signal made by the towing vessel.

(e) When a pushing vessel and a vessel being pushed ahead are rigidly connected in a composite unit they shall be regarded as a power-driven vessel and shall give the signals prescribed in paragraphs (a) or (b) of this Rule.

(f) A vessel at anchor shall at intervals of not more than 1 minute ring the bell rapidly for about 5 seconds. In a vessel of 100 meters or more in length the bell shall be sounded in the forepart of the vessel and immediately after the ringing of the bell the gong shall be sounded rapidly for about 5 seconds in the after part of the vessel. A vessel at anchor may in addition sound three blasts in succession; namely, one short, one prolonged and one short blast, to give warning of her position and of the possibility of collision to an approaching vessel.

(g) A vessel aground shall give the bell signal and if required the gong signal prescribed in paragraph (f) of this Rule and shall, in addition, give three separate and distinct strokes on the bell immediately before and after the rapid ringing of the bell. A vessel aground may in addition sound an appropriate whistle signal.

(h) A vessel of less than 12 meters in length shall not be obliged to give the above-mentioned signals but, if she does not, shall make some other efficient sound signal at intervals of not more than 2 minutes.

(i) A pilot vessel when engaged on pilotage duty may in addition to the signals prescribed in paragraphs (a), (b) or (f) of this Rule sound an identity signal consisting of four short blasts.

(j) The following vessels shall not be required to sound signals as prescribed in paragraph (f) of this Rule when anchored in a special anchorage area designated by the Secretary:

    (i) a vessel of less than 20 meters in length; and

    (ii) a barge, canal boat, scow, or other nondescript craft.

Our first observation should be that these signals are required day or night when in or near an area of restricted visibility. Just as Rule 19's code of conduct applies when skirting a fogbank so do the requirements for whistle signals. Second, note that although the COLREGS and Inland statements are not identical they are reasonably so. And third, we should recall some realities about sound in fog. To hear a loud noise in fog is no reliable evidence that the source is closeby. More important, a faint sound in fog is not a guarantee that the source is far away. Fog does strange things to sound waves. We should not expect them to offer any safe grounds for judging range or bearing. Sound can warn that something is hidden nearby and the sequence of blasts can give a clue to identity, but we cannot expect sound to do much more. Nor need we expect any more preamble to our study of Rule 35 so here are its patterns.

A power-driven vessel making way through the water sounds one prolonged blast. And reading this requirement might nudge a memory of our discussion long ago about the word "underway." Standing alone it means no more than that a vessel has no connection to the bottom or to the shore. But for a power-driven vessel to sound one prolonged blast she must also be making way through the water. When, although underway, she is not moving through the water her signal changes to two prolonged blasts. In either case the specified interval is no more than 2 minutes. The frequency may be shorter but it may not be longer. And the pattern is surely not complicated: one prolonged blast means power-driven moving through the water, two prolonged mean power-driven lying-to dead in the water.

In the Morse Code the sequence of a dash followed by two dots or "dah-dit-dit" signifies the letter "D" (Delta). And to that letter the International Code of Signals assigns the meaning "Keep clear of me; I am maneuvering with difficulty." The Rules of the Road make use of this sequence to identify a fogbound vessel operating under an impediment. COLREGS has its say in Rule 35(c) and (d) while Inland uses 35(c). But there is one difference. We should read the two COLREGS paragraphs first before noting a contrast. The roster of those required to make this signal is comprised of these vessels: those not under command, restricted in ability to maneuver whether underway or at anchor, constrained by draft, sailing, engaged in fishing whether underway or at anchor, and engaged in towing or pushing. This makes very good sense, for each is plagued with a difficulty in maneuvering. The maximum interval is again 2 minutes, which squares with the frequency used throughout Rule 35 for vessels underway. And back before us is the problem of how these vessels relate to the planet when they sound the signal. Are they suffering their impediment while underway? If so, do they signal only when making way? Or do they make this signal even when at anchor? Two of the classes give us no trouble. A vessel restricted in her ability to maneuver sounds "dah-dit-dit" whether underway or at anchor. That takes care of a host of activities including the cablelayer, the buoy tender, the dredge, the diving mother ship, the aircraft carrier, and the vessel clearing mines. The same sounds are made by a vessel engaged in fishing whether underway or at anchor. And although the point is not crystal-clear, we should not expect them to make any other sound signals. Not spelled out at all is any guidance to the other classes subject to Rule 35(c) and (d). Is "dah-dit-dit" a signal to be used by them when underway but not to be used when at anchor? Does the factor of making way have any influence? Here are the answers we should accept. Vessels not under command, constrained by draft, sailing, and engaged in towing or pushing sound "dah-dit-dit" when underway, whether making way or not. But they do *not* sound that signal when at anchor. Instead they make normal anchor signals, which are still to come. A contrast between COLREGS and Inland should come as no surprise. The vessel constrained by draft is recognized on international waters and told to make the same sound as any other maneuvering with difficulty. Inland, though, extends no deference to such a vessel and makes her just another power-driven. And we are ready for some examples to start placing all these sound patterns in focus.

Suppose a power-driven vessel in fog is underway and making way. Her signal would then be one prolonged blast at 2-minute intervals. Even if she were moving astern the signal would be unchanged so long as no one else was in sight. Next, though, she stops her engines and begins to slow down. While she is still in motion the signal is unchanged, but when she becomes dead in the water her fog signal changes. She is still underway but not making way, so the signal becomes two prolonged blasts at 2-minute intervals. When she again starts moving she reverts to the one-prolonged signal. But suddenly disaster strikes! Her rudder falls off. Now she is not under command, so the fog signal becomes one prolonged followed by two shorts and continues so whether she is making way or not.

Let's vary the facts and make her an aircraft carrier. First she is steaming along making way but not practicing her profession. The signal is one prolonged blast. Next comes a neat trick in the fog, for she begins to recover aircraft. The signal changes to one prolonged followed by two shorts. Still at work, she comes dead in the water but her "D" signal continues. Now she drops her anchor but is still accepting her brood of planes. The "D" signal continues. She lifts the anchor and gets underway while aircraft are still alighting. "D" still continues. Next, her engine fails and she is not under command. The signal of one prolonged followed by two shorts continues whether she is still handling aircraft or not. The last jet lands and she drops the anchor. But her engine is still out of commission. This would require her to change her fog signal from the status of "not under command" to "at anchor." No more "dah-dit-dit" will be heard; instead the anchor signals (still to come) would be heard.

One further example should suffice to get the idea. A multipurpose sailing vessel in fog experiences a rudder casualty. To begin with she is sailing along but not engaged in any special operation and has no equipment problems. Her signal, as a sailing vessel, is one prolonged followed by two shorts. Next she decides to engage in fishing. Out go the nets but the signal is not changed. A helicopter perched on her midship house is prepared for takeoff. The signal remains the same. She is directed to a good fishing spot and drops the anchor while her nets are out. Still the signal is the same. A diver on board stands ready to descend, so she is a mother ship engaged in an underwater operation. The fog signal continues as "dah-dit-dit." What now happens is that she raises her anchor and becomes underway. But for so long as she is still engaged in fishing the signal doesn't change. Next comes a rudder casualty, but what doesn't come is a fog signal change. Her sails are hauled down, her diver is hauled up, her nets are hauled in. But for so long as she remains rudderless and underway she is not under command, so the fog signal is unchanged. At last, though, she throws in the sponge and drops the anchor to await a tow. This finally changes her fog signal. She has changed status to a vessel at anchor and begins to sound the anchor signals (yet to be discussed).

Here in recap is the pattern. The following vessels, whether making way or not, sound one prolonged followed by two shorts but switch to anchor signals when they come to anchor: not under command, sail, towing or pushing, and (on the high seas only) a vessel constrained by draft. Those restricted in ability to maneuver and those engaged in fishing keep sounding that "D" signal whether they are underway or at anchor. COLREGS achieved this by amending an original rule to include a new paragraph. This nudged some existing paragraphs deeper into the alphabet and caused them to fall out of step with Inland. By now, though, we should be quite expert in playing the numbers and letters game of the Rules. Farragut would say, "Damn the designations! Full speed ahead!" He would also rather face Confederate torpedoes in Mobile Bay than be confronted with "chapter and verse" of the modern Rules. Not having his options, we must plunge ahead. So, heedless of whether the paragraph is (d) or (e), we carry on to the next subject.

Vessels being towed, say Rule 35(d) of Inland and (e) of COLREGS, sound one prolonged blast followed by three short blasts. In Morse Code this is the letter "B" (Bravo). The International Code defines that as "I am taking in or discharging dangerous goods." Admiral Farragut might agree with this meaning but that is not true of the Rules of the Road, for there is no intended correlation with the Code of Signals. Even so, we can fashion one. A vessel in tow might be a barge, and that word starts with "B." More important to us is a discussion of who gives the signal and when. "B" is sounded by a vessel in tow provided she is the last in line and is manned. No signal is required if no crewmember is present to sound it. And none is allowed from the middle of a line of vessels being towed astern. The idea is to identify the end of the line, and then only if identification is feasible.

Rule 35(e) in Inland—which is 35(f) in COLREGS—harks back to our earlier discussion of modern technology. A tug pushing ahead and its pushee can be so connected that they become a rigid composite unit. In that case, says this paragraph, they become one power-driven vessel and sound the fog signals detailed in Rule 35(a) and (b) for normal power-driven vessels.

The next paragraph of each rule, whether (g) of COLREGS or (f) of Inland, prescribes the signals for vessels at anchor. Those 100 meters or more long sound a bell forward and a gong aft. The period is 5 seconds for each sound and the interval is shortened from the underway maximum of 2 minutes to no longer than 1 minute. When the length is under 100 meters all that need be sounded is the bell. Note, though, that the bell need not then be sounded forward. Only when the vessel is 100 meters or more long and will also be sounding a gong need the bell be clanged in the fore part of the vessel.

This paragraph also provides for making a whistle signal of one short followed by one prolonged and then followed by one short. The purpose is to warn others of the anchored vessel's position and of the danger of collision. A possible impact on the rulemakers might well have been frustration. "Dit-dah-dit" in Morse Code is the letter "R" (Romeo), and years ago its International Code meaning was "The way is off my vessel; you may feel your way past me." In the 1960s the rulemakers looked over at the code and considered the warning worthy of incorporation into the sound patterns for a vessel at anchor. The reasoning was sound but the timing was wrong. In retrospect the ink seemed not dry on adoption of "R" by the Rules of the Road before the signal codemakers changed the meaning of that letter. Nowadays all it says to a signalman is that a signal has been received. Undaunted, though, both COLREGS and Inland carry on its heritage. To them "R" retains the spirit of its original intent; "dit-dah-dit" is an option given to vessels at anchor.

Rule 35(g) in Inland and 35(h) in COLREGS set out the signals for a vessel aground. In addition to the anchor signal required for a vessel of her length, she sounds three strokes of the bell before 5 seconds of clanging and then three strokes afterward. No wonder the equipment requirements of Rule 33 make provision for automatic signaling! Imagine the predicament of two able seamen on a vessel 1100 feet long and aground. In a muffling fog they are expected to maintain a 60-second rhythm of three strokes of the bell before 5 seconds of ringing and then three more strokes of the bell to be followed by 5 seconds of gonging from a station more than three football fields distant. Few would look forward to a long anchor watch on such a ship.

The paragraph describing signals for vessels aground allows for a whistle signal appropriate to the circumstances. But that word "appropriate" is vague. It is easy to conclude what such a signal cannot be. One already assigned for use in fog would not be allowed. That would exclude one prolonged, two prolonged, and one prolonged followed by two or three shorts. It might also exclude the "R" signal of short-prolonged-short, for we've been told it is allowed a vessel at anchor to warn of her position and of the danger of collision. On the other hand since "R" does warn of position and danger, there are those who consider it appropriate whether the position and danger are caused by being anchored or aground. Another signal offered by the International Code of Signals is less controversial. The letter "U" (Uniform) means "You are standing into danger." Its short-short-prolonged pattern is not used elsewhere in the Rules and would seem a likely candidate. Frumping in the wings are advocates of the use of the doubt signal in fog. "What about it?" say they. Our reply should be "Cite us some modern authority." The picture is beginning to cloud again so we should hurry on.

It would be more accurate to say that we must hurry back, for next to be studied is the matter of the small vessel exemption already discussed. Vessels less than 12 meters long are not required to make the above-mentioned signals. But if they don't, they must sound some efficient noise at 2-minute intervals. Now comes a high-pitched wail of anguish from the true student of the Rules. Specified ahead of Inland's Rule 35(h) are (a) through (g). Perched on top of COLREGS Rule 35(i) are (a) through (h). Does this paragraph exempt small vessels only from sounding the signals of the preceding paragraph or does it absolve them from giving any of the foregoing all the way back to the beginning of the rule? Artful reading provides an answer. Back in Rule 33(b) we read that vessels less than 12 meters long need not carry a whistle, a bell, or a gong. That means they need not have any equipment to make the "above-mentioned" signals. The cat with the touchy tail would not be able to emit short or prolonged blasts any more than to sound like a bell or a gong. We should give this part of the Rules a literal meaning. "Above-mentioned" refers to all other signals mentioned in Rule 35.

Next considered is a pilot vessel. Whether underway or at anchor she is allowed to identify herself by sounding four short blasts. Here is another merger of the Morse Code with the International Code of Signals. Four shorts is the letter "H" (Hotel), and that means "I have a pilot on board." Our friend the nitpicker now reappears. In addition to the signals in COLREGS Rules 35(a), (b), and (g)—which are Inland Rules 35(a), (b), and (f)—this signal can be made. The literal reference tells us that in addition to the signals for a power-driven vessel underway and making way, and for a power-driven vessel underway but stopped, and for any vessel at anchor, a pilot vessel can add "H." Where does that leave a sailing pilot vessel? Is this a presumption that all modern pilot vessels are power-driven? If so the presumption is not well taken. There must be hundreds of sail pilot vessels throughout the world. During an energy crunch they might even increase in the United States. But the question now raised is whether a sail pilot vessel may sound the identity signal of four shorts. It is not logical to accept that a power-driven vessel can identify herself as carrying a pilot while a sail vessel cannot. It is less reasonable that a sail pilot vessel is invited to alter her basic signal of one prolonged followed by two shorts when she exercises an option to add the supplementary signal of four shorts. That would give sail a license to masquerade as power-driven when in a fog. Good seamanship would indicate that declaration of propulsion is more important than an advertisement of cargo. But need she make a choice? What would be wrong with a sail pilot vessel's sounding prolonged-short-short in fog to announce her difficulty and then to add four shorts to say she is carrying a pilot? Our reading should be that nothing is wrong with that view. A blemish in the Rules might disturb the scrupulous, but it should not upset the rest of us. A pilot vessel on duty should be allowed to supplement her normal fog signal, whether for power or sail, with the sounding of four shorts for identity.

Now, though, comes another topic for speculation. What about an on-duty pilot vessel which has run aground? Has she the option to sound four short blasts? Prudent public relations would recommend that she forgo professional advertising for a while. Pilots aground on their own vessels hardly engender confidence. Such a vessel will stroke a bell before and after a vigorous ringing. She might even sound a gong. Whistle blasts could be added to warn others that they are standing into danger by getting anywhere near her. But she will not become a public penitent by blowing four shorts.

"Channel fever" is upon us, for we approach the end of this tortuous study. Only three numbered rules lie between us and the final hazards of surveying the annexes. Our next subject, Rule 36, seems harmless enough, but we have grown accustomed to deception. After studying the words of this rule we discuss its meaning.

RULE 36—Signals to Attract Attention
COLREGS

If necessary to attract the attention of another vessel, any vessel may make light or sound signals that cannot be mistaken for any signal authorized elsewhere in these Rules, or may direct the beam of her searchlight in the direction of the danger, in such a way as not to embarrass any vessel. Any light to attract the attention of another vessel shall be such that it cannot be mistaken for any aid to navigation. For the purpose of this Rule the use of high intensity intermittent or revolving lights, such as strobe lights, shall be avoided.

INLAND

If necessary to attract the attention of another vessel, any vessel may make light or sound signals that cannot be mistaken for any signal authorized elsewhere in these Rules, or may direct the beam of her searchlight in the direction of the danger, in such a way as not to embarrass any vessel.

The matter of strobe lights has driven a wedge between international thought and that in the United States. High-seas rules consider such high-intensity devices so blinding as to mask normal navigation lights. So the COLREGS recommendation is that their use be avoided. The rebuttal presented on our waters is that they certainly achieve the aim of attracting attention. Inland contains no recommendation that a damper be put on their use. The U.S. view, as we'll learn in the next chapter, seems directly opposed. COLREGS request we not use a strobe light to attract attention. They approve any sound or light pattern which does not conflict with an already-assigned signal. A searchlight carefully directed is considered acceptable. But a strobe light? COLREGS say, "We'd rather you not use it." Inland, by silence, would seem to say, "Why not use it if it attracts attention?" Here, though, is more evidence that indeed things are not always what they seem to be. Rule 36 requires that attention-getters be such that they cannot be mistaken for signals authorized elsewhere. There is no "elsewhere" mention of a strobe light within COLREGS, and the discouragement from use found in Rule 36 is not an inflexible prohibition. The result is that on international waters, although use shall be avoided it is not flat-out forbidden. The contrast on inland waters is ironical. The use of the strobe light will come up again when we discuss the distress signals of Annex IV. For now we should note that Inland lists a specific strobe display as an authorized distress signal. What results is that to use a high-intensity white light flashing 50–70 times a minute as a signal to attract attention on inland waters is to violate the Rules, for Inland has authorized it elsewhere. On waters where a strobe light is welcome it cannot be used to attract attention. On waters where that light is snubbed no such absolute prohibition exists.

With that statement we have our first encounter with distress signals. Rule 37 of both COLREGS and Inland does no more than tell us that we should look to Annex IV for details. Here are the official statements.

RULE 37—Distress Signals
COLREGS

When a vessel is in distress and requires assistance she shall use or exhibit the signals described in Annex IV to these Rules.

INLAND

When a vessel is in distress and requires assistance she shall use or exhibit the signals described in Annex IV to these Regulations.

We'll defer any further discussion of this rule until we meet the next chapter.

Part E—Exemptions contains the last numbered rule. And if Rule 38 crumbled into dust the mariner's command of knowledge adequate for onboard operation would hardly be affected. We could easily be coaxed into disregarding the whole works, for at midnight on a dark and stormy night the mariner would find little use for what is said. By now, though, our compulsion for thoroughness is too strong. Gloss over we may, but ignore we must not. Here are the uninspiring details

RULE 38—Exemptions

COLREGS

Any vessel (or class of vessels) provided that she complies with the requirements of the International Regulations for Preventing Collisions at Sea, 1960, the keel of which is laid or which is at a corresponding stage of construction before the entry into force of these Regulations may be exempted from compliance therewith as follows:

(a) The installation of lights with ranges prescribed in Rule 22, until four years after the date of entry into force of these Regulations.

(b) The installation of lights with color specifications as prescribed in Section 7 of Annex I to these Regulations, until four years after the date of entry into force of these Regulations.

(c) The repositioning of lights as a result of conversion from Imperial to metric units and rounding off measurement figures, permanent exemption.

(d)(i) The repositioning of masthead lights on vessels of less than 150 meters in length, resulting from the prescriptions of Section 3(a) of Annex I to these Regulations, permanent exemption.

(ii) The repositioning of masthead lights on vessels of 150 meters or more in length, resulting from the prescriptions of Section 3(a) of Annex I to these Regulations, until 9 years after the date of entry into force of these Regulations.

(e) The repositioning of masthead lights resulting from the prescriptions of Section 2(b) of Annex I to these Regulations, until 9 years after the date of entry into force of these Regulations.

(f) The repositioning of sidelights resulting from the prescriptions of Sections 2(g) and 3(b) of Annex I to these Regulations, until 9 years after the date of entry into force of these Regulations.

(g) The requirements for sound signal appliances prescribed in Annex III to these Regulations, until 9 years after the date of entry into force of these Regulations.

(h) The repositioning of all-round lights resulting from the prescription of Section 9(b) of Annex I to these Regulations, permanent exemption.

INLAND

Any vessel or class of vessels, the keel of which is laid or which is at a corresponding stage of construction before the date of enactment of this Act, provided that she complies with the requirements of—

(a) The Act of June 7, 1897 (30 Stat. 96), as amended (33 U.S.C. 154–232) for vessels navigating the waters subject to that statute;

(b) Section 4233 of the Revised Statutes (33 U.S.C. 301–356) for vessels navigating the waters subject to that statute;

(c) The Act of February 8, 1895 (28 Stat. 645), as amended (33 U.S.C. 241–295) for vessels navigating the waters subject to that statute; or

(d) Sections 3, 4, and 5 of the Act of April 25, 1940 (54 Stat. 163), as amended (46 U.S.C. 526 b, c, and d) for motorboats navigating the waters subject to that statute; shall be exempted from compliance with the technical Annexes to these Rules as follows:

(i) the installation of lights with ranges prescribed in Rule 22, until 4 years after the effective date of these Rules, except that vessels of less than 20 meters in length are permanently exempt;

(ii) the installation of lights with color specifications as prescribed in Annex I to these Rules, until 4 years after the effective date of these Rules, except that vessels of less than 20 meters in length are permanently exempt;

(iii) the repositioning of lights as a result of conversion to metric units and rounding off measurement figures, are permanently exempt; and

(iv) the horizontal repositioning of masthead lights prescribed by Annex I to these Rules:

(1) on vessels of less than 150 meters in length, permanent exemption.

(2) on vessels of 150 meters or more in length, until 9 years after the effective date of these Rules.

(v) the restructuring or repositioning of all lights to meet the prescriptions of Annex I to these Rules, until 9 years after the effective date of these Rules;

(vi) power-driven vessels of 12 meters or more but less than 20 meters in length are permanently exempt from the provisions of Rule 23(a)(i) and 23 (a)(iv) provided that, in place of these lights, the vessel exhibits a white light aft visible all round the horizon; and

(vii) the requirements for sound signal appliances prescribed in Annex III to these Rules, until 9 years after the effective date of these Rules.

The impact of COLREGS Rule 38 is far less than that of the Inland rule, for the international regulations have been updated about once a generation. Not so with Inland. Its basic structure was a jury-rigged antique held together by baling wire and soft patches for decades. Gutting it back to the bare bulkheads required extensive demolition with sling-loads of laws and regulations dumped overboard. We have no need to rush to a law library to identify exactly what statutes dating back to August 19, 1890, are now flotsam and jetsam. It is sufficient to note that a new broom swept very clean.

Rule 38 of COLREGS restricts itself to granting amnesties and stays of execution from imposition of equipment requirements, and some of those have already expired. Compliance with new rules on light ranges and color specifications by vessels conforming to the older 1960 International Rules was delayed until four years after COLREGS became effective. That stay expired in July 1981. Relief from repositioning some light placement and sound appliance installation was extended for nine years, until July 1986. And a few rearrangements on existing vessels were permanently suspended. If we have further interest we can read the fine print.

No matriarch of the age of luxury yachts need conform to the letter of modern equipment rules. [Photo by Beken & Son, Cowes]

Rule 38 of Inland parallels COLREGS with amnesties and stays, and grants particular consideration to smaller vessels. Any craft constructed after the effective date of the new rules must of course meet their requirements. But if the keel was laid prior to the enactment date of the new rules, then exemptions apply only so long as the fittings placed aboard meet the demands of the older Inland Rules and related laws. Owners of those preexisting vessels who have already jettisoned their copies of the old requirements had better grab a boat-hook and start hauling them back on board.

The general idea is that light ranges and color specifications can remain as is on vessels 20 meters or more long until December 24, 1985. The smaller vessels which predate the new rules are given a lifetime exemption from compliance. The onslaught of the metric system is stemmed by a permanent suspension of requirements to align preexisting measurements in feet to meters. Vessels under 150 meters long and existing in whole or in part when Inland went to work need never reposition masthead lights to comply with the new Annex I. Longer ships can wait for nine years after December 1981. Compliance with new requirements for sound signal appliances is delayed for the same nine years, so the old bellows foghorn might not become extinct until December 24, 1990.

Of special interest to owners of preexisting small power-driven vessels is subparagraph vi of Inland's Rule 38 recital of exemptions. The old Motorboat Act prescribed for Classes 2 and 3 a 20-point white light forward and a 32-point white light aft accompanied by separate sidelights. Those two classes embraced vessels at least 40 feet and no more than 65 feet long. Translated to metric measurement, 40 feet is a hair more than 12 meters and 65 feet is just shy of 20 meters. Subparagraph vi grants them a permanent exemption from some of the requirements of the new Inland Rule 23. There, in 23(a)(i), they are told to show a 225° white light (a masthead light) as far forward as possible. And 23(a)(iv) demands that they show a 135° white light (a sternlight) pointing aft. The burden of Rule 38 is to say that they need not show either of those lights if they have an all-around white light aft. So when already rigged for the gutted Motorboat Act, power-driven vessels at least 12 meters long but less than 20 meters need only turn off their existing 20-point light forward and they will meet the new requirements for the life of the vessel. One other thing in this connection is worth recalling. Rule 21(b) allows vessels less than 20 meters long to show, if they choose, a combined red-and-green lantern in lieu of separate sidelights. The Motorboat Act required the 12-to-20 group to show separate sidelights. The result, then, is a stay for them on the white light requirements and the inheritance of an option regarding their sidelights.

A statement found in Rule 1(b)(ii) of Inland expresses an exemption far more sweeping than any found in Rule 38. It seems to say that compliance with Inland's construction and equipment requirements is *optional!* Are we being told that the time spent mastering the details of Inland's lights, shapes, and sound patterns was unnecessary? If so, mutinous notions will be stewing from prow to poopdeck. Long ago in studying Rule 1 we met its paragraph (b)(ii). Menaced as we are by unruliness, we'd better take a second look to learn if that rule really does make a lot of other rules unruly. Here are the exact words used:

> All vessels complying with the construction and equipment requirements of the International Regulations are considered to be in compliance with these Rules.

First we should try to find out why any such concession need be made. It doesn't take much deliberation to conclude that the motive is well founded.

A vessel crossing a line of demarcation between COLREGS and Inland could otherwise be faced with the task of rearranging the way in which some signaling equipment was fitted. That prospect would discourage high-seas shipping from coming in and inland shipping from going out. The remedy is to allow one set of requirements to be used on both sides of the line. No single nation has the right to decide for itself what should not be done on international waters, so we cannot allow vessels rigged for Inland Rules to disregard conflicting demands when operating under COLREGS. But we don't have to be hard-nosed by insisting that those rigged for COLREGS must change things around when they enter inland waters. So Rule 1(b)(ii) authorizes substituting some COLREGS specifics for some Inland counterparts.

How far, though, may this replacement process go? The expressed application is to construction and equipment requirements, and that does not include codes of conduct and maneuvering signals. So a vessel ascending a Western River may not capriciously elect to follow COLREGS Rule 9. Nor may an overtaking vessel on an inland narrow channel start blowing the "G" signal of COLREGS Rules 9 and 34 to the ship ahead of her. On the other hand should the whistle used be located according to COLREGS dictates it need not be relocated on inland waters. More involved is consideration of problems such as would confront a towboat in the following circumstances. She has been pushing ahead on international waters and crosses over the line to inland waters. During the COLREGS leg of the voyage she would display only a white light at her stern and would not be required to mount a special flashing yellow light on the forepart of the vessel being pushed ahead. Inland's Rule 24, however, requires two towing lights in a vertical line as the stern display and insists that the flashing yellow light appear on the vessel being pushed. The requirements of Inland Rules reflect a considered judgment of the rulemakers. They thought vessels being pushed ahead should have a distinctive signal of identification. They concluded that vessels doing the pushing should have an identity pattern visible from astern. For whatever reason, the COLREGS rulemakers reached different conclusions. In the case of these signals it would seem that the Inland requirements are very worthwhile. In fact they are almost invaluable, as we discovered when discussing Rule 24. Is it then good sense for Inland to allow the use of a COLREGS pattern rejected by the makers of the rules as inadequate?

An opinion has been voiced that options granted by Rule 1(b)(ii) should not in any case apply to a vessel which spends her entire life on the inland side of the line of demarcation. That view seems to reflect unassailable logic. A vessel penned in by the shores of Lake Tahoe should not be allowed to rig under COLREGS in any manner. But there still remains the problem of the "sometime outside, sometime inside" vessel. Those who would engage in dual operation should check with a Coast Guard district office before presuming too much on the basis of this paragraph of Rule 1.

We should presume no longer on our powers of perseverance. The end of this wearying chapter is at hand. During our watch below we can splice the main brace, grab a few winks in the bunk, and be ready to rise and shine for the next chapter's conclusion of our study. Did someone just remind us of a quiz? It can't have been Teacher's Pet, for he has been "normalized." Why, it was that treacherous Tom Sawyer! The old sailor was right when he said that no one is more insufferable than the reformed.

QUESTIONS

Since this chapter has ended on the tedious note of legislative trivia, we should empanel a trio of virtuosos to present our test. Gen. Henry M. Robert, USA, draws on his expertise in rules of order to chair the tribunal. Edmond Hoyle will keep an eye on how we play the game. And J. Wellington Hammurabi returns from ancient Babylonia to ensure that substance will not be concealed by form. The law firm of Hammurabi, Hoyle & Robert, judges pro tem, is ready to decide our fate. Ten interrogatories having been prepared, the judges overrule all objections and the trial proceeds.

1. A vessel 15 meters long is required to be equipped with
   a. a whistle
   b. a bell
   c. both of the above
   d. none of the above

2. A power-driven vessel is in sight of a sail vessel on her starboard bow and crossing her course. The power-driven vessel is maneuvering to keep clear. She decides to change course to the right. The rules specify that she sound one short blast
   a. on the high seas
   b. on inland waters
   c. both of the above
   d. none of the above

3. The maneuvering light
   a. can be used to supplement the one, two, three, and at least five short-blast signals
   b. can be yellow on inland waters
   c. both of the above
   d. none of the above

4. The signal of one prolonged blast followed by two short blasts is specified to be given in restricted visibility by a sail vessel
   a. on inland waters
   b. on the high seas
   c. both of the above
   d. none of the above

5. The doubt signal of at least five short and rapid blasts is required of all vessels, regardless of propulsion, in sight of another and in doubt
   a. on the high seas
   b. on inland waters
   c. both of the above
   d. none of the above

6. The one-short-blast and two-short-blasts maneuvering signals given by a power-driven vessel
   a. indicate execution of the maneuver on inland waters
   b. indicate execution of the maneuver on the high seas
   c. both of the above
   d. none of the above

7. The fog signal of one prolonged followed by two short blasts is to be given when underway on both high seas and inland waters by
   a. a power-driven vessel engaged in fishing
   b. a sail vessel engaged in fishing
   c. a sail vessel not under command
   d. all of the above

8. A vessel 15 meters long and aground must
   a. ring a bell
   b. sound one short blast followed by one prolonged blast followed by one short blast ("R")
   c. both of the above
   d. none of the above

9. The sound signal of one prolonged blast on a whistle is specified by COLREGS as the signal for
   a. a vessel nearing a channel bend
   b. a power-driven vessel leaving a dock or berth
   c. both of the above
   d. none of the above

10. In fog a vessel less than 12 meters long is required to make a sound signal
    a. by COLREGS
    b. by Inland
    c. by both of the above
    d. by none of the above

AND ANSWERS

The judges have collected their yellow notepads and retired to chambers for deliberation. They will allow 10 points for each correct response and use this schedule to guide their decision:

90–100	orderly, according to Hoyle, and acceptable by both the Tigris and the Euphrates
80	slightly galling to the general but substantively sound
70	the Tigris is satisfied but the Euphrates is undecided
under 70	raise bail quickly!

1. c   2. a   3. c   4. c   5. c   6. b   7. d   8. a   9. a   10. c

9
THE ANNEXES

THE ANNEXES to the Rules of the Road are like vessels in tow astern of the main body. The "towlines" connecting them with the numbered rules they serve are well marked, as we've already learned in earlier chapters. Most of the time a mariner's reference to an annex will only be when equipment is being selected and put in place. Since that is not always true, we must make a quick survey and concentrate on salient points. But it won't be necessary in this chapter to wade through reprints of all the annexes. When necessary we'll thumb back to the Appendix section of this book to find the official text for COLREGS' four annexes and the five attached to Inland.

ANNEX I

If our interest lies in fitting out a vessel with lights and shapes we must carefully read Annex I. But operational knowledge need emphasize only the variations on basic patterns which might be observed. In Chapter 6 we wrestled with Rule 24's instructions to power-driven towboats and observed that tugs may rig their identity white lights aligned with either the forward masthead light or the after one. We also considered how such an option can change the patterns an observer might see. All we need do here is remind ourselves that Rule 24 grants options and Annex I is the guide for the measuring tape when an option has been selected.

The impact of Annex I on Rule 27 is quite substantial. Also in Chapter 6 we learned about the vertical string of all-round lights used to identify vessels restricted in their ability to maneuver by the nature of their work. The display consists of red-white-red, and Annex I details how it will be placed. A careful reading of those details reveals some surprises. Suppose a large power-driven vessel is engaged in surveying at night while underway and making way. She displays her sidelights, sternlight, and both the forward and after masthead lights because she is making way. Also burning is a vertical row of red-white-red lights. But where should they hang? Rule 27(b)(i) instructs no more than "where they can best be seen." It is for Annex I to answer the "where" in the instruction. A complete specification would refer to height, to athwartships displacement from the keel, and to distance abaft the bow. Surprisingly, though, the annex is not that detailed. No longitudinal limitation is mentioned, but special attention is given to height and athwartships positioning. The customary placement is lower than the masthead lights, and when so placed, "red-white-red" may be in a vertical line with them or offset to one side or the other. But allowance is made for feasibility. If the red-white-red string cannot conveniently be located below the masthead lights it can be between them or

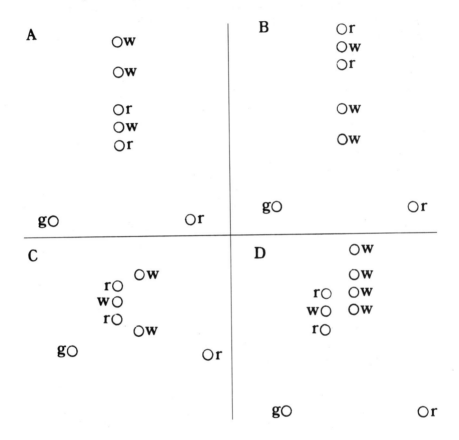

Fig. 60. Lights of Vessels Restricted in Ability to Maneuver. (A) Customary bow view of a power-driven vessel 50 meters or more long while making way and restricted in ability to maneuver (COLREGS and Inland); *(B) optional bow view of power-driven vessel 50 meters or more long showing lights for "restricted in ability to maneuver" above the masthead lights* (COLREGS and Inland); *(C) optional bow view of power-driven vessel 50 meters or more showing lights for "restricted in ability to maneuver" vertically between the masthead lights* (COLREGS and Inland); *(D) optional bow view of a tug 50 meters or more long with a tow over 200 meters astern while severely restricted in ability to change course* (COLREGS and Inland).

above them. But that allows for some arrangements which will significantly change the entire array. If the red-white-red string is higher than the masthead lights it can be in their same vertical plane or it can be offset. But if that string has a height which is higher than the forward masthead light but lower than the after one, then it *cannot* be located in their same vertical plane. Figure 60 shows the scope of displays, and here is the reason for offset. We've already considered the neat manner in which masthead lights fitted on separate masts may act as a range to show direction or aspect. For example, when appearing in a vertical line they indicate a bow-on view. But if a string of "red-white-red" clutters up the space between them their value as a range is lessened. So Annex I requires that when the height of the string places it vertically between a forward and an after masthead light display the red-white-red pattern must be offset to port or starboard from their fore-and-aft plane.

A study of Annex I is tedious and we should be grateful that there is no need to absorb every slight detail. But Inland's Section 84.11(a)(3) harbors an eccentricity which will catch the eye of even a casual reader. There a cylinder is described as being at least 0.6 meters in diameter and twice as high. What startles the reader is not the description but the fact that Inland bothers to say anything at all. Cylinders are shapes which COLREGS allows to be shown by vessels constrained by draft. But Inland Rules consider such vessels not worthy of special identification. Yet nowhere else in either set of rules does a cylinder appear. Why then does Inland bother to set out a description? One possible explanation is editorial oversight; another could be a portent of things to come. Does Inland, after all, secretly question its view on the issue of vessels constrained by draft? We should think not. Perhaps, since a cylinder is a distinctive shape, Inland keeps its options open for future assignment in a Pilot Rule. Whatever the "why," the appearance of a cylinder's description, even if inadvertent, is hardly momentous.

ANNEX II

Our study of Rule 26 and its commands to vessels engaged in fishing leaves nothing left to say about Annex II. In Chapter 7 we discussed the unique patterns required of trawlers and those engaged in fishing by other means. There we also learned of the colorful scene when a pair of large trawlers might be working together. This annex tells us where and how some optional lights might appear. What is possibly worth noting is that the additional lights are not intended to tell the entire maritime world what is taking place. Section 1. "General" specifies that the extra lights shall have ranges less than those of the normal patterns required by Rule 26. The message is that the displays of Rule 26 are to inform the world of being engaged in fishing while the displays allowed by Annex II are intramural. They are intended only as a signal to other vessels fishing in close proximity that an impeding fishing procedure is being carried out.

ANNEX III

While slogging through Chapter 8 we exhausted ourselves delving into the intricacies of high- and low-pitched whistles, single whistles, and combined whistle signals. What Annex III adds is wearisome detail. Having "paid our dues" by careful attention to all that has gone before, we're entitled to skim quickly over the impact of "2×10^{-5} n/m²" on a $\frac{1}{3}$-octave band. The fact that whether a vessel will peep or roar depends on her length is worth recall. It could also be worthwhile to remember that huge ships might have a complex of sound sources. But the fact that a Hertz frequency might qualify for $\pm 1\%$ is best left to Annex III or perhaps to that other car-rental company. The bulk of this annex is only for manufacturers and those who fit out ships.

ANNEX IV—DISTRESS SIGNALS

Our holiday is over! We can leave to the shipbuilder and purchasing agent the details of the first three annexes, but the content of Annex IV is too critical to be ignored. Rule 37 does no more than refer us to this annex to learn the signals used by a vessel in distress and requiring assistance. The time has come for us to look carefully at what is provided.

COLREGS

1. Need of assistance

The following signals, used or exhibited either together or separately, indicate distress and need of assistance:

(a) a gun or other explosive signal fired at intervals of about a minute;

(b) a continuous sounding with any fog-signalling apparatus;

(c) rockets or shells, throwing red stars fired one at a time at short intervals;

(d) a signal made by radiotelegraphy or by any other signaling method consisting of the group . . . — — — . . . (SOS) in the Morse Code;

(e) a signal sent by radiotelephony consisting of the spoken word "Mayday";

(f) the International Code Signal of distress indicated by N.C.;

(g) a signal consisting of a square flag having above or below it a ball or anything resembling a ball;

(h) flames on the vessel (as from a burning tar barrel, oil barrel, etc.);

(i) a rocket parachute flare or a hand flare showing a red light;

(j) a smoke signal giving off orange-colored smoke;

(k) slowly and repeatedly raising and lowering arms outstretched to each side;

(l) the radiotelegraph alarm signal;

(m) the radiotelephone alarm signal;

(n) signals transmitted by emergency position-indicating radio beacons.

2. The use or exhibition of any of the foregoing signals except for the purpose of indicating distress and need of assistance and the use of other signals which may be confused with any of the above signals is prohibited.

3. Attention is drawn to the relevant sections of the

INLAND

§ 87.1 Need of assistance.

The following signals, used or exhibited either together or separately, indicate distress and need of assistance:

(a) A gun or other explosive signal fired at intervals of about a minute;

(b) A continuous sounding with any fog-signalling apparatus;

(c) Rockets or shells, throwing red stars fired one at a time at short intervals;

(d) A signal made by radiotelegraphy or by any other signaling method consisting of the group . . . — — — . . . (SOS) in the Morse Code;

(e) A signal sent by radiotelephony consisting of the spoken word "Mayday";

(f) The International Code Signal of distress indicated by N.C.;

(g) A signal consisting of a square flag having above or below it a ball or anything resembling a ball;

(h) Flames on the vessel (as from a burning tar barrel, oil barrel, etc.);

(i) A rocket parachute flare or a hand flare showing a red light;

(j) A smoke signal giving off orange-colored smoke;

(k) Slowly and repeatedly raising and lowering arms outstretched to each side;

(l) The radiotelegraph alarm signal;

(m) The radiotelephone alarm signal;

(n) Signals transmitted by emergency position-indicating radio beacons;

(o) A high intensity white light flashing at regular intervals from 50 to 70 times per minute.

§ 87.3 Exclusive use.

The use or exhibition of any of the foregoing signals except for the purpose of indicating distress and need of assistance and the use of other signals which may be confused with any of the above signals is prohibited.

§ 87.5 Supplemental signals.

Attention is drawn to the relevant sections of the International Code of Signals, the Merchant Ship Search and Rescue Manual and the following signals:

(a) A piece of orange-colored canvas with either a black square and circle or other appropriate symbol (for identification from the air);

(b) A dye marker.

First, observe that the distress signals listed are not just to be used one by one. The troubled mariner is allowed to use them singly or in any combination. Second, although they are in fact signals to attract attention, they must only be made when in distress and requiring assistance. To employ them under the authority of Rule 36 to attract attention without need of help is forbidden. These are signals made pursuant to Rule 37 and no other numbered rule. That prohibition cannot be overemphasized. Maritime distress is too scary to allow any sham. On the other hand no one is to be considered as emotionless as a being from the planet Vulcan. Every Earthling mariner is given the license to indulge in some panic. When he honestly feels distressed and in need of help he can invoke the signals even if he overstates the urgency. Still, he is not allowed to cry "Wolf!"

With her back broken, a foundering tanker awaits assistance. [USCG photo]

We need not go over the signals one after the other, for many are expressed in very clear terms. A few, though, justify discussion. An example is 1(b), which seems to howl for attention. There the *continuous sounding of any fog-signaling apparatus* is mentioned. What immediately comes to mind is the image of a mariner hauling down on a whistle lanyard, but the provision goes further. A bell and a gong are also within the category of "any fog-signaling apparatus." Continuous ringing of a bell and constant sounding of a gong would be included. After all, the whistle might depend on a reserve of steam or air or some kind of aerosol substance under pressure. The situation is grave when boilers and air tanks are ruptured and aerosol cans are spent. Then perhaps the only noisemakers left are bells and gongs.

In Chapter 6 we discussed the problem created by having no color assigned to paragraph 1(g)'s *square flag and ball.* Years ago it was named the "distance signal" since its contrasting shapes, regardless of color or placement, are readily discernible at a distance. We should now remind ourselves of that discussion and note that the "Henry Ford Rule" does not apply. They are not required to be any color so long as it is black, as seems inferred by Annex I. They can be any color and can differ in color. The only requirement is that one shape be a square and that the other be ball-shaped, and that one be above the other.

Gutted by fire and explosion, a cruise liner wallows with her last lifeboat dangling from unmanned davits. [USCG photo]

Should our choice be *flames on the vessel* to indicate need, we should recall how a hapless mariner once compounded his distress. His vessel, a small wooden craft, suffered an irreparable engine failure and was being swept pitilessly toward jagged rocks. His frantic waving of arms went unnoticed by nearby traffic, so he betook the final solution. Soaking a pillow in lighter fluid he lit a match and produced flames on his vessel. In fact he produced flames *of* his vessel by accidentally igniting the hull. Good seamanlike practices dictate a measure of discretion.

The issue of color arises again. Star shells and flares, say paragraphs 1(c) and (i), must be red, but 1(j) specifies that a *smoke signal* shall be orange. Paragraph 3, in drawing our attention to the International Code of Signals and to the Merchant Ship Search and Rescue Manual, mentions an orange-colored canvas backdrop for black symbols and also mentions a dye marker. The hue of the dye can be any color but we are impelled to consider why, for the others, the shade is sometimes orange and at other times red. The answer probably lies in the chemistry of manufacturing pyrotechnics and the science of chromatics. Over the years there has appeared such a swatch of color tones as to make amber fade almost to white. Fire-engine red seemed universally acceptable as of the highest visibility but then came the likes of chrome yellow, Indian orange, and International orange. Those schooled in chromatics might weigh the relative merits but the rest of us can use a less busy palette. The annex demands no more than red star shells and flares along with orange smoke and canvas backdrops. We have no concern whether the red is type A, B, or O, nor with its Rh factor. The orange can be from California, Florida, or for that matter, the sunny shores of Spain.

Subparagraphs (l) and (m) return us to the early part of our century. The *Titanic* disaster spawned more than a succession of movies with the stalwart singing of "Nearer, My God, to Thee" as icy waters flooded the coal bunkers. Barely over the horizon was a radio-equipped steamer able to undertake a rescue if only she had known of the liner's plight. But her single radio operator had secured his set and turned in after a long watch of monitoring dots and dashes. An aftermath of this calamity was introduction of the *radiotelegraph alarm signal.* Following it in later years was one fashioned for radiotelephone equipment. Their specifications can be found, among other places, in *Radio Navigational Aids* prepared by the Defense Mapping Agency in two parts as Publications 117a and 117b. Our present aim is a brief sketch of what those signals amount to. The receiver on a modern ship carrying radiotelegraph equipment is fitted with an automatic alarm to alert off-duty operators to an incoming distress call. When not in use the set is tuned to the distress frequency of 500 kHz. A distressed vessel also equipped for radiotelegraph transmissions sends a series of 12 4-second dashes interspersed with 1-second periods of silence. This triggers the auto alarm at a receiver and tumbles the radio operator out of his bunk. The auto alarm designed for radiotelephone equipment is a distinctive signal of varying high to low pitch.

Subparagraph (m) injects the *emergency position-indicating radio beacon.* Usually abbreviated as *EPIRB,* this most valuable lifesaving device is a floatable radio transmitter which will automatically send out a call whose bearing can easily be measured. The specifications of such equipment are spelled out in Coast Guard regulations and some generalities on operating procedures appear in *Radio Navigational Aids.*

Now we come to the matter of a wrangle between COLREGS and Inland. Annex IV of the rules for inland waters contains one signal not found on the international roster. In Section 87.1(o) we find the inclusion of a high-intensity white light flashing from 50 to 70 times per minute. This is the *strobe light* which is frowned upon by international rulemakers. In fact, as we learned in studying COLREGS Rule 36, the high-seas rules urge that use of the strobe light to attract attention be discouraged. The shapers of the Inland Rules, undaunted by such an admonition, list use of the strobe light as a distress signal. Since the Inland view seems so much at odds with that of the rest of the world we should make inquiry. The "War of the Strobe" has probably just begun. When mention is made that COLREGS Rule 36 would dissuade mariners from using the light, Inland retorts that a signal to attract attention under Rule 36 is not a distress signal under Rule 37 and Annex IV. That response would have us accept the COLREGS discouragement as referring only to signals to attract attention and not to signals of distress. There is no denying that the strobe light is a very effective attention-getter. There is little doubt that its signal offers a most valuable means to announce distress. The problem is not so much with the strobe light as it is with its popularity. The COLREGS view expressed in Rule 36 makes sense. A signal to attract attention (but not rescuers!) should not be so strong that it masks normal patterns required by the Rules. On the other hand when a vessel is in distress she hardly has any reason to worry about whether her desperate signals outshine sidelights or a sternlight. The primary concern is to pass the word of her dire straits. Few signals will then outperform the strobe light. Without doubt there will be more debate on the issue. The War of the Strobe will continue and we can look forward to a series of skirmishes between the cohorts of COLREGS and those of Inland. Since we are rule users and not makers, however, what should we conclude? Indiscriminate use of a strobe light on inland waters will surely bring confusion. Here is an example. On that dark and stormy night when disaster strikes, *A* aims his small strobe light outward and sends off what he fervently hopes are between 50 and 70 flashes per minute. *B* has been observing high-intensity flashes for some time from a nearby fishing fleet. Now he must distinguish between such inconsequential signals and those of genuine distress. A count of 50 to 70 flashes per minute would galvanize him into action. However, should the number be less than 50 or over 70 his reaction might be different. Only a latter-day Don Quixote would risk the ripping of nets and fouling of propeller by plunging through a fishing fleet on a needless rescue mission. The utility of a distress signal should not hinge on an accurate count of light flashes. It would be better if flashing white strobe lights were used *only* when in distress. That view has been officially fostered with a resolution urging the Coast Guard to seek a COLREGS amendment making the use of strobe lights acceptable as an international distress signal.

ANNEX V (INLAND)

Having thrown down the gauntlet over strobe lights, COLREGS withdraws into frosty silence. Its parade of annexes is complete. But Inland has one more. Its Annex V presently contains the Pilot Rules, but over the years to come can be expected to expand. It now consists of seven sections and we've already met some of them. Even so, a quick recap is worthwhile.

M.V. Spokane, *a vessel of the Washington State Ferries system, carries 2000 passengers and more than 200 vehicles on Puget Sound. [Courtesy Washington State Ferries]*

Section 88.01 defines the scope of application of Pilot Rules. They govern all vessels on U.S. inland waters and U.S. vessels on Canadian waters of the Great Lakes to the extent that there is no conflict with Canadian law. 88.03 does no more than refer us to the numbered Inland Rules for definitions. 88.05 orders each self-propelled vessel 12 meters or more in length to have a copy of the Inland Navigation Rules on board. This instruction has been on the books for years, but three changes have been made. The demand now applies to vessels as short as 12 meters, which is just below 40 feet in length. In the past the dividing line was 65 feet. Second, the old rules excluded small *power-driven,* but now the exemption is keyed to *self-propelled.* That would include those under sails and oars. The last change? The Coast Guard booklet on the Rules of the Road is no longer available without charge. Now the only way to get the publication from the government is by purchase. But the rulemakers did not consider cost an impediment, so 88.05 orders that it be on board.

The numbering of sections within Inland annexes is interesting. All of them are contained in Title 33 of the Code of Federal Regulations and are cited as "33 CFR and so forth." As for the "and so forth," it consists of a whole number and a decimal to identify the Part of 33 CFR and the section of that part. Annex I is Part 84; its full designation is 33 CFR 84. As we would expect, Annex II is 33 CFR 85, Annex III is 86, Annex IV is 87, and Annex V is 88. The decimal in a full number indicates the section. So the first paragraph in Annex V is also known as 33 CFR 88.01. A study of these number patterns reveals that odd-numbered decimals prevail. Annex V 88.01 is followed by 88.03 after which comes 88.05. The purpose is to allow slack for future fill-ins. The same allowance for expansion appears in all the other Inland annexes. So

Annex I progresses through every odd number from 84.01 via .03, .05, .07, and .09 all the way to .25. A reading of the last few sentences might suggest that we are caving in under the pressure of our studies. Who cares what numbers are used, whether they be Roman or Arabic, or for that matter whether numbers are used at all? We must concede that there are more important

The S.S. Exxon Lexington *churns her way through fractured ice. [Courtesy Exxon Corp.]*

topics. Perhaps we're reaching the end of our studies just in the nick of time. We'd better resist the urge to consider why four of the annexes start out with .01 and Annex IV begins its listing of distress signals with .1. The answer probably could be found in some handbook of federal numerology, but we had better not look. Already there might be the suspicion that we are playing with less than a full deck and paddling with only one oar.

But more than an obsession with numbers is involved now, and the last paragraph is an overlong introduction to a more important topic. As we look through Annex V we should note that there is no Section 88.07. After 88.05 comes 88.09 and the inevitable question "What happened to 88.07?" It appeared in the *proposed* content of Annex V but was deleted in the final selection of Pilot Rules. The subject matter was cross signals, and that needs discussion. During the dialogue of sound between power-driven vessels on inland waters an occasional mariner, dissatisfied with the announcement of intention he heard, would issue a contradiction as his reply. This practice of "cross signaling" by answering one blast with two or two with one led to confusion. Often the mariner who had first sounded the one-blast signal didn't bother to note the reply. Considering that no one would deign to contradict his proposal he was unaware of the unexpected reply and proceeded into a collision. For many years the use of cross signals was expressly prohibited by older Pilot Rules. No alternative pattern was specified, but mariners fashioned their own. If one blast or two is the offer and you would rather have two blasts or one, you must first politely reject the offer by sounding the doubt signal. Then you may offer your own proposal, with the other mariner reserving the right to decline by sounding his own doubt signal. Carried to an illogical conclusion this conversation of blasts would immobilize the vessels until either one mariner concedes or both whistles wear out. The point, though, is that meanwhile you would not be moving heedlessly toward a collision. All this reinforces the value of voice exchanges by VHF radiotelephone, but doesn't explain why any mention of cross signals was deleted from the Pilot Rules of Annex V. In summarizing comment received before adoption of the final rule, the Coast Guard accepted the argument that mention of cross signals would be redundant. Rule 34(a), (c), and (d) spell out the sequence of signals exchanged by power-driven vessels when involved in meeting, crossing, or overtaking one another on inland waters. There it is specified that whatever one might sound the other uses as a reply unless there is doubt. To reemphasize the sequence in Annex V was not considered necessary. But even if redundant, the express prohibition of cross signals would bring greater assurance that all hands understood what is forbidden, and as a result would be more aware of what is to be expected. In any case the problem should not arise for us after this postmortem examination of the late cross signal rule.

We find in section 88.09 of Annex V a reassuring touch of common sense. It allows a vessel to lower her navigation lights and shapes if necessary in order to pass under a bridge. Wear and tear on the top hamper of ships as well as the undersides of low bridges is thereby kept at a minimum.

In earlier chapters we sampled the contents of the remaining three sections in Annex V. Section 88.11 describes a flashing blue light for law enforcement vessels (we discussed that in Chapter 6). Section 88.13 gives the details for lights on barges at a bank or dock and 88.15 tells of the light displays on pipelines leading from a dredge (those patterns were found in Chapter 7. Perhaps, though, we should note a gap in Section 88.15. No day shape is prescribed, and the omission has brought problems. Leading from a dredge at work in a seaboard port was a pipeline designed to sink to the bottom when full and to float on the surface when empty. The inevitable happened: a succession of vessels ran over the empty pipeline in daylight. The ensuing inquiry searched for specification of a day shape to be mounted on the pipeline. Good seamanship dictated that the hazard be somehow marked, but Annex V gave no hint of how. A future modification of Section 88.15 might provide a cure, but meanwhile the mariner should take heed. Daytime passage by an operating dredge should be made with extra care. Modified or not, this section completes Annex V and the Inland Rules. Giddy with expectation, we should look at the chart and fix our position.

Little remains to be studied, but it is laced with a sprig of annoyance. We suggested earlier that the very nature of seafaring might make official penalties for misconduct unnecessary. The threat of damage, injury, and death, added to increased insurance premiums, should admonish all but the foolhardy. Even so there are statutory restraints. Scattered through the *United States Code* (USC) are congressional pronouncements; in the Code of Federal Regulations (CFR) are agency rules to price misdeeds out of the market. Here are some of the hedges.

The basic "hit-and-run" laws are found in Sections 367 and 368, Title 33, of the *United States Code* (33 USC 367 and 368). After a collision the participants must stand by, identify themselves, and give such aid as is feasible. Failure to do so exposes any mariner, regardless of nationality, to liability for the collision. Should he be a U.S. citizen he can be dealt the further punishment of a hefty fine and imprisonment.

Violation of a COLREG, says 33 USC 1608, raises the spectre of a $5000 civil penalty, and with it seizure of the vessel for payment. Added is the considerable deterrent that the collector of customs might withhold clearance from port until the matter is adjusted. Similar penalties for violation of an Inland rule are found in 33 USC 2072.

Miscreants can find themselves under attack from a battery of laws and regulations. For example, the Federal Boat Safety Act includes its own penalty for foul play. And always hovering overhead is action by the Coast Guard against a mariner's document or license. The price of noncompliance is high.

Tucked away in 33 CFR 100 is a pattern for control of marine regattas. The staging of any such performance is subject to Coast Guard supervision. Ground rules are set and then published in *Local Notice to Mariners*. Traffic in the area during the activity is held cognizant of the requirements, and miscues are dealt with by Coast Guard investigation units. Overregulation is the bane of modern life; on the other hand there are valid reasons for some official controls. Nor need one be an attorney-at-law to uncover the key restraints. A visit to a fair-size public library should be enough to learn about general requirements.

Found in 33 CFR 86 will be Coast Guard interpretive rulings to clarify ambiguities in the Rules of the Road. The secretary of the navy announces in 32 CFR 707 those special signals one might expect from ships of war. Demarcation lines between international and inland waters are defined in 33 CFR 80.

Even the most dedicated seaman may be in danger of confusion after muddling through a jumble of citations to this title of USC and that of CFR. Yet we who live in a complicated world are expected to have some knowledge of the complications. On the other hand we need not have instant recall of every requirement. But we should know where to look for guidance. At the top of list of sources is the district office of the U.S. Coast Guard. Then we can, if so inclined, visit a public library to check the USC and CFR titles and sections already cited.

All systems of navigation agree! We are at the end of our trip! It has been a long voyage and the demands on our attention have been many. When a tough passage is over, seamen often take their leave vowing never to sail that route again. What a temptation for us now to consider our job done and over with once and for all, vowing never to look at another numbered rule or annex. But we cannot afford such thoughts. While we have been studying the rules, people in Washington and London have been studying possible changes. Of course that should come as no surprise, for COLREGS and Inland are not chiseled on stone tablets. They can change a bit from year to year of their own volition and will be shaped by court interpretations. Since we are now armed with a sound knowledge of the rules, however, we should encounter no distress in keeping up with modifications as they might come along.

It's time now to indulge ourselves. The study is complete and the Old Man is ready to sign off the crew. Let's not delay him further by fussing with a chapter quiz. Instead, let's exchange congratulations for having finished the voyage. At the end of a trip the master pays off the crew according to the terms of the Shipping Articles. Our payoff need not be limited by what is specified in any contract of engagement. In fact the rewards for all the watches we've stood in fair weather and foul throughout the chapters are really up to us. Stand ready, then, to pay off with safe passages as we put the rules to work.

Awaiting a pilot in the Panama Canal. [Photo by Lawrence Wyatt]

HEADINGS OF ANOTHER BY BEARINGS OF HER RUNNING LIGHTS

Sidelights, masthead lights, and a sternlight display a pattern to key the *general* aspect of another being observed. By combining knowledge of running light arcs with an observed bearing of another vessel the mariner can estimate the limits of that vessel's possible courses. The procedure is not complicated and is based on Rule 21's definition of light arcs as 112.5° for each sidelight, 135° for the sternlight, and 225° for a masthead light. The *true* bearing of the other vessel (a compass bearing corrected for compass error) is the best to use, although the compass bearing without correction can usually serve. But a relative bearing (measured from your ship's bow) cannot be used. Here are the steps to follow.

When Only a Red Light Is Observed

Reverse the true bearing and add 112.5°. The other vessel's possible courses are within that arc.

Example: A red light is observed bearing 045° True. What are the limits of that vessel's courses?

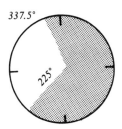

045° reversed = (045° + 180°) = 225°

225° + 112.5° = 337.5°

Her course is from 225° through 270° to 337.5°.

When Only a Green Light Is Observed

Reverse the true bearing and subtract 112.5°. The other vessel's possible courses are within that arc.

Example: A green light is observed bearing 315° True. What are the limits of that vessel's courses?

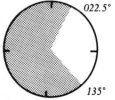

315° reversed = (315° − 180°) = 135°

135° − 112.5° = 022.5°

Her course is from 022.5° through 090° to 135°.

When a White Light Is Observed

A. If it is judged to be a *masthead* light, reverse the true bearing then add 112.5° to find one limit and subtract 112.5° to find the other.

Example: A white light, judged to be a masthead light, is observed bearing 200° True. What are the limits of that vessel's courses?

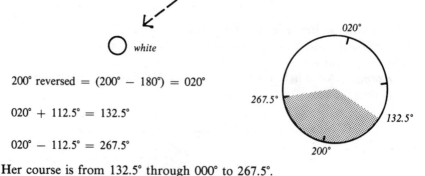

200° reversed = (200° − 180°) = 020°

020° + 112.5° = 132.5°

020° − 112.5° = 267.5°

Her course is from 132.5° through 000° to 267.5°.

B. If it is judged to be a *sternlight,* do *not* reverse the true bearing; just add 67.5° to find one limit and subtract 67.5° to find the other.

Example: A white light, judged to be a sternlight, is observed bearing 200° True. What are the limits of that vessel's courses?

200° + 67.5° = 267.5°

200° − 67.5° = 132.5°

Her course is from 132.5° through 180° to 267.5°.

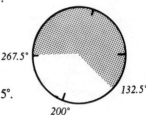

Shortcut Using the Compass Rose on a Chart or Plotting Sheet

1. Reverse the true bearing in all cases and mark that angle on the compass rose.

2. Measure 112.5° to the right and mark that arc as *red*.

3. Measure 112.5° to the left and mark that arc as *green*.

4. Mark the remaining arc as *stern*.

If a red light is observed that vessel's possible courses are in the *red* arc. If a green light is seen the courses are in the *green* arc. If a white light is observed and judged to be a sternlight, the course limits are in the *stern* arc; if the white light is judged to be a masthead light the possible courses are in both the *red* and *green* arcs.

Example: A segment of a running light display is observed bearing 090° True. What would be the courses, depending on the color of the light observed?

090° reversed = (090° + 180°) = 270°

If a *red* light, courses are from 270° through 000° to 022.5°.
If a *green* light, courses are from 270° through 180° to 157.5°.
If a *sternlight*, courses are from 022.5° through 090° to 157.5°.
If a *masthead* light, courses are from 157.5° through 270° to 022.5°.

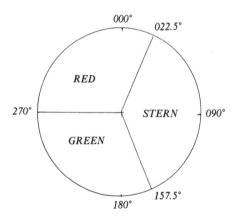

TIME, SPEED, DISTANCE, AND THE RULES OF THE ROAD

Piloting is a subject to be found in a book on navigation and not one on the Rules of the Road. But some of the navigator's formulas can be very important during a Rules of the Road maneuvering situation. When meeting, crossing, or overtaking another vessel the mariner must know something about how much time and how much distance is involved. Here is a restatement of basic procedures. The factors 0.6 and 1.8 are rounded off to the nearest tenth so answers will not be precise. But mathematical exactness is not necessary. The solutions reached by the following formulas are adequate for our present use.

Miles, Minutes, and Knots

1. Distance in nautical miles $= \dfrac{\text{speed in knots} \times \text{time in minutes}}{60}$

2. Time in minutes $= \dfrac{\text{distance in nautical miles} \times 60}{\text{speed in knots}}$

Yards, Seconds, and Knots

1. Distance in yards $= \dfrac{\text{speed in knots} \times \text{time in seconds}}{1.8}$

2. Time in seconds $= \dfrac{\text{distance in yards} \times 1.8}{\text{speed in knots}}$

Feet, Seconds, and Knots

1. Distance in feet $= \dfrac{\text{speed in knots} \times \text{time in seconds}}{0.6}$

2. Time in seconds $= \dfrac{\text{distance in feet} \times 0.6}{\text{speed in knots}}$

Examples:

1. A vessel is traveling at 12 knots and observes another at anchor a half mile dead ahead. How long will it take to zero range?

Time in minutes $= \dfrac{\text{distance in miles} \times 60}{\text{speed in knots}} = \dfrac{0.5 \times 60}{12} = 2.5 \text{ minutes}$

2. A vessel is traveling at 15 knots and observes dead ahead a fishing vessel tending its nets. The range is 500 yards. How long will it be to zero range?

Time in seconds $= \dfrac{\text{distance in yards} \times 1.8}{\text{speed in knots}} = \dfrac{500 \times 1.8}{15} = 60 \text{ seconds}$

3. A vessel is traveling at 8 knots. How many feet will she move in 37 seconds?

Distance in feet $= \dfrac{\text{speed in knots} \times \text{time in seconds}}{0.6} = \dfrac{8 \times 37}{0.6} = 493 \text{ feet}$

THE CROSSING SITUATION

Appearing here is a very handy table for a quick conn aboard any vessel from a day sailer to an ocean liner. All that's needed to gain data supplementing the overrated "seaman's eye" cast on a crossing vessel is some means to measure an angle on the bow. The table handles bearings from 10° to 80° on either bow and at convenient increments. A hand calculator reading out sines, cosines, and tangents will expand the scope to any angle between 0° and 90° . Trigonometry has no more direct connection with the Rules of the Road than does any other part of mathematics, but there are some trig tidbits which should not be overlooked. Even mariners who find the relationships between sides and angles in a triangle somewhat alien have no cause to hurry on, for the table is very simple to use. And those more familiar with plane trigonometry might find that our discussion of basics reminds them how mathematics can be applied in other ways to gain important clues without a cabin filled with electronics.

First off we should identify the various parts of the relationships as defined by mathematics and as applied to our Rules of the Road usage.

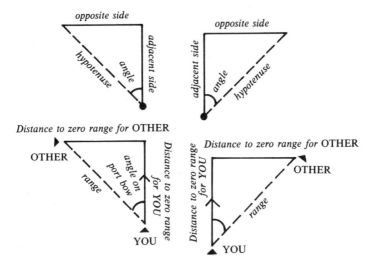

Opposite side = sine of angle × hypotenuse

Other's distance to zero range = sine of angle on bow × initial range

Adjacent side = cosine of angle × hypotenuse

Your distance to zero range = cosine of angle on bow × initial range

Tangent of angle = $\dfrac{\text{opposite side}}{\text{adjacent side}}$

Tangent of angle on bow = $\dfrac{\textit{Other's distance to zero range}}{\textit{Your distance to zero range}}$

Tangent of angle on bow = ratio of *Other*'s speed to *Your* speed

All of this is put to work in Table RR1, but first we need recognize the following assumptions for its use:

1.   that the *Other*'s course differs from yours by 90° or nearly so; that is, the tracks converge at a right angle.
2.   that the bearing on the bow remains constant or nearly so.
3.   that each vessel maintains a constant speed or nearly so.
4.   that the initial range is 1 mile and is decreasing.

Our encounter with Rule 14 introduced us to the problem with such words as "nearly so." In the case of Table RR1 they tell us that accuracy depends on the existence of the assumed circumstances. But since our goal is a workable "quick conn," answers will be acceptable so long as we stay close to the assumptions. The last assumption controls the two columns dealing with distance to zero range. If that range differs from 1 mile the answers are to be prorated. So if the initial range is 2 miles, double the distances to zero range. If the initial range is 0.5 mile, divide the tabulated distances by 2. Note also that since the decimal factors in the table are expressed only to the nearest tenth, answers will not be exact. Where a trigonometric function would be 0.866025403 it mercifully became 0.9 in the table. Where the precise value was found as 2.74747742 our table was satisfied with 2.7.

Table RR1. Distance to Zero Range When Crossing

ANGLE ON YOUR BOW	SPEED OF OTHER VESSEL	INITIAL RANGE	YOUR DISTANCE TO ZERO RANGE	OTHER'S DISTANCE TO ZERO RANGE
10°	0.2 × Yours	1 mile	1.0 mile	0.2 mile
20°	0.4 × Yours	1 mile	0.9 mile	0.3 mile
30°	0.6 × Yours	1 mile	0.9 mile	0.5 mile
40°	0.8 × Yours	1 mile	0.8 mile	0.6 mile
45°	1.0 × Yours	1 mile	0.7 mile	0.7 mile
50°	1.2 × Yours	1 mile	0.6 mile	0.8 mile
60°	1.7 × Yours	1 mile	0.5 mile	0.9 mile
70°	2.7 × Yours	1 mile	0.3 mile	0.9 mile
80°	5.7 × Yours	1 mile	0.2 mile	1.0 mile

Having determined speed and the distance to zero range, the mariner can use time, speed, and distance formulas to compute the time available for avoidance. Here are some examples of what the table does:

1. You are heading north at 10 knots. You observe another vessel heading west and with a steady bearing of 40° on your starboard bow. What is her estimated speed?

Look under the "Angle on Your Bow" column at 40°. In the "Speed of Other

Vessel" column find "0.8 × Yours." The other's speed is 0.8 × your 10 knots, or 8 knots.

2. You are heading south at 6 knots. Another vessel appears to be on a course of west and bearing a constant 70° on your port bow. What is her estimated speed?

Look under the "Angle on Your Bow" column at 70°. In the "Speed of Other Vessel" column find "2.7 × Yours." The other's speed is 2.7 × your 6 knots, or 16.2 knots.

Seeing double while the Puget Sound double-ended ferry M.V. Hyak *stands on to cross ahead with her interchangeable bow to the left and stern to the right. [Courtesy Washington State Ferries]*

3. Your course is 220° and your speed is 12 knots. You observe another bearing a steady 50° on your starboard bow. She appears to be on a course at a right angle to your track; that is, you estimate her course to be about 110°. The range is 1.5 miles and is decreasing.

a. What is her speed? The table shows, for a 50° angle, her speed is 1.2 × Yours, or 14.4 knots.

b. What are the distances to zero range or collision? *Your* distance to zero range is tabulated as 0.6 miles for each 1 mile of initial range. Since the actual range is 1.5, *Your* distance to zero range is 1.5 × 0.6, or 0.9 miles. *Other*'s distance to zero range is tabulated as 0.8 miles for each 1 mile of initial range. Converted to an actual range of 1.5, the distance is 1.5 × 0.8, or 1.2 miles.

c. What is the time interval to zero range; that is, how long in minutes do the vessels have to take avoiding action? *Based on You:* 0.9 miles to zero range at a speed of 12 knots means (0.9 × 60)/12 or 4.5 minutes. Rounded off, this is 5 minutes. *Based on Other:* 1.2 miles to zero range at a speed of 14.4 knots means (1.2 × 60)/14.4 or 5 minutes.

4. Any table of trigonometric functions or (even better) a hand calculator displaying sines, cosines, and tangents increases the bearing coverage this way:

You are on a course of east at 10 knots. Another vessel bears a constant 33° on your starboard bow at an initial range of 1 mile. Her course appears to be 000°.

a. What is her speed? Press the hand calculator buttons for the tangent of 33°. That value (0.6494 . . .) is the ratio of her speed to yours. She is traveling at 0.6494 × your 10 knots, or 6.494 knots.

b. What are the distances to zero range? By hand calculator or otherwise the cosine of 33° is found as 0.83867; . . . that is your distance to zero range. The sine of 33° is found as 0.54463; . . . that is the other's distance to zero range.

Tables RR2 and RR3 recap a mathematical approach to collision avoidance. They present distance to zero range when vessels are meeting and overtaking. There is nothing profound about them, for they do no more than tabulate time, speed, and distance. And a necessary "known" is the speed of the other ship. That means either advice by VHF radiotelephone or radar. In any case here are the other conditions which must be assumed:

1.　　That the initial range is 1 mile. If it is greater, increase the times in proportion; if it is less, pro-rate them. So if the initial range is 2 miles, double the times; if the initial range is 0.5 mile, divide them in half.
2.　　That each vessel maintains a constant course and speed.
3.　　That speed of approach is
　　　a. when meeting, *Your* speed plus *Other*'s speed;
　　　b. in overtaking, the greater speed minus the lesser speed.

Table RR2. Distance to Zero Range When Meeting			Table RR3. Distance to Zero Range When Overtaking		
SPEED OF APPROACH	INITIAL RANGE	TIME TO ZERO RANGE	SPEED OF APPROACH	INITIAL RANGE	TIME TO ZERO RANGE
10 kn.	1 mile	6 min.	1 kn.	1 mile	60 min.
15 kn.	1 mile	4 min.	2 kn.	1 mile	30 min.
20 kn.	1 mile	3 min.	3 kn.	1 mile	20 min.
25 kn.	1 mile	2 min. 24 sec.	4 kn.	1 mile	15 min.
30 kn.	1 mile	2 min.	5 kn.	1 mile	12 min.
35 kn.	1 mile	1 min. 42 sec.	10 kn.	1 mile	6 min.
40 kn.	1 mile	1 min. 30 sec.	15 kn.	1 mile	4 min.

The formula used (and to be used to increase the coverage) is

$$\text{Time in minutes to zero range} = \frac{60 \times \text{initial range}}{\text{speed of approach}}$$

NOTES ON DEFENSIVE SEAFARING

Appearing throughout the book are photographs of many different types of vessels. The purpose is more than decoration, for safe passage involves recognition. Just as important, though, is some understanding of their unusual operation. This is not a catalog of abnormal behavior, but these comments should aid when in the presence of an uncommon ship.

MILITARY VESSELS

In General

Most people are relieved that almost the entire life of a warship is devoted to peacetime practice. But mariners should remember that a naval exercise is not a sporting event. It often includes maneuvers which under other circumstances would be imprudent and in violation of the Rules of the Road. An earlier chapter introduced SELMA, our unofficial guide for standing ready to depart from normal maneuvering rules. "L" for "*L*imitations of vessels involved" and "A" for "*A*ny situation not not covered by the Rules" will nearly always apply when one is approaching naval activity. A simpler maxim used by merchantmen warns, "If it's gray, stay away!" No matter how expressed, the message is clear: the demands of naval operations must be taken into account. For example, no mariner can expect that a zigzaging formation of gray ships will call off an exercise while a red light crosses ahead from right to left. Here are some worthwhile observations on coexistence with military vessels.

During a NATO training exercise a naval escort risks the dangers of refueling at close range in heavy seas. [USN photo]

1. Charts and *Coast Pilot* should be consulted to learn the descriptions of military operating areas and transit zones, the most likely places to meet up with naval vessels.

2. No warship is exempt from following the Rules of the Road, but allowance is made for her mode of operation. At night she will probably display running lights, but she need not if the commanding officer judges that her mission is best served when she is blacked out.

3. Rule 1 allows military vessels and those operating under military escort to show unusual patterns of lights and shapes. What has been specified for U.S. vessels can be found by searching through such sources as the Code of Federal Regulations, but an easier means is a study of *Notice to Mariners.* Most navigators know of this weekly publication of the Defense Mapping Agency Hydrographic/Topographic Center as a periodical to keep nautical charts and publications up to date. What is not so well known is that its first issue each year, *Notice to Mariners No. 1,* contains an annual recap of many special signals authorized for vessels of special purpose. The dedicated student of the Rules of the Road should acquire this first issue each January to be advised of the unusual displays. What all students should conclude is that the customary signals prescribed by such regulations as Rule 27 are by no means definitive of the vessel on which they appear.

A submarine operating out of her element in Arctic pancake ice. [USN photo]

Here are some examples of what a recent *Notice to Mariners No. 1* had to say. Naval vessels in convoy may show a blue sternlight in lieu of the white one specified by the Rules of the Road. Incidentally, an aircraft carrier might also mount such a blue light when engaged in landing planes. Apparently it has been found that white lights distract the pilots, so for their safety the blue sternlight may be used. Two pulsating red lights in a vertical line can signify that a man fell overboard from a naval craft. A minesweeper might show two white lights in a vertical line as a guide to station-keeping. A helicopter engaged in mineclearing can be as low as 50 feet off the water and towing screw-snagging cables. Her signal could be a rotating yellow beacon. A large red flag can indicate a naval target vessel upon which a sharp-eyed submarine commander is taking a bead. All this confirms that old merchantman's precept. When a vessel is painted gray, the rest of us should stay far, far away.

In Particular

1. *Aircraft carriers* are powerful ships whose function is to align a runway with the axis of the wind for the takeoff and landing of aircraft. On the flat-topped flight deck of a large carrier the runway is usually slanted about 10° to the left of her keel. When handling aircraft she will probably be on a course with the wind about 10° on her port bow. Jet planes require more wind speed than do propeller-driven, so the carrier's speed can vary as she creates the best relative wind force for handling her aircraft. When she is launching planes of any kind she is greatly restricted in maneuverability. The best to expect under any such conditions is that she can make a 20° change in course. And no mariner should disregard the overhang of her flight deck. The officer of the deck cannot see anything closer than about 1000 feet ahead and 300 feet on the port side. Ideally the carrier will operate with no list, for then nested aircraft will not roll around. Should she have a list when changing course, she will turn toward the low side so that the physical forces at work during her turn will not increase the angle.

Should an aircraft go into the sea the carrier will probably turn sharply away from the crash and launch a helicopter to recover survivors. And as the ship is turning she will use hundreds of yards of ocean while advancing forward and transferring to the right or left of her original course. The mariner who finds himself within a mile of a ditched carrier aircraft can be in extreme danger. He would probably be listening to imprecations by loudspeaker from a helicopter overhead. He might well find that the carrier is bearing down at 30 knots during an emergency turn. Perhaps his best action would be to stop while the war group maneuvers at increasing ranges. Anticipation of the danger by an exercise of defensive seafaring would be better.

2. *Submarines* on the surface belie their true nature. In their underwater element they cavort with the adroitness of sea creatures but on the surface they seem small and unwieldy. While changing from the submerged mode to surfaced their sophisticated electronic gear might even be blind.

When in a submarine operating area mariners should be particularly alert for the identity signal of a flashing yellow beacon. It might announce the nearby presence of a nuclear-powered narwhal whose missile cells hold the means to destroy a nation. It would hardly be an exercise of good seamanship to sightsee and rubberneck close aboard.

Here are important signals which a submarine gives to warn surface vessels of her condition:

a. A *green flare or star cluster* appearing several hundred feet above the water or a *green or black smoke bomb* burning on the surface warns that torpedo practice is underway. The mariner, being reassured of no hostile intent, continues on his way. If power-driven, he keeps his propeller turning.

b. A *yellow flare, star group, or smoke bomb* announces that a submarine is about to surface. The observing mariner moves out of the way with his propeller turning.

c. When a *red flare, star cluster, or smoke bomb* is seen the mariner should consider that a submarine is in distress and is trying to surface. This is a distress signal, just as much as any detailed in Annex IV. Mariners should clear the immediate area but must not go away. If possible they should immediately send a radio message to the naval authorities indicating time, location, and circumstances. Meanwhile they stand off to give the submarine a chance to bob up in the clear. If that doesn't happen, they gingerly approach the area of the signal looking for a dumbbell-shaped buoy. Attached to it will be instructions on what to do next.

3. *Mineclearing vessels* are to be avoided at all costs. What they do for a living is not the business of the rest of us. They clear mines by snipping cables; they do it by acoustics and electronics. But whatever they do is certainly none of our affair. Inland Rule 27 cautions that mariners should approach no closer than 500 meters on either side and no closer than 1000 meters astern. COL-REGS prescribes 1000 meters on any bearing. But good seamanship demands a wider berth. Sighting the triangular signal of three black balls by day and three green lights by night is not a cue to stand 1001 meters off the port beam of a minesweeper. A better practice would be to move away in the opposite direction.

4. *Military vessels restricted in ability to maneuver* are not always aircraft carriers. Rule 27's signals of a ball-diamond-ball by day and a vertical string of red-white-red lights by night can mark such differing pursuits as fueling a missile frigate, keeping tabs on a spy satellite, and tending a school of frogmen. By day the most inexperienced should have no difficulty distinguishing the mother ship for an underwater demolition team from a navy oiler, but on a hazy night the distinction might not be so apparent. A fingertip knowledge of the signals described in *Notice to Mariners No. 1* would settle the issues, yet we need not be so learned. The answer again is to accept that military operations are dangerous and should be given a wide berth. An album of snapshots taken of a submarine's crash dive or the launching of a jet squadron would

enhance a coffee table. On the other hand the defense establishment is not maintained to entertain the citizenry. If you must take photos of naval operations, do so with a powerful telescopic lens at a very, very long range. Better still would be to read about these activities in an unclassified publication. Coastal waters are not teeming with dangers but they do hold more than a few hazards both to the military and to thoughtless bystanders.

U.S.N.S. Albert J. Myer *riding at anchor between assignments as a naval underwater cable tender. [USN photo]*

Coast Guard Vessels

When servicing an aid to navigation a USCG buoy tender is more than just restricted in ability to maneuver. Her signal patterns as prescribed by Rule 27 are black ball–black diamond–black ball by day and a vertical string of red-white-red lights by night, but those displays are too general to indicate her singular concerns. A buoy is anchored with great care, for navigators will place some reliance on its position as shown on a chart. The mariner should be quick to recognize the tender at work and be prepared to allow her free rein to do her job. The same must be true of a law enforcement cutter. They come in all sizes, from powerful high-endurance vessels on patrol from the Bering Sea to Reykjavik to small craft policing inland waters. Annex V of the Inland Rules grants them the use of a blue light display to signal their activity. But the response of a prudent mariner is not delayed until he sees a particular array of shapes or lights. The appearance of the distinctive USCG "badge" of crossed anchors and shield within a diagonal swatch should be enough to recommend that he stay clear.

One of a class of high-endurance cutters, the U.S.C.G.C. Mellon combines missions of search and rescue, research, and ocean patrol. [USCG photo]

Restricted Vessels in General

A vessel not under command is literally what the words mean. She is unable to control her actions in a normal manner. No one should conclude that she needs help; on the other hand no one should assume that she is normal. The risks created when nearby are related to unpredictability. Since she cannot guarantee what she will do next, there is no call for anyone else to be more optimistic. A vertical line of two black balls by day and two red lights by night is every bit as startling as a signal of distress. Within sight is a vessel out of control. The prudent mariner must react by getting as far away as possible.

We've already discussed some of the military vessels which will display the signals of Rule 27, but those signals are not reserved for armed shipping. The appearance of ball-diamond-ball by day and red-white-red by night will cue more risks than running afoul of a clutch of warships. Dredges at work can be surrounded by a variety of perils. Anchor chain might lead out on all quarters and floating pipelines often project from one side or another. Both sets of rules prescribe lights and shapes for the dredge and Inland's Annex V specifies lights to be shown on the pipeline. But no prudent mariner will rely solely on the appearance of such patterns. Some pipelines, for example, sink to the bottom when loaded with dredged material but float on the surface when empty. Only Inland assigns them a night signal and no rule yet prescribes a day pattern. But that is no excuse for becoming entangled. Mariners near what appears to be a dredge at work should expect something to be jutting out. Good seamanship requires recognition of the craft by type and signal, and then allowance for her unusual behavior.

Notice to Mariners No. 1 gives warning of perhaps the ultimate in offshoots from a restricted vessel. One engaged in seismographic surveying might be towing a cable tail more than two miles long! It might be marked by buoys, but on the other hand it might not. It might be submerged or surfaced. Its great length often is to afford protection to the survey vessel from shock waves set off by charges attached to the cable. No Rule 27 signal gives warning of that sort of danger.

In fact official attention has been directed toward whether the red-white-red lights and the ball-diamond-ball shapes required by that rule are sufficient warning. The view has been advanced that she is a vessel with a tow astern and severly restricted in ability to change course. That, we've learned, would add the towing patterns of Rule 24. Whether or not the outcome will require such a combination, defensive seafaring dictates an answer. The prudent mariner approaches any survey vessel with extreme caution. He should be particularly wary when abaft the beam of such a craft. The state of the oceanographer's art has progressed far beyond taking bearings and soundings. Any display from a vessel identified as engaged in surveying should be taken as a command not to get close, and certainly not to cut across her wake.

A NOAA research ship carrying small craft, deck cranes, winches, and reels of cable for underwater surveying. [NOAA photo]

Fishing Vessels

The distinguishing feature of a vessel engaged in fishing as defined by Rule 3(d) is that her gear restricts her maneuverability. Mariners in her vicinity should also keep in mind that such appliances also limit their scope of action by projecting outboard a considerable distance. The trawler's green-over-white lights warn of cables and drag nets streaming from her stern or quarter. The nontrawler's red-over-white lights announce the likelihood of nets and gear in any direction. Should another white light appear, she gives notice that her gear extends outboard 500 or more feet. A day-shape pattern of either two black cones point-to-point or a basket indicates that impediments may be ahead, abeam, or astern.

Prudent seamen approach *any* vessel engaged in fishing with extreme caution. In fact they draw no line between those engaged in fishing and those, such as trollers, who are considered by Rule 3 to be unrestricted fishing vessels. Even though the more nimble fishing craft is expected to play normal Rules of the Road roles without difficulty, she is still taking up more of the waterway than just her length and beam.

Manned by a crew of two, this vessel is ready to engage in fishing. [USCG photo]

Also worth remembering is the nature of a fishing expedition. Usually the ship's complement is minimal and those on board are inclined to be preoccupied with tending acres of nets or cablelengths of line. The vessel and her appliances should be viewed as an unwieldy complex and should always be given as wide a berth as possible.

With sidelights canted and lee rail under, a sail vessel heels in a stiff breeze.
[Photo by Harry Merrick]

Sailing Vessels

These have obvious limitations. Since motion depends on artful use of the wind which Nature provides, both the art of the sailor and the largesse of Nature will control how and where she heads. The Rules of the Road don't expect that every sailor be a member of a windjammer club, nor do they require that all nearby mariners be experts in canvas. But the ordinary practice of seamen does include recognition of some basic principles.

Rule 25's red-over-green pattern is a valuable light signal, but it may not always appear as the rulemakers intended. First of all we should remember that since the signal is optional it need not appear at all. The second consideration is that a vertical alignment of the two lights is not to be expected. All vessels roll, so no vertical string of lights will ever stay vertical. But a sail vessel does more than roll. By nature she relishes heeling her lee rail down toward the sea at angles other ships consider verging on disaster. The inevitable result is that lights in a vertical line are no longer so. Annex I sets the minimum vertical distance between such lights as 1 meter, and the COLREGS version pegs it for vessels 20 meters or more long at 2 meters. Some basic trigonometry now tells us that on a sailing vessel showing red-over-green and heeled to 30°, the red light will be more than 1½ feet outboard to the low side from being over the green. Whatever the actual vertical distance between the lights, the horizontal displacement would be half as much. The result? Nearby mariners would see a diagonal pattern with red higher than green but visibly offset.

An observer with an overactive imagination might interpret that as a low-flying aircraft banking sharply with its right wingtip scraping whitecaps. That may be too far-fetched for the rest of us perhaps, but we would at least be surprised. And surprise could become alarm when another factor is considered. Sidelights will heel with all other lights, and the one on the low side might be canted down so much toward the sea that it is visible, if at all, only at short

Harbor pilot peers over the starboard wing of a huge freighter's bridge. [USCG photo]

range. The number of possible combinations is quite large. The pattern could be only a diagonal line with red higher than green. It could also be triangular, for the missing corner could be a white sternlight or a colored sidelight. But no matter what its geometric form, any offbeat display evokes the same reaction from a prudent seaman. He navigates with extra caution while resolving his doubts.

Large Vessels

Throughout this book we've read so much about the dangers of being near large ships that we should now require no more than a review. But some concerns warrant frequent repetition. For example, we should reconsider the issue of what is a large ship. Some mariners define it as one which is larger than theirs, but that approach misses the point. The definition depends more on clumsiness than relative size. Perhaps a definition close to the mark is that a large ship is one of good size which requires considerable time and distance within which to perform her collision-avoidance duties. And a second look at the singular "her" in the last sentence is necessary. In choosing a workable description of a large vessel we must recognize that included is a group of two or more single vessels linked together so they more or less move along in company. High on the list of those invoking extra caution must be a tug struggling along with one or more vessels in tow.

Size is of course the fundamental cause of increased danger. A large ship requires more time and distance to maneuver. The power of her engines and her steering gear is increased, but by no means enough to make her as handy as a smaller vessel. She has limitations and they must be recognized. But her bridge complement is not increased in proportion to her size. The principle followed is that piloting any vessel in motion requires a helmsman, a lookout, and someone in charge. Smaller vessels can assign those duties to one person. The largest merchant ship will often have no more than two people on watch. Whether the rudder weighs 20 pounds or 20 tons, only one seaman is needed to turn the wheel. Moreover, until maneuvering she might engage automatic steering equipment. And electronic aids will share the task of looking out. Even the well-manned aircraft carrier is no better off. Only one person steers and there should be no more than one senior watch officer making decisions. As for lookouts, they only report. Were they shoulder-to-shoulder on the bridge wings they could probably detect no more than an alert officer of the deck with a radar. At anytime all but a few of the carrier's thousand-plus complement have no more to do with actual navigating than does the cook on a merchant ship.

An approach to *any* large vessel demands consideration of her limitations. She cannot stop or turn readily. She can have "blind spots" created by her superstructure. Nothing will be visible under the overhang of a carrier's flight deck. At night a large vessel might not even be aware that small craft are

Even without a tow, tugs plunge and twist in a seaway. [Courtesy McDermott Incorporated]

nearby. Bigness and right-of-way are not expressly equated by the Rules of the Road, but the general prudence demanded by Rule 2 includes allowance for limitations. And again, large ships *are* limited in their actions. The rest of us cannot ignore their size. It is a seafaring reality and must be accommodated. No more equated are girth and extra crew. Whether the mission is military or commercial, the large ship will have no more operational personnel on deck than that necessary to man the wheel, look around, and make a decision.

Before we conclude this review, we must attend to the plight of a tug with one or more barges in tow astern. Not many "vessels" will be more encumbered. A barge astern is not steered like a hook-and-ladder firetruck. No one sits in an after cockpit steering the tail around corners. The helm of a barge is the towing hawser and "whither goest thou" states the lifestyle. In fact, though, the obedience of the two is not instant. It will follow the tug, but not immediately. After the tug changes course it will forge ahead on the original track before responding to the hawser pull by swinging through a wide arc.

Moreover it has no separate power to slow down or to go astern. A crash stop by a tug means little to her tow. Should the foolish tug be able to dodge oncoming barges, she might well find their roles reversed for a time while "the cart pulls the horse." No mariner can expect tugs with tows astern to be able to perform assigned maneuvering roles with any degree of smartness.

Lights

It is unconscionable that *any* mariner not recognize light patterns specified by the Rules. They warn of dangers, and the mariner who either disregards or is ignorant of warnings is not a good seaman. Yet ambiguity is unavoidable, as we have learned while progressing through the text. And at the top of the roster of perplexing signals is a single white light. The range of possible meanings seems endless.

First suggested might be a sternlight. Should it appear dead ahead and closing, a mariner would expect the range to decrease slowly while he overtook whatever is on his track. But then it could be the masthead light of an oncoming power-driven vessel beyond the range of sidelights. Now the range could drop rapidly and the time for defensive maneuvers would be lessened. Of course another possibility is a small craft showing only an all-round white light. Now the manner of approach is indefinite. In shallow water it could be an anchor light. Perhaps it is no more than a deck lamp or one over a bunk and shining through an open porthole. In a harbor it might even be a buoy or a street lamp or a porch light on a seaside home. Context is very important when interpreting the meaning, for porch lights are hard to come by on the high seas. But no mariner who has once been too casual in strange waters at night will ever be so again. Picking up a single white light grants a license to be upset. The very color of the light is disarming, for no threat seems associated with whiteness. To the prudent mariner *any* unidentified light, whatever its hue, poses a threat.

Conclusion

These past few pages have spotlighted some of the practical factors to be considered in the real world where the Rules of the Road are applied. Much could be discussed, but at least our thought processes should by now be functioning. Defensive seafaring means seamanlike caution. And that means careful navigation until doubts are resolved. Part D of the Rules affords doubtful vessels the use of five or more short and rapid whistle blasts to warn others of their concern. It even grants the option of making such a signal by light to emphasize uncertainty. Within each careful seafarer should be a private doubt signal to alert not others, but himself. The price to pay for safe navigation is modest; the penalty for being in default is out of all proportion. Being sensitive to a call to caution is, in substance, what the Rules of the Road are all about.

Appendix A—

THE RULES OF THE ROAD

Official statements of the Rules of the Road can be found in several federal publications, but they all stem from two sources of U.S. codified laws. What the United States accepts as COLREGS will be found in Sections 1601 and 1602, Title 33, of the United States Code (33 USC 1601–1602). The Inland Rules appear in 33 USC 2001–2038. But we need not shape a course for the nearest law library, for next to follow is a full reprint of both sets of rules.

INTERNATIONAL
PART A—GENERAL

RULE 1
Application

(a) These Rules shall apply to all vessels upon the high seas and in all waters connected therewith navigable by seagoing vessels.

(b) Nothing in these Rules shall interfere with the operation of special rules made by an appropriate authority for roadsteads, harbors, rivers, lakes or inland waterways connected with the high seas and navigable by seagoing vessels. Such special rules shall conform as closely as possible to these Rules.

(c) Nothing in these Rules shall interfere with the operation of any special rules made by the Government of any State with respect to additional station or signal lights, shapes or whistle signals for ships of war and vessels proceeding under convoy, or with respect to additional station or signal lights or shapes for fishing vessels engaged in fishing as a fleet. These additional station or signal lights, shapes or whistle signals shall, so far as possible, be such that they cannot be mistaken for any light, shape or signal authorized elsewhere under these Rules.

(d) Traffic separation schemes may be adopted by the Organization for the purpose of these Rules.

(e) Whenever the Government concerned shall have determined that a vessel of special construction or purpose cannot comply fully with the provisions of any of these Rules with respect to the number, position, range or arc of visibility of lights or shapes, as well as to the disposition and characteristics of sound-signalling appliances, without interfering with the special function of the vessel, such vessel shall comply with such other provisions in regard to the number, position, range or arc of visibility of lights or shapes, as well as to the disposition and characteristics of sound-signalling appliances, as her Government shall have determined to be the closest possible compliance with these Rules in respect to that vessel.

INLAND
PART A—GENERAL

RULE 1
Application

(a) These Rules apply to all vessels upon the inland waters of the United States, and to vessels of the United States on the Canadian waters of the Great Lakes to the extent that there is no conflict with Canadian law.

(b)(i) These Rules constitute special rules made by an appropriate authority within the meaning of Rule 1(b) of the International Regulations.

(ii) All vessels complying with the construction and equipment requirements of the International Regulations are considered to be in compliance with these Rules.

(c) Nothing in these Rules shall interfere with the operation of any special rules made by the Secretary of the Navy with respect to additional station or signal lights and shapes or whistle signals for ships of war and vessels proceeding under convoy, or by the Secretary with respect to additional station or signal lights and shapes for fishing vessels engaged in fishing as a fleet. These additional station or signal lights and shapes or whistle signals shall, so far as possible, be such that they cannot be mistaken for any light, shape, or signal authorized elsewhere under these Rules. Notice of such special rules shall be published in the Federal Register and, after the effective date specified in such notice, they shall have effect as if they were a part of these Rules.

(d) Vessel traffic service regulations may be in effect in certain areas.

(e) Whenever the Secretary determines that a vessel or class of vessels of special construction or purpose cannot comply fully with the provisions of any of these Rules with respect to the number, position, range, or arc of visibility of lights or shapes, as well as to the disposition and characteristics of sound-signalling appliances, without interfering with the special function of the vessel, the vessel shall comply with such other provisions in

INTERNATIONAL

RULE 2
Responsibility

(a) Nothing in these Rules shall exonerate any vessel, or the owner, master or crew thereof, from the consequences of any neglect to comply with these Rules or of the neglect of any precaution which may be required by the ordinary practice of seamen, or by the special circumstances of the case.

(b) In construing and complying with these Rules due regard shall be had to all dangers of navigation and collision and to any special circumstances, including the limitations of the vessels involved, which may make a departure from these Rules necessary to avoid immediate danger.

RULE 3
General Definitions

For the purpose of these Rules, except where the context otherwise requires:

(a) The word "vessel" includes every description of water craft, including nondisplacement craft and seaplanes, used or capable of being used as a means of transportation on water.

INLAND

regard to the number, position, range, or arc of visibility of lights or shapes, as well as to the disposition and characteristics of sound-signalling appliances, as the Secretary shall have determined to be the closest possible compliance with these Rules. The Secretary may issue a certificate of alternative compliance for a vessel or class of vessels specifying the closest possible compliance with these Rules. The Secretary of the Navy shall make these determinations and issue certificates of alternative compliance for vessels of the Navy.

(f) The Secretary may accept a certificate of alternative compliance issued by a contracting party to the International Regulations if he determines that the alternative compliance standards of the contracting party are substantially the same as those of the United States.

RULE 2
Responsibility

(a) Nothing in these Rules shall exonerate any vessel, or the owner, master, or crew thereof, from the consequences of any neglect to comply with these Rules or of the neglect of any precaution which may be required by the ordinary practice of seamen, or by the special circumstances of the case.

(b) In construing and complying with these Rules due regard shall be had to all dangers of navigation and collision and to any special circumstances, including the limitations of the vessels involved, which may make a departure from these Rules necessary to avoid immediate danger.

RULE 3
General Definitions

For the purpose of these Rules and this Act, except where the context otherwise requires:

(a) The word "vessel" includes every description of water craft, including nondisplacement craft and seaplanes, used or capable of being used as a means of transportation on water;

(b) The term "power-driven vessel" means any vessel propelled by machinery.

(c) The term "sailing vessel" means any vessel under sail provided that propelling machinery, if fitted, is not being used.

(d) The term "vessel engaged in fishing" means any vessel fishing with nets, lines, trawls or other fishing apparatus which restrict maneuverability, but does not include a vessel fishing with trolling lines or other fishing apparatus which do not restrict maneuverability.

(e) The word "seaplane" includes any aircraft designed to maneuver on the water.

(f) The term "vessel not under command" means a vessel which through some exceptional circumstance is unable to maneuver as required by these Rules and is therefore unable to keep out of the way of another vessel.

(g) The term "vessel restricted in her ability to maneuver" means a vessel which from the nature of her work is restricted in her ability to maneuver as required by these Rules and is therefore unable to keep out of the way of another vessel.

The term 'vessels restricted in their ability to maneuver' shall include but not be limited to:

(i) a vessel engaged in laying, servicing or picking up a navigation mark, submarine cable or pipeline;

(ii) a vessel engaged in dredging, surveying or underwater operations;

(iii) a vessel engaged in replenishment or transferring persons, provisions or cargo while underway;

(iv) a vessel engaged in the launching or recovery of aircraft;

(v) a vessel engaged in mineclearance operations;

(vi) a vessel engaged in a towing operation such as severely restricts the towing vessel and her tow in their ability to deviate from their course.

(h) The term "vessel constrained by her draft" means a power-driven vessel which because of her draft in relation to the available depth of water is severely restricted in her ability to deviate from the course she is following.

(b) The term "power-driven vessel" means any vessel propelled by machinery;

(c) The term "sailing vessel" means any vessel under sail provided that propelling machinery, if fitted, is not being used;

(d) The term "vessel engaged in fishing" means any vessel fishing with nets, lines, trawls, or other fishing apparatus which restrict maneuverability, but does not include a vessel fishing with trolling lines or other fishing apparatus which do not restrict maneuverability;

(e) The word "seaplane" includes any aircraft designed to maneuver on the water;

(f) The term "vessel not under command" means a vessel which through some exceptional circumstance is unable to maneuver as required by these Rules and is therefore unable to keep out of the way of another vessel;

(g) The term "vessel restricted in her ability to maneuver" means a vessel which from the nature of her work is restricted in her ability to maneuver as required by these Rules and is therefore unable to keep out of the way of another vessel; vessels restricted in their ability to maneuver include, but are not limited to:

(i) a vessel engaged in laying, servicing, or picking up a navigation mark, submarine cable, or pipeline;

(ii) a vessel engaged in dredging, surveying, or underwater operations;

(iii) a vessel engaged in replenishment or transferring persons, provisions, or cargo while underway;

(iv) a vessel engaged in the launching or recovery of aircraft;

(v) a vessel engaged in minesweeping operations; and

(vi) a vessel engaged in a towing operation such as severely restricts the towing vessel and her tow in their ability to deviate from their course.

(h) The word "underway" means that a vessel is not at anchor, or made fast to the shore, or aground;

(i) The words "length" and "breadth" of a vessel means her length overall and greatest breadth;

(j) Vessels shall be deemed to be in sight of one another only when one can be observed visually from the other;

INTERNATIONAL

(i) The word "underway" means that a vessel is not at anchor, or made fast to the shore, or aground.

(j) The words "length" and "breadth" of a vessel means her length overall and greatest breadth.

(k) Vessels shall be deemed to be in sight of one another only when one can be observed visually from the other.

(l) The term "restricted visibility" means any condition in which visibility is restricted by fog, mist, falling snow, heavy rainstorms, sandstorms or any other similar causes.

PART B—STEERING AND SAILING RULES

Subpart I—Conduct of Vessels in Any Condition of Visibility

INLAND

(k) The term "restricted visibility" means any condition in which visibility is restricted by fog, mist, falling snow, heavy rainstorms, sandstorms, or any other similar causes;

(l) "Western Rivers" means the Mississippi River, its tributaries, South Pass, and Southwest Pass, to the navigational demarcation lines dividing the high seas from harbors, rivers, and other inland waters of the United States, and the Port Allen-Morgan City Alternate Route, and that part of the Atchafalaya River above its junction with the Port Allen-Morgan City Alternate Route including the Old River and the Red River;

(m) "Great Lakes" means the Great Lakes and their connecting and tributary waters including the Calumet River as far as the Thomas J. O'Brien Lock and Controlling Works (between mile 326 and 327), the Chicago River as far as the east side of the Ashland Avenue Bridge (between mile 321 and 322), and the Saint Lawrence River as far east as the lower exit of Saint Lambert Lock;

(n) "Secretary" means the Secretary of the department in which the Coast Guard is operating;

(o) "Inland Waters" means the navigable waters of the United States shoreward of the navigational demarcation lines dividing the high seas from harbors, rivers, and other inland waters of the United States and the waters of the Great Lakes on the United States side of the International Boundary;

(p) "Inland Rules" or "Rules" mean the Inland Navigational Rules and the annexes thereto, which govern the conduct of vessels and specify the lights, shapes, and sound signals that apply on inland waters; and

(q) "International Regulations" means the International Regulations for Preventing Collisions at Sea, 1972, including annexes currently in force for the United States.

PART B—STEERING AND SAILING RULES

Section I—Conduct of Vessels in Any Condition of Visibility

RULE 4

Application

Rules in this Section apply to any condition of visibility.

RULE 5

Look-out

Every vessel shall at all times maintain a proper look-out by sight and hearing as well as by all available means appropriate in the prevailing circumstances and conditions so as to make a full appraisal of the situation and of the risk of collision.

RULE 6

Safe Speed

Every vessel shall at all times proceed at a safe speed so that she can take proper and effective action to avoid collision and be stopped within a distance appropriate to the prevailing circumstances and conditions.

In determining a safe speed the following factors shall be among those taken into account:

(a) By all vessels:

(i) the state of visibility;

(ii) the traffic density including concentrations of fishing vessels or any other vessels;

(iii) the maneuverability of the vessel with special reference to stopping distance and turning ability in the prevailing conditions;

(iv) at night the presence of background light such as from shore lights or from back scatter of her own lights;

(v) the state of wind, sea and current, and the proximity of navigational hazards;

(vi) the draft in relation to the available depth of water.

(b) Additionally, by vessels with operational radar:

(i) the characteristics, efficiency and limitations of the radar equipment;

(ii) any constraints imposed by the radar range scale in use;

RULE 4

Application

Rules in this subpart apply in any condition of visibility.

RULE 5

Look-out

Every vessel shall at all times maintain a proper look-out by sight and hearing as well as by all available means appropriate in the prevailing circumstances and conditions so as to make a full appraisal of the situation and of the risk of collision.

RULE 6

Safe Speed

Every vessel shall at all times proceed at a safe speed so that she can take proper and effective action to avoid collision and be stopped within a distance appropriate to the prevailing circumstances and conditions.

In determining a safe speed the following factors shall be among those taken into account:

(a) By all vessels:

(i) the state of visibility;

(ii) the traffic density including concentration of fishing vessels or any other vessels;

(iii) the maneuverability of the vessel with special reference to stopping distance and turning ability in the prevailing conditions;

(iv) at night the presence of background light such as from shore lights or from back scatter of her own lights;

(v) the state of wind, sea, and current, and the proximity of navigational hazards;

(vi) the draft in relation to the available depth of water.

(b) Additionally, by vessels with operational radar:

(i) the characteristics, efficiency and limitations of the radar equipment;

(ii) any constraints imposed by the radar range scale in use;

INTERNATIONAL

(iii) the effect on radar detection of the sea state, weather and other sources of interference;

(iv) the possibility that small vessels, ice and other floating objects may not be detected by radar at an adequate range;

(v) the number, location and movement of vessels detected by radar;

(vi) the more exact assessment of the visibility that may be possible when radar is used to determine the range of vessels or other objects in the vicinity.

RULE 7

Risk of Collision

(a) Every vessel shall use all available means appropriate to the prevailing circumstances and conditions to determine if risk of collision exists. If there is any doubt such risk shall be deemed to exist.

(b) Proper use shall be made of radar equipment if fitted and operational, including long-range scanning to obtain early warning of risk of collision and radar plotting or equivalent systematic observation of detected objects.

(c) Assumptions shall not be made on the basis of scanty information, especially scanty radar information.

(d) In determining if risk of collision exists the following considerations shall be among those taken into account:

(i) such risk shall be deemed to exist if the compass bearing of an approaching vessel does not appreciably change;

(ii) such risk may sometimes exist even when an appreciable bearing change is evident, particularly when approaching a very large vessel or a tow or when approaching a vessel at close range.

RULE 8

Action to Avoid Collision

(a) Any action taken to avoid collision shall, if the circumstances of the case admit, be positive, made in ample time and with due regard to the observance of good seamanship.

INLAND

(iii) the effect on radar detection of the sea state, weather, and other sources of interference;

(iv) the possibility that small vessels, ice and other floating objects may not be detected by radar at an adequate range;

(v) the number, location, and movement of vessels detected by radar; and

(vi) the more exact assessment of the visibility that may be possible when radar is used to determine the range of vessels or other objects in the vicinity.

RULE 7

Risk of Collision

(a) Every vessel shall use all available means appropriate to the prevailing circumstances and conditions to determine if risk of collision exists. If there is any doubt such risk shall be deemed to exist.

(b) Proper use shall be made of radar equipment if fitted and operational, including long-range scanning to obtain early warning of risk of collision and radar plotting or equivalent systematic observation of detected objects.

(c) Assumptions shall not be made on the basis of scanty information, especially scanty radar information.

(d) In determining if risk of collision exists the following considerations shall be among those taken into account:

(i) such risk shall be deemed to exist if the compass bearing of an approaching vessel does not appreciably change; and

(ii) such risk may sometimes exist even when an appreciable bearing change is evident, particularly when approaching a very large vessel or a tow or when approaching a vessel at close range.

RULE 8

Action to Avoid Collision

(a) Any action taken to avoid collision shall, if the circumstances of the case admit, be positive, made in ample time and with due regard to the observance of good seamanship.

(b) Any alteration of course and/or speed to avoid collision shall, if the circumstances of the case admit, be large enough to be readily apparent to another vessel observing visually or by radar; a succession of small alterations of course and/or speed should be avoided.

(c) If there is sufficient sea room, alteration of course alone may be the most effective action to avoid a close-quarters situation provided that it is made in good time, is substantial and does not result in another close-quarters situation.

(d) Action taken to avoid collision with another vessel shall be such as to result in passing at a safe distance. The effectiveness of the action shall be carefully checked until the other vessel is finally past and clear.

(e) If necessary to avoid collision or allow more time to assess the situation, a vessel shall slacken her speed or take all way off by stopping or reversing her means of propulsion.

RULE 9

Narrow Channels

(a) A vessel proceeding along the course of a narrow channel or fairway shall keep as near to the outer limit of the channel or fairway which lies on her starboard side as is safe and practicable.

(b) A vessel of less than 20 meters in length or a sailing vessel shall not impede the passage of a vessel which can safely navigate only within a narrow channel or fairway.

(c) A vessel engaged in fishing shall not impede the passage of any other vessel navigating within a narrow channel or fairway.

(d) A vessel shall not cross a narrow channel or fairway if such crossing impedes the passage of a vessel which can safely navigate only within such channel or fairway. The latter vessel may use the sound signal prescribed in Rule 34(d) if in doubt as to the intention of the crossing vessel.

(e)(i) In a narrow channel or fairway when overtaking can take place only if the vessel to be overtaken has to take action to permit safe passing, the vessel intending to overtake shall indicate her intention by sounding the appropriate signal prescribed in Rule 34(c)(i). The vessel to be overtaken shall, if in agreement, sound

(b) Any alteration of course or speed to avoid collision shall, if the circumstances of the case admit, be large enough to be readily apparent to another vessel observing visually or by radar; a succession of small alterations of course or speed should be avoided.

(c) If there is sufficient sea room, alteration of course alone may be the most effective action to avoid a close-quarters situation provided that it is made in good time, is substantial and does not result in another close-quarters situation.

(d) Action taken to avoid collision with another vessel shall be such as to result in passing at a safe distance. The effectiveness of the action shall be carefully checked until the other vessel is finally past and clear.

(e) If necessary to avoid collision or allow more time to assess the situation, a vessel shall slacken her speed or take all way off by stopping or reversing her means of propulsion.

RULE 9

Narrow Channels

(a)(i) A vessel proceeding along the course of a narrow channel or fairway shall keep as near to the outer limit of the channel or fairway which lies on her starboard side as is safe and practicable.

(ii) Notwithstanding paragraph (a)(i) and Rule 14(a), a power-driven vessel operating in narrow channels or fairways on the Great Lakes, Western Rivers, or waters specified by the Secretary, and proceeding downbound with a following current shall have the right-of-way over an upbound vessel, shall propose the manner and place of passage, and shall initiate the maneuvering signals prescribed by Rule 34(a)(i), as appropriate. The vessel proceeding upbound against the current shall hold as necessary to permit safe passing.

(b) A vessel of less than 20 meters in length or a sailing vessel shall not impede the passage of a vessel that can safely navigate only within a narrow channel or fairway.

(c) A vessel engaged in fishing shall not impede the passage of any other vessel navigating within a narrow channel or fairway.

(d) A vessel shall not cross a narrow channel or fairway if such

INTERNATIONAL

the appropriate signal prescribed in Rule 34(c)(ii) and take steps to permit safe passing. If in doubt she may sound the signals prescribed in Rule 34(d).

(ii) This Rule does not relieve the overtaking vessel of her obligation under Rule 13.

(f) A vessel nearing a bend or an area of a narrow channel or fairway where other vessels may be obscured by an intervening obstruction shall navigate with particular alertness and caution and shall sound the appropriate signal prescribed in Rule 34(e).

(g) Any vessel shall, if the circumstances of the case admit, avoid anchoring in a narrow channel.

RULE 10

Traffic Separation Schemes

(a) This Rule applies to traffic separation schemes adopted by the Organization.

(b) A vessel using a traffic separation scheme shall:

(i) proceed in the appropriate traffic lane in the general direction of traffic flow for that lane;

(ii) so far as practicable keep clear of a traffic separation line or separation zone;

(iii) normally join or leave a traffic lane at the termination of the lane, but when joining or leaving from either side shall do so at as small an angle to the general direction of traffic flow as practicable.

(c) A vessel shall so far as practicable avoid crossing traffic lanes, but if obliged to do so shall cross as nearly as practicable at right angles to the general direction of traffic flow.

(d) Inshore traffic zones shall not normally be used by through

INLAND

crossing impedes the passage of a vessel which can safely navigate only within that channel or fairway. The latter vessel shall use the danger signal prescribed in Rule 34(d) if in doubt as to the intention of the crossing vessel.

(e)(i) In a narrow channel or fairway when overtaking, the vessel intending to overtake shall indicate her intention by sounding the appropriate signal prescribed in Rule 34(c) and take steps to permit safe passing. The overtaken vessel, if in agreement, shall sound the same signal. If in doubt she shall sound the danger signal prescribed in Rule 34(d).

(ii) This Rule does not relieve the overtaking vessel of her obligation under Rule 13.

(f) A vessel nearing a bend or an area of a narrow channel or fairway where other vessels may be obscured by an intervening obstruction shall navigate with particular alertness and caution and shall sound the appropriate signal prescribed in Rule 34(e).

(g) Every vessel shall, if the circumstances of the case admit, avoid anchoring in a narrow channel.

RULE 10

Vessel Traffic Services

Each vessel required by regulation to participate in a vessel traffic service shall comply with the applicable regulations.

traffic which can safely use the appropriate traffic lane within the adjacent traffic separation scheme. However, vessels of less than 20 meters in length and sailing vessels may under all circumstances use inshore traffic zones.

(e) A vessel other than a crossing vessel or a vessel joining or leaving a lane shall not normally enter a separation zone or cross a separation line except:

(i) in cases of emergency to avoid immediate danger;

(ii) to engage in fishing within a separation zone.

(f) A vessel navigating in areas near the terminations of traffic separation schemes shall do so with particular caution.

(g) A vessel shall so far as practicable avoid anchoring in a traffic separation scheme or in areas near its terminations.

(h) A vessel not using a traffic separation scheme shall avoid it by as wide a margin as is practicable.

(i) A vessel engaged in fishing shall not impede the passage of any vessel following a traffic lane.

(j) A vessel of less than 20 meters in length or a sailing vessel shall not impede the safe passage of a power-driven vessel following a traffic lane.

(k) A vessel restricted in her ability to maneuver when engaged in an operation for the maintenance of safety of navigation in a traffic separation scheme is exempted from complying with this Rule to the extent necessary to carry out the operation.

(l) A vessel restricted in her ability to maneuver when engaged in an operation for the laying, servicing or picking up of a submarine cable, within a traffic separation scheme, is exempted from complying with this Rule to the extent necessary to carry out the operation.

Section II—Conduct of Vessels in Sight of One Another

RULE 11

Application

Rules in this Section apply to vessels in sight of one another.

Subpart II—Conduct of Vessels in Sight of One Another

RULE 11

Application

Rules in this subpart apply to vessels in sight of one another.

INTERNATIONAL
RULE 12

Sailing Vessels

(a) When two sailing vessels are approaching one another, so as to involve risk of collision, one of them shall keep out of the way of the other as follows:

(i) when each has the wind on a different side, the vessel which has the wind on the port side shall keep out of the way of the other;

(ii) when both have the wind on the same side, the vessel which is to windward shall keep out of the way of the vessel which is to leeward;

(iii) if a vessel with the wind on the port side sees a vessel to windward and cannot determine with certainty whether the other vessel has the wind on the port or on the starboard side, she shall keep out of the way of the other.

(b) For the purposes of this Rule the windward side shall be deemed to be the side opposite to that on which the mainsail is carried or, in the case of a square-rigged vessel, the side opposite to that on which the largest fore-and-aft sail is carried.

RULE 13

Overtaking

(a) Notwithstanding anything contained in the Rules of Part B, Sections I and II, any vessel overtaking any other shall keep out of the way of the vessel being overtaken.

(b) A vessel shall be deemed to be overtaking when coming up with another vessel from a direction more than 22.5 degrees abaft her beam, that is, in such a position with reference to the vessel she is overtaking, that at night she would be able to see only the sternlight of that vessel but neither of her sidelights.

(c) When a vessel is in any doubt as to whether she is overtaking another, she shall assume that this is the case and act accordingly.

INLAND
RULE 12

Sailing Vessels

(a) When two sailing vessels are approaching one another, so as to involve risk of collision, one of them shall keep out of the way of the other as follows:

(i) when each has the wind on a different side, the vessel which has the wind on the port side shall keep out of the way of the other;

(ii) when both have the wind on the same side, the vessel which is to windward shall keep out of the way of the vessel which is to leeward; and

(iii) if a vessel with the wind on the port side sees a vessel to windward and cannot determine with certainty whether the other vessel has the wind on the port or on the starboard side, she shall keep out of the way of the other.

(b) For the purpose of this Rule the windward side shall be deemed to be the side opposite to that on which the mainsail is carried or, in the case of a square-rigged vessel, the side opposite to that on which the largest fore-and-aft sail is carried.

RULE 13

Overtaking

(a) Notwithstanding anything contained in Rules 4 through 18, any vessel overtaking any other shall keep out of the way of the vessel being overtaken.

(c) When a vessel is in any doubt as to whether she is overtaking another, she shall assume that this is the case and act accordingly.

(b) A vessel shall be deemed to be overtaking when coming up with another vessel from a direction more than 22.5 degrees abaft her beam; that is, in such a position with reference to the vessel she is overtaking, that at night she would be able to see only the sternlight of that vessel but neither of her sidelights.

(d) Any subsequent alteration of the bearing between the two vessels shall not make the overtaking vessel a crossing vessel within the meaning of these Rules or relieve her of the duty of keeping clear of the overtaken vessel until she is finally past and clear.

RULE 14

Head-on Situation

(a) When two power-driven vessels are meeting on reciprocal or nearly reciprocal courses so as to involve risk of collision each shall alter her course to starboard so that each shall pass on the port side of the other.

(b) Such a situation shall be deemed to exist when a vessel sees the other ahead or nearly ahead and by night she could see the masthead lights of the other in a line or nearly in a line or both sidelights and by day she observes the corresponding aspect of the other vessel.

(c) When a vessel is in any doubt as to whether such a situation exists she shall assume that it does exist and act accordingly.

RULE 15

Crossing Situation

(a) When two power-driven vessels are crossing so as to involve risk of collision, the vessel which has the other on her starboard side shall keep out of the way and shall, if the circumstances of the case admit, avoid crossing ahead of the other vessel.

(b) Notwithstanding paragraph (a), on the Great Lakes, Western Rivers, or water specified by the Secretary, a vessel crossing a river shall keep out of the way of a power-driven vessel ascending or descending the river.

RULE 16

Action by Give-way Vessel

Every vessel which is directed to keep out of the way of another vessel shall, so far as possible, take early and substantial action to keep well clear.

(d) Any subsequent alteration of the bearing between the two vessels shall not make the overtaking vessel a crossing vessel within the meaning of these Rules or relieve her of the duty of keeping clear of the overtaken vessel until she is finally past and clear.

RULE 14

Head-on Situation

(a) When two power-driven vessels are meeting on reciprocal or nearly reciprocal courses so as to involve risk of collision each shall alter her course to starboard so that each shall pass on the port side of the other.

(b) Such a situation shall be deemed to exist when a vessel sees the other ahead or nearly ahead and by night she could see the masthead lights of the other in a line or nearly in a line and/or both sidelights and by day she observes the corresponding aspect of the other vessel.

(c) When a vessel is in any doubt as to whether such a situation exists she shall assume that it does exist and act accordingly.

RULE 15

Crossing Situation

When two power-driven vessels are crossing so as to involve risk of collision, the vessel which has the other on her own starboard side shall keep out of the way and shall, if the circumstances of the case admit, avoid crossing ahead of the other vessel.

RULE 16

Action by Give-way Vessel

Every vessel which is directed to keep out of the way of another vessel shall, so far as possible, take early and substantial action to keep well clear.

RULE 17

Action by Stand-on Vessel

(a)(i) Where one of two vessels is to keep out of the way, the other shall keep her course and speed.

(ii) The latter vessel may, however, take action to avoid collision by her maneuver alone, as soon as it becomes apparent to her that the vessel required to keep out of the way is not taking appropriate action in compliance with these Rules.

(b) When, from any cause, the vessel required to keep her course and speed finds herself so close that collision cannot be avoided by the action of the give-way vessel alone, she shall take such action as will best aid to avoid collision.

(c) A power-driven vessel which takes action in a crossing situation in accordance with subparagraph (a)(ii) of this Rule to avoid collision with another power-driven vessel shall, if the circumstances of the case admit, not alter course to port for a vessel on her own port side.

(d) This Rule does not relieve the give-way vessel of her obligation to keep out of the way.

RULE 18

Responsibilities Between Vessels

Except where Rules 9, 10, and 13 otherwise require:

(a) A power-driven vessel underway shall keep out of the way of:
(i) a vessel not under command;
(ii) a vessel restricted in her ability to maneuver;
(iii) a vessel engaged in fishing; and
(iv) a sailing vessel.

(b) A sailing vessel underway shall keep out of the way of:
(i) a vessel not under command;
(ii) a vessel restricted in her ability to maneuver; and
(iii) a vessel engaged in fishing.

RULE 17

Action by Stand-on Vessel

(a)(i) Where one of two vessels is to keep out of the way, the other shall keep her course and speed.

(ii) The latter vessel may, however, take action to avoid collision by her maneuver alone, as soon as it becomes apparent to her that the vessel required to keep out of the way is not taking appropriate action in compliance with these Rules.

(b) When, from any cause, the vessel required to keep her course and speed finds herself so close that collision cannot be avoided by the action of the give-way vessel alone, she shall take such action as will best aid to avoid collision.

(c) A power-driven vessel which takes action in a crossing situation in accordance with subparagraph (a)(ii) of this Rule to avoid collision with another power-driven vessel shall, if the circumstances of the case admit, not alter course to port for a vessel on her own port side.

(d) This Rule does not relieve the give-way vessel of her obligation to keep out of the way.

RULE 18

Responsibilities Between Vessels

Except where Rules 9, 10, and 13 otherwise require:

(a) A power-driven vessel underway shall keep out of the way of:
(i) a vessel not under command;
(ii) a vessel restricted in her ability to maneuver;
(iii) a vessel engaged in fishing; and
(iv) a sailing vessel.

(b) A sailing vessel underway shall keep out of the way of:
(i) a vessel not under command;
(ii) a vessel restricted in her ability to maneuver; and
(iii) a vessel engaged in fishing.

(c) A vessel engaged in fishing when underway shall, so far as possible, keep out of the way of:

(i) a vessel not under command;

(ii) a vessel restricted in her ability to maneuver.

(d)(i) Any vessel other than a vessel not under command or a vessel restricted in her ability to maneuver shall, if the circumstances of the case admit, avoid impeding the safe passage of a vessel constrained by her draft, exhibiting the signals in Rule 28.

(ii) A vessel constrained by her draft shall navigate with particular caution having full regard to her special condition.

(e) A seaplane on the water shall, in general, keep well clear of all vessels and avoid impeding their navigation. In circumstances, however, where risk of collision exists, she shall comply with the Rules of this Part.

Section III—Conduct of Vessels in Restricted Visibility

RULE 19

Conduct of Vessels in Restricted Visibility

(a) This Rule applies to vessels not in sight of one another when navigating in or near an area of restricted visibility.

(b) Every vessel shall proceed at a safe speed adapted to the prevailing circumstances and conditions of restricted visibilty. A power-driven vessel shall have her engines ready for immediate maneuver.

(c) Every vessel shall have due regard to the prevailing circumstances and conditions of restricted visibility when complying with the Rules of Section I of this Part.

(d) A vessel which detects by radar alone the presence of another vessel shall determine if a close-quarters situation is developing and/or risk of collision exists. If so, she shall take avoiding action in ample time, provided that when such action consists of an alteration of course, so far as possible the following shall be avoided:

(c) A vessel engaged in fishing when underway shall, so far as possible, keep out of the way of:

(i) a vessel not under command; and

(ii) a vessel restricted in her ability to maneuver.

(d) A seaplane on the water shall, in general, keep well clear of all vessels and avoid impeding their navigation. In circumstances, however, where risk of collision exists, she shall comply with the Rules of this Part.

Subpart III—Conduct of Vessels in Restricted Visibility

RULE 19

Conduct of Vessels in Restricted Visibility

(a) This Rule applies to vessels not in sight of one another when navigating in or near an area of restricted visibility.

(b) Every vessel shall proceed at a safe speed adapted to the prevailing circumstances and conditions of restricted visibility. A power-driven vessel shall have her engines ready for immediate maneuver.

(c) Every vessel shall have due regard to the prevailing circumstances and conditions of restricted visibility when complying with Rules 4 through 10.

(d) A vessel which detects by radar alone the presence of another vessel shall determine if a close-quarters situation is developing or risk of collision exists. If so, she shall take avoiding action in ample time, provided that when such action consists of an alteration of course, so far as possible the following shall be avoided:

INTERNATIONAL

(i) an alteration of course to port for a vessel forward of the beam, other than for a vessel being overtaken;

(ii) an alteration of course towards a vessel abeam or abaft the beam.

(e) Except where it has been determined that a risk of collision does not exist, every vessel which hears apparently forward of her beam the fog signal of another vessel, or which cannot avoid a close-quarters situation with another vessel forward of her beam, shall reduce her speed to the minimum at which she can be kept on her course. She shall if necessary take all her way off and in any event navigate with extreme caution until danger of collision is over.

PART C—LIGHTS AND SHAPES

RULE 20

Application

(a) Rules in this Part shall be complied with in all weathers.

(b) The Rules concerning lights shall be complied with from sunset to sunrise, and during such times no other lights shall be exhibited, except such lights as cannot be mistaken for the lights specified in these Rules or do not impair their visibility or distinctive character, or interfere with the keeping of a proper look-out.

(c) The lights prescribed by these Rules shall, if carried, also be exhibited from sunrise to sunset in restricted visibility and may be exhibited in all other circumstances when it is deemed necessary.

(d) The Rules concerning shapes shall be complied with by day.

(e) The lights and shapes specified in these Rules shall comply with the provisions of Annex I to these Regulations.

RULE 21

Definitions

(a) "Masthead light" means a white light placed over the fore and aft centerline of the vessel showing an unbroken light over an

INLAND

(i) an alteration of course to port for a vessel forward of the beam, other than for a vessel being overtaken; and

(ii) an alteration of course toward a vessel abeam or abaft the beam.

(e) Except where it has been determined that a risk of collision does not exist, every vessel which hears apparently forward of her beam the fog signal of another vessel, or which cannot avoid a close-quarters situation with another vessel forward of her beam, shall reduce her speed to the minimum at which she can be kept on course. She shall if necessary take all her way off and, in any event, navigate with extreme caution until danger of collision is over.

PART C—LIGHTS AND SHAPES

RULE 20

Application

(a) Rules in this Part shall be complied with in all weathers.

(b) The Rules concerning lights shall be complied with from sunset to sunrise, and during such times no other lights shall be exhibited, except such lights as cannot be mistaken for the lights specified in these Rules or do not impair their visibility or distinctive character, or interfere with the keeping of a proper look-out.

(c) The lights prescribed by these Rules shall, if carried, also be exhibited from sunrise to sunset in restricted visibility and may be exhibited in all other circumstances when it is deemed necessary.

(d) The Rules concerning shapes shall be complied with by day.

(e) The lights and shapes specified in these Rules shall comply with the provisions of Annex I of these Rules.

RULE 21

Definitions

(a) "Masthead light" means a white light placed over the fore and aft centerline of the vessel showing an unbroken light over an arc of the horizon of 225 degrees and so fixed as to show the light from right ahead to 22.5 degrees abaft the beam on either side of the vessel, except that on a vessel of less than 12 meters in length the masthead light shall be placed as nearly as practicable to the fore and aft centerline of the vessel.

(b) "Sidelights" mean a green light on the starboard side and a red light on the port side each showing an unbroken light over an arc of the horizon of 112.5 degrees and so fixed as to show the light from right ahead to 22.5 degrees abaft the beam on its respective side. On a vessel of less than 20 meters in length the sidelights may be combined in one lantern carried on the fore and aft centerline of the vessel, except that on a vessel of less than 12 meters in length the sidelights when combined in one lantern shall be placed as nearly as practicable to the fore and aft centerline of the vessel.

(c) "Sternlight" means a white light placed as nearly as practicable at the stern showing an unbroken light over an arc of the horizon of 135 degrees and so fixed as to show the light 67.5 degrees from right aft on each side of the vessel.

(d) "Towing light" means a yellow light having the same characteristics as the "sternlight" defined in paragraph (c) of this Rule.

(e) "All-round light" means a light showing an unbroken light over an arc of the horizon of 360 degrees.

(f) "Flashing light" means a light flashing at regular intervals at a frequency of 120 flashes or more per minute.

(g) "Special flashing light" means a yellow light flashing at regular intervals at a frequency of 50 to 70 flashes per minute, placed as far forward and as nearly as practicable on the fore and aft centerline of the tow and showing an unbroken light over an arc of the horizon of not less than 180 degrees nor more than 225 degrees and so fixed as to show the light from right ahead to abeam and no more than 22.5 degrees abaft the beam on either side of the vessel.

arc of the horizon of 225 degrees and so fixed as to show the light from right ahead to 22.5 degrees abaft the beam on either side of the vessel.

(b) "Sidelights" means a green light on the starboard side and a red light on the port side each showing an unbroken light over an arc of the horizon of 112.5 degrees and so fixed as to show the light from right ahead to 22.5 degrees abaft the beam on its respective side. In a vessel of less than 20 meters in length the sidelights may be combined in one lantern carried on the fore and aft centerline of the vessel.

(c) "Sternlight" means a white light placed as nearly as practicable at the stern showing an unbroken light over an arc of the horizon of 135 degrees and so fixed as to show the light 67.5 degrees from right aft on each side of the vessel.

(d) "Towing light" means a yellow light having the same characteristics as the "sternlight" defined in paragraph (c) of this Rule.

(e) "All-round light" means a light showing an unbroken light over an arc of the horizon of 360 degrees.

(f) "Flashing light" means a light flashing at regular intervals at a frequency of 120 flashes or more per minute.

INTERNATIONAL
RULE 22

Visibility of Lights

The lights prescribed in these Rules shall have an intensity as specified in Section 8 of Annex I to these Regulations so as to be visible at the following minimum ranges:

(a) In vessels of 50 meters or more in length:

—a masthead light, 6 miles;

—a sidelight, 3 miles;

—a sternlight, 3 miles;

—a towing light, 3 miles;

—a white, red, green or yellow all-round light, 3 miles.

(b) In vessels of 12 meters or more in length but less than 50 meters in length:

—a masthead light, 5 miles; except that where the length of the vessel is less than 20 meters, 3 miles;

—a sidelight, 2 miles;

—a sternlight, 2 miles;

—a towing light, 2 miles;

—a white, red, green or yellow all-round light, 2 miles.

(c) In vessels of less than 12 meters in length:

—a masthead light, 2 miles;

—a sidelight, 1 mile;

—a sternlight, 2 miles;

—a towing light, 2 miles;

—a white, red, green or yellow all-round light, 2 miles.

(d) In inconspicuous, partly submerged vessels or objects being towed:

—a white all-round light, 3 miles.

INLAND
RULE 22

Visibility of Lights

The lights prescribed in these Rules shall have an intensity as specified in Annex I to these Rules, so as to be visible at the following minimum ranges:

(a) In a vessel of 50 meters or more in length:

—a masthead light, 6 miles;

—a sidelight, 3 miles;

—a sternlight, 3 miles;

—a towing light, 3 miles;

—a white, red, green or yellow all-round light, 3 miles; and a special flashing light, 2 miles.

(b) In a vessel of 12 meters or more in length but less than 50 meters in length:

—a masthead light, 5 miles; except that where the length of the vessel is less than 20 meters, 3 miles;

—a sidelight, 2 miles;

—a sternlight, 2 miles;

—a towing light, 2 miles;

—a white, red, green or yellow all-round light, 2 miles; and a special flashing light, 2 miles.

(c) In a vessel of less than 12 meters in length:

—a masthead light, 2 miles;

—a sidelight, 1 mile;

—a sternlight, 2 miles;

—a towing light, 2 miles;

—a white, red, green or yellow all-round light, 2 miles; and a special flashing light, 2 miles.

(d) In an inconspicuous, partly submerged vessel or object being towed:

—a white all-round light, 3 miles.

RULE 23

Power-driven Vessels Underway

(a) A power-driven vessel underway shall exhibit:

(i) a masthead light forward;

(ii) a second masthead light abaft of and higher than the forward one; except that a vessel of less than 50 meters in length shall not be obliged to exhibit such light but may do so;

(iii) sidelights;

(iv) a sternlight.

(b) An air-cushion vessel when operating in the non-displacement mode shall, in addition to the lights prescribed in paragraph (a) of this Rule, exhibit an all-round flashing yellow light.

(c)(i) A power-driven vessel of less than 12 meters in length may in lieu of the lights prescribed in paragraph (a) of this Rule exhibit an all-round white light and sidelights;

(ii) a power-driven vessel of less than 7 meters in length whose maximum speed does not exceed 7 knots may in lieu of the lights prescribed in paragraph (a) of this Rule exhibit an all-round white light and shall, if practicable, also exhibit sidelights;

(iii) the masthead light or all-round white light on a power-driven vessel of less than 12 meters in length may be displaced from the fore and aft centerline of the vessel if centerline fitting is not practicable, provided that the sidelights are combined in one lantern which shall be carried on the fore and aft centerline of the vessel or located as nearly as practicable in the same fore and aft line as the masthead light or the all-round white light.

RULE 24

Towing and Pushing

(a) A power-driven vessel when towing shall exhibit:

(i) instead of the light prescribed in Rule 23(a)(i) or (a)(ii), two masthead lights in a vertical line. When the length of the tow,

RULE 23

Power-driven Vessels Underway

(a) A power-driven vessel underway shall exhibit:

(i) a masthead light forward; except that a vessel of less than 20 meters in length need not exhibit this light forward of amidships but shall exhibit it as far forward as is practicable;

(ii) a second masthead light abaft of and higher than the forward one; except that a vessel of less than 50 meters in length shall not be obliged to exhibit such light but may do so;

(iii) sidelights; and

(iv) a sternlight.

(b) An air-cushion vessel when operating in the nondisplacement mode shall, in addition to the lights prescribed in paragraph (a) of this Rule, exhibit an all-round flashing yellow light where it can best be seen.

(c) A power-driven vessel of less than 12 meters in length may in lieu of the lights prescribed in paragraph (a) of this Rule, exhibit an all-round white light and sidelights.

(d) A power-driven vessel when operating on the Great Lakes may carry an all-round white light in lieu of the second masthead light and sternlight prescribed in paragraph (a) of this Rule. The light shall be carried in the position of the second masthead light and be visible at the same minimum range.

RULE 24

Towing and Pushing

(a) A power-driven vessel when towing astern shall exhibit:

(i) instead of the light prescribed either in Rule 23(a)(i) or 23(a)(ii), two masthead lights in a vertical line. When the length of

INTERNATIONAL

measuring from the stern of the towing vessel to the after end of the tow exceeds 200 meters, three such lights in a vertical line;

   (ii) sidelights;

   (iii) a sternlight;

   (iv) a towing light in a vertical line above the sternlight;

   (v) when the length of the tow exceeds 200 meters, a diamond shape where it can best be seen.

(b) When a pushing vessel and a vessel being pushed ahead are rigidly connected in a composite unit they shall be regarded as a power-driven vessel and exhibit the lights prescribed in Rule 23.

(c) A power-driven vessel when pushing ahead or towing alongside, except in the case of a composite unit, shall exhibit:

   (i) instead of the light prescribed in Rule 23(a)(i) or (a)(ii), two masthead lights in a vertical line;

   (ii) sidelights;

   (iii) a sternlight.

(d) A power-driven vessel to which paragraph (a) or (c) of this Rule apply shall also comply with Rule 23(a)(ii).

(e) A vessel or object being towed, other than those mentioned in paragraph (g) of this Rule, shall exhibit:

   (i) sidelights;

   (ii) a sternlight;

   (iii) when the length of the tow exceeds 200 meters, a diamond shape where it can best be seen.

(f) Provided that any number of vessels being towed alongside or pushed in a group shall be lighted as one vessel,

   (i) a vessel being pushed ahead, not being part of a composite unit, shall exhibit at the forward end, sidelights;

   (ii) a vessel being towed alongside shall exhibit a sternlight and at the forward end, sidelights.

(g) An inconspicuous, partly submerged vessel or object, or combination of such vessels or objects being towed, shall exhibit:

   (i) if it is less than 25 meters in breadth, one all-round white

INLAND

the tow, measuring from the stern of the towing vessel to the after end of the tow exceeds 200 meters, three such lights in a vertical line;

   (ii) sidelights;

   (iii) a sternlight;

   (iv) a towing light in a vertical line above the sternlight; and

   (v) when the length of the tow exceeds 200 meters, a diamond shape where it can best be seen.

(b) When a pushing vessel and a vessel being pushed ahead are rigidly connected in a composite unit they shall be regarded as a power-driven vessel and exhibit the lights prescribed in Rule 23.

(c) A power-driven vessel when pushing ahead or towing alongside, except as required by paragraphs (b) and (i) of this Rule, shall exhibit:

   (i) instead of the light prescribed either in Rule 23(a)(i) or 23(a)(ii), two masthead lights in a vertical line;

   (ii) sidelights; and

   (iii) two towing lights in a vertical line.

(d) A power-driven vessel to which paragraphs (a) or (c) of this Rule apply shall also comply with Rule 23(a)(i) and 23(a)(ii).

(e) A vessel or object other than those referred to in paragraph (g) of this Rule being towed shall exhibit:

   (i) sidelights;

   (ii) a sternlight; and

   (iii) when the length of the tow exceeds 200 meters, a diamond shape where it can best be seen.

(f) Provided that any number of vessels being towed alongside or pushed in a group shall be lighted as one vessel:

   (i) a vessel being pushed ahead, not being part of a composite unit, shall exhibit at the forward end sidelights, and a special flashing light; and

   (ii) a vessel being towed alongside shall exhibit a sternlight and at the forward end sidelights.

light at or near the forward end and one at or near the after end except that dracones need not exhibit a light at or near the forward end;

(ii) if it is 25 meters or more in breadth, two additional all-round white lights at or near the extremities of its breadth;

(iii) if it exceeds 100 meters in length, additional all-round white lights between the lights prescribed in subparagraphs (i) and (ii) so that the distance between the lights shall not exceed 100 meters;

(iv) a diamond shape at or near the aftermost extremity of the last vessel or object being towed and if the length of the tow exceeds 200 meters an additional diamond shape where it can best be seen and located as far forward as is practicable.

(h) Where from any sufficient cause it is impracticable for a vessel or object being towed to exhibit the lights or shapes prescribed in paragraph (e) or (g) of this Rule, all possible measures shall be taken to light the vessel or object towed or at least to indicate the presence of such vessel or object.

(i) Where from any sufficient cause it is impracticable for a vessel not normally engaged in towing operations to display the lights prescribed in paragraph (a) or (c) of this Rule, such vessel shall not be required to exhibit those lights when engaged in towing another vessel in distress or otherwise in need of assistance. All possible measures shall be taken to indicate the nature of the relationship between the towing vessel and the vessel being towed as authorized by Rule 36, in particular by illuminating the towline.

(g) An inconspicuous, partly submerged vessel or object being towed shall exhibit:

(i) if it is less than 25 meters in breadth, one all-round white light at or near each end;

(ii) if it is 25 meters or more in breadth, four all-round white lights to mark its length and breadth;

(iii) if it exceeds 100 meters in length, additional all-round white lights between the lights prescribed in subparagraphs (i) and (ii) so that the distance between the lights shall not exceed 100 meters: *Provided,* That any vessels or objects being towed alongside each other shall be lighted as one vessel or object;

(iv) a diamond shape at or near the aftermost extremity of the last vessel or object being towed; and

(v) the towing vessel may direct a searchlight in the direction of the tow to indicate its presence to an approaching vessel.

(h) Where from any sufficient cause it is impracticable for a vessel or object being towed to exhibit the lights prescribed in paragraph (e) or (g) of this Rule, all possible measures shall be taken to light the vessel or object towed or at least to indicate the presence of the unlighted vessel or object.

(i) Notwithstanding paragraph (c), on the Western Rivers and on waters specified by the Secretary, a power-driven vessel when pushing ahead or towing alongside, except as paragraph (b) applies, shall exhibit:

(i) sidelights; and

(ii) two towing lights in a vertical line.

(j) Where from any sufficient cause it is impracticable for a vessel not normally engaged in towing operations to display the lights prescribed by paragraph (a), (c) or (i) of this Rule, such vessel shall not be required to exhibit those lights when engaged in towing another vessel in distress or otherwise in need of assistance. All possible measures shall be taken to indicate the nature of the relationship between the towing vessel and the vessel being assisted. The searchlight authorized by Rule 36 may be used to illuminate the tow.

INTERNATIONAL
RULE 25

Sailing Vessels Underway and Vessels Under Oars

(a) A sailing vessel underway shall exhibit:

   (i) sidelights;

   (ii) a sternlight.

(b) In a sailing vessel of less than 20 meters in length the lights prescribed in paragraph (a) of this Rule may be combined in one lantern carried at or near the top of the mast where it can best be seen.

(c) A sailing vessel underway may, in addition to the lights prescribed in paragraph (a) of this Rule, exhibit at or near the top of the mast, where they can best be seen, two all-round lights in a vertical line, the upper being red and the lower green, but these lights shall not be exhibited in conjunction with the combined lantern permitted by paragraph (b) of this Rule.

(d)(i) A sailing vessel of less than 7 meters in length shall, if practicable, exhibit the lights prescribed in paragraph (a) or (b) of this Rule, but if she does not, she shall have ready at hand an electric torch or lighted lantern showing a white light which shall be exhibited in sufficient time to prevent collision.

   (ii) A vessel under oars may exhibit the lights prescribed in this Rule for sailing vessels, but if she does not, she shall have ready at hand an electric torch or lighted lantern showing a white light which shall be exhibited in sufficient time to prevent collision.

(e) A vessel proceeding under sail when also being propelled by machinery shall exhibit forward where it can best be seen a conical shape, apex downwards.

RULE 26

Fishing Vessels

(a) A vessel engaged in fishing, whether underway or at anchor, shall exhibit only the lights and shapes prescribed in this Rule.

INLAND
RULE 25

Sailing Vessels Underway and Vessels Under Oars

(a) A sailing vessel underway shall exhibit:

   (i) sidelights; and

   (ii) a sternlight.

(b) In a sailing vessel of less than 20 meters in length the lights prescribed in paragraph (a) of this Rule may be combined in one lantern carried at or near the top of the mast where it can best be seen.

(c) A sailing vessel underway may, in addition to the lights prescribed in paragraph (a) of this Rule, exhibit at or near the top of the mast, where they can best be seen, two all-round lights in a vertical line, the upper being red and the lower green, but these lights shall not be exhibited in conjunction with the combined lantern permitted by paragraph (b) of this Rule.

(d)(i) A sailing vessel of less than 7 meters in length shall, if practicable, exhibit the lights prescribed in paragraph (a) or (b) of this Rule, but if she does not, she shall have ready at hand an electric torch or lighted lantern showing a white light which shall be exhibited in sufficient time to prevent collision.

   (ii) A vessel under oars may exhibit the lights prescribed in this Rule for sailing vessels, but if she does not, she shall have ready at hand an electric torch or lighted lantern showing a white light which shall be exhibited in sufficient time to prevent collision.

(e) A vessel proceeding under sail when also being propelled by machinery shall exhibit forward where it can best be seen a conical shape, apex downward. A vessel of less than 12 meters in length is not required to exhibit this shape, but may do so.

RULE 26

Fishing Vessels

(a) A vessel engaged in fishing, whether underway or at anchor, shall exhibit only the lights and shapes prescribed in this Rule.

(b) A vessel when engaged in trawling, by which is meant the dragging through the water of a dredge net or other apparatus used as a fishing appliance, shall exhibit:

(i) two all-round lights in a vertical line, the upper being green and the lower white, or a shape consisting of two cones with their apexes together in a vertical line one above the other; a vessel of less than 20 meters in length may instead of this shape exhibit a basket;

(ii) a masthead light abaft of and higher than the all-round green light; a vessel of less than 50 meters in length shall not be obliged to exhibit such a light but may do so; and

(iii) when making way through the water, in addition to the lights prescribed in this paragraph, sidelights and a sternlight.

(c) A vessel engaged in fishing, other than trawling, shall exhibit:

(i) two all-round lights in a vertical line, the upper being red and the lower white, or a shape consisting of two cones with apexes together in a vertical line one above the other; a vessel of less than 20 meters in length may instead of this shape exhibit a basket;

(ii) when there is outlying gear extending more than 150 meters horizontally from the vessel, an all-round white light or a cone apex upward in the direction of the gear; and

(iii) when making way through the water, in addition to the lights prescribed in this paragraph, sidelights and a sternlight.

(d) A vessel engaged in fishing in close proximity to other vessels engaged in fishing may exhibit the additional signals described in Annex II to these Rules.

(e) A vessel when not engaged in fishing shall not exhibit the lights or shapes prescribed in this Rule, but only those prescribed for a vessel of her length.

(b) A vessel when engaged in trawling, by which is meant the dragging through the water of a dredge net or other apparatus used as a fishing appliance, shall exhibit:

(i) two all-round lights in a vertical line, the upper being green and the lower white, or a shape consisting of two cones with their apexes together in a vertical line one above the other; a vessel of less than 20 meters in length may instead of this shape exhibit a basket;

(ii) a masthead light abaft of and higher than the all-round green light; a vessel of less than 50 meters in length shall not be obliged to exhibit such a light but may do so;

(iii) when making way through the water, in addition to the lights prescribed in this paragraph, sidelights and a sternlight.

(c) A vessel engaged in fishing, other than trawling, shall exhibit:

(i) two all-round lights in a vertical line, the upper being red and the lower white, or a shape consisting of two cones with apexes together in a vertical line one above the other; a vessel of less than 20 meters in length may instead of this shape exhibit a basket;

(ii) when there is outlying gear extending more than 150 meters horizontally from the vessel, an all-round white light or a cone apex upwards in the direction of the gear;

(iii) when making way through the water, in addition to the lights prescribed in this paragraph, sidelights and a sternlight.

(d) A vessel engaged in fishing in close proximity to other vessels engaged in fishing may exhibit the additional signals described in Annex II to these Regulations.

(e) A vessel when not engaged in fishing shall not exhibit the lights or shapes prescribed in this Rule, but only those prescribed for a vessel of her length.

INTERNATIONAL
RULE 27

Vessels Not Under Command or Restricted in Their Ability to Maneuver

(a) A vessel not under command shall exhibit:

(i) two all-round red lights in a vertical line where they can best be seen;

(ii) two balls or similar shapes in a vertical line where they can best be seen;

(iii) when making way through the water, in addition to the lights prescribed in this paragraph, sidelights and a sternlight.

(b) A vessel restricted in her ability to maneuver, except a vessel engaged in mineclearance operations, shall exhibit:

(i) three all-round lights in a vertical line where they can best be seen. The highest and lowest of these lights shall be red and the middle light shall be white;

(ii) three shapes in a vertical line where they can best be seen. The highest and lowest of these shapes shall be balls and the middle one a diamond;

(iii) when making way through the water, a masthead light or lights, sidelights and a sternlight, in addition to the lights prescribed in subparagraph (i);

(iv) when at anchor, in addition to the lights or shapes prescribed in subparagraphs (i) and (ii), the light, lights or shape prescribed in Rule 30.

(c) A power-driven vessel engaged in a towing operation such as severely restricts the towing vessel and her tow in their ability to deviate from their course shall, in addition to the lights or shapes prescribed in Rule 24(a), exhibit the lights or shapes prescribed in subparagraphs (b)(i) and (ii) of this Rule.

(d) A vessel engaged in dredging or underwater operations, when restricted in her ability to maneuver, shall exhibit the lights and shapes prescribed in subparagraphs (b)(i), (ii) and (iii) of this Rule and shall in addition, when an obstruction exists, exhibit:

INLAND
RULE 27

Vessels Not Under Command or Restricted in Their Ability to Maneuver

(a) A vessel not under command shall exhibit:

(i) two all-round red lights in a vertical line where they can best be seen;

(ii) two balls or similar shapes in a vertical line where they can best be seen; and

(iii) when making way through the water, in addition to the lights prescribed in this paragraph, sidelights and a sternlight.

(b) A vessel restricted in her ability to maneuver, except a vessel engaged in minesweeping operations, shall exhibit:

(i) three all-round lights in a vertical line where they can best be seen. The highest and lowest of these lights shall be red and the middle light shall be white;

(ii) three shapes in a vertical line where they can best be seen. The highest and lowest of these shapes shall be balls and the middle one a diamond;

(iii) when making way through the water, masthead lights, sidelights and a sternlight, in addition to the lights prescribed in subparagraph (b)(i); and

(iv) when at anchor, in addition to the lights or shapes prescribed in subparagraphs (b)(i) and (ii), the light, lights or shapes prescribed in Rule 30.

(c) A vessel engaged in a towing operation which severely restricts the towing vessel and her tow in their ability to deviate from their course shall, in addition to the lights or shapes prescribed in subparagraphs (b)(i) and (ii) of this Rule, exhibit the lights or shape prescribed in Rule 24.

(d) A vessel engaged in dredging or underwater operations, when restricted in her ability to maneuver, shall exhibit the lights and shapes prescribed in subparagraphs (b)(i), (ii), and (iii) of this Rule and shall in addition, when an obstruction exists, exhibit:

(i) two all-round red lights or two balls in a vertical line to indicate the side on which the obstruction exists;

(ii) two all-round green lights or two diamonds in a vertical line to indicate the side on which another vessel may pass;

(iii) when at anchor, the lights or shapes prescribed in this paragraph instead of the lights or shape prescribed in Rule 30.

(e) Whenever the size of a vessel engaged in diving operations makes it impracticable to exhibit all lights and shapes prescribed in paragraph (d) of this Rule, the following shall be exhibited:

(i) three all-round lights in a vertical line where they can best be seen. The highest and lowest of these lights shall be red and the middle light shall be white;

(ii) a rigid replica of the International Code flag "A" not less than 1 meter in height. Measures shall be taken to ensure its all-round visibility.

(f) A vessel engaged in mineclearance operations shall in addition to the lights prescribed for a power-driven vessel in Rule 23 or to the lights or shape prescribed for a vessel at anchor in Rule 30 as appropriate, exhibit three all-round green lights or three balls. One of these lights or shapes shall be exhibited near the foremast head and one at each end of the fore yard. These lights or shapes indicate that it is dangerous for another vessel to approach within 1000 meters of the mineclearance vessel.

(g) Vessels of less than 12 meters in length, except those engaged in diving operations, shall not be required to exhibit the lights and shapes prescribed in this Rule.

(h) The signals prescribed in this Rule are not signals of vessels in distress and requiring assistance. Such signals are contained in Annex IV to these Regulations.

RULE 28

Vessels Constrained by their Draft

A vessel constrained by her draft may, in addition to the lights prescribed for power-driven vessels in Rule 23, exhibit where they can best be seen three all-round red lights in a vertical line, or a cylinder.

(i) two all-round red lights or two balls in a vertical line to indicate the side on which the obstruction exists;

(ii) two all-round green lights or two diamonds in a vertical line to indicate the side on which another vessel may pass; and

(iii) when at anchor, the lights or shape prescribed by this paragraph, instead of the lights or shapes prescribed in Rule 30 for anchored vessels.

(e) Whenever the size of a vessel engaged in diving operations makes it impracticable to exhibit all lights and shapes prescribed in paragraph (d) of this Rule, the following shall instead be exhibited:

(i) Three all-round lights in a vertical line where they can best be seen. The highest and lowest of these lights shall be red and the middle light shall be white;

(ii) A rigid replica of the international Code flag "A" not less than 1 meter in height. Measures shall be taken to insure its all-round visibility.

(f) A vessel engaged in minesweeping operations shall, in addition to the lights prescribed for a power-driven vessel in Rule 23, exhibit three all-round green lights or three balls. One of these lights or shapes shall be exhibited near the foremast head and one at each end of the fore yard. These lights or shapes indicate that it is dangerous for another vessel to approach closer than 1,000 meters astern or 500 meters on either side of the minesweeper.

(g) A vessel of less than 12 meters in length, except when engaged in diving operations, is not required to exhibit the lights or shapes prescribed in this Rule.

(h) The signals prescribed in this Rule are not signals of vessels in distress and requiring assistance. Such signals are contained in Annex IV to these Rules.

RULE 28

[Reserved]

INTERNATIONAL
RULE 29

Pilot Vessels

(a) A vessel engaged on pilotage duty shall exhibit:

(i) at or near the masthead, two all-round lights in a vertical line, the upper being white and the lower red;

(ii) when underway, in addition, sidelights and a sternlight;

(iii) when at anchor, in addition to the lights prescribed in subparagraph (i), the light, lights or shape prescribed in Rule 30 for vessels at anchor.

(b) A pilot vessel when not engaged on pilotage duty shall exhibit the lights or shapes prescribed for a similar vessel of her length.

RULE 30

Anchored Vessels and Vessels Aground

(a) A vessel at anchor shall exhibit where it can best be seen:

(i) in the fore part, an all-round white light or one ball;

(ii) at or near the stern and at a lower level than the light prescribed in subparagraph (i), an all-round white light.

(b) A vessel of less than 50 meters in length may exhibit an all-round white light where it can best be seen instead of the lights prescribed in paragraph (a) of this Rule.

(c) A vessel at anchor may, and a vessel of 100 meters and more in length shall, also use the available working or equivalent lights to illuminate her decks.

(d) A vessel aground shall exhibit the lights prescribed in paragraph (a) or (b) of this Rule and in addition, where they can best be seen:

(i) two all-round red lights in a vertical line;

(ii) three balls in a vertical line.

(e) A vessel of less than 7 meters in length, when at anchor, not in or near a narrow channel, fairway or anchorage, or where other

INLAND
RULE 29

Pilot Vessels

(a) A vessel engaged on pilotage duty shall exhibit:

(i) at or near the masthead, two all-round lights in a vertical line, the upper being white and the lower red;

(ii) when underway, in addition, sidelights and a sternlight; and

(iii) when at anchor, in addition to the lights prescribed in subparagraph (i), the anchor light, lights, or shape prescribed in Rule 30 for anchored vessels.

(b) A pilot vessel when not engaged on pilotage duty shall exhibit the lights or shapes prescribed for a vessel of her length.

RULE 30

Anchored Vessels and Vessels Aground

(a) A vessel at anchor shall exhibit where it can best be seen:

(i) in the fore part, an all-round white light or one ball; and

(ii) at or near the stern and at a lower level than the light prescribed in subparagraph (i), an all-round white light.

(b) A vessel of less than 50 meters in length may exhibit an all-round white light where it can best be seen instead of the lights prescribed in paragraph (a) of this Rule.

(c) A vessel at anchor may, and a vessel of 100 meters or more in length shall, also use the available working or equivalent lights to illuminate her decks.

(d) A vessel aground shall exhibit the lights prescribed in paragraph (a) or (b) of this Rule and in addition, if practicable, where they can best be seen:

(i) two all-round red lights in a vertical line; and

(ii) three balls in a vertical line.

(e) A vessel of less than 7 meters in length, when at anchor, not in or near a narrow channel, fairway, anchorage, or where other vessels normally navigate, shall not be required to exhibit the lights or shape prescribed in paragraphs (a) and (b) of this Rule.

(f) A vessel of less than 12 meters in length, when aground, shall not be required to exhibit the lights or shapes prescribed in subparagraphs (d)(i) and (ii) of this Rule.

PART D—SOUND AND LIGHT SIGNALS

RULE 31

Seaplanes

Where it is impracticable for a seaplane to exhibit lights and shapes of the characteristics or in the positions prescribed in the Rules of this Part she shall exhibit lights and shapes as closely similar in characteristics and position as is possible.

RULE 32

Definitions

(a) The word "whistle" means any sound signalling appliance capable of producing the prescribed blasts and which complies with the specifications in Annex III to these Regulations.

(b) The term "short blast" means a blast of about one second's duration.

(c) The term "prolonged blast" means a blast of from four to six seconds' duration.

RULE 33

Equipment for Sound Signals

(a) A vessel of 12 meters or more in length shall be provided with a whistle and a bell and a vessel of 100 meters or more in length shall, in addition, be provided with a gong, the tone and sound of which cannot be confused with that of the bell. The

---

vessels normally navigate, shall not be required to exhibit the lights or shape prescribed in paragraphs (a) and (b) of this Rule.

(f) A vessel of less than 12 meters in length when aground shall not be required to exhibit the lights or shapes prescribed in subparagraphs (d)(i) and (ii) of this Rule.

(g) A vessel of less than 20 meters in length, when at anchor in a special anchorage area designated by the Secretary, shall not be required to exhibit the anchor lights and shapes required by this Rule.

PART D—SOUND AND LIGHT SIGNALS

RULE 31

Seaplanes

Where it is impracticable for a seaplane to exhibit lights and shapes of the characteristics or in the positions prescribed in the Rules of this Part she shall exhibit lights and shapes as closely similar in characteristics and position as is possible.

RULE 32

Definitions

(a) The word "whistle" means any sound signaling appliance capable of producing the prescribed blasts and which complies with specifications in Annex III to these Rules.

(b) The term "short blast" means a blast of about 1 second's duration.

(c) The term "prolonged blast" means a blast of from 4 to 6 seconds' duration.

RULE 33

Equipment for Sound Signals

(a) A vessel of 12 meters or more in length shall be provided with a whistle and a bell and a vessel of 100 meters or more in length shall, in addition, be provided with a gong, the tone and sound of which cannot be confused with that of the bell. The

INTERNATIONAL

whistle, bell and gong shall comply with the specifications in Annex III to these Regulations. The bell or gong or both may be replaced by other equipment having the same respective sound characteristics, provided that manual sounding of the prescribed signals shall always be possible.

(b) A vessel of less than 12 meters in length shall not be obliged to carry the sound signalling appliances prescribed in paragraph (a) of this Rule but if she does not, she shall be provided with some other means of making an efficient sound signal.

RULE 34

Maneuvering and Warning Signals

(a) When vessels are in sight of one another, a power-driven vessel underway, when maneuvering as authorized or required by these Rules, shall indicate that maneuver by the following signals on her whistle:

—one short blast to mean "I am altering my course to starboard";

—two short blasts to mean "I am altering my course to port";

—three short blasts to mean "I am operating astern propulsion".

(b) Any vessel may supplement the whistle signals prescribed in paragraph (a) of this Rule by light signals, repeated as appropriate, whilst the maneuver is being carried out:

(i) these light signals shall have the following significance:

—one flash to mean "I am altering my course to starboard";

—two flashes to mean "I am altering my course to port";

—three flashes to mean "I am operating astern propulsion";

(ii) the duration of each flash shall be about one second, the interval between flashes shall be about one second, and the

INLAND

whistle, bell and gong shall comply with the specifications in Annex III to these Rules. The bell or gong or both may be replaced by other equipment having the same respective sound characteristics, provided that manual sounding of the prescribed signals shall always be possible.

(b) A vessel of less than 12 meters in length shall not be obliged to carry the sound signaling appliances prescribed in paragraph (a) of this Rule but if she does not, she shall be provided with some other means of making an efficient sound signal.

RULE 34

Maneuvering and Warning Signals

(a) When power-driven vessels are in sight of one another and meeting or crossing at a distance within half a mile of each other, each vessel underway, when maneuvering as authorized or required by these Rules:

(i) shall indicate that maneuver by the following signals on her whistle: one short blast to mean "I intend to leave you on my port side"; two short blasts to mean "I intend to leave you on my starboard side"; and three short blasts to mean "I am operating astern propulsion".

(ii) upon hearing the one or two blast signal of the other shall, if in agreement, sound the same whistle signal and take the steps necessary to effect a safe passing. If, however, from any cause, the vessel doubts the safety of the proposed maneuver, she shall sound the danger signal specified in paragraph (d) of this Rule and each vessel shall take appropriate precautionary action until a safe passing agreement is made.

(b) A vessel may supplement the whistle signals prescribed in paragraph (a) of this Rule by light signals:

(i) These signals shall have the following significance: one flash to mean "I intend to leave you on my port side"; two flashes to mean "I intend to leave you on my starboard side"; three flashes to mean "I am operating astern propulsion";

interval between successive signals shall be not less than ten seconds;

(iii) the light used for this signal shall, if fitted, be an all-round white light, visible at a minimum range of 5 miles, and shall comply with the provisions of Annex I to these Regulations.

(c) When in sight of one another in a narrow channel or fairway:

(i) a vessel intending to overtake another shall in compliance with Rule 9(e)(i) indicate her intention by the following signals on her whistle:

—two prolonged blasts followed by one short blast to mean "I intend to overtake you on your starboard side";

—two prolonged blasts followed by two short blasts to mean "I intend to overtake you on your port side".

(ii) the vessel about to be overtaken when acting in accordance with Rule 9(e)(i) shall indicate her agreement by the following signal on her whistle:

—one prolonged, one short, one prolonged and one short blast, in that order.

(d) When vessels in sight of one another are approaching each other and from any cause either vessel fails to understand the intentions or actions of the other, or is in doubt whether sufficient action is being taken by the other to avoid collision, the vessel in doubt shall immediately indicate such doubt by giving at least five short and rapid blasts on the whistle. Such signal may be supplemented by a light signal of at least five short and rapid flashes.

(e) A vessel nearing a bend or an area of a channel or fairway where other vessels may be obscured by an intervening obstruction shall sound one prolonged blast. Such signal shall be answered with a prolonged blast by any approaching vessel that may be within hearing around the bend or behind the intervening obstruction.

(f) If whistles are fitted on a vessel at a distance apart of more than 100 meters, one whistle only shall be used for giving maneuvering and warning signals.

(ii) The duration of each flash shall be about 1 second; and

(iii) The light used for this signal shall, if fitted, be one all-round white or yellow light, visible at a minimum range of 2 miles, synchronized with the whistle, and shall comply with the provisions of Annex I to these Rules.

(c) When in sight of one another:

(i) a power-driven vessel intending to overtake another power-driven vessel shall indicate her intention by the following signals on her whistle: one short blast to mean "I intend to overtake you on your starboard side"; two short blasts to mean "I intend to overtake you on your port side"; and

(ii) the power-driven vessel about to be overtaken shall, if in agreement, sound a similar sound signal. If in doubt she shall sound the danger signal prescribed in paragraph (d).

(d) When vessels in sight of one another are approaching each other and from any cause either vessel fails to understand the intentions or actions of the other, or is in doubt whether sufficient action is being taken by the other to avoid collision, the vessel in doubt shall immediately indicate such doubt by giving at least five short and rapid blasts on the whistle. This signal may be supplemented by a light signal of at least five short and rapid flashes.

(e) A vessel nearing a bend or an area of a channel or fairway where other vessels may be obscured by an intervening obstruction shall sound one prolonged blast. This signal shall be answered with a prolonged blast by any approaching vessel that may be within hearing around the bend or behind the intervening obstruction.

(f) If whistles are fitted on a vessel at a distance apart of more than 100 meters, one whistle only shall be used for giving maneuvering and warning signals.

(g) When a power-driven vessel is leaving a dock or berth, she shall sound one prolonged blast.

(h) A vessel that reaches agreement with another vessel in a meeting, crossing, or overtaking situation by using the radiotelephone as prescribed by the Bridge-to-Bridge

INTERNATIONAL

RULE 35

Sound Signals in Restricted Visibility

In or near an area of restricted visibility, whether by day or night, the signals prescribed in this Rule shall be used as follows:

(a) A power-driven vessel making way through the water shall sound at intervals of not more than 2 minutes one prolonged blast.

(b) A power-driven vessel underway but stopped and making no way through the water shall sound at intervals of not more than 2 minutes two prolonged blasts in succession with an interval of about 2 seconds between them.

(c) A vessel not under command, a vessel restricted in her ability to maneuver, a vessel constrained by her draft, a sailing vessel, a vessel engaged in fishing and a vessel engaged in towing or pushing another vessel shall, instead of the signals prescribed in paragraphs (a) or (b) of this Rule, sound at intervals of not more than 2 minutes three blasts in succession, namely one prolonged followed by two short blasts.

(d) A vessel engaged in fishing, when at anchor, and a vessel restricted in her ability to maneuver when carrying out her work at anchor, shall instead of the signals prescribed in paragraph (g) of this Rule sound the signal prescribed in paragraph (c) of this Rule.

(e) A vessel towed or if more than one vessel is towed the last vessel of the tow, if manned, shall at intervals of not more than 2 minutes sound four blasts in succession, namely one prolonged followed by three short blasts. When practicable, this signal shall be made immediately after the signal made by the towing vessel.

(f) When a pushing vessel and a vessel being pushed ahead are rigidly connected in a composite unit they shall be regarded as

INLAND

Radiotelephone Act (85 Stat. 165; 33 U.S.C. 1207), is not obliged to sound the whistle signals prescribed by this Rule, but may do so. If agreement is not reached, then whistle signals shall be exchanged in a timely manner and shall prevail.

RULE 35

Sound Signals in Restricted Visibility

In or near an area of restricted visibility, whether by day or night, the signals prescribed in this Rule shall be used as follows:

(a) A power-driven vessel making way through the water shall sound at intervals of not more than 2 minutes one prolonged blast.

(b) A power-driven vessel underway but stopped and making no way through the water shall sound at intervals of not more than 2 minutes two prolonged blasts in succession with an interval of about 2 seconds between them.

(c) A vessel not under command; a vessel restricted in her ability to maneuver, whether underway or at anchor; a sailing vessel; a vessel engaged in fishing, whether underway or at anchor; and a vessel engaged in towing or pushing another vessel shall, instead of the signals prescribed in paragraphs (a) or (b) of this Rule, sound at intervals of not more than 2 minutes, three blasts in succession; namely, one prolonged followed by two short blasts.

(d) A vessel towed or if more than one vessel is towed the last vessel of the tow, if manned, shall at intervals of not more than 2 minutes sound four blasts in succession; namely, one prolonged followed by three short blasts. When practicable, this signal shall be made immediately after the signal made by the towing vessel.

(e) When a pushing vessel and a vessel being pushed ahead are rigidly connected in a composite unit they shall be regarded as a power-driven vessel and shall give the signals prescribed in paragraphs (a) or (b) of this Rule.

(f) A vessel at anchor shall at intervals of not more than 1 minute ring the bell rapidly for about 5 seconds. In a vessel of 100 meters or more in length the bell shall be sounded in the forepart of the vessel and immediately after the ringing of the bell the gong shall be sounded rapidly for about 5 seconds in the after part of the vessel. A vessel at anchor may in addition sound three blasts in succession; namely, one short, one prolonged and one short blast, to give warning of her position and of the possibility of collision to an approaching vessel.

(g) A vessel aground shall give the bell signal and if required the gong signal prescribed in paragraph (f) of this Rule and shall, in addition, give three separate and distinct strokes on the bell immediately before and after the rapid ringing of the bell. A vessel aground may in addition sound an appropriate whistle signal.

(h) A vessel of less than 12 meters in length shall not be obliged to give the above-mentioned signals but, if she does not, shall make some other efficient sound signal at intervals of not more than 2 minutes.

(i) A pilot vessel when engaged on pilotage duty may in addition to the signals prescribed in paragraphs (a), (b) or (f) of this Rule sound an identity signal consisting of four short blasts.

(j) The following vessels shall not be required to sound signals as prescribed in paragraph (f) of this Rule when anchored in a special anchorage area designated by the Secretary:

(i) a vessel of less than 20 meters in length; and

(ii) a barge, canal boat, scow, or other nondescript craft.

RULE 36

Signals to Attract Attention

If necessary to attract the attention of another vessel, any vessel may make light or sound signals that cannot be mistaken for any signal authorized elsewhere in these Rules, or may direct the beam of her searchlight in the direction of the danger, in such a way as not to embarrass any vessel.

---

a power-driven vessel and shall give the signals prescribed in paragraphs (a) or (b) of this Rule.

(g)   A vessel at anchor shall at intervals of not more than one minute ring the bell rapidly for about 5 seconds. In a vessel of 100 meters or more in length the bell shall be sounded in the forepart of the vessel and immediately after the ringing of the bell the gong shall be sounded rapidly for about 5 seconds in the after part of the vessel. A vessel at anchor may in addition sound three blasts in succession, namely one short, one prolonged and one short blast, to give warning of her position and of the possibility of collision to an approaching vessel.

(h)   A vessel aground shall give the bell signal and if required the gong signal prescribed in paragraph (g)   of this Rule and shall, in addition, give three separate and distinct strokes on the bell immediately before and after the rapid ringing of the bell. A vessel aground may in addition sound an appropriate whistle signal.

(i)   A vessel of less than 12 meters in length shall not be obliged to give the above-mentioned signals but, if she does not, shall make some other efficient sound signal at intervals of not more than 2 minutes.

(j)   A pilot vessel when engaged on pilotage duty may in addition to the signals prescribed in paragraphs (a), (b) or (g)   of this Rule sound an identity signal consisting of four short blasts.

RULE 36

Signals to Attract Attention

If necessary to attract the attention of another vessel, any vessel may make light or sound signals that cannot be mistaken for any signal authorized elsewhere in these Rules, or may direct the beam of her searchlight in the direction of the danger, in such a way as not to embarrass any vessel. Any light to attract the attention of another vessel shall be such that it cannot be mistaken for any aid to navigation. For the purpose of this Rule the use of high intensity intermittent or revolving lights, such as strobe lights, shall be avoided.

INTERNATIONAL
RULE 37

Distress Signals

When a vessel is in distress and requires assistance she shall use or exhibit the signals described in Annex IV to these Regulations.

PART E—EXEMPTIONS
RULE 38

Exemptions

Any vessel (or class of vessels) provided that she complies with the requirements of the International Regulations for Preventing Collisions at Sea, 1960, the keel of which is laid or which is at a corresponding stage of construction before the entry into force of these Regulations may be exempted from compliance therewith as follows:

(a) The installation of lights with ranges prescribed in Rule 22, until four years after the date of entry into force of these Regulations.

(b) The installation of lights with color specifications as prescribed in Section 7 of Annex I to these Regulations, until four years after the date of entry into force of these Regulations.

(c) The repositioning of lights as a result of conversion from Imperial to metric units and rounding off measurement figures, permanent exemption.

(d)(i) The repositioning of masthead lights on vessels of less than 150 meters in length, resulting from the prescriptions of Section 3(a) of Annex I to these Regulations, permanent exemption.

(ii) The repositioning of masthead lights on vessels of 150 meters or more in length, resulting from the prescriptions of Section 3(a) of Annex I to these Regulations, until 9 years after the date of entry into force of these Regulations.

(e) The repositioning of masthead lights resulting from the prescriptions of Section 2(b) of Annex I to these Regulations, until

INLAND
RULE 37

Distress Signals

When a vessel is in distress and requires assistance she shall use or exhibit the signals described in Annex IV to these Rules.

PART E—EXEMPTIONS
RULE 38

Exemptions

Any vessel or class of vessels, the keel of which is laid or which is at a corresponding stage of construction before the date of enactment of this Act, provided that she complies with the requirements of—

(a) The Act of June 7, 1897 (30 Stat. 96), as amended (33 U.S.C. 154–232) for vessels navigating the waters subject to that statute;

(b) Section 4233 of the Revised Statutes (33 U.S.C. 301–356) for vessels navigating the waters subject to that statute;

(c) The Act of February 8, 1895 (28 Stat. 645), as amended (33 U.S.C. 241–295) for vessels navigating the waters subject to that statute; or

(d) Sections 3, 4, and 5 of the Act of April 25, 1940 (54 Stat. 163), as amended (46 U.S.C. 526 b, c, and d) for motorboats navigating the waters subject to that statute; shall be exempted from compliance with the technical Annexes to these Rules as follows:

(i) the installation of lights with ranges prescribed in Rule 22, until 4 years after the effective date of these Rules, except that vessels of less than 20 meters in length are permanently exempt;

(ii) the installation of lights with color specifications as prescribed in Annex I to these Rules, until 4 years after the effective date of these Rules, except that vessels of less than 20 meters in length are permanently exempt;

(iii) the repositioning of lights as a result of conversion to metric units and rounding off measurement figures, are permanently exempt; and

9 years after the date of entry into force of these Regulations.

(f) The repositioning of sidelights resulting from the prescriptions of Sections 2(g) and 3(b) of Annex I to these Regulations, until 9 years after the date of entry into force of these Regulations.

(g) The requirements for sound signal appliances prescribed in Annex III to these Regulations, until 9 years after the date of entry into force of these Regulations.

(h) The repositioning of all-round lights resulting from the prescription of Section 9(b) of Annex I to these Regulations, permanent exemption.

ANNEX I

Positioning and Technical Details of Lights and Shapes

1. Definition

The term "height above the hull" means height above the uppermost continuous deck. This height shall be measured from the position vertically beneath the location of the light.

2. Vertical positioning and spacing of lights

(a) On a power-driven vessel of 20 meters or more in length the masthead lights shall be placed as follows:

(i) the forward masthead light, or if only one masthead light is carried, then that light, at a height above the hull of not less than 6 meters, and, if the breadth of the vessel exceeds 6 meters, then at a height above the hull not less than such breadth, so however that the light need not be placed at a greater height above the hull than 12 meters;

(ii) when two masthead lights are carried the after one shall be at least 4.5 meters vertically higher than the forward one.

(iv) the horizontal repositioning of masthead lights prescribed by Annex I to these Rules:

(1) on vessels of less than 150 meters in length, permanent exemption.

(2) on vessels of 150 meters or more in length, until 9 years after the effective date of these Rules.

(v) the restructuring or repositioning of all lights to meet the prescriptions of Annex I to these Rules, until 9 years after the effective date of these Rules;

(vi) power-driven vessels of 12 meters or more but less than 20 meters in length are permanently exempt from the provisions of Rule 23(a)(i) and 23 (a)(iv) provided that, in place of these lights, the vessel exhibits a white light aft visible all round the horizon; and

(vii) the requirements for sound signal appliances prescribed in Annex III to these Rules, until 9 years after the effective date of these Rules.

ANNEX I

Positioning and Technical Details of Lights and Shapes

§ 84.01 Definitions.

(a) The term "height above the hull" means height above the uppermost continuous deck. This height shall be measured from the position vertically beneath the location of the light.

(b) The term "practical cut-off" means, for vessels 20 meters or more in length, 12.5 percent of the minimum luminous intensity (Table 84.15(b)) corresponding to the greatest range of visibility for which the requirements of Annex I are met.

(c) The term "Rule" or "Rules" means the Inland Navigation Rules contained in Sec. 2 of the Inland Navigational Rules Act of 1980 (Pub. L. 96-591, 94 Stat. 3415, 33 U.S.C. 2001, December 24, 1980) as amended.

§ 84.03 Vertical positioning and spacing of lights.

(a) On a power-driven vessel of 20 meters or more in length the masthead lights shall be placed as follows:

INTERNATIONAL

(b) The vertical separation of masthead lights of power-driven vessels shall be such that in all normal conditions of trim the after light will be seen over and separate from the forward light at a distance of 1000 meters from the stem when viewed from sea level.

(c) The masthead light of a power-driven vessel of 12 meters but less than 20 meters in length shall be placed at a height above the gunwale of not less than 2.5 meters.

(d) A power-driven vessel of less than 12 meters in length may carry the uppermost light at a height of less than 2.5 meters above the gunwale. When however a masthead light is carried in addition to sidelights and a sternlight, then such masthead light shall be carried at least 1 meter higher than the sidelights.

(e) One of the two or three masthead lights prescribed for a power-driven vessel when engaged in towing or pushing another vessel shall be placed in the same position as either the forward masthead light or the after masthead light; provided that, if carried on the aftermast, the lowest after masthead light shall be at least 4.5 meters vertically higher than the forward masthead light.

(f)(i) The masthead light or lights prescribed in Rule 23(a) shall be so placed as to be above and clear of all other lights and obstructions except as described in subparagraph (ii).

(ii) When it is impracticable to carry the all-round lights prescribed by Rule 27(b)(i) or Rule 28 below the masthead lights, they may be carried above the after masthead light(s) or vertically in between the forward masthead light(s) and after masthead light(s), provided that in the latter case the requirement of Section 3(c) of this Annex shall be complied with.

(g) The sidelights of a power-driven vessel shall be placed at a height above the hull not greater than three quarters of that of the forward masthead light. They shall not be so low as to be interfered with by deck lights.

(h) The sidelights, if in a combined lantern and carried on a power-driven vessel of less than 20 meters in length, shall be placed not less than 1 meter below the masthead light.

INLAND

(1) The forward masthead light, or if only one masthead light is carried, then that light, at a height above the hull of not less than 5 meters, and, if the breadth of the vessel exceeds 5 meters, then at a height above the hull not less than such breadth, so however that the light need not be placed at a greater height above the hull than 8 meters;

(2) When two masthead lights are carried the after one shall be at least 2 meters vertically higher than the forward one.

(b) The vertical separation of the masthead lights of power-driven vessels shall be such that in all normal conditions of trim the after light will be seen over and separate from the forward light at a distance of 1000 meters from the stem when viewed from water level.

(c) The masthead light of a power-driven vessel of 12 meters but less than 20 meters in length shall be placed at a height above the gunwale of not less than 2.5 meters.

(d) The masthead light, or the all-round light described in Rule 23(c), of a power-driven vessel of less than 12 meters in length shall be carried at least one meter higher than the sidelights.

(e) One of the two or three masthead lights prescribed for a power-driven vessel when engaged in towing or pushing another vessel shall be placed in the same position as either the forward masthead light or the after masthead light, provided that the lowest after masthead light shall be at least 2 meters vertically higher than the highest forward masthead light.

(f)(1) The masthead light or lights prescribed in Rule 23(a) shall be so placed as to be above and clear of all other lights and obstructions except as described in paragraph (f)(2) of this section.

(2) When it is impracticable to carry the all-round lights prescribed in Rule 27(b)(i) below the masthead lights, they may be carried above the after masthead light(s) or vertically in between the forward masthead light(s) and after masthead light(s), provided that in the latter case the requirement of § 84.05(d) shall be complied with.

(g) The sidelights of a power-driven vessel shall be placed at

(i) When the Rules prescribe two or three lights to be carried in a vertical line, they shall be spaced as follows:

(i) on a vessel of 20 meters in length or more such lights shall be spaced not less than 2 meters apart, and the lowest of these lights shall, except where a towing light is required, be placed at a height of not less than 4 meters above the hull;

(ii) on a vessel of less than 20 meters in length such lights shall be spaced not less than 1 meter apart and the lowest of these lights shall, except where a towing light is required, be placed at a height of not less than 2 meters above the hull;

(iii) when three lights are carried they shall be equally spaced.

(j) The lower of the two all-round lights prescribed for a vessel when engaged in fishing shall be at a height above the sidelights not less than twice the distance between the two vertical lights.

(k) The forward anchor light prescribed in Rule 30(a)(i), when two are carried, shall not be less than 4.5 meters above the after one. On a vessel of 50 meters or more in length this forward anchor light shall be placed at a height of not less than 6 meters above the hull.

3. Horizontal positioning and spacing of lights

(a) When two masthead lights are prescribed for a power-driven vessel, the horizontal distance between them shall not be less than one half of the length of the vessel but need not be more than 100 meters. The forward light shall be placed not more than one quarter of the length of the vessel from the stem.

(b) On a power-driven vessel of 20 meters or more in length the sidelights shall not be placed in front of the forward masthead lights. They shall be placed at or near the side of the vessel.

(c) When the lights prescribed in Rule 27(b)(i) or Rule 28 are placed vertically between the forward masthead light(s) and the after masthead lights(s) these all-round lights shall be placed at a horizontal distance of not less than 2 meters from the fore and aft centerline of the vessel in the athwartship direction.

4. Details of location of direction-indicating lights for fishing vessels, dredgers and vessels engaged in underwater operations

(a) The light indicating the direction of the outlying gear from a

least one meter lower than the forward masthead light. They shall not be so low as to be interfered with by deck lights.

(h) [Reserved]

(i) When the Rules prescribe two or three lights to be carried in a vertical line, they shall be spaced as follows:

(1) On a vessel of 20 meters in length or more such lights shall be spaced not less than 1 meter apart, and the lowest of these lights shall, except where a towing light is required, be placed at a height of not less than 4 meters above the hull;

(2) On a vessel of less than 20 meters in length such lights shall be spaced not less than 1 meter apart and the lowest of these lights shall, except where a towing light is required, be placed at a height of not less than 2 meters above the hull;

(3) When three lights are carried they shall be equally spaced.

(j) The lower of the two all-round lights prescribed for a vessel when engaged in fishing shall be at a height above the sidelights not less than twice the distance between the two vertical lights.

(k) The forward anchor light prescribed in Rule 30(a)(i), when two are carried, shall not be less than 4.5 meters above the after one. On a vessel of 50 meters or more in length this forward anchor light shall be placed at a height of not less than 6 meters above the hull.

§ 84.05 Horizontal positioning and spacing of lights

(a) Except as specified in paragraph (b) of this section, when two masthead lights are prescribed for a power-driven vessel, the horizontal distance between them shall not be less than one quarter of the length of the vessel but need not be more than 50 meters. The forward light shall be placed not more than one half of the length of the vessel from the stem.

(b) On power-driven vessels 50 meters but less than 60 meters in length operated on the Western Rivers, the horizontal distance between masthead lights shall not be less than 10 meters.

(c) On a power-driven vessel of 20 meters or more in length the sidelights shall not be placed in front of the forward masthead lights. They shall be placed at or near the side of the vessel.

(d) When the lights prescribed in Rule 27(b)(i) are placed vertically between the forward masthead light(s) and the after

INTERNATIONAL

vessel engaged in fishing as prescribed in Rule 26(c)(ii) shall be placed at a horizontal distance of not less than 2 meters and not more than 6 meters away from the two all-round red and white lights. This light shall be placed not higher than the all-round white light prescribed in Rule 26(c)(i) and not lower than the sidelights.

(b) The lights and shapes on a vessel engaged in dredging or underwater operations to indicate the obstructed side and/or the side on which it is safe to pass, as prescribed in Rule 27(d)(i) and (ii), shall be placed at the maximum practical horizontal distance, but in no case less than 2 meters, from the lights or shapes prescribed in Rule 27(b)(i) and (ii). In no case shall the upper of these lights or shapes be at a greater height than the lower of the three lights or shapes prescribed in Rule 27(b)(i) and (ii).

5. Screens for sidelights

The sidelights of vessels of 20 meters or more in length shall be fitted with inboard screens painted matt black, and meeting the requirements of Section 9 of this Annex. On vessels of less than 20 meters in length the sidelights, if necessary to meet the requirements of Section 9 of this Annex, shall be fitted with inboard matt black screens. With a combined lantern, using a single vertical filament and a very narrow division between the green and red sections, external screens need not be fitted.

6. Shapes

(a) Shapes shall be black and of the following sizes:

(i) a ball shall have a diameter of not less than 0.6 meter;

(ii) a cone shall have a base diameter of not less than 0.6 meter and a height equal to its diameter;

(iii) a cylinder shall have a diameter of at least 0.6 meter and a height of twice its diameter;

(iv) a diamond shape shall consist of two cones as defined in (ii) above having a common base.

(b) The vertical distance between shapes shall be at least 1.5 meter.

(c) In a vessel of less than 20 meters in length shapes of lesser

INLAND

masthead light(s) these all-round lights shall be placed at a horizontal distance of not less than 2 meters from the fore and aft centerline of the vessel in the athwartship direction.

§ 84.07 Details of location of direction-indicating lights for fishing vessels, dredgers and vessels engaged in underwater operations

(a) The light indicating the direction of the outlying gear from a vessel engaged in fishing as prescribed in Rule 26(c)(ii) shall be placed at a horizontal distance of not less than 2 meters and not more than 6 meters away from the two all-round red and white lights. This light shall be placed not higher than the all-round white light prescribed in Rule 26(c)(i) and not lower than the sidelights.

(b) The lights and shapes on a vessel engaged in dredging or underwater operations to indicate the obstructed side and/or the side on which it is safe to pass, as prescribed in Rule 27(d)(i) and (ii), shall be placed at the maximum practical horizontal distance, but in no case less than 2 meters, from the lights or shapes prescribed in Rule 27(b)(i) and (ii). In no case shall the upper of these lights or shapes be at a greater height than the lower of the three lights or shapes prescribed in Rule 27(b)(i) and (ii).

§ 84.09 Screens

(a) The sidelights of vessels of 20 meters or more in length shall be fitted with mat black inboard screens and meet the requirements of § 84.17. On vessels of less than 20 meters in length, the sidelights, if necessary to meet the requirements of § 84.17, shall be fitted with mat black inboard screens. With a combined lantern, using a single vertical filament and a very narrow division between the green and red sections, external screens need not be fitted.

(b) On power-driven vessels less than 12 meters in length constructed after July 31, 1983, the masthead light, or the all-round light described in Rule 23(c) shall be screened to prevent direct illumination of the vessel forward of the operator's position.

§ 84.11 Shapes

(a) Shapes shall be black and of the following sizes:

(1) A ball shall have a diameter of not less than 0.6 meter;

(2) A cone shall have a base diameter of not less than 0.6 meter and a height equal to its diameter;

(3) A diamond shape shall consist of two cones (as defined in paragraph (a)(2) of this section) having a common base.

(b) The vertical distance between shapes shall be at least 1.5 meter.

(c) In a vessel of less than 20 meters in length shapes of lesser dimensions but commensurate with the size of the vessel may be used and the distance apart may be correspondingly reduced.

§ 84.13 Color specification of lights

(a) The chromaticity of all navigation lights shall conform to the following standards, which lie within the boundaries of the area of the diagram specified for each color by the International Commission on Illumination (CIE), in the "Colors of Light Signals", which is incorporated by reference. It is Publication CIE No. 2.2. (TC–1.6), 1975, and is available from the Illumination Engineering Society, 345 East 47th Street, New York, NY 10017. It is also available for inspection at the Office of the Federal Register, Room 8401, 1100 L Street N.W., Washington, D.C. 20408. This incorporation by reference was approved by the Director of the Federal Register.

(b) The boundaries of the area for each color are given by indicating the corner coordinates, which are as follows:

(1) *White:*

x	0.525	0.525	0.452	0.310	0.310	0.443
y	0.382	0.440	0.440	0.348	0.283	0.382

(2) *Green:*

x	0.028	0.009	0.300	0.203
y	0.385	0.723	0.511	0.356

(3) *Red:*

x	0.680	0.660	0.735	0.721
y	0.320	0.320	0.265	0.259

(4) *Yellow:*

x	0.612	0.618	0.575	0.575
y	0.382	0.382	0.425	0.406

---

dimensions but commensurate with the size of the vessel may be used and the distance apart may be correspondingly reduced.

7. Color specification of lights

The chromaticity of all navigation lights shall conform to the following standards, which lie within the boundaries of the area of the diagram specified for each color by the International Commission on Illumination (CIE).

The boundaries of the area for each color are given by indicating the corner coordinates, which are as follows:

(i) *White:*

x	0.525	0.525	0.452	0.310	0.310	0.443
y	0.382	0.440	0.440	0.348	0.283	0.382

(ii) *Green:*

x	0.028	0.009	0.300	0.203
y	0.385	0.723	0.511	0.356

(iii) *Red:*

x	0.680	0.660	0.735	0.721
y	0.320	0.320	0.265	0.259

(iv) *Yellow:*

x	0.612	0.618	0.575	0.575
y	0.382	0.382	0.425	0.406

8. Intensity of lights

(a) The minimum luminous intensity of lights shall be calculated by using the formula:

$$I = 3.43 \times 10^6 \times T \times D^2 \times K^{-D}$$

where I is luminous intensity in candelas under service conditions,

T is threshold factor 2×10^{-7} lux,

D is range of visibility (luminous range) of the light in nautical miles,

K is atmospheric transmissivity. For prescribed lights the value of K shall be 0.8, corresponding to a meteorological visibility of approximately 13 nautical miles.

(b) A selection of figures derived from the formula is given in the following table:

INTERNATIONAL

Range of visibility (luminous range) of light in nautical miles D	Luminous intensity of light in candelas for K = 0.8 I
1	0.9
2	4.3
3	12
4	27
5	52
6	94

Note: The maximum luminous intensity of navigation lights should be limited to avoid undue glare. This shall not be achieved by a variable control of the luminous intensity.

9. Horizontal sectors

(a)(i) In the forward direction, sidelights as fitted on the vessel shall show the minimum required intensities. The intensities shall decrease to reach practical cut-off between 1 degree and 3 degrees outside the prescribed sectors.

(ii) For sternlights and masthead lights and at 22.5 degrees abaft the beam for sidelights, the minimum required intensities shall be maintained over the arc of the horizon up to 5 degrees within the limits of the sectors prescribed in Rule 21. From 5 degrees within the prescribed sectors the intensity may decrease by 50 percent up to the prescribed limits; it shall decrease steadily to reach practical cut-off at not more than 5 degrees outside the prescribed sectors.

(b) All-round lights shall be so located as not to be obscured by masts, topmasts or structures within angular sectors of more than 6 degrees, except anchor lights prescribed in Rule 30, which need not be placed at an impracticable height above the hull.

10. Vertical sectors

(a) The vertical sectors of electric lights as fitted, with the exception of lights on sailing vessels shall ensure that:

INLAND

§ 84.15 Intensity of lights

(a) The minimum luminous intensity of lights shall be calculated by using the formula:

$$I = 3.43 \times 10^6 \times T \times D^2 \times K^{-D}$$

where I is luminous intensity in candelas under service conditions,

T is threshold factor 2×10^{-7} lux,

D is range of visibility (luminous range) of the light in nautical miles,

K is atmospheric transmissivity. For prescribed lights the value of K shall be 0.8, corresponding to a meteorological visibility of approximately 13 nautical miles.

(b) A selection of figures derived from the formula is given in Table 84.15(b).

Table 84.15(b)

Range of visibility (luminous range) of light in nautical miles D	Minimum luminous intensity of light in candelas for K = 0.8 I
1	0.9
2	4.3
3	12
4	27
5	52
6	94

§ 84.17 Horizontal sectors

(a)(1) In the forward direction, sidelights as fitted on the vessel shall show the minimum required intensities. The intensities shall decrease to reach practical cut-off between 1 and 3 degrees outside the prescribed sectors.

(2) For sternlights and masthead lights and at 22.5 degrees abaft the beam for sidelights, the minimum required intensities shall be maintained over the arc of the horizon up to 5 degrees within the limits of the sectors prescribed in Rule 21. From 5 degrees within the prescribed sectors the intensity may decrease

(i) at least the required minimum intensity is maintained at all angles from 5 degrees above to 5 degrees below the horizontal;

(ii) at least 60 percent of the required minimum intensity is maintained from 7.5 degrees above to 7.5 degrees below the horizontal.

(b) In the case of sailing vessels the vertical sectors of electric lights as fitted shall ensure that:

(i) at least the required minimum intensity is maintained at all angles from 5 degrees above to 5 degrees below the horizontal;

(ii) at least 50 percent of the required minimum intensity is maintained from 25 degrees above to 25 degrees below the horizontal.

(c) In the case of lights other than electric these specifications shall be met as closely as possible.

11. Intensity of non-electric lights

Non-electric lights shall so far as practicable comply with the minimum intensities, as specified in the Table given in Section 8 of this Annex.

12. Maneuvering light

Notwithstanding the provisions of paragraph 2(f) of this Annex the maneuvering light described in Rule 34(b) shall be placed in the same fore and aft vertical plane as the masthead light or lights and, where practicable, at a minimum height of 2 meters vertically above the forward masthead light, provided that it shall be carried not less than 2 meters vertically above or below the after masthead light. On a vessel where only one masthead light is carried the maneuvering light, if fitted, shall be carried where it can best be seen, not less than 2 meters vertically apart from the masthead light.

13. Approval

The construction of lights and shapes and the installation of lights on board the vessel shall be to the satisfaction of the appropriate authority of the State whose flag the vessel is entitled to fly.

by 50 percent up to the prescribed limits; it shall decrease steadily to reach practical cut-off at not more than 5 degrees outside the prescribed sectors.

(b) All-round lights shall be so located as not to be obscured by masts, topmasts or structures within angular sectors of more than 6 degrees, except anchor lights prescribed in Rule 30, which need not be placed at an impracticable height above the hull, and the all-round white light described in Rule 23(d), which may not be obscured at all.

§ 84.19 Vertical sectors

(a) The vertical sectors of electric lights as fitted, with the exception of lights on sailing vessels and on unmanned barges, shall ensure that:

(1) At least the required minimum intensity is maintained at all angles from 5 degrees above to 5 degrees below the horizontal;

(2) At least 60 percent of the required minimum intensity is maintained from 7.5 degrees above to 7.5 degrees below the horizontal.

(b) In the case of sailing vessels the vertical sectors of electric lights as fitted shall ensure that:

(1) At least the required minimum intensity is maintained at all angles from 5 degrees above to 5 degrees below the horizontal;

(2) At least 50 percent of the required minimum intensity is maintained from 25 degrees above to 25 degrees below the horizontal.

(c) In the case of unmanned barges the minimum required intensity of electric lights as fitted shall be maintained on the horizontal.

(d) In the case of lights other than electric lights these specifications shall be met as closely as possible.

§ 84.21 Intensity of non-electric lights

Non-electric lights shall so far as practicable comply with the minimum intensities, as specified in the Table given in § 84.15.

§ 84.23 Maneuvering light

Notwithstanding the provisions of § 84.03(f), the maneuvering light described in Rule 34(b) shall be placed approximately in the

INTERNATIONAL

ANNEX II

Additional Signals for Fishing Vessels Fishing in Close Proximity

1. General

The lights mentioned herein shall, if exhibited in pursuance of Rule 26(d), be placed where they can best be seen. They shall be at least 0.9 meter apart but at a lower level than lights prescribed in Rule 26(b)(i) and (c)(i). The lights shall be visible all around the horizon at a distance of at least 1 mile but at a lesser distance from the lights prescribed by these Rules for fishing vessels.

2. Signals for trawlers

(a) Vessels when engaged in trawling, whether using demersal or pelagic gear, may exhibit:

(i) when shooting their nets: two white lights in a vertical line;

(ii) when hauling their nets: one white light over one red light in a vertical line;

(iii) when the net has come fast upon an obstruction: two red lights in a vertical line.

(b) Each vessel engaged in pair trawling may exhibit:

(i) by night, a searchlight directed forward and in the direction of the other vessel of the pair;

(ii) when shooting or hauling their nets or when their nets have come fast upon an obstruction, the lights prescribed in 2(a) above.

INLAND

same fore and aft vertical plane as the masthead light or lights and, where practicable, at a minimum height of one-half meter vertically above the forward masthead light, provided that it shall be carried not less than one-half meter vertically above or below the after masthead light. On a vessel where only one masthead light is carried the maneuvering light, if fitted, shall be carried where it can best be seen, not less than one-half meter vertically apart from the masthead light.

§ 84.25 Approval. [Reserved]

ANNEX II

Additional Signals for Fishing Vessels Fishing in Close Proximity

§ 85.1. General

The lights mentioned herein shall, if exhibited in pursuance of Rule 26(d), be placed where they can best be seen. They shall be at least 0.9 meter apart but at a lower level than lights prescribed in Rule 26(b)(i) and (c)(i) contained in the Inland Navigational Rules Act of 1980. The lights shall be visible all around the horizon at a distance of at least 1 mile but at a lesser distance from the lights prescribed by these Rules for fishing vessels.

§ 85.3 Signals for trawlers

(a) Vessels when engaged in trawling, whether using demersal or pelagic gear, may exhibit:

(1) When shooting their nets: two white lights in a vertical line;

(2) When hauling their nets: one white light over one red light in a vertical line.

(3) When the net has come fast upon an obstruction: two red lights in a vertical line.

(b) Each vessel engaged in pair trawling may exhibit:

(1) By night, a searchlight directed forward and in the direction of the other vessel of the pair;

(2) When shooting or hauling their nets or when their nets

have come fast upon an obstruction, the lights prescribed in paragraph (a) above.

§ 85.5 Signals for purse seiners

Vessels engaged in fishing with purse seine gear may exhibit two yellow lights in a vertical line. These lights shall flash alternately every second and with equal light and occultation duration. These lights may be exhibited only when the vessel is hampered by its fishing gear.

ANNEX III

Technical Details of Sound Signal Appliances

Subpart A—Whistles

§ 86.01 Frequencies and range of audibility. The fundamental frequency of the signal shall lie within the range 70–525 Hz. The range of audibility of the signal from a whistle shall be determined by those frequencies, which may include the fundamental and/or one or more higher frequencies, which lie within the frequency ranges and provide the sound pressure levels specified in § 86.05.

§ 86.03 Limits of fundamental frequencies. To ensure a wide variety of whistle characteristics, the fundamental frequency of a whistle shall be between the following limits:

(a) 70–200 Hz, for a vessel 200 meters or more in length;

(b) 130–350 Hz, for a vessel 75 meters but less than 200 meters in length;

(c) 250–525 Hz, for a vessel less than 75 meters in length.

§ 86.05 Sound signal intensity and range of audibility. A whistle on a vessel shall provide, in the direction of the forward axis of the whistle and at a distance of 1 meter from it, a sound pressure level in at least one 1/3-octave band of not less than the appropriate figure given in Table 86.05 within the following frequency ranges (±1 percent):

---

3. Signals for purse seiners

Vessels engaged in fishing with purse seine gear may exhibit two yellow lights in a vertical line. These lights shall flash alternately every second and with equal light and occultation duration. These lights may be exhibited only when the vessel is hampered by its fishing gear.

ANNEX III

Technical Details of Sound Signal Appliances

1. Whistles

(a) **Frequencies and range of audibility.** The fundamental frequency of the signal shall lie within the range 70–700 Hz.

The range of audibility of the signal from a whistle shall be determined by those frequencies, which may include the fundamental and/or one or more higher frequencies, which lie within the range 180–700 Hz (±1 percent) and which provide the sound pressure levels specified in paragraph 1(c) below.

(b) **Limits of fundamental frequencies.** To ensure a wide variety of whistle characteristics, the fundamental frequency of a whistle shall be between the following limits:

(i) 70–200 Hz, for a vessel 200 meters or more in length;

(ii) 130–350 Hz, for a vessel 75 meters but less than 200 meters in length;

(iii) 250–700 Hz, for a vessel less than 75 meters in length.

(c) **Sound signal intensity and range of audibility.** A whistle fitted in a vessel shall provide, in the direction of maximum intensity of the whistle and at a distance of 1 meter from it, a sound pressure level in at least one 1/3-octave band within the

INTERNATIONAL

range of frequencies 180–700 Hz (± 1 percent) of not less than the appropriate figure given in the table below.

Length of vessel in meters	⅓-octave band level at 1 meter in dB referred to 2x10⁻⁴ N/m²	Audibility range in nautical miles
200 or more..........	143	2
75 but less than 200....	138	1.5
20 but less than 75....	130	1
Less than 20....	120	0.5

The range of audibility in the table above is for information and is approximately the range at which a whistle may be heard on its forward axis with 90 percent probability in conditions of still air on board a vessel having average background noise level at the listening posts (taken to be 68 dB in the octave band centered on 250 Hz and 63 dB in the octave band centered on 500 Hz).

In practice the range at which a whistle may be heard is extremely variable and depends critically on weather conditions; the values given can be regarded as typical but under conditions of strong wind or high ambient noise level at the listening post the range may be much reduced.

(d) **Directional properties.** The sound pressure level of a directional whistle shall be not more than 4 dB below the prescribed sound pressure level on the axis at any direction in the horizontal plane within ±45 degrees of the axis. The sound pressure level at any other direction in the horizontal plane shall be not more than 10 dB below the prescribed sound pressure level on the axis, so that the range in any direction will be at least half the range on the forward axis. The sound pressure level shall be

INLAND

(a) 130–1200 Hz, for a vessel 75 meters or more in length;

(b) 250–1600 Hz, for a vessel 20 meters but less than 75 meters in length;

(c) 250–2100 Hz, for a vessel 12 meters but less than 20 meters in length.

Table 86.05

Length of vessel in meters	Fundamental frequency range (Hz)	For measured frequencies (Hz)	⅓-octave band level at 1 meter in dB referred to 2x10⁻⁴ N/m²	Audibility range in nautical miles
200 or more	70–200	130–180 180–250 250–1200	145 143 140	2
75 but less than 200	130–350	130–180 180–250 250–1200	140 138 134	1.5
20 but less than 75	250–525	250–450 450–800 800–1600	130 125 121	1.0
12 but less than 20	250–525	250–450 450–800 800–2100	120 115 111	0.5

NOTE: The range of audibility in the table above is for information and is approximately the range at which a whistle may usually be heard on its forward axis in conditions of still air on board a vessel having average background noise level at the listening posts (taken to be 68 dB in the octave band centered on 250 Hz and 63 dB in the octave band centered on 500 Hz).

In practice the range at which a whistle may be heard is extremely variable and depends critically on weather conditions; the values given can be regarded as typical but under conditions measured in that one-third octave band which determines the audibility range.

(e) **Positioning of whistles.** When a directional whistle is to be used as the only whistle on a vessel, it shall be installed with its maximum intensity directed straight ahead.

A whistle shall be placed as high as practicable on a vessel, in order to reduce interception of the emitted sound by obstructions and also to minimize hearing damage risk to personnel. The sound pressure level of the vessel's own signal at listening posts shall not exceed 110 dB (A) and so far as practicable should not exceed 100 dB (A).

(f) **Fitting of more than one whistle.** If whistles are fitted at a distance apart of more than 100 meters, it shall be so arranged that they are not sounded simultaneously.

(g) **Combined whistle systems.** If due to the presence of obstructions the sound field of a single whistle or of one of the whistles referred to in paragraph 1(f) above is likely to have a zone of greatly reduced signal level, it is recommended that a combined whistle system be fitted so as to overcome this reduction. For the purposes of the Rules a combined whistle system is to be regarded as a single whistle. The whistles of a combined whistle system shall be located at a distance apart of not more than 100 meters and arranged to be sounded simultaneously. The frequency of any one whistle shall differ from those of the others by at least 10 Hz.

2. Bell or gong

(a) **Intensity of signal.** A bell or gong, or other device having similar sound characteristics shall produce a sound pressure level of not less than 110 dB at a distance of 1 meter from it

(b) **Construction.** Bells and gongs shall be made of corrosion-resistant material and designed to give a clear tone. The diameter of the mouth of the bell shall be not less than 300 mm for vessels of 20 meters or more in length, and shall be not less than 200 mm for vessels of 12 meters or more but of less than 20 meters in length. Where practicable, a power-driven bell striker is recommended to ensure constant force but manual operation

of strong wind or high ambient noise level at the listening post the range may be much reduced.

§ 86.07 Directional properties.

The sound pressure level of a directional whistle shall be not more than 4 dB below the sound pressure level specified in § 86.05 in any direction in the horizontal plane within ±45 degrees of the forward axis. The sound pressure level of the whistle at any other direction in the horizontal plane shall not be more than 10 dB less than the sound pressure level specified for the forward axis, so that the range of audibility in any direction will be at least half the range required on the forward axis. The sound pressure level shall be measured in that one-third octave band which determines the audibility range.

§ 86.09 Positioning of whistles.

(a) When a directional whistle is to be used as the only whistle on the vessel and is permanently installed, it shall be installed with its forward axis directed forward.

(b) A whistle shall be placed as high as practicable on a vessel, in order to reduce interception of the emitted sound by obstructions and also to minimize hearing damage risk to personnel. The sound pressure level of the vessel's own signal at listening posts shall not exceed 110 dB (A) and so far as practicable should not exceed 100 dB (A).

§ 86.11 Fitting of more than one whistle.

If whistles are fitted at a distance apart of more than 100 meters, they shall not be sounded simultaneously.

§ 86.13 Combined whistle systems.

(a) A combined whistle system is a number of whistles (sound emitting sources) operated together. For the purposes of the Rules a combined whistle system is to be regarded as a single whistle.

(b) The whistles of a combined system shall—

(1) Be located at a distance apart of not more than 100 meters,

(2) Be sounded simultaneously,

INTERNATIONAL

shall be possible. The mass of the striker shall be not less than 3 percent of the mass of the bell.

3. Approval

The construction of sound signal appliances, their performance and their installation on board the vessel shall be to the satisfaction of the appropriate authority of the State whose flag the vessel is entitled to fly.

INLAND

(3) Each have a fundamental frequency different from those of the others by at least 10 Hz, and

(4) Have a tonal characteristic appropriate for the length of vessel which shall be evidenced by at least two-thirds of the whistles in the combined system having fundamental frequencies falling within the limits prescribed in § 86.03, or if there are only two whistles in the combined system, by the higher fundamental frequency falling within the limits prescribed in § 86.03.

NOTE: If due to the presence of obstructions the sound field of a single whistle or of one of the whistles referred to in § 86.11 is likely to have a zone of greatly reduced signal level, a combined whistle system should be fitted so as to overcome this reduction.

§ 86.15 Towing vessel whistles.

A power-driven vessel normally engaged in pushing ahead or towing alongside may, at all times, use a whistle whose characteristic falls within the limits prescribed by § 86.03 for the longest customary composite length of the vessel and its tow.

Subpart B—Bell or gong

§ 86.21 Intensity of signal.

A bell or gong, or other device having similar sound characteristics shall produce a sound pressure level of not less than 110 dB at 1 meter.

§ 86.23 Construction.

Bells and gongs shall be made of corrosion-resistant material and designed to give a clear tone. The diameter of the mouth of the bell shall be not less than 300 mm for vessels of more than 20 meters in length, and shall be not less than 200 mm for vessels of 12 to 20 meters in length. The mass of the striker shall be not less than 3 percent of the mass of the bell. The striker shall be capable of manual operation.

NOTE: When practicable, a power-driven bell striker is recommended to ensure constant force.

Subpart C—Approval

§ 86.31 Approval. [Reserved]

ANNEX IV
Distress Signals

§ 87.1 Need of assistance.

The following signals, used or exhibited either together or separately, indicate distress and need of assistance:

(a) A gun or other explosive signal fired at intervals of about a minute;

(b) A continuous sounding with any fog-signalling apparatus;

(c) Rockets or shells, throwing red stars fired one at a time at short intervals;

(d) A signal made by radiotelegraphy or by any other signaling method consisting of the group . . . — — — . . . (SOS) in the Morse Code;

(e) A signal sent by radiotelephony consisting of the spoken word "Mayday";

(f) The International Code Signal of distress indicated by N.C.;

(g) A signal consisting of a square flag having above or below it a ball or anything resembling a ball;

(h) Flames on the vessel (as from a burning tar barrel, oil barrel, etc.);

(i) A rocket parachute flare or a hand flare showing a red light;

(j) A smoke signal giving off orange-colored smoke;

(k) Slowly and repeatedly raising and lowering arms outstretched to each side;

(l) The radiotelegraph alarm signal;

(m) The radiotelephone alarm signal;

(n) Signals transmitted by emergency position-indicating radio beacons;

(o) A high intensity white light flashing at regular intervals from 50 to 70 times per minute.

§ 87.3 Exclusive use.

The use or exhibition of any of the foregoing signals except for the purpose of indicating distress and need of assistance and the

ANNEX IV
Distress Signals

1. Need of assistance

The following signals, used or exhibited either together or separately, indicate distress and need of assistance:

(a) a gun or other explosive signal fired at intervals of about a minute;

(b) a continuous sounding with any fog-signalling apparatus;

(c) rockets or shells, throwing red stars fired one at a time at short intervals;

(d) a signal made by radiotelegraphy or by any other signaling method consisting of the group . . . — — — . . . (SOS) in the Morse Code;

(e) a signal sent by radiotelephony consisting of the spoken word "Mayday";

(f) the International Code Signal of distress indicated by N.C.;

(g) a signal consisting of a square flag having above or below it a ball or anything resembling a ball;

(h) flames on the vessel (as from a burning tar barrel, oil barrel, etc.);

(i) a rocket parachute flare or a hand flare showing a red light;

(j) a smoke signal giving off orange-colored smoke;

(k) slowly and repeatedly raising and lowering arms outstretched to each side;

(l) the radiotelegraph alarm signal;

(m) the radiotelephone alarm signal;

(n) signals transmitted by emergency position-indicating radio beacons.

2. The use or exhibition of any of the foregoing signals except for the purpose of indicating distress and need of assistance and the use of other signals which may be confused with any of the above signals is prohibited.

3. Attention is drawn to the relevant sections of the

INTERNATIONAL

International Code of Signals, the Merchant Ship Search and Rescue Manual and the following signals:

(a) a piece of orange-colored canvas with either a black square and circle or other appropriate symbol (for identification from the air);

(b) a dye marker.

INLAND

use of other signals which may be confused with any of the above signals is prohibited.

§ 87.5 **Supplemental signals.**

Attention is drawn to the relevant sections of the International Code of Signals, the Merchant Ship Search and Rescue Manual and the following signals:

(a) A piece of orange-colored canvas with either a black square and circle or other appropriate symbol (for identification from the air);

(b) A dye marker.

INLAND

ANNEX V *Pilot Rules*

§ 88.01 **Purpose and applicability.**

This Part applies to all vessels operating on United States inland waters and to United States vessels operating on the Canadian waters of the Great Lakes to the extent there is no conflict with Canadian law.

§ 88.03 **Definitions.**

The terms used in this part have the same meaning as defined in the Inland Navigational Rules Act of 1980.

§ 88.05 **Copy of Rules.**

After January 1, 1983, the operator of each self-propelled vessel 12 meters or more in length shall carry on board and maintain for ready reference a copy of the Inland Navigation Rules.

§ 88.09 **Temporary exemption from light and shape requirements when operating under bridges.**

A vessel's navigation lights and shapes may be lowered if necessary to pass under a bridge.

§ 88.11 **Law enforcement vessels.**

(a) Law enforcement vessels may display a flashing blue light when engaged in direct law enforcement activities. This light shall

(d) Barges moored in well-illuminated areas are exempt from the lighting requirements of this section. These areas are as follows:

Chicago Sanitary Ship Canal

(1) Mile 293.2 to 293.9
(3) Mile 295.2 to 296.1
(5) Mile 297.5 to 297.8
(7) Mile 298 to 298.2
(9) Mile 298.6 to 298.8
(11) Mile 299.3 to 299.4
(13) Mile 299.8 to 300.5
(15) Mile 303 to 303.2
(17) Mile 303.7 to 303.9
(19) Mile 305.7 to 305.8
(21) Mile 310.7 to 310.9
(23) Mile 311 to 311.2
(25) Mile 312.5 to 312.6
(27) Mile 313.8 to 314.2
(29) Mile 314.6
(31) Mile 314.8 to 315.3

(43) Mile 318.7 to 318.8
(45) Mile 320 to 320.3
(47) Mile 320.6
(49) Mile 322.3 to 322.4
(51) Mile 322.8
(53) Mile 322.9 to 327.2

Calumet Sag Channel

(61) Mile 316.5

Little Calumet River

(71) Mile 321.2
(73) Mile 322.3

Calumet River

(81) Mile 328.5 to 328.7
(83) Mile 329.2 to 329.4
(85) Mile 330, west bank to 330.2
(87) Mile 331.4 to 331.6

(33) Mile 315.7 to 316	(89) Mile 332.2 to 332.4
(35) Mile 316.8	(91) Mile 332.6 to 332.8
(37) Mile 316.85 to 317.05	*Cumberland River*
(39) Mile 317.5	(101) Mile 126.8
(41) Mile 318.4 to 318.9	(103) Mile 191

§ 88.15 Lights on dredge pipelines.

Dredge pipelines that are floating or supported on trestles shall display the following lights at night and in periods of restricted visibility.

(a) One row of yellow lights. The lights must be—

(1) Flashing 50 to 70 times per minute,

(2) Visible all around the horizon,

(3) Visible for at least 2 miles on a clear dark night,

(4) Not less than 1 and not more than 3.5 meters above the water,

(5) Approximately equally spaced, and

(6) Not more than 10 meters apart where the pipeline crosses a navigable channel. Where the pipeline does not cross a navigable channel the lights must be sufficient in number to clearly show the pipeline's length and course.

(b) Two red lights at each end of the pipeline, including the ends in a channel where the pipeline is separated to allow vessels to pass (whether open or closed). The lights must be—

(1) Visible all around the horizon, and

(2) Visible for at least 2 miles on a clear dark night, and

(3) One meter apart in a vertical line with the lower light at the same height above the water as the flashing yellow light.

be located so that it does not interfere with the visibility of the vessel's navigation lights.

(b) The blue light described in this section may be displayed by law enforcement vessels of the United States and the States and their political subdivisions.

§ 88.13 Lights on barges at bank or dock.

(a) The following barges shall display at night and, if practicable, in periods of restricted visibility the lights described in paragraph (b) of this section—

(1) Every barge projecting into a buoyed or restricted channel.

(2) Every barge so moored that it reduces the available navigable width of any channel to less than 80 meters.

(3) Barges moored in groups more than two barges wide or to a maximum width of over 25 meters.

(4) Every barge not moored parallel to the bank or dock.

(b) Barges described in paragraph (a) shall carry two unobstructed white lights of an intensity to be visible for at least one mile on a clear dark night, and arranged as follows:

(1) On a single moored barge, lights shall be placed on the two corners farthest from the bank or dock.

(2) On barges moored in group formation, a light shall be placed on each of the upstream and downstream ends of the group, on the corners farthest from the bank or dock.

(3) Any barge in a group, projecting from the main body of the group toward the channel, shall be lighted as a single barge.

(c) Barges moored in any slip or slough which is used primarily for mooring purposes are exempt from the lighting requirements of this section.

Appendix B—
RULE INTERPRETATIONS

GUIDANCE STATEMENTS

The following statements have been issued as guides toward uniform application of COLREGS. Reference to vessels constrained by draft and to traffic separation schemes are not relevant to the Inland Rules, so Clarifications 1, 4, 5, 6, and 7 have no bearing on U.S. waters. However, Clarifications 2 and 3 should be considered appropriate when applying Inland.

The Maritime Safety Committee of the International Maritime Organization (IMO) decided at its forty-sixth session to bring the attached Guidance for the Uniform Application of Certain Rules of the 1972 Collision Regulations to the attention of Member Governments by MSC/Circ. 320.

The following guidance is provided to assist seafarers and all others concerned in the application of certain rules of the International Regulations for Preventing Collisions ar Sea, 1972:

1. Clarification of the definition "Vessel constrained by her draft," Rule 3(h)

Not only the depth of water but also the available navigable water width should be used as a factor to determine whether a vessel may be regarded as constrained by her draft. When determining this, due account should also be taken of the effect of a small underkeel clearance on maneuverability of the vessel and thus her ability to deviate from the course she is following. A vessel navigating in an area with a small underkeel clearance but with adequate space to take avoiding action should not be regarded as a vessel constrained by her draft.

2. Clarification of the application of the word "underway," Rule 3(i)

When applying the definition of the term "underway" mariners should also have regard to Rule 35(b) where it is indicated that a vessel may be underway but stopped and making no way through the water.

3. Clarification of the implication of the words "not to impede" as appearing in Rules 9(b), (c), and (d), 10(i) and (j), and 18(d)

When a vessel is required not to impede the passage of another vessel, such vessel shall so far as practicable navigate in such a way as to avoid the development of risk of collision. If, however, a situation has developed so as to involve risk of collision, the relevant Steering and Sailing Rules shall be complied with.

4. Clarification of the relation between Rule 10 and the Rules of Part B, Sections II and III

A vessel navigating in or near a traffic separation scheme adopted by the Organization shall, in particular, comply with Rule 10 of the International Regulations for Preventing Collisions at Sea, 1972, to minimize the development of risk of collision with another vessel. The other Rules of the 1972 Collision Regulations apply in all respects, and particularly the Rules of Part B, Sections II and III, if risk of collision with another vessel is deemed to exist.

5. Clarification of the transference within a lane, Rule 10(b)(i)

It is within the ordinary practice of prudent seamanship and in keeping with the provisions of Rule 10 of the 1972 Collision Regulations that a vessel using a traffic lane may make a transfer within a lane from one side to the other, provided such a transfer is accomplished at as small an angle to the general direction of traffic flow as is practicable.

6. Clarification on the use of inshore traffic zones by small vessels, Rule 10(d)

To comply with Rule 10(j) and for reasons of safe navigation a vessel of less than 20 meters in length or a sailing vessel, even when through traffic, may use inshore traffic zones.

7. Clarification of the relation between Rule 18(d) and the Rules of Part B, Sections II and III

A vessel constrained by her draft shall, when risk of collision with another vessel in a crossing or head-on situation exists, apply the relevant Steering and Sailing Rules as a power-driven vessel. She should, when showing the signals prescribed by Rule 28, have her engines ready for immediate maneuver and proceed at a safe speed as required by Rule 6.

U.S. COAST GUARD INTERPRETIVE RULING

The U.S. Coast Guard is authorized to promulgate interpretive rulings for guidance in applying the Rules of the Road. A violation of such a ruling is considered a violation of the rule which it interprets. The following is an exercise of that authority as found in the Code of Federal Regulations (CFR):

§ 88.1 Purpose.
This part contains the interpretative rules concerning the 72 COLREGS that are adopted by the Coast Guard for the guidance of the public.

§ 88.3 Pushing vessel and vessel being pushed: Composite unit.
Rule 24(b) of the 72 COLREGS states that when a pushing vessel and a vessel being pushed ahead are rigidly connected in a composite unit, they are regarded as a power-driven vessel and must exhibit the lights under Rule 23. A "composite unit" is interpreted to be a pushing vessel that is rigidly connected by mechanical means to a vessel being pushed so they react to sea and swell as one vessel. "Mechanical means" does not include the following:

(a) Lines.
(b) Hawsers.
(c) Wires.
(d) Chains.

TRAFFIC SEPARATION SCHEMES NEAR U.S. WATERS

Vessel routing measures existing on the high seas near U.S. waters and which, by IMO adoption, are considered Traffic Separation Schemes subject to COLREGS Rule 10 are:

In the approaches to Portland, Maine
In the approaches to Boston, Massachusetts
In the approaches to Narragansett Bay, Rhode Island, and Buzzards Bay
Off New York
Off Delaware Bay
In the approaches to Chesapeake Bay
Off San Francisco
In the Santa Barbara Channel
In the approaches to Los Angeles–Long Beach
In the Strait of Juan de Fuca